"Either America will destroy ignorance or ignorance
will destroy the United States."

—W.E.B. DuBois

BITTER ROOT™ LEGACY, VOL. 3. First printing: October 2021. Published by Image Comics, Inc. Office of publication: PO BOX 14457, Portland, OR 97293. Copyright © 2021 David F. Walker, Chuck Brown, and Sanford Greene. All rights reserved. Contains material originally published in single magazine form as BITTER ROOT™ #11-15. "Bitter Root™," its logos, and the likenesses of all characters herein are trademarks of David F. Walker, Chuck Brown, and Sanford Greene, unless otherwise noted. "Image" and the Image Comics logos are registered trademarks of Image Comics, Inc. No part of this publication may be reproduced or transmitted, in any form or by any means (except for short excerpts for journalistic or review purposes), without the express written permission of David F. Walker, Chuck Brown, and Sanford Greene, or Image Comics, Inc. All names, characters, events, and locales in this publication are entirely fictional. Any resemblance to actual persons (living or dead), events, or places, without satirical intent, is coincidental. Printed in the USA. For international rights, contact: foreignlicensing@imagecomics.com. ISBN: 978-1-5343-1917-2.

BITTER ROOT

VOLUME THREE:
LEGACY

DAVID F. WALKER,
CHUCK BROWN &
SANFORD GREENE
creators

SOFIE DODGSON
color artist

HASSAN OTSMANE-ELHAOU
letterer

SANFORD GREENE
cover artist

JOHN JENNINGS
backmatter

SHELLY BOND
editor

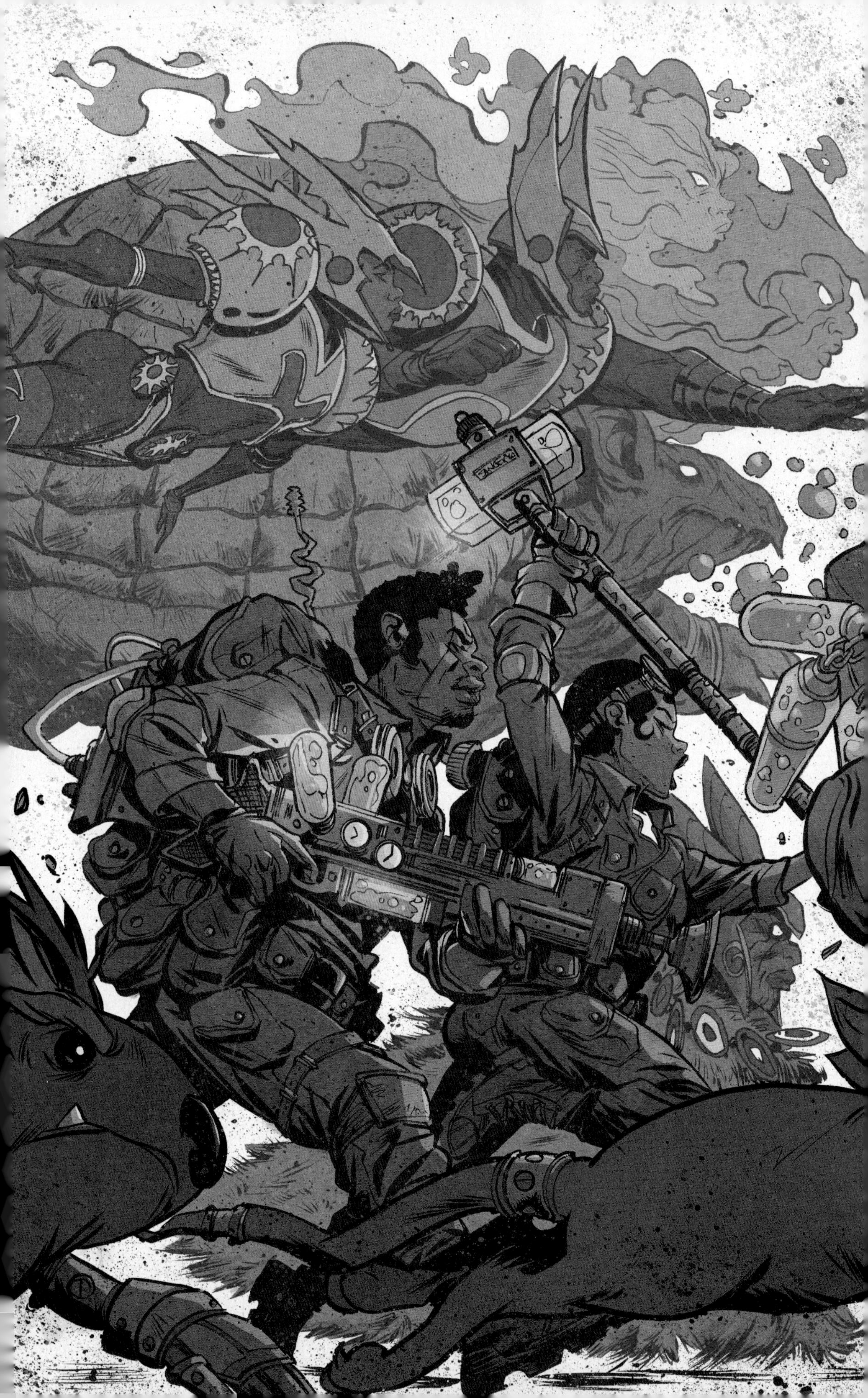

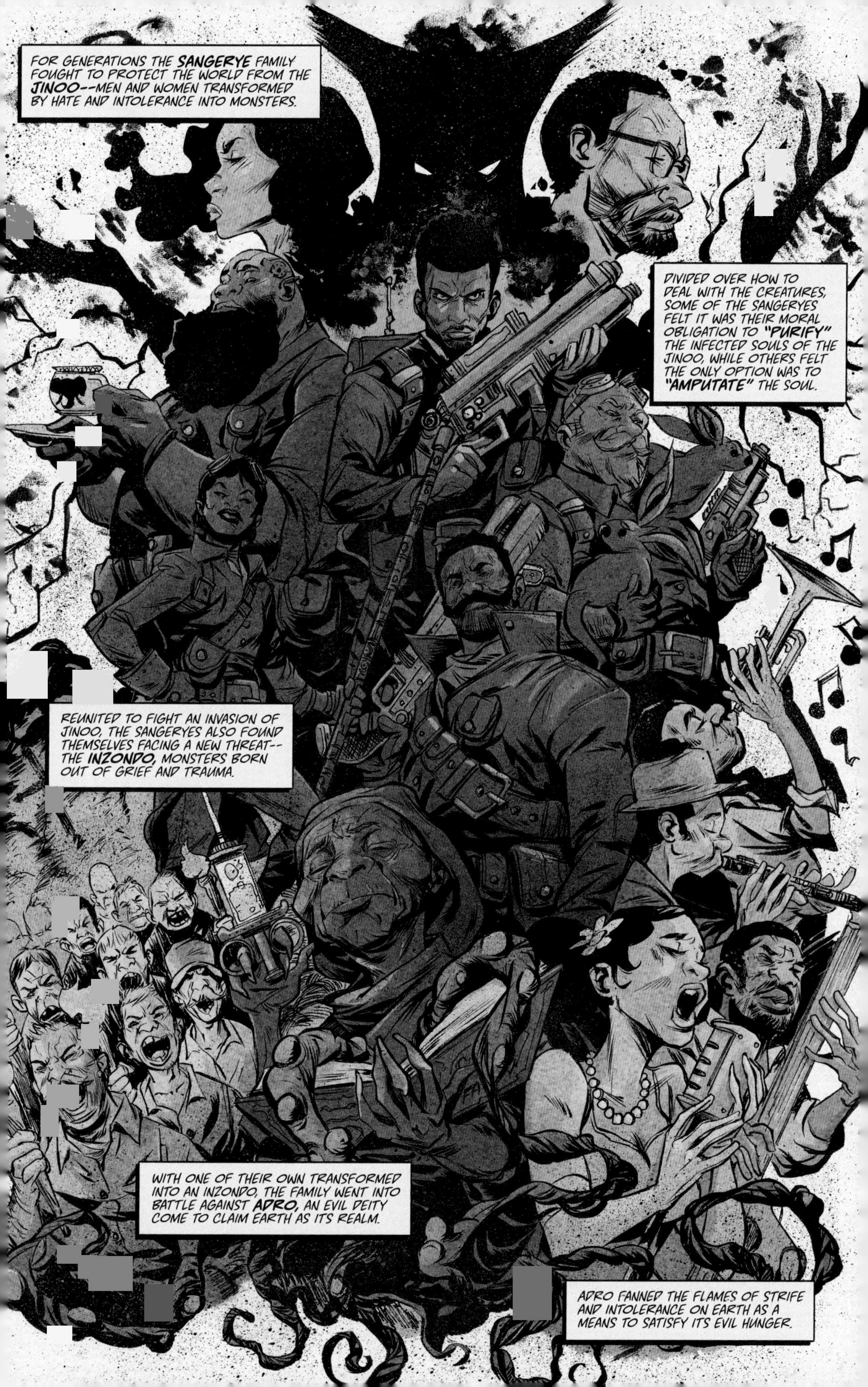
FOR GENERATIONS THE SANGERYE FAMILY FOUGHT TO PROTECT THE WORLD FROM THE JINOO--MEN AND WOMEN TRANSFORMED BY HATE AND INTOLERANCE INTO MONSTERS.
DIVIDED OVER HOW TO DEAL WITH THE CREATURES, SOME OF THE SANGERYES FELT IT WAS THEIR MORAL OBLIGATION TO "PURIFY" THE INFECTED SOULS OF THE JINOO, WHILE OTHERS FELT THE ONLY OPTION WAS TO "AMPUTATE" THE SOUL.
REUNITED TO FIGHT AN INVASION OF JINOO, THE SANGERYES ALSO FOUND THEMSELVES FACING A NEW THREAT--THE INZONDO, MONSTERS BORN OUT OF GRIEF AND TRAUMA.
WITH ONE OF THEIR OWN TRANSFORMED INTO AN INZONDO, THE FAMILY WENT INTO BATTLE AGAINST ADRO, AN EVIL DEITY COME TO CLAIM EARTH AS ITS REALM.
ADRO FANNED THE FLAMES OF STRIFE AND INTOLERANCE ON EARTH AS A MEANS TO SATISFY ITS EVIL HUNGER.

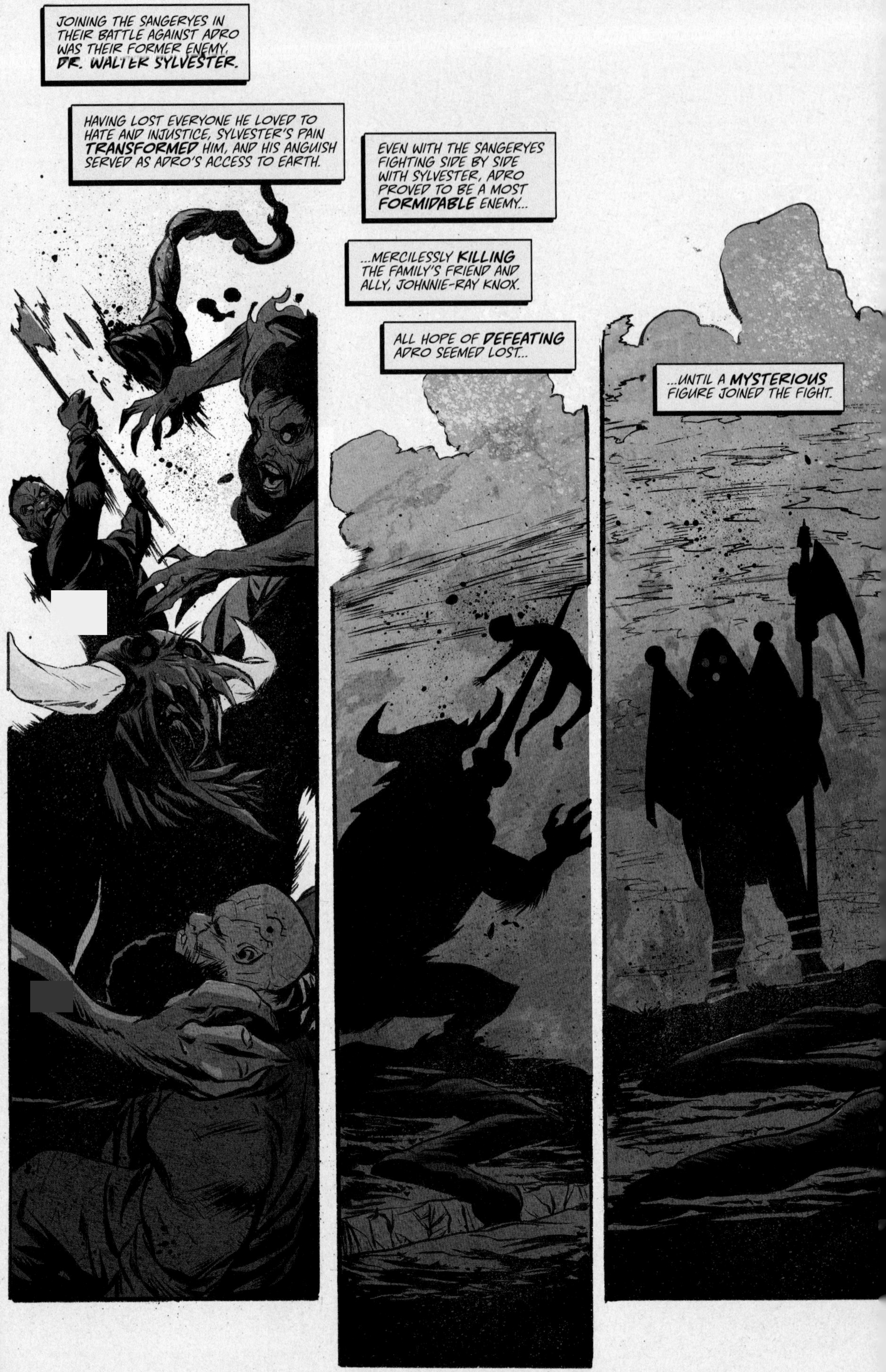
JOINING THE SANGERYES IN THEIR BATTLE AGAINST ADRO WAS THEIR FORMER ENEMY, DR. WALTER SYLVESTER.
HAVING LOST EVERYONE HE LOVED TO HATE AND INJUSTICE, SYLVESTER'S PAIN TRANSFORMED HIM, AND HIS ANGUISH SERVED AS ADRO'S ACCESS TO EARTH.
EVEN WITH THE SANGERYES FIGHTING SIDE BY SIDE WITH SYLVESTER, ADRO PROVED TO BE A MOST FORMIDABLE ENEMY...
...MERCILESSLY KILLING THE FAMILY'S FRIEND AND ALLY, JOHNNIE-RAY KNOX.
ALL HOPE OF DEFEATING ADRO SEEMED LOST...
...UNTIL A MYSTERIOUS FIGURE JOINED THE FIGHT.

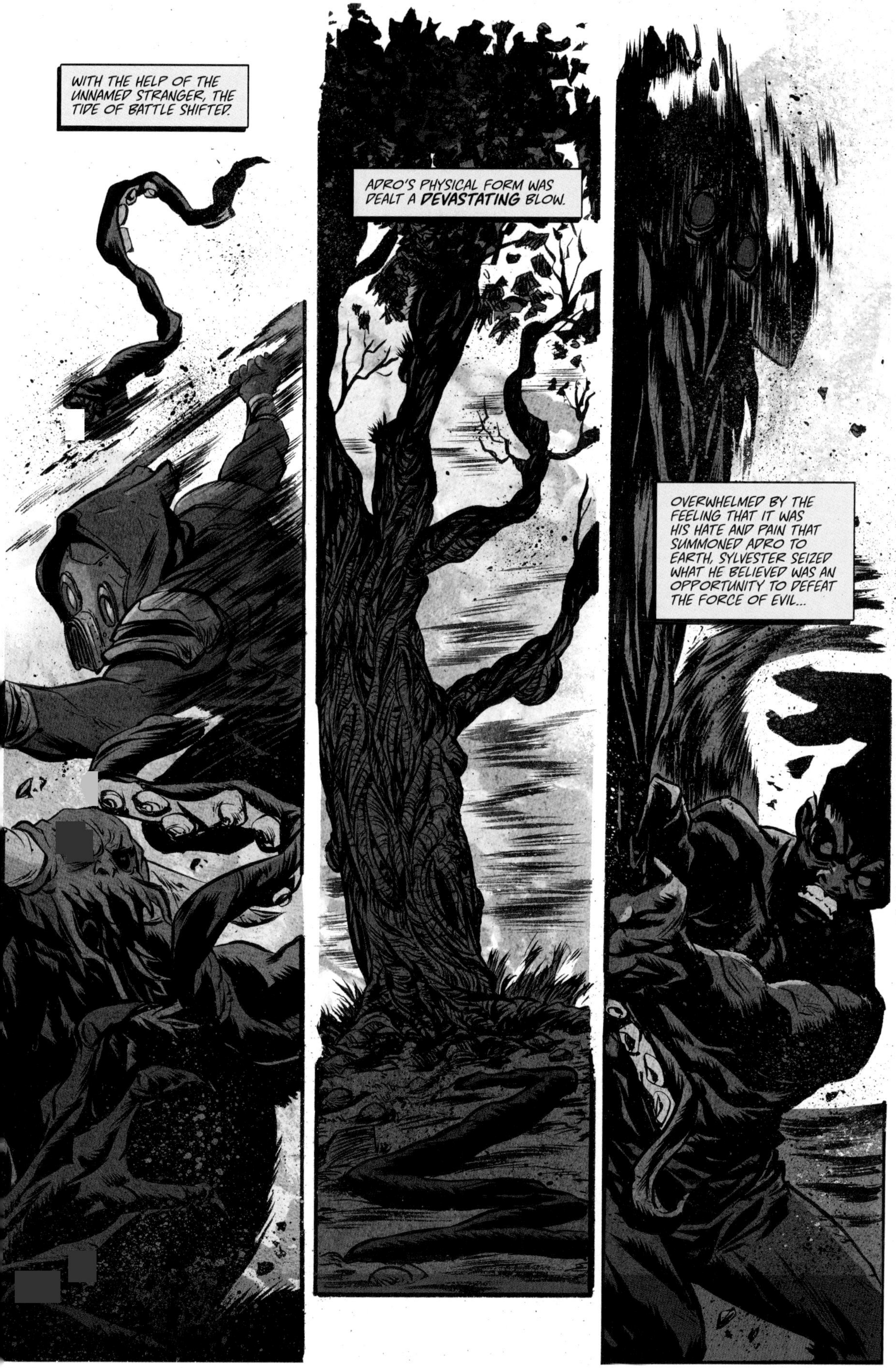
WITH THE HELP OF THE UNNAMED STRANGER, THE TIDE OF BATTLE SHIFTED.
ADRO'S PHYSICAL FORM WAS DEALT A **DEVASTATING** BLOW.
OVERWHELMED BY THE FEELING THAT IT WAS HIS HATE AND PAIN THAT SUMMONED ADRO TO EARTH, SYLVESTER SEIZED WHAT HE BELIEVED WAS AN OPPORTUNITY TO DEFEAT THE FORCE OF EVIL...

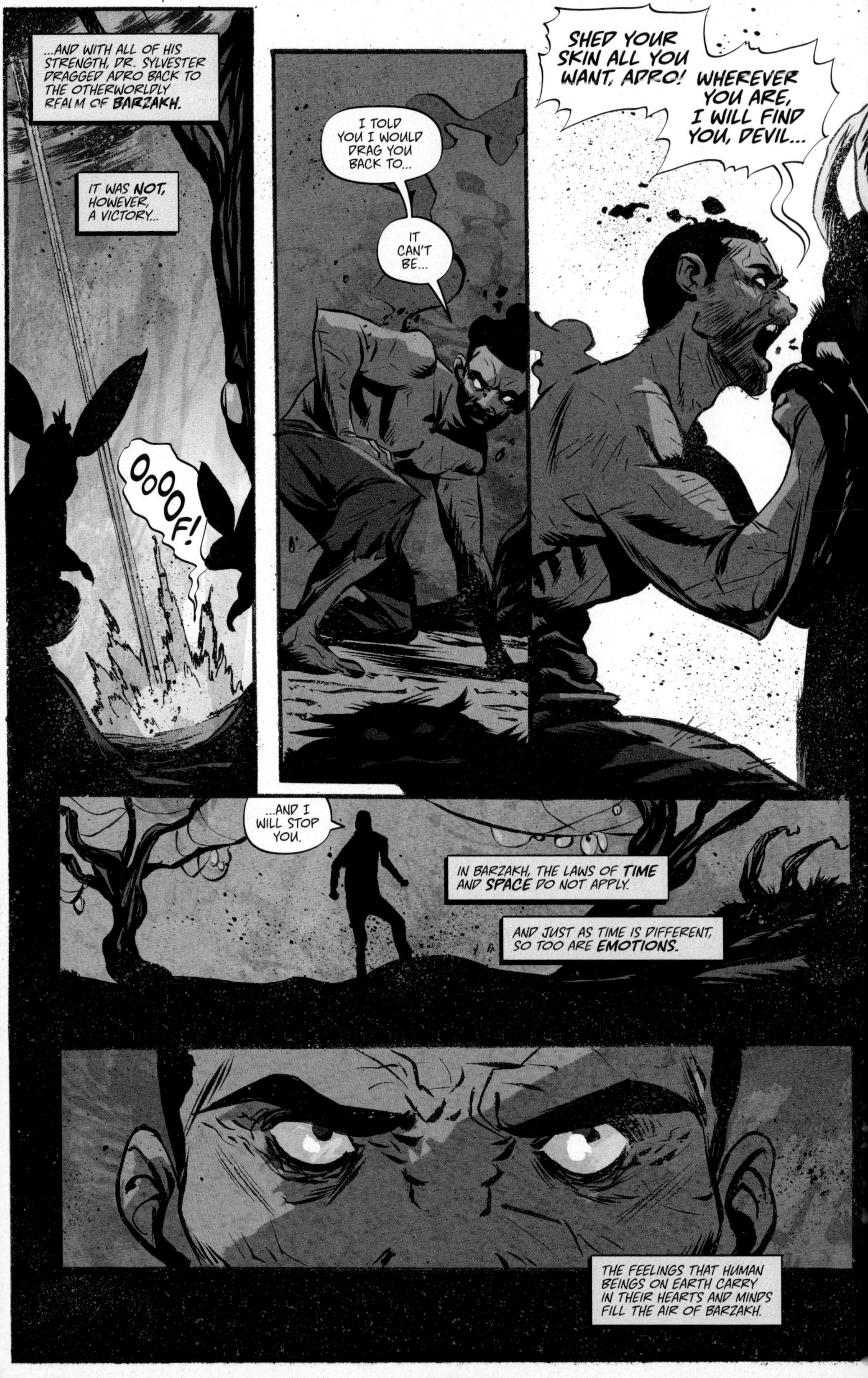
...AND WITH ALL OF HIS STRENGTH, DR. SYLVESTER DRAGGED ADRO BACK TO THE OTHERWORLDLY REALM OF BARZAKH.
IT WAS NOT, HOWEVER, A VICTORY...
OOOOF!
I TOLD YOU I WOULD DRAG YOU BACK TO...
IT CAN'T BE...
SHED YOUR SKIN ALL YOU WANT, ADRO!
WHEREVER YOU ARE, I WILL FIND YOU, DEVIL...
...AND I WILL STOP YOU.
IN BARZAKH, THE LAWS OF TIME AND SPACE DO NOT APPLY.
AND JUST AS TIME IS DIFFERENT, SO TOO ARE EMOTIONS.
THE FEELINGS THAT HUMAN BEINGS ON EARTH CARRY IN THEIR HEARTS AND MINDS FILL THE AIR OF BARZAKH.

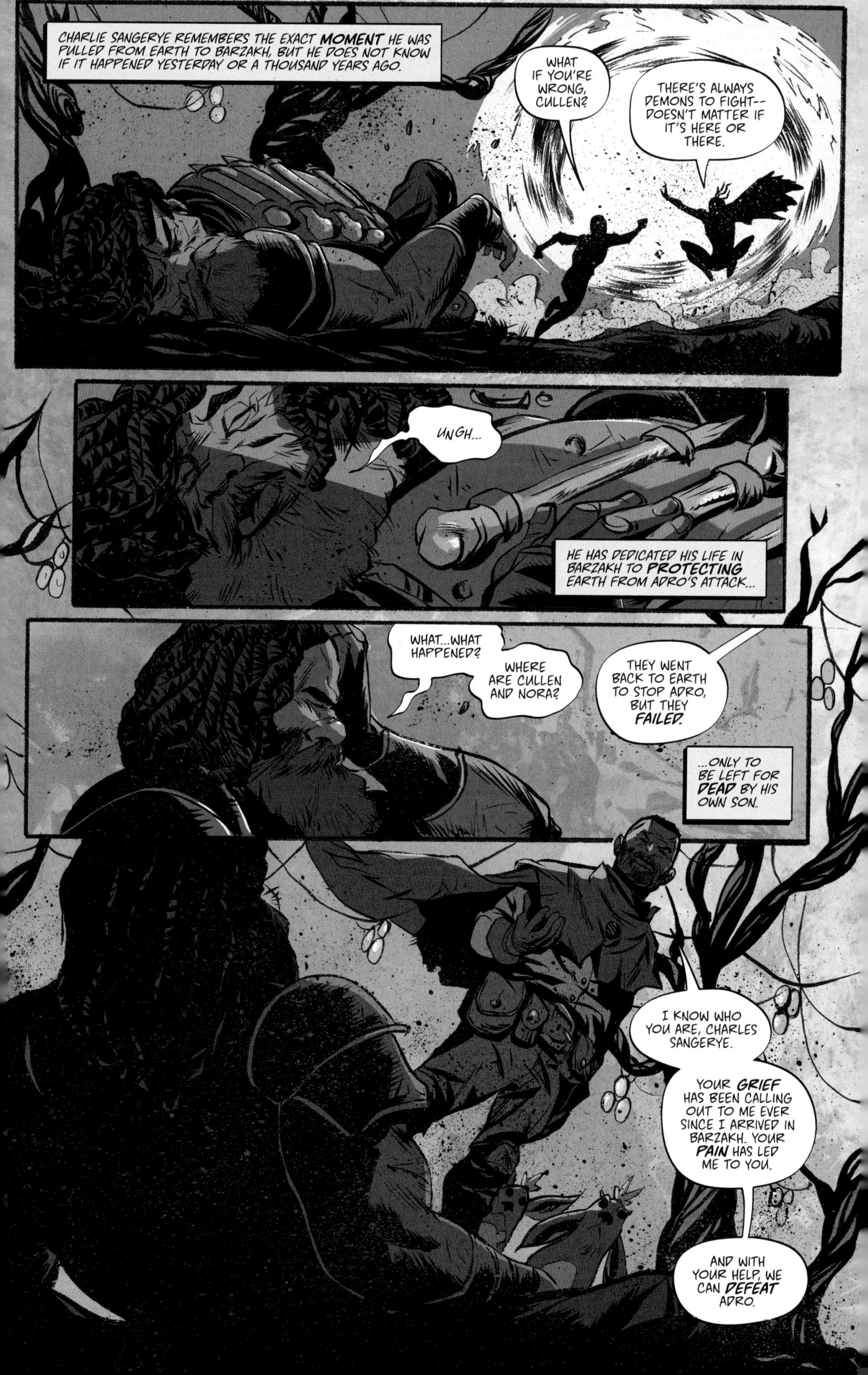

CHARLIE SANGERYE REMEMBERS THE EXACT MOMENT HE WAS PULLED FROM EARTH TO BARZAKH, BUT HE DOES NOT KNOW IF IT HAPPENED YESTERDAY OR A THOUSAND YEARS AGO.
WHAT IF YOU'RE WRONG, CULLEN?
THERE'S ALWAYS DEMONS TO FIGHT-- DOESN'T MATTER IF IT'S HERE OR THERE.
UNGH...
HE HAS DEDICATED HIS LIFE IN BARZAKH TO PROTECTING EARTH FROM ADRO'S ATTACK...
WHAT...WHAT HAPPENED?
WHERE ARE CULLEN AND NORA?
THEY WENT BACK TO EARTH TO STOP ADRO, BUT THEY FAILED.
...ONLY TO BE LEFT FOR DEAD BY HIS OWN SON.
I KNOW WHO YOU ARE, CHARLES SANGERYE.
YOUR GRIEF HAS BEEN CALLING OUT TO ME EVER SINCE I ARRIVED IN BARZAKH. YOUR PAIN HAS LED ME TO YOU.
AND WITH YOUR HELP, WE CAN DEFEAT ADRO.

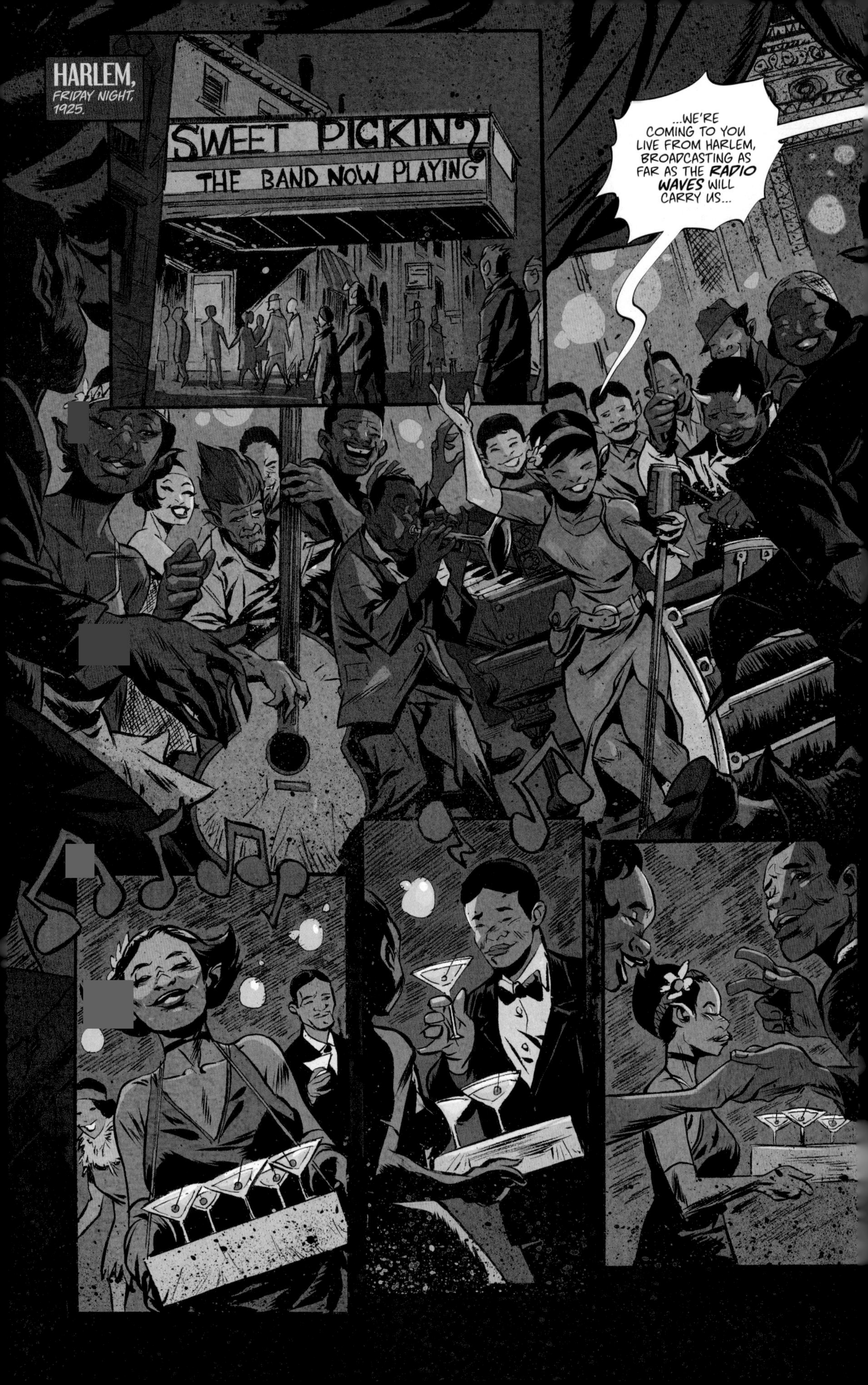
HARLEM, FRIDAY NIGHT, 1925.
SWEET PICKIN'
THE BAND NOW PLAYING
...WE'RE COMING TO YOU LIVE FROM HARLEM, BROADCASTING AS FAR AS THE RADIO WAVES WILL CARRY US...

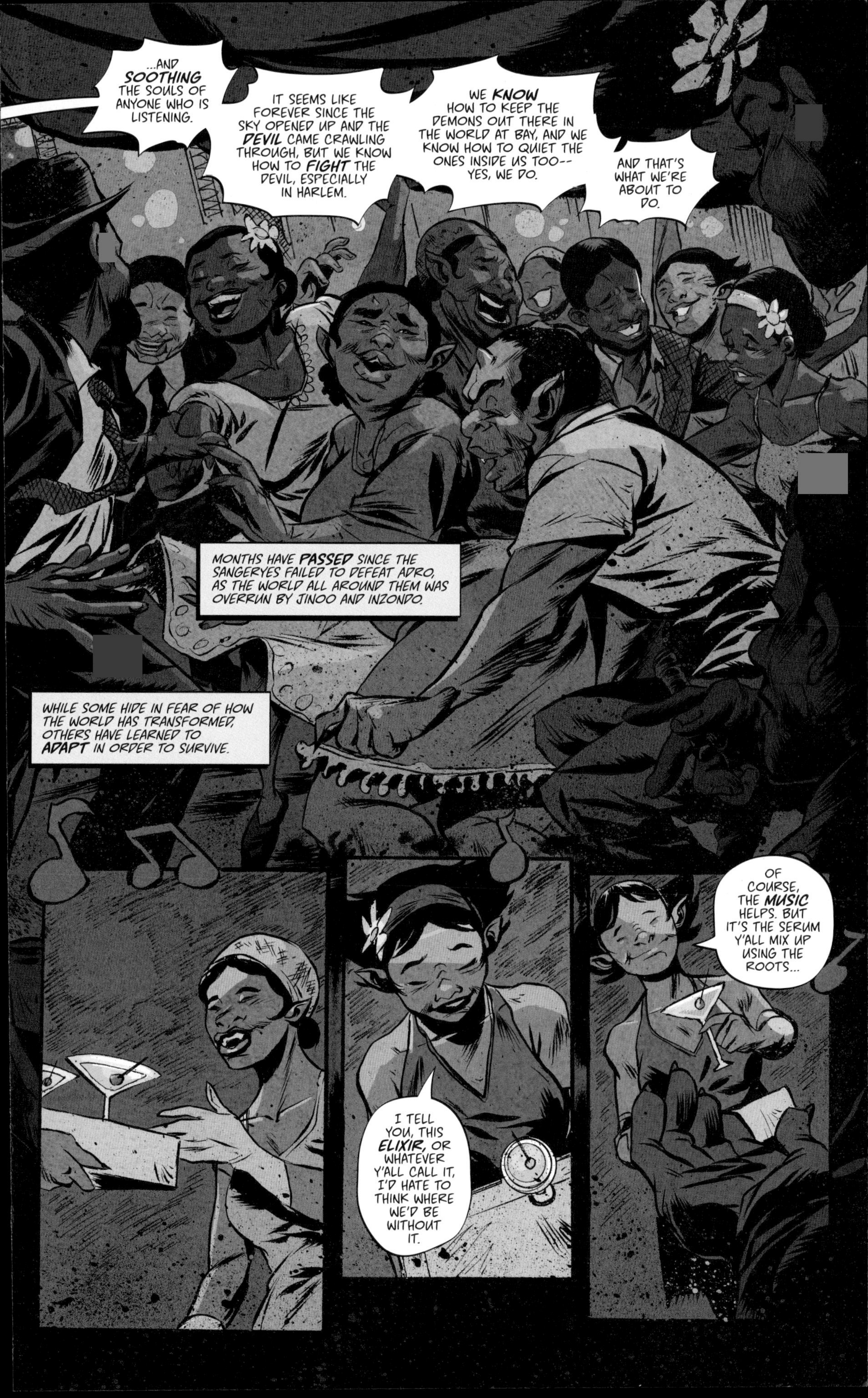
...AND SOOTHING THE SOULS OF ANYONE WHO IS LISTENING.
IT SEEMS LIKE FOREVER SINCE THE SKY OPENED UP AND THE DEVIL CAME CRAWLING THROUGH, BUT WE KNOW HOW TO FIGHT THE DEVIL, ESPECIALLY IN HARLEM.
WE KNOW HOW TO KEEP THE DEMONS OUT THERE IN THE WORLD AT BAY, AND WE KNOW HOW TO QUIET THE ONES INSIDE US TOO-- YES, WE DO.
AND THAT'S WHAT WE'RE ABOUT TO DO.
MONTHS HAVE PASSED SINCE THE SANGERYES FAILED TO DEFEAT ADRO, AS THE WORLD ALL AROUND THEM WAS OVERRUN BY JINOO AND INZONDO.
WHILE SOME HIDE IN FEAR OF HOW THE WORLD HAS TRANSFORMED, OTHERS HAVE LEARNED TO ADAPT IN ORDER TO SURVIVE.
I TELL YOU, THIS ELIXIR, OR WHATEVER Y'ALL CALL IT, I'D HATE TO THINK WHERE WE'D BE WITHOUT IT.
OF COURSE, THE MUSIC HELPS. BUT IT'S THE SERUM Y'ALL MIX UP USING THE ROOTS...

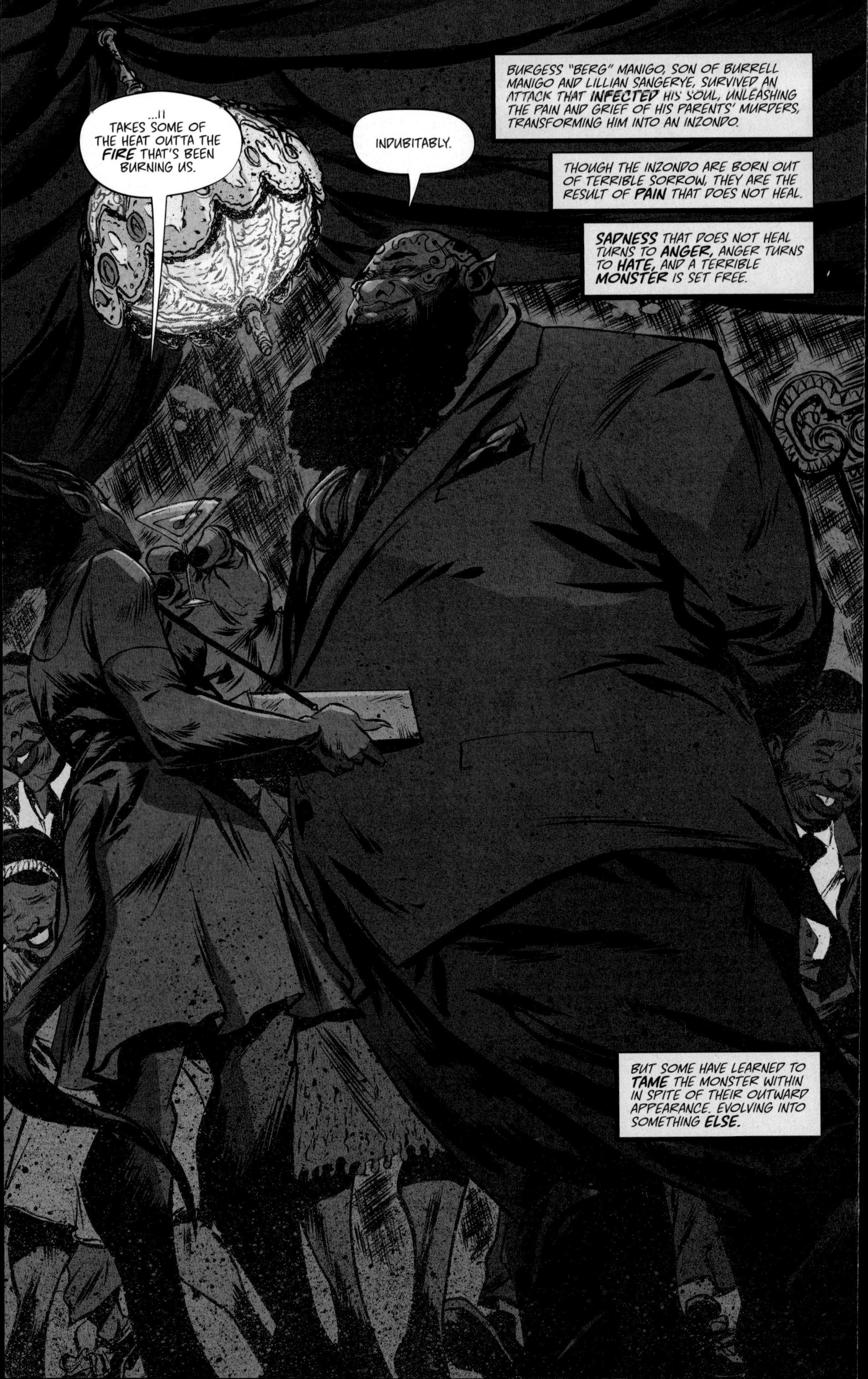
BURGESS "BERG" MANIGO, SON OF BURRELL MANIGO AND LILLIAN SANGERYE, SURVIVED AN ATTACK THAT INFECTED HIS SOUL, UNLEASHING THE PAIN AND GRIEF OF HIS PARENTS' MURDERS, TRANSFORMING HIM INTO AN INZONDO.
...IT TAKES SOME OF THE HEAT OUTTA THE FIRE THAT'S BEEN BURNING US.
INDUBITABLY.
THOUGH THE INZONDO ARE BORN OUT OF TERRIBLE SORROW, THEY ARE THE RESULT OF PAIN THAT DOES NOT HEAL.
SADNESS THAT DOES NOT HEAL TURNS TO ANGER, ANGER TURNS TO HATE, AND A TERRIBLE MONSTER IS SET FREE.
BUT SOME HAVE LEARNED TO TAME THE MONSTER WITHIN IN SPITE OF THEIR OUTWARD APPEARANCE. EVOLVING INTO SOMETHING ELSE.

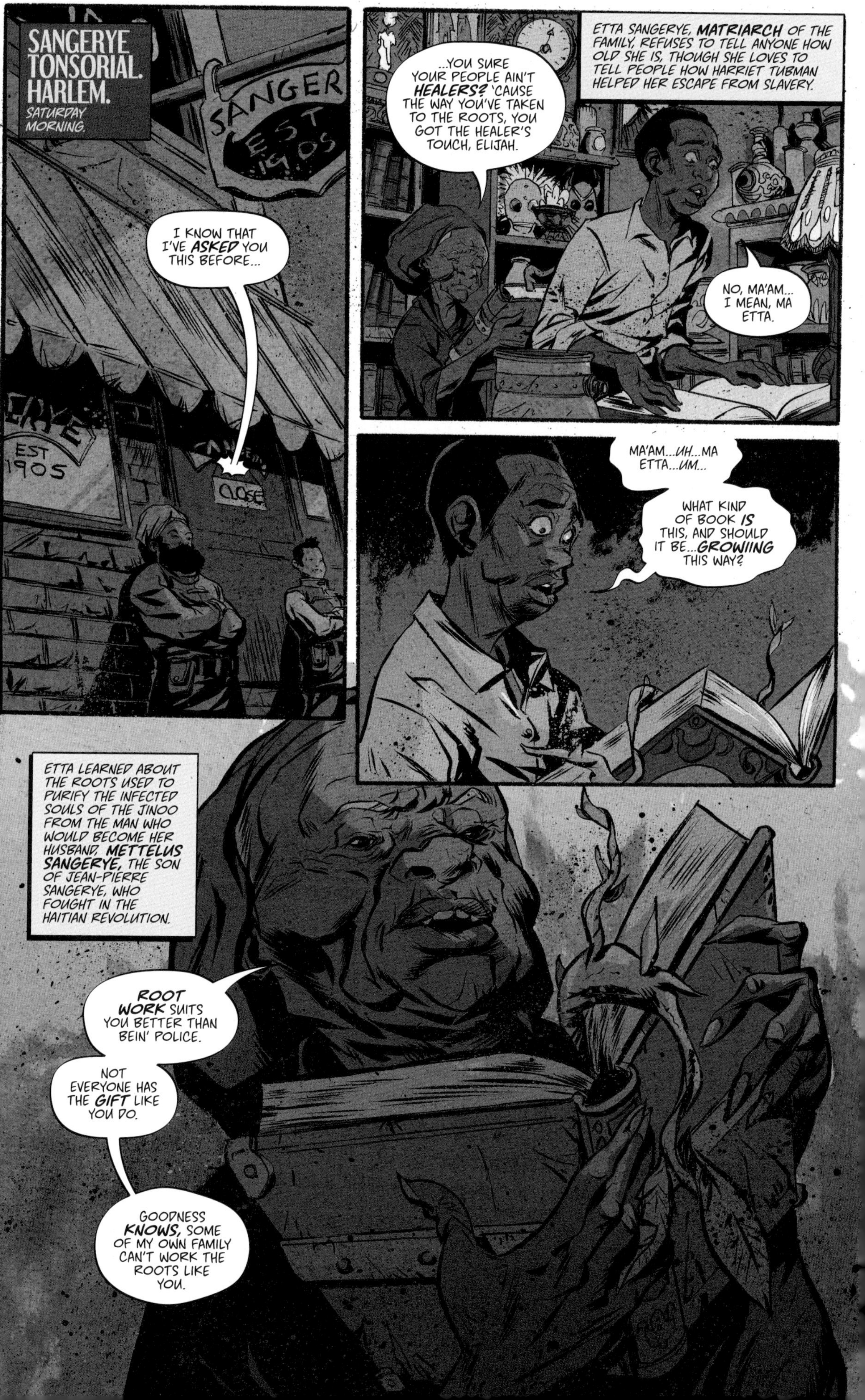
SANGERYE TONSORIAL. HARLEM.
SATURDAY MORNING.
SANGER EST 1905
I KNOW THAT I'VE ASKED YOU THIS BEFORE...
ERYE EST 1905
CLOSE
...YOU SURE YOUR PEOPLE AIN'T HEALERS? 'CAUSE THE WAY YOU'VE TAKEN TO THE ROOTS, YOU GOT THE HEALER'S TOUCH, ELIJAH.
ETTA SANGERYE, MATRIARCH OF THE FAMILY, REFUSES TO TELL ANYONE HOW OLD SHE IS, THOUGH SHE LOVES TO TELL PEOPLE HOW HARRIET TUBMAN HELPED HER ESCAPE FROM SLAVERY.
NO, MA'AM... I MEAN, MA ETTA.
MA'AM...UH...MA ETTA...UM...
WHAT KIND OF BOOK IS THIS, AND SHOULD IT BE...GROWIING THIS WAY?
ETTA LEARNED ABOUT THE ROOTS USED TO PURIFY THE INFECTED SOULS OF THE JINOO FROM THE MAN WHO WOULD BECOME HER HUSBAND, METTELUS SANGERYE, THE SON OF JEAN-PIERRE SANGERYE, WHO FOUGHT IN THE HAITIAN REVOLUTION.
ROOT WORK SUITS YOU BETTER THAN BEIN' POLICE.
NOT EVERYONE HAS THE GIFT LIKE YOU DO.
GOODNESS KNOWS, SOME OF MY OWN FAMILY CAN'T WORK THE ROOTS LIKE YOU.

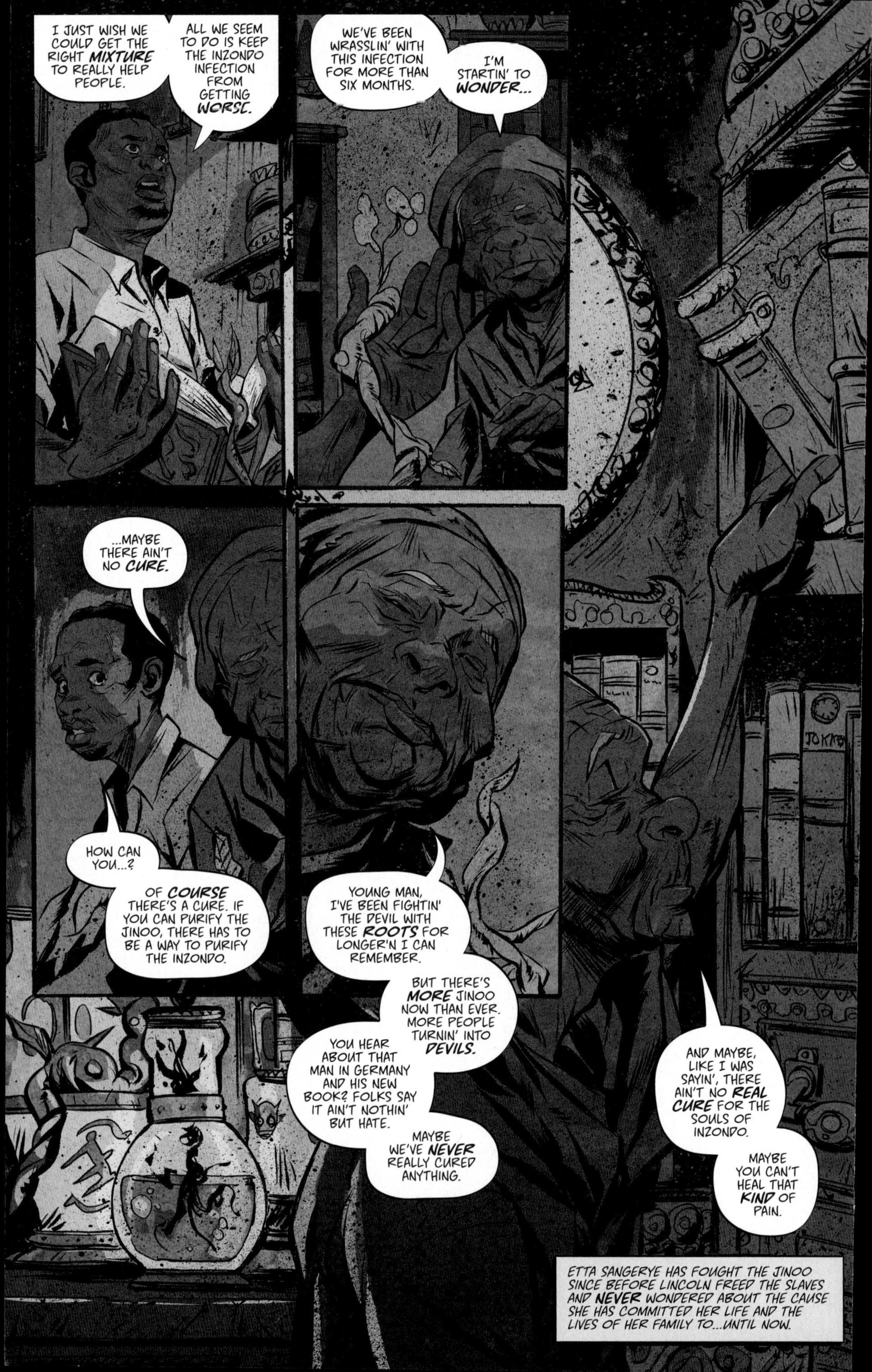
I JUST WISH WE COULD GET THE RIGHT MIXTURE TO REALLY HELP PEOPLE.
ALL WE SEEM TO DO IS KEEP THE INZONDO INFECTION FROM GETTING WORSE.
WE'VE BEEN WRASSLIN' WITH THIS INFECTION FOR MORE THAN SIX MONTHS.
I'M STARTIN' TO WONDER...
...MAYBE THERE AIN'T NO CURE.
HOW CAN YOU...?
OF COURSE THERE'S A CURE. IF YOU CAN PURIFY THE JINOO, THERE HAS TO BE A WAY TO PURIFY THE INZONDO.
YOUNG MAN, I'VE BEEN FIGHTIN' THE DEVIL WITH THESE ROOTS FOR LONGER'N I CAN REMEMBER.
BUT THERE'S MORE JINOO NOW THAN EVER. MORE PEOPLE TURNIN' INTO DEVILS.
YOU HEAR ABOUT THAT MAN IN GERMANY AND HIS NEW BOOK? FOLKS SAY IT AIN'T NOTHIN' BUT HATE.
MAYBE WE'VE NEVER REALLY CURED ANYTHING.
AND MAYBE, LIKE I WAS SAYIN', THERE AIN'T NO REAL CURE FOR THE SOULS OF INZONDO.
MAYBE YOU CAN'T HEAL THAT KIND OF PAIN.
ETTA SANGERYE HAS FOUGHT THE JINOO SINCE BEFORE LINCOLN FREED THE SLAVES AND NEVER WONDERED ABOUT THE CAUSE SHE HAS COMMITTED HER LIFE AND THE LIVES OF HER FAMILY TO...UNTIL NOW.

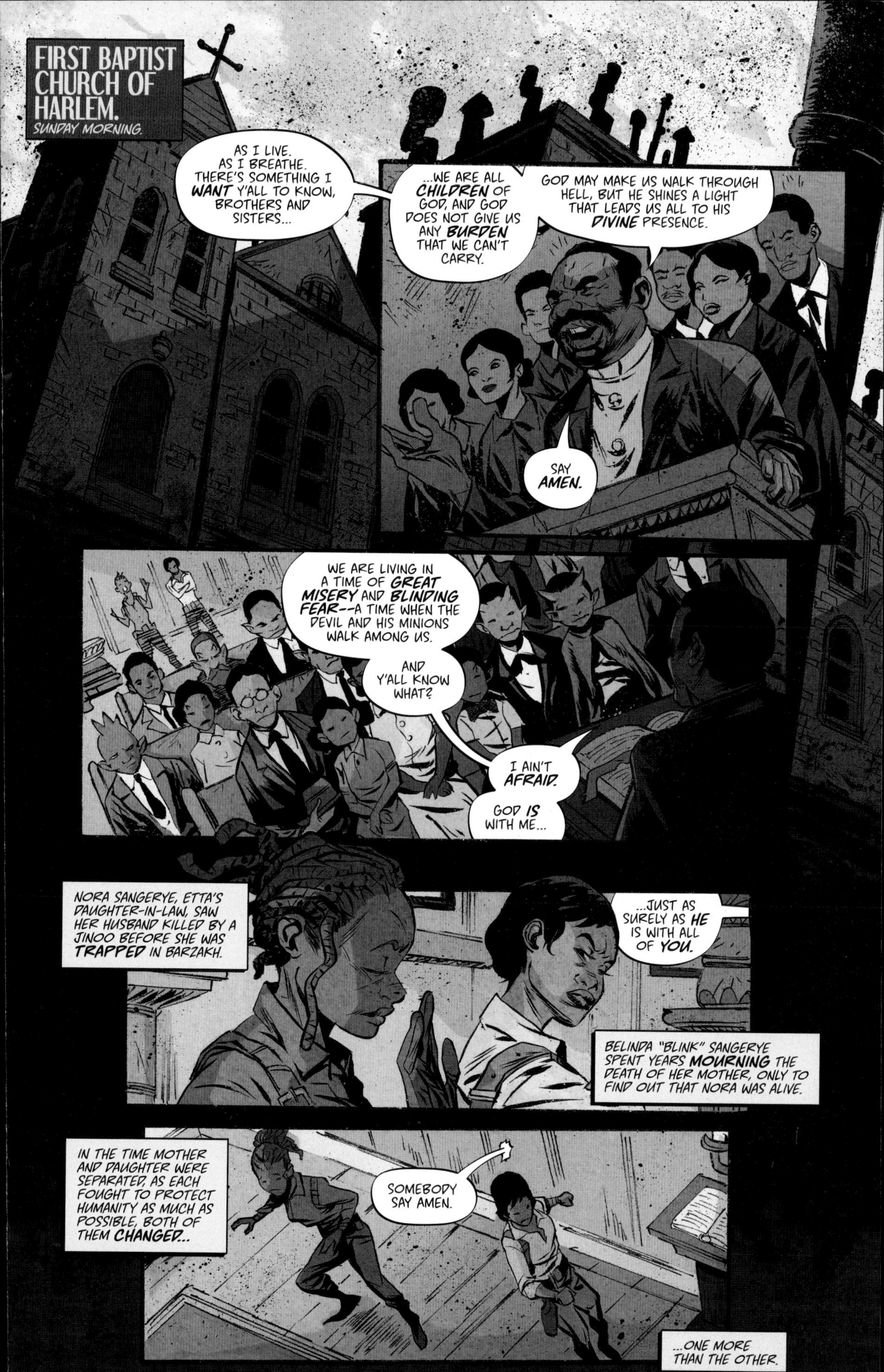
FIRST BAPTIST CHURCH OF HARLEM.
SUNDAY MORNING.
AS I LIVE. AS I BREATHE. THERE'S SOMETHING I WANT Y'ALL TO KNOW, BROTHERS AND SISTERS...
...WE ARE ALL CHILDREN OF GOD, AND GOD DOES NOT GIVE US ANY BURDEN THAT WE CAN'T CARRY.
GOD MAY MAKE US WALK THROUGH HELL, BUT HE SHINES A LIGHT THAT LEADS US ALL TO HIS DIVINE PRESENCE.
SAY AMEN.
WE ARE LIVING IN A TIME OF GREAT MISERY AND BLINDING FEAR--A TIME WHEN THE DEVIL AND HIS MINIONS WALK AMONG US.
AND Y'ALL KNOW WHAT?
I AIN'T AFRAID.
GOD IS WITH ME...
NORA SANGERYE, ETTA'S DAUGHTER-IN-LAW, SAW HER HUSBAND KILLED BY A JINOO BEFORE SHE WAS TRAPPED IN BARZAKH.
...JUST AS SURELY AS HE IS WITH ALL OF YOU.
BELINDA "BLINK" SANGERYE SPENT YEARS MOURNING THE DEATH OF HER MOTHER, ONLY TO FIND OUT THAT NORA WAS ALIVE.
IN THE TIME MOTHER AND DAUGHTER WERE SEPARATED, AS EACH FOUGHT TO PROTECT HUMANITY AS MUCH AS POSSIBLE, BOTH OF THEM CHANGED...
SOMEBODY SAY AMEN.
...ONE MORE THAN THE OTHER.

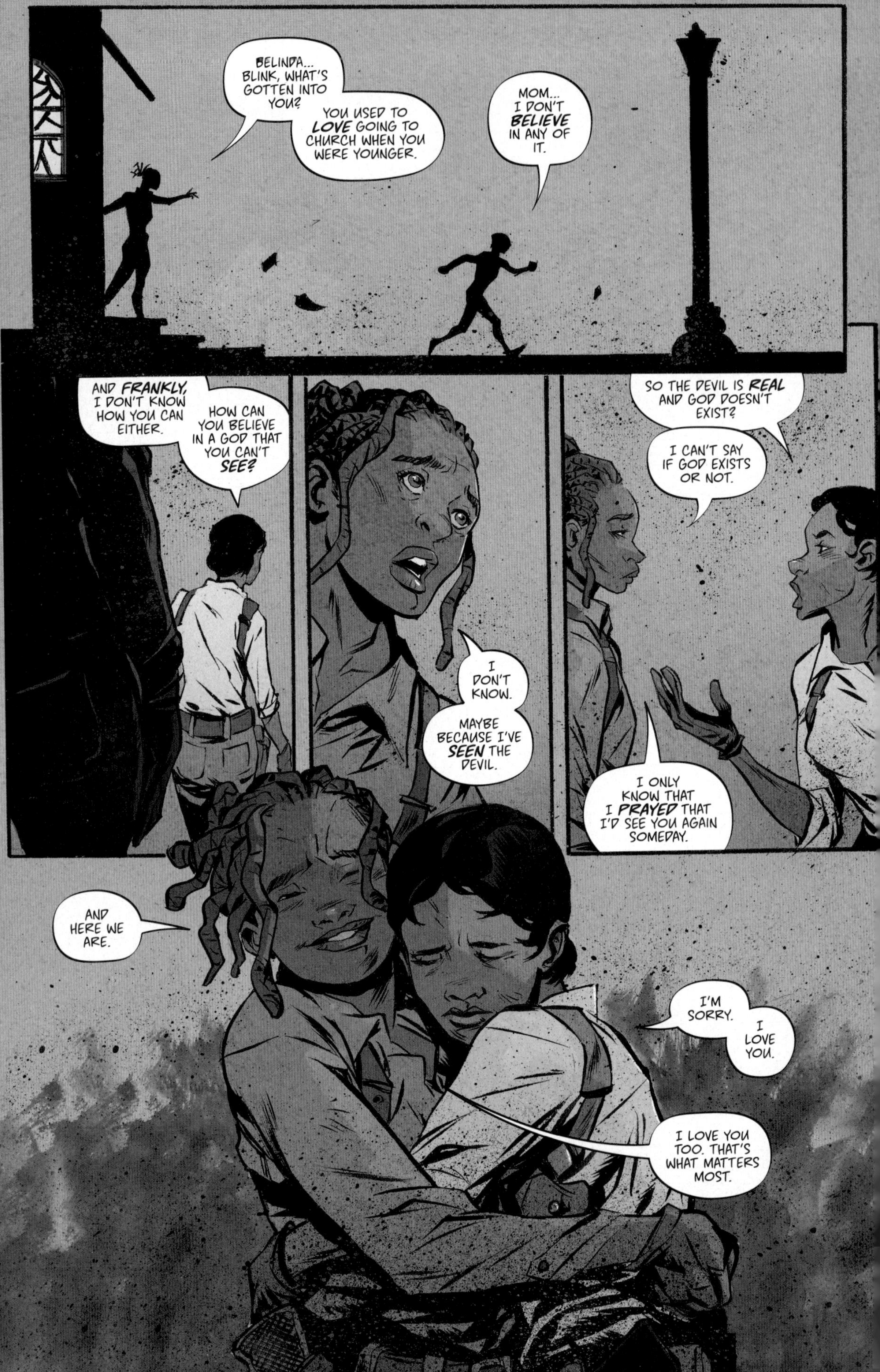
BELINDA... BLINK, WHAT'S GOTTEN INTO YOU?
YOU USED TO LOVE GOING TO CHURCH WHEN YOU WERE YOUNGER.
MOM... I DON'T BELIEVE IN ANY OF IT.
AND FRANKLY, I DON'T KNOW HOW YOU CAN EITHER.
HOW CAN YOU BELIEVE IN A GOD THAT YOU CAN'T SEE?
I DON'T KNOW.
MAYBE BECAUSE I'VE SEEN THE DEVIL.
SO THE DEVIL IS REAL AND GOD DOESN'T EXIST?
I CAN'T SAY IF GOD EXISTS OR NOT.
I ONLY KNOW THAT I PRAYED THAT I'D SEE YOU AGAIN SOMEDAY.
AND HERE WE ARE.
I'M SORRY.
I LOVE YOU.
I LOVE YOU TOO. THAT'S WHAT MATTERS MOST.

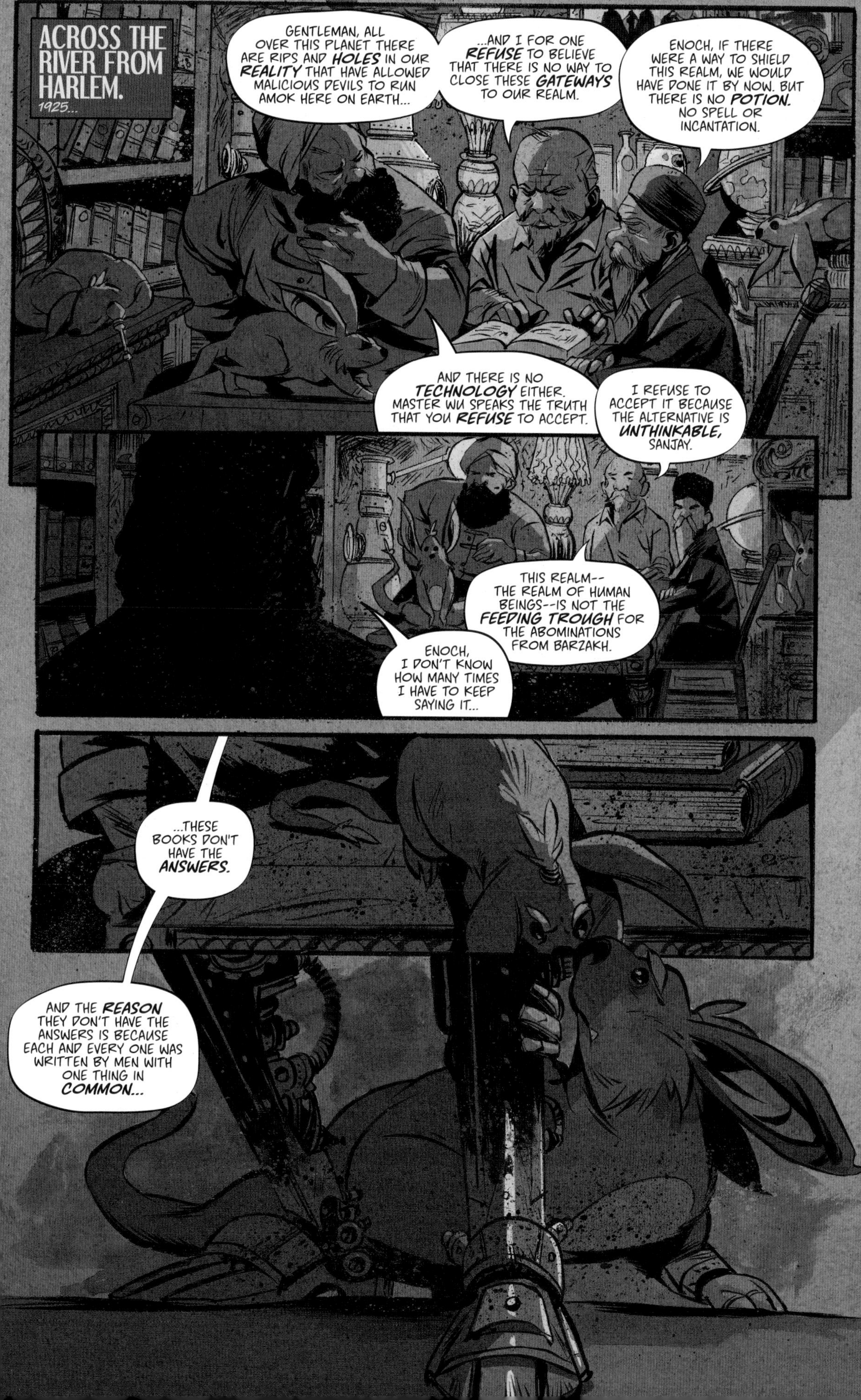
ACROSS THE RIVER FROM HARLEM.
1925...
GENTLEMAN, ALL OVER THIS PLANET THERE ARE RIPS AND HOLES IN OUR REALITY THAT HAVE ALLOWED MALICIOUS DEVILS TO RUN AMOK HERE ON EARTH...
...AND I FOR ONE REFUSE TO BELIEVE THAT THERE IS NO WAY TO CLOSE THESE GATEWAYS TO OUR REALM.
ENOCH, IF THERE WERE A WAY TO SHIELD THIS REALM, WE WOULD HAVE DONE IT BY NOW. BUT THERE IS NO POTION. NO SPELL OR INCANTATION.
AND THERE IS NO TECHNOLOGY EITHER. MASTER WU SPEAKS THE TRUTH THAT YOU REFUSE TO ACCEPT.
I REFUSE TO ACCEPT IT BECAUSE THE ALTERNATIVE IS UNTHINKABLE, SANJAY.
THIS REALM-- THE REALM OF HUMAN BEINGS--IS NOT THE FEEDING TROUGH FOR THE ABOMINATIONS FROM BARZAKH.
ENOCH, I DON'T KNOW HOW MANY TIMES I HAVE TO KEEP SAYING IT...
...THESE BOOKS DON'T HAVE THE ANSWERS.
AND THE REASON THEY DON'T HAVE THE ANSWERS IS BECAUSE EACH AND EVERY ONE WAS WRITTEN BY MEN WITH ONE THING IN COMMON...

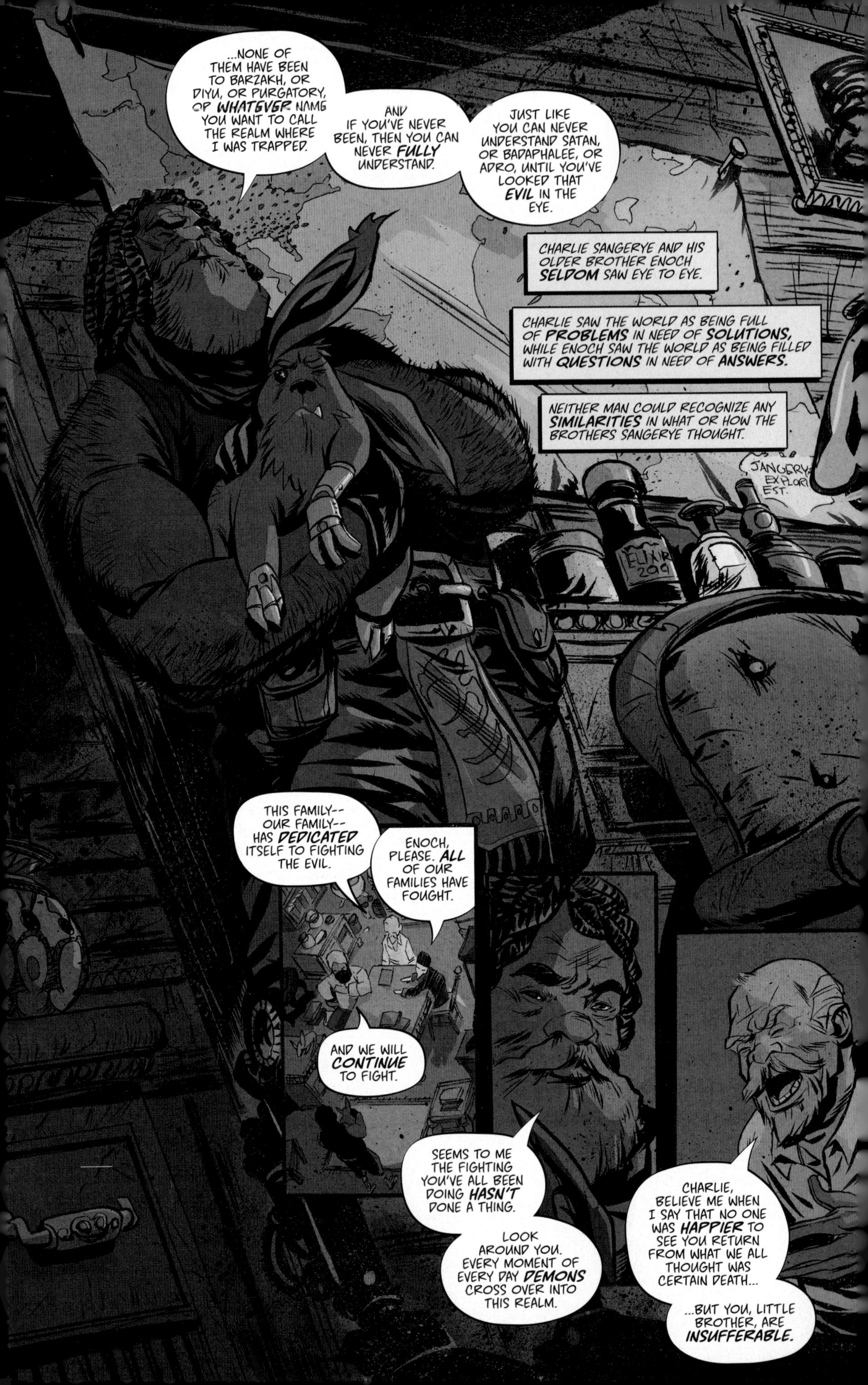
...NONE OF THEM HAVE BEEN TO BARZAKH, OR DIYU, OR PURGATORY, OR WHATEVER NAME YOU WANT TO CALL THE REALM WHERE I WAS TRAPPED.
AND IF YOU'VE NEVER BEEN, THEN YOU CAN NEVER FULLY UNDERSTAND.
JUST LIKE YOU CAN NEVER UNDERSTAND SATAN, OR BADAPHALEE, OR ADRO, UNTIL YOU'VE LOOKED THAT EVIL IN THE EYE.
CHARLIE SANGERYE AND HIS OLDER BROTHER ENOCH SELDOM SAW EYE TO EYE.
CHARLIE SAW THE WORLD AS BEING FULL OF PROBLEMS IN NEED OF SOLUTIONS, WHILE ENOCH SAW THE WORLD AS BEING FILLED WITH QUESTIONS IN NEED OF ANSWERS.
NEITHER MAN COULD RECOGNIZE ANY SIMILARITIES IN WHAT OR HOW THE BROTHERS SANGERYE THOUGHT.
ELIXIR
THIS FAMILY-- OUR FAMILY-- HAS DEDICATED ITSELF TO FIGHTING THE EVIL.
ENOCH, PLEASE. ALL OF OUR FAMILIES HAVE FOUGHT.
AND WE WILL CONTINUE TO FIGHT.
SEEMS TO ME THE FIGHTING YOU'VE ALL BEEN DOING HASN'T DONE A THING.
LOOK AROUND YOU. EVERY MOMENT OF EVERY DAY DEMONS CROSS OVER INTO THIS REALM.
CHARLIE, BELIEVE ME WHEN I SAY THAT NO ONE WAS HAPPIER TO SEE YOU RETURN FROM WHAT WE ALL THOUGHT WAS CERTAIN DEATH...
...BUT YOU, LITTLE BROTHER, ARE INSUFFERABLE.

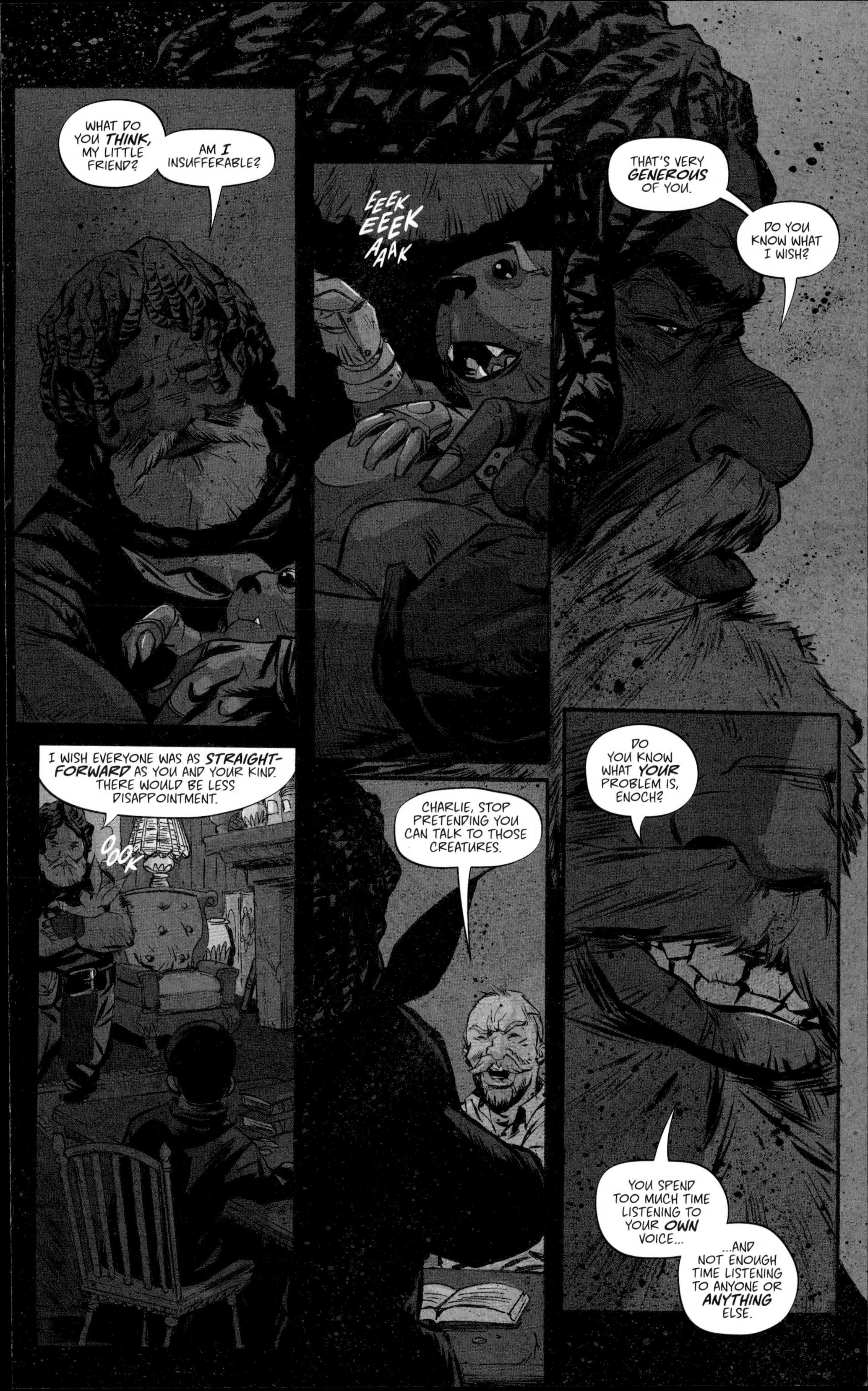
WHAT DO YOU THINK, MY LITTLE FRIEND?
AM I INSUFFERABLE?
EEEK EEEK AAAK
THAT'S VERY GENEROUS OF YOU.
DO YOU KNOW WHAT I WISH?
I WISH EVERYONE WAS AS STRAIGHT-FORWARD AS YOU AND YOUR KIND. THERE WOULD BE LESS DISAPPOINTMENT.
OOOK
CHARLIE, STOP PRETENDING YOU CAN TALK TO THOSE CREATURES.
DO YOU KNOW WHAT YOUR PROBLEM IS, ENOCH?
YOU SPEND TOO MUCH TIME LISTENING TO YOUR OWN VOICE...
...AND NOT ENOUGH TIME LISTENING TO ANYONE OR ANYTHING ELSE.

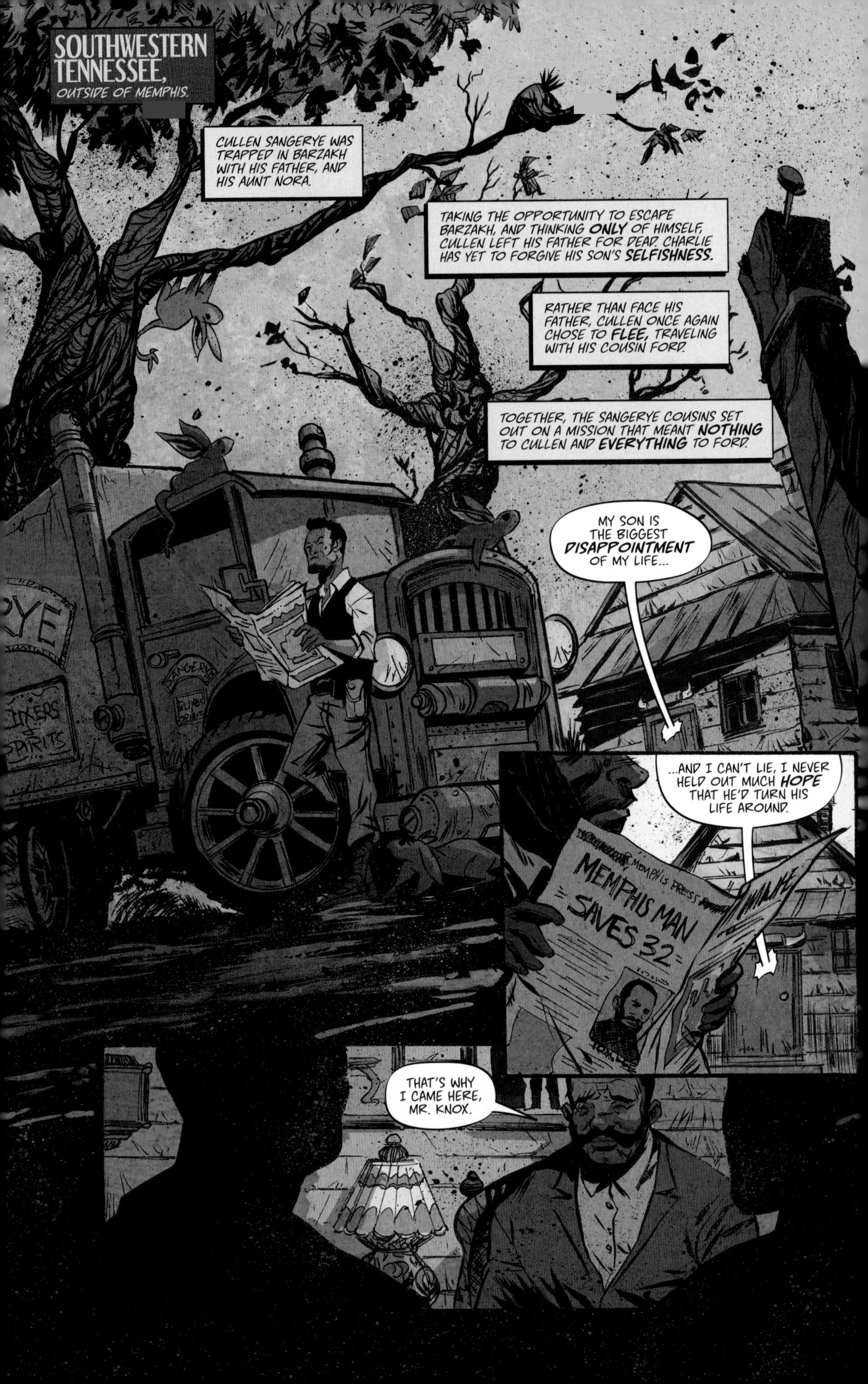
SOUTHWESTERN TENNESSEE,
OUTSIDE OF MEMPHIS.
CULLEN SANGERYE WAS TRAPPED IN BARZAKH WITH HIS FATHER, AND HIS AUNT NORA.
TAKING THE OPPORTUNITY TO ESCAPE BARZAKH, AND THINKING ONLY OF HIMSELF, CULLEN LEFT HIS FATHER FOR DEAD. CHARLIE HAS YET TO FORGIVE HIS SON'S SELFISHNESS.
RATHER THAN FACE HIS FATHER, CULLEN ONCE AGAIN CHOSE TO FLEE, TRAVELING WITH HIS COUSIN FORD.
TOGETHER, THE SANGERYE COUSINS SET OUT ON A MISSION THAT MEANT NOTHING TO CULLEN AND EVERYTHING TO FORD.
MY SON IS THE BIGGEST DISAPPOINTMENT OF MY LIFE...
...AND I CAN'T LIE, I NEVER HELD OUT MUCH HOPE THAT HE'D TURN HIS LIFE AROUND.
MEMPHIS PRESS
MEMPHIS MAN SAVES 32
THAT'S WHY I CAME HERE, MR. KNOX.

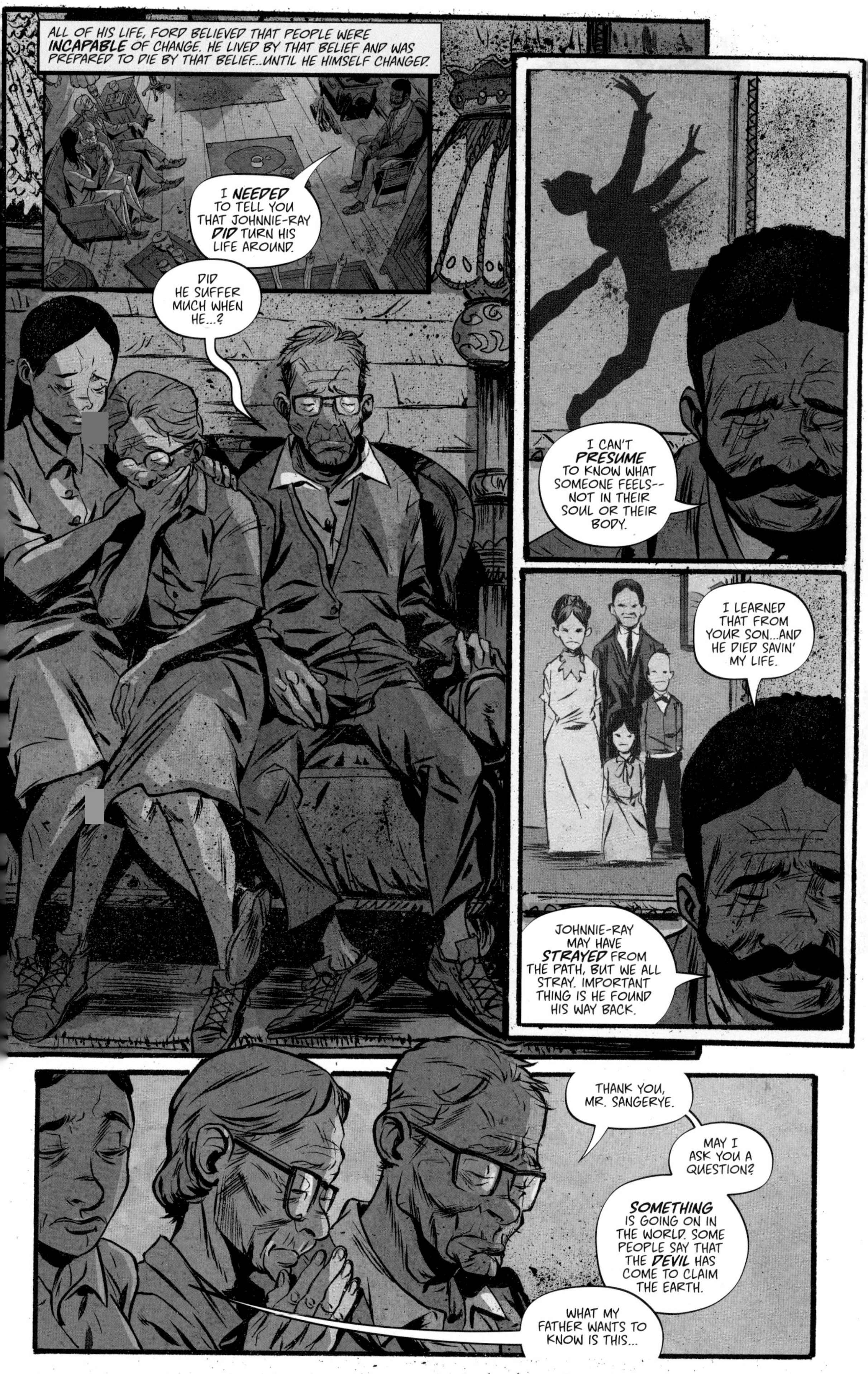

ALL OF HIS LIFE, FORD BELIEVED THAT PEOPLE WERE INCAPABLE OF CHANGE. HE LIVED BY THAT BELIEF AND WAS PREPARED TO DIE BY THAT BELIEF...UNTIL HE HIMSELF CHANGED.
I NEEDED TO TELL YOU THAT JOHNNIE-RAY DID TURN HIS LIFE AROUND.
DID HE SUFFER MUCH WHEN HE...?
I CAN'T PRESUME TO KNOW WHAT SOMEONE FEELS--NOT IN THEIR SOUL OR THEIR BODY.
I LEARNED THAT FROM YOUR SON...AND HE DIED SAVIN' MY LIFE.
JOHNNIE-RAY MAY HAVE STRAYED FROM THE PATH, BUT WE ALL STRAY. IMPORTANT THING IS HE FOUND HIS WAY BACK.
THANK YOU, MR. SANGERYE.
MAY I ASK YOU A QUESTION?
SOMETHING IS GOING ON IN THE WORLD. SOME PEOPLE SAY THAT THE DEVIL HAS COME TO CLAIM THE EARTH.
WHAT MY FATHER WANTS TO KNOW IS THIS...

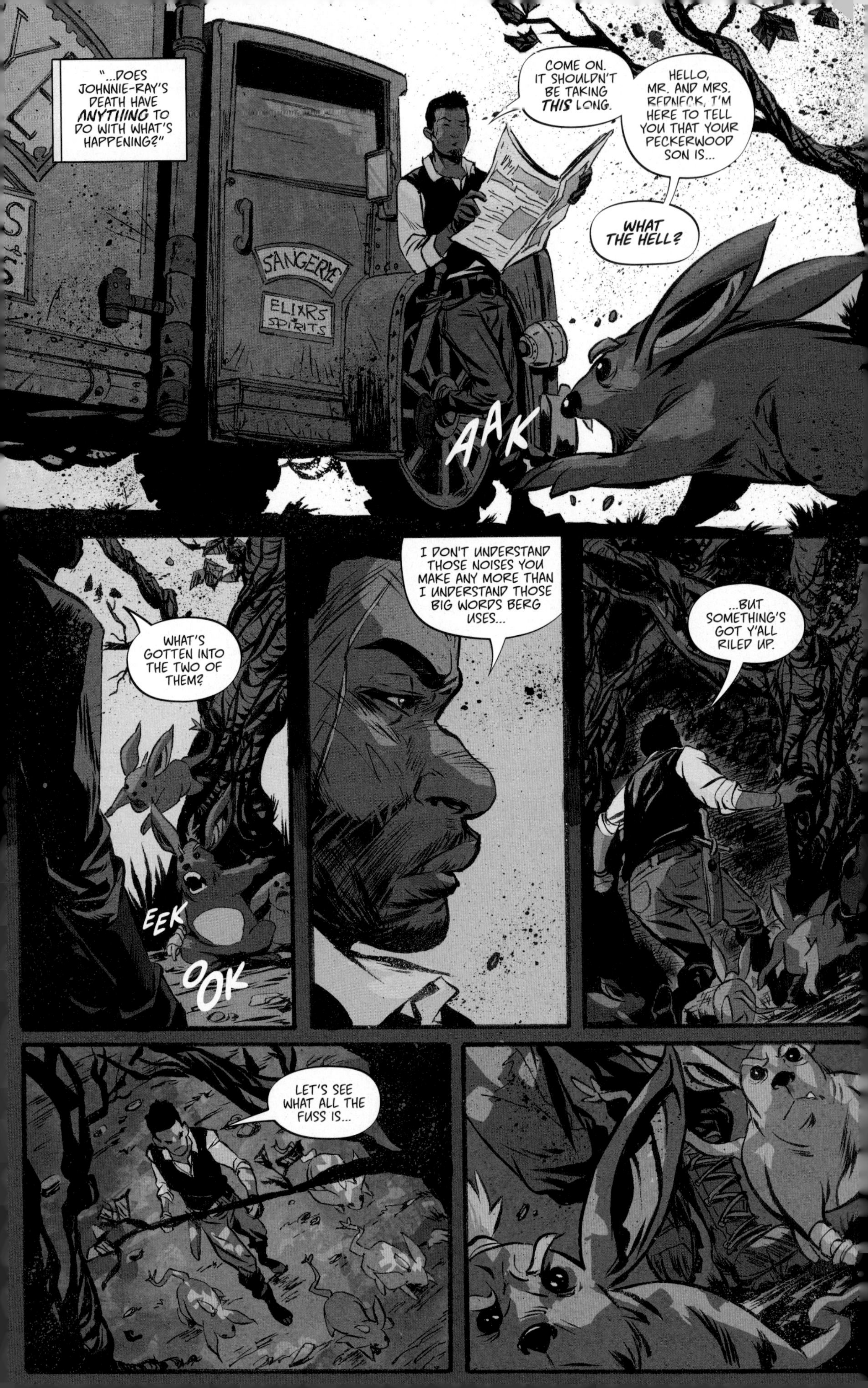
"...DOES JOHNNIE-RAY'S DEATH HAVE ANYTHING TO DO WITH WHAT'S HAPPENING?"
COME ON. IT SHOULDN'T BE TAKING THIS LONG.
HELLO, MR. AND MRS. REDNECK, I'M HERE TO TELL YOU THAT YOUR PECKERWOOD SON IS...
WHAT THE HELL?
SANGERYE
ELIXRS SPIRITS
AAK
WHAT'S GOTTEN INTO THE TWO OF THEM?
EEK
OOK
I DON'T UNDERSTAND THOSE NOISES YOU MAKE ANY MORE THAN I UNDERSTAND THOSE BIG WORDS BERG USES...
...BUT SOMETHING'S GOT Y'ALL RILED UP.
LET'S SEE WHAT ALL THE FUSS IS...

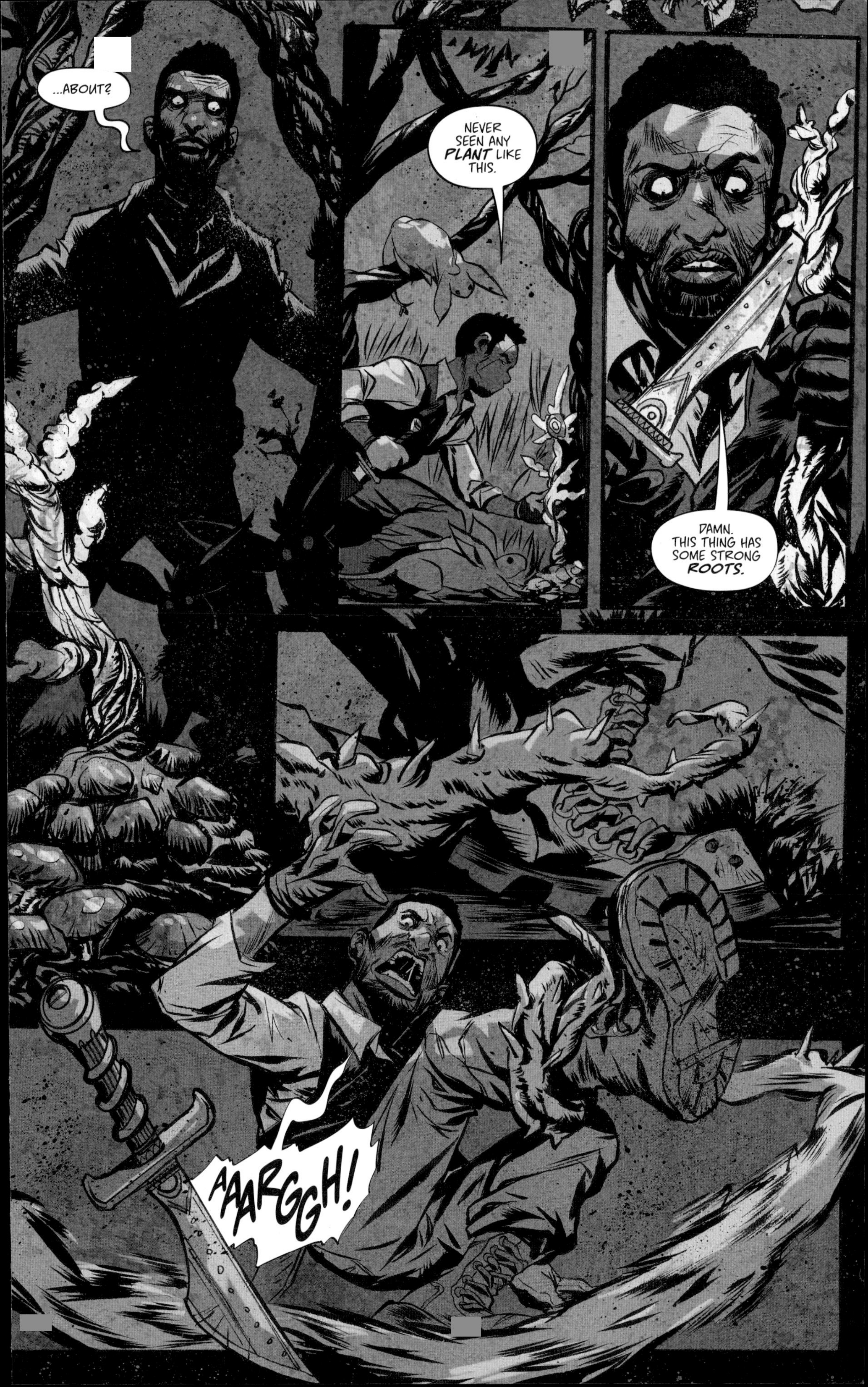

...ABOUT?
NEVER SEEN ANY PLANT LIKE THIS.
DAMN. THIS THING HAS SOME STRONG ROOTS.
AAARGGH!

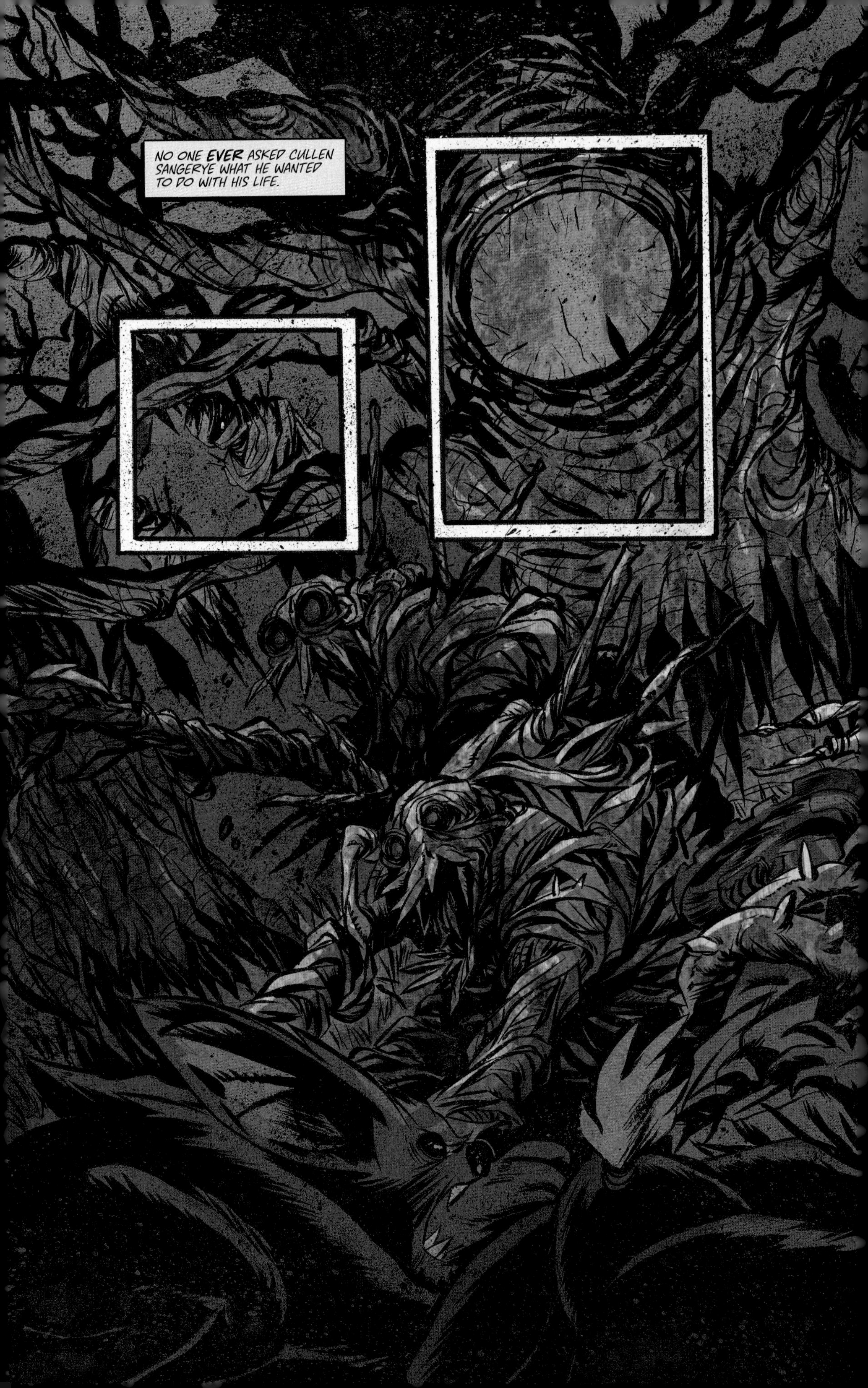
NO ONE EVER ASKED CULLEN SANGERYE WHAT HE WANTED TO DO WITH HIS LIFE.

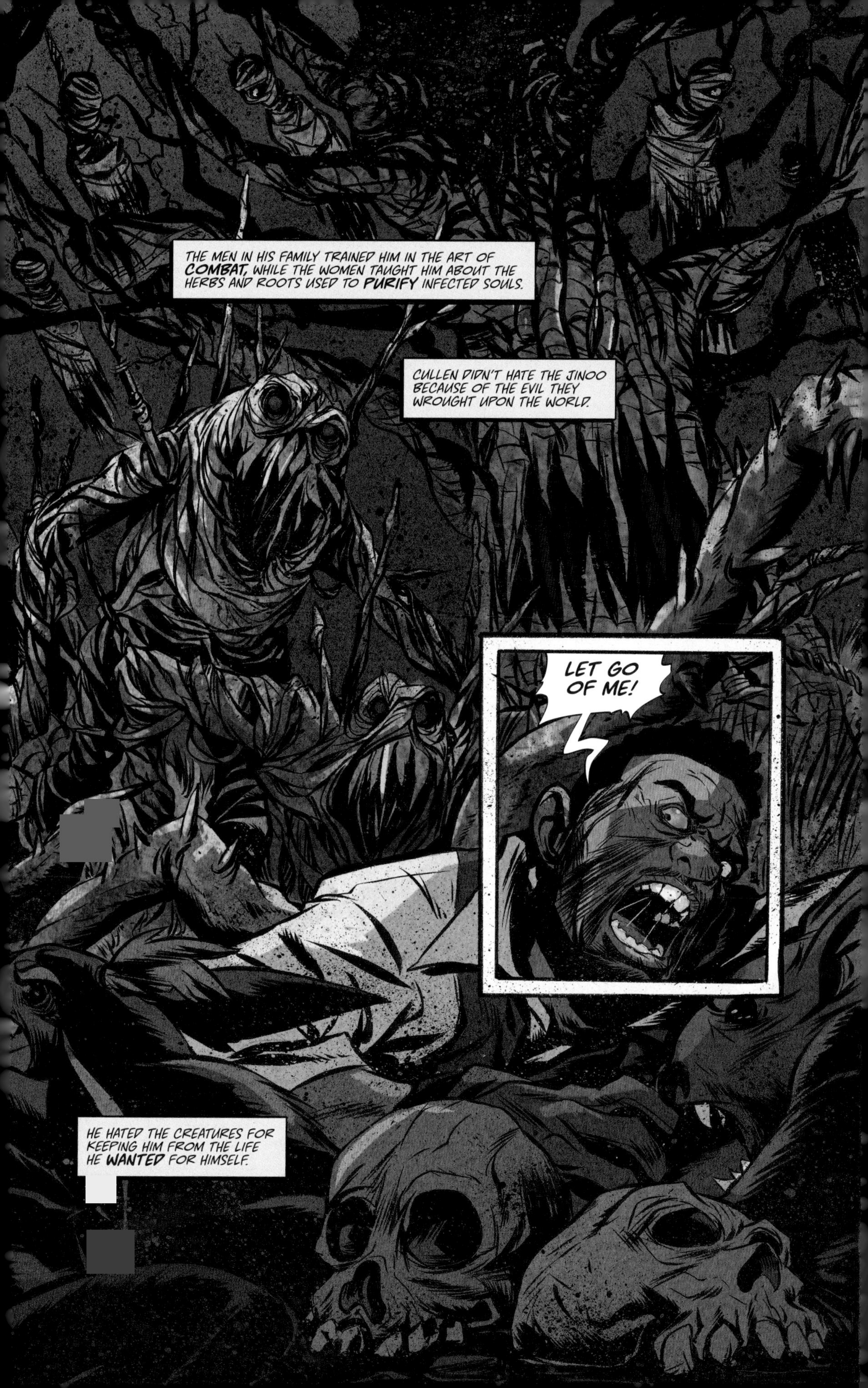
THE MEN IN HIS FAMILY TRAINED HIM IN THE ART OF COMBAT, WHILE THE WOMEN TAUGHT HIM ABOUT THE HERBS AND ROOTS USED TO PURIFY INFECTED SOULS.
CULLEN DIDN'T HATE THE JINOO BECAUSE OF THE EVIL THEY WROUGHT UPON THE WORLD.
LET GO OF ME!
HE HATED THE CREATURES FOR KEEPING HIM FROM THE LIFE HE WANTED FOR HIMSELF.

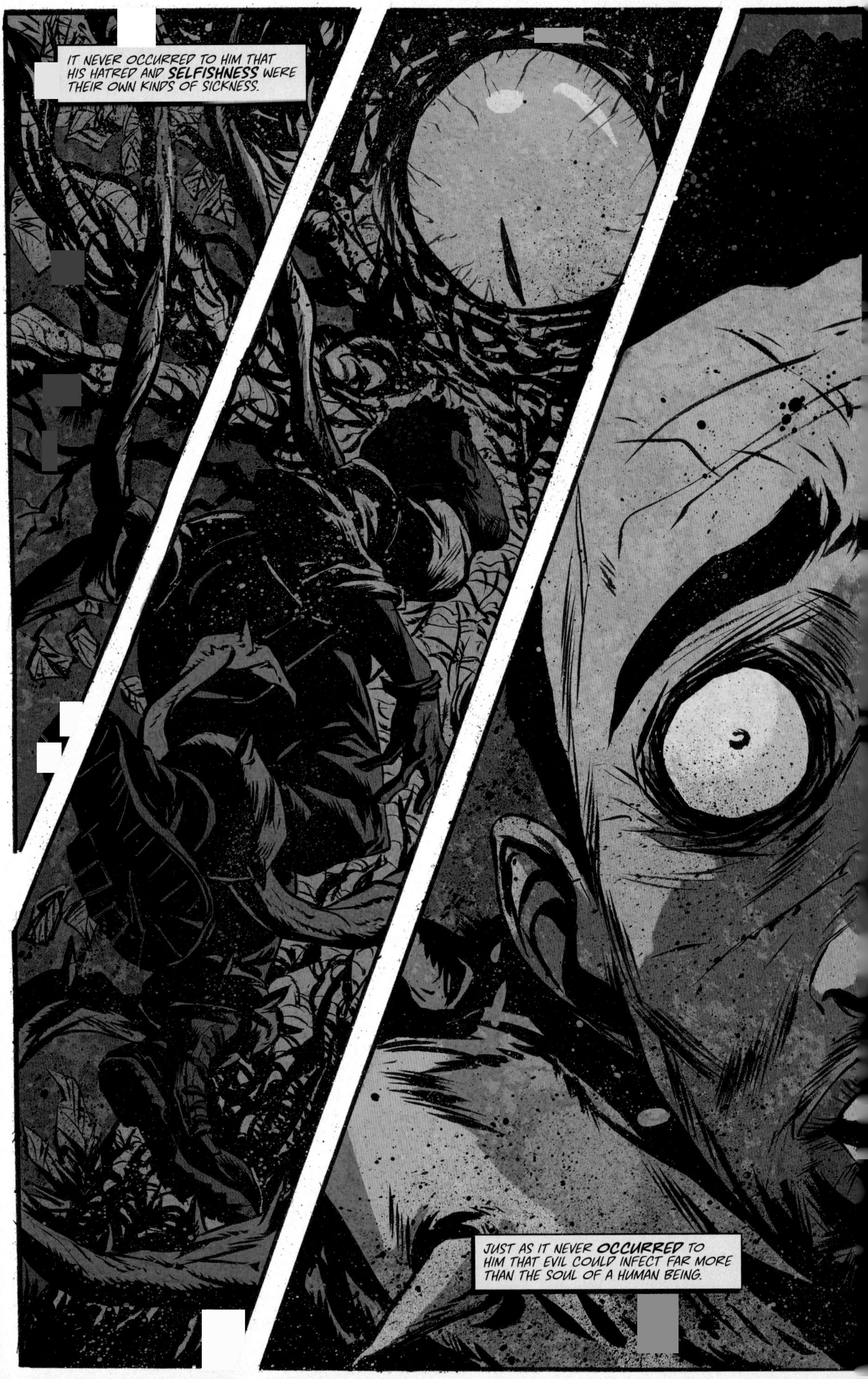
IT NEVER OCCURRED TO HIM THAT HIS HATRED AND SELFISHNESS WERE THEIR OWN KINDS OF SICKNESS.
JUST AS IT NEVER OCCURRED TO HIM THAT EVIL COULD INFECT FAR MORE THAN THE SOUL OF A HUMAN BEING.

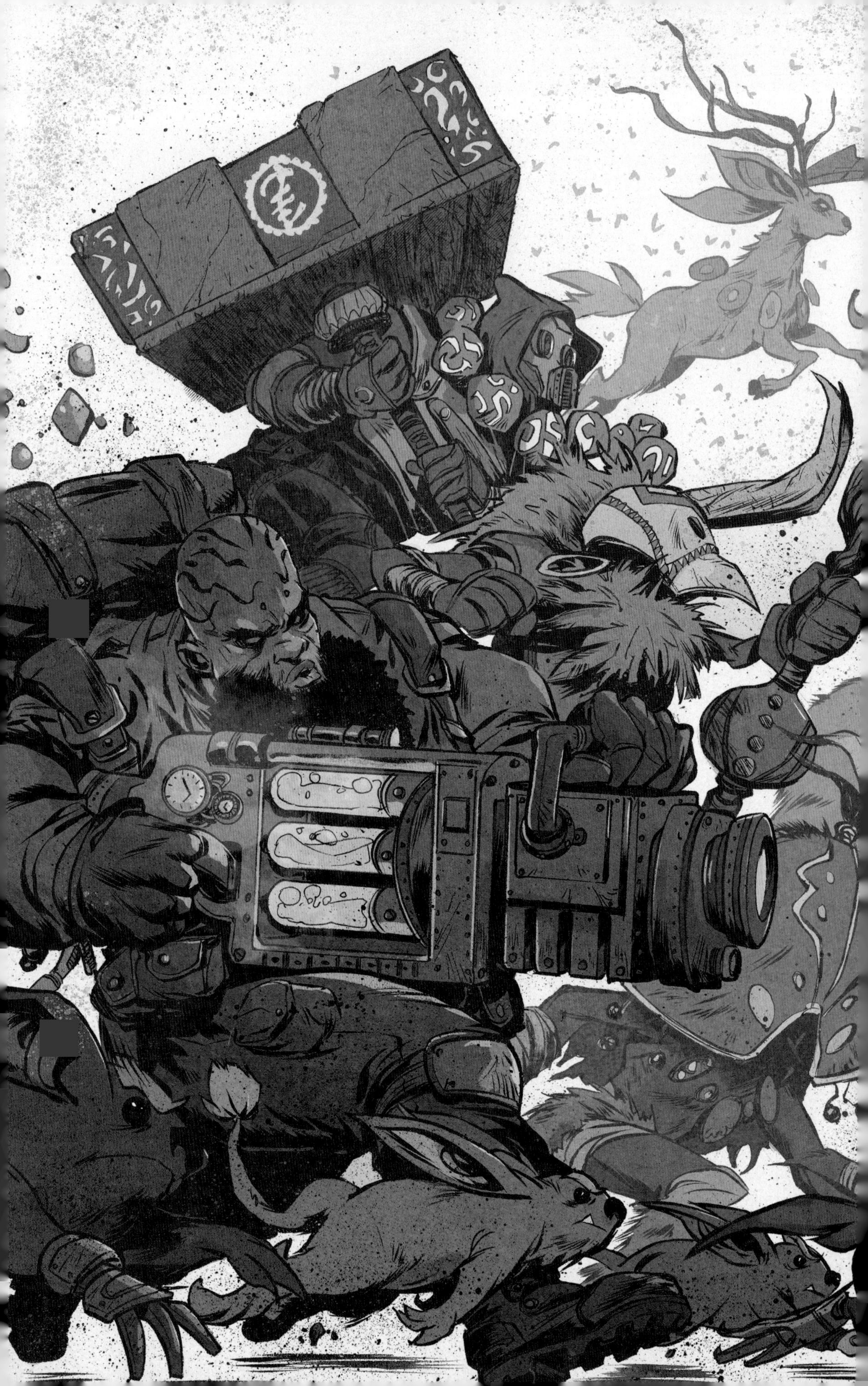

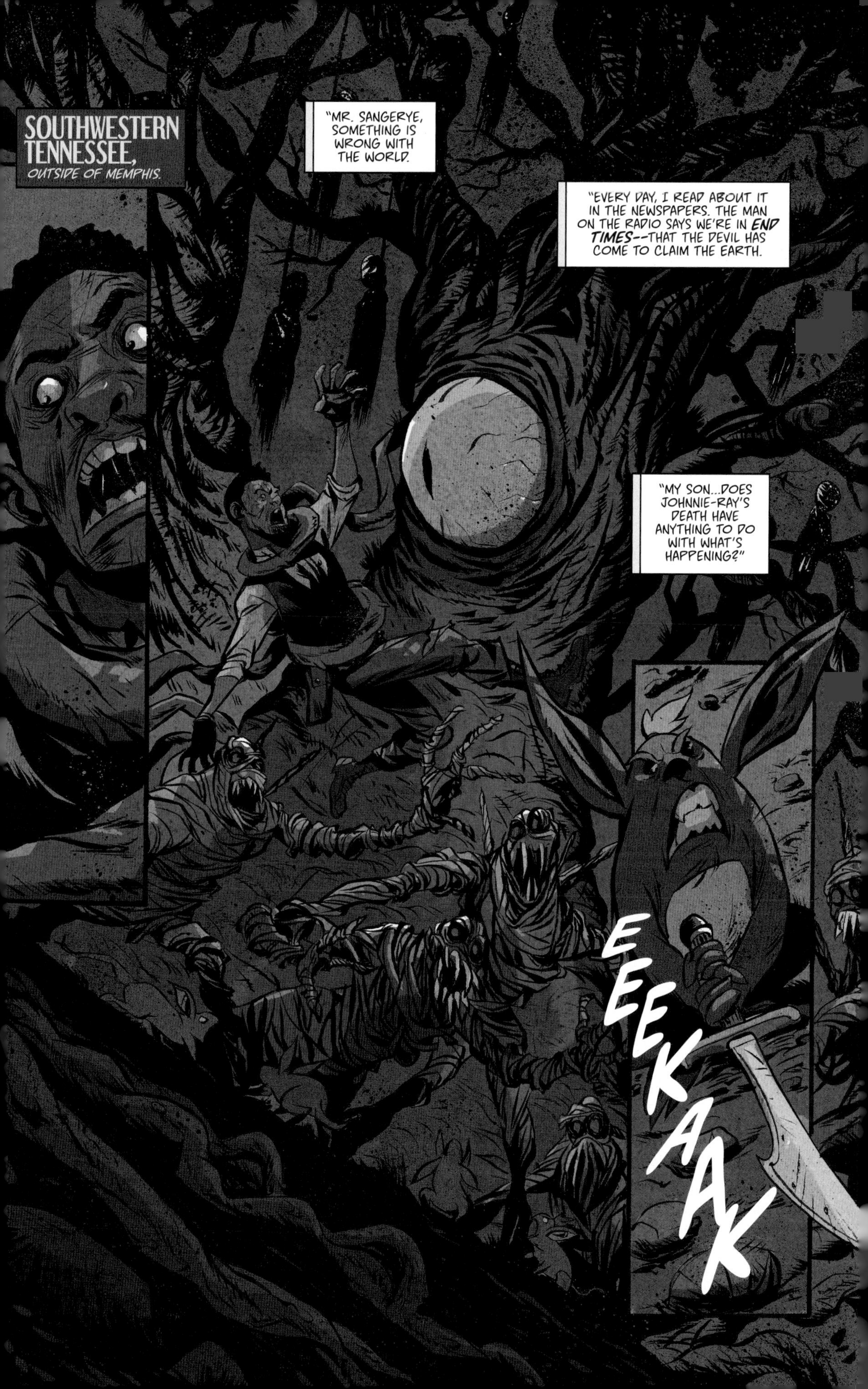
SOUTHWESTERN TENNESSEE,
OUTSIDE OF MEMPHIS.
"MR. SANGERYE, SOMETHING IS WRONG WITH THE WORLD.
"EVERY DAY, I READ ABOUT IT IN THE NEWSPAPERS. THE MAN ON THE RADIO SAYS WE'RE IN END TIMES--THAT THE DEVIL HAS COME TO CLAIM THE EARTH.
"MY SON...DOES JOHNNIE-RAY'S DEATH HAVE ANYTHING TO DO WITH WHAT'S HAPPENING?"
EEEKAAAK

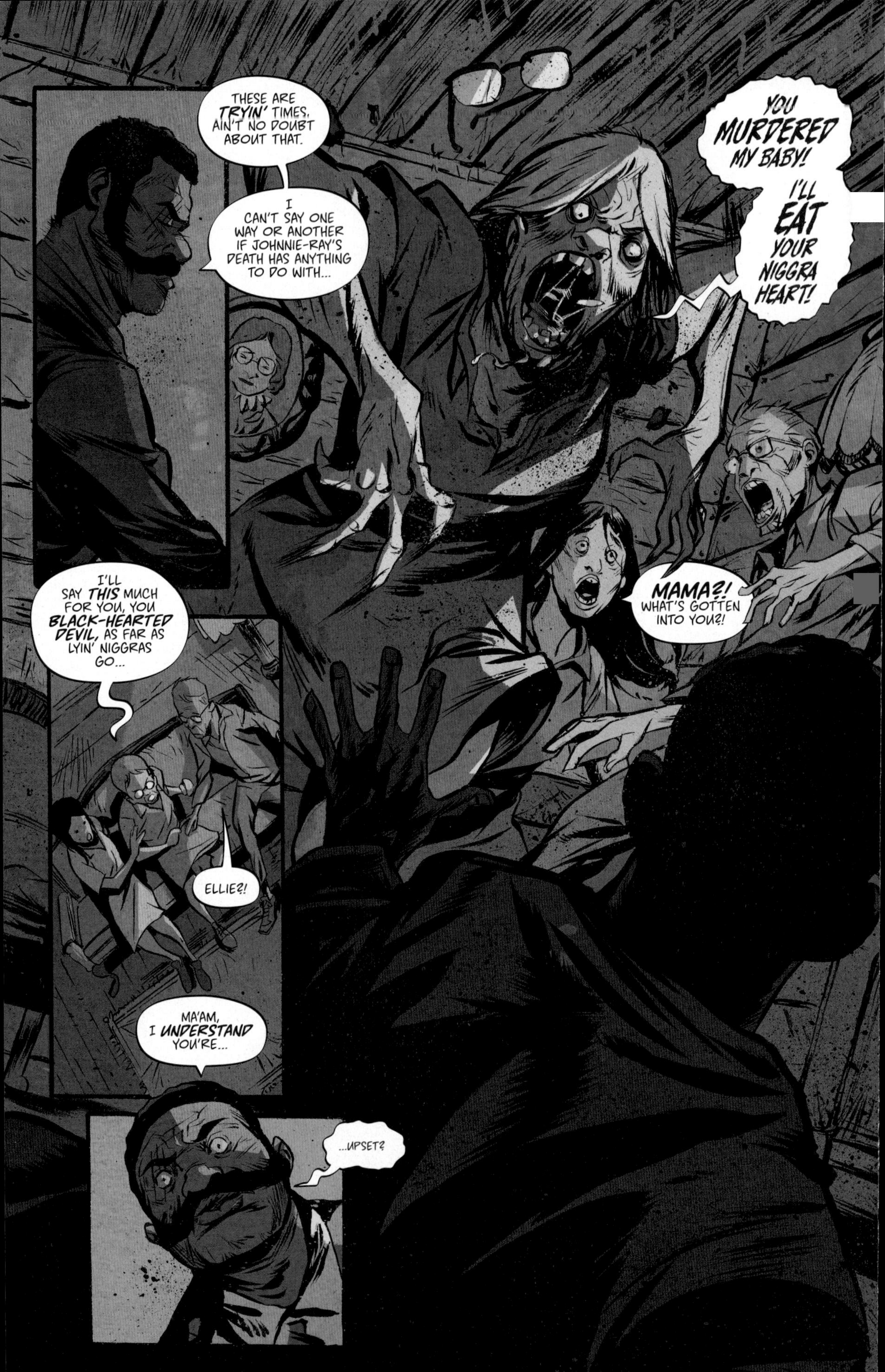
THESE ARE TRYIN' TIMES. AIN'T NO DOUBT ABOUT THAT.
I CAN'T SAY ONE WAY OR ANOTHER IF JOHNNIE-RAY'S DEATH HAS ANYTHING TO DO WITH...
YOU MURDERED MY BABY!
I'LL EAT YOUR NIGGRA HEART!
I'LL SAY THIS MUCH FOR YOU, YOU BLACK-HEARTED DEVIL, AS FAR AS LYIN' NIGGRAS GO...
MAMA?! WHAT'S GOTTEN INTO YOU?!
ELLIE?!
MA'AM, I UNDERSTAND YOU'RE...
...UPSET?

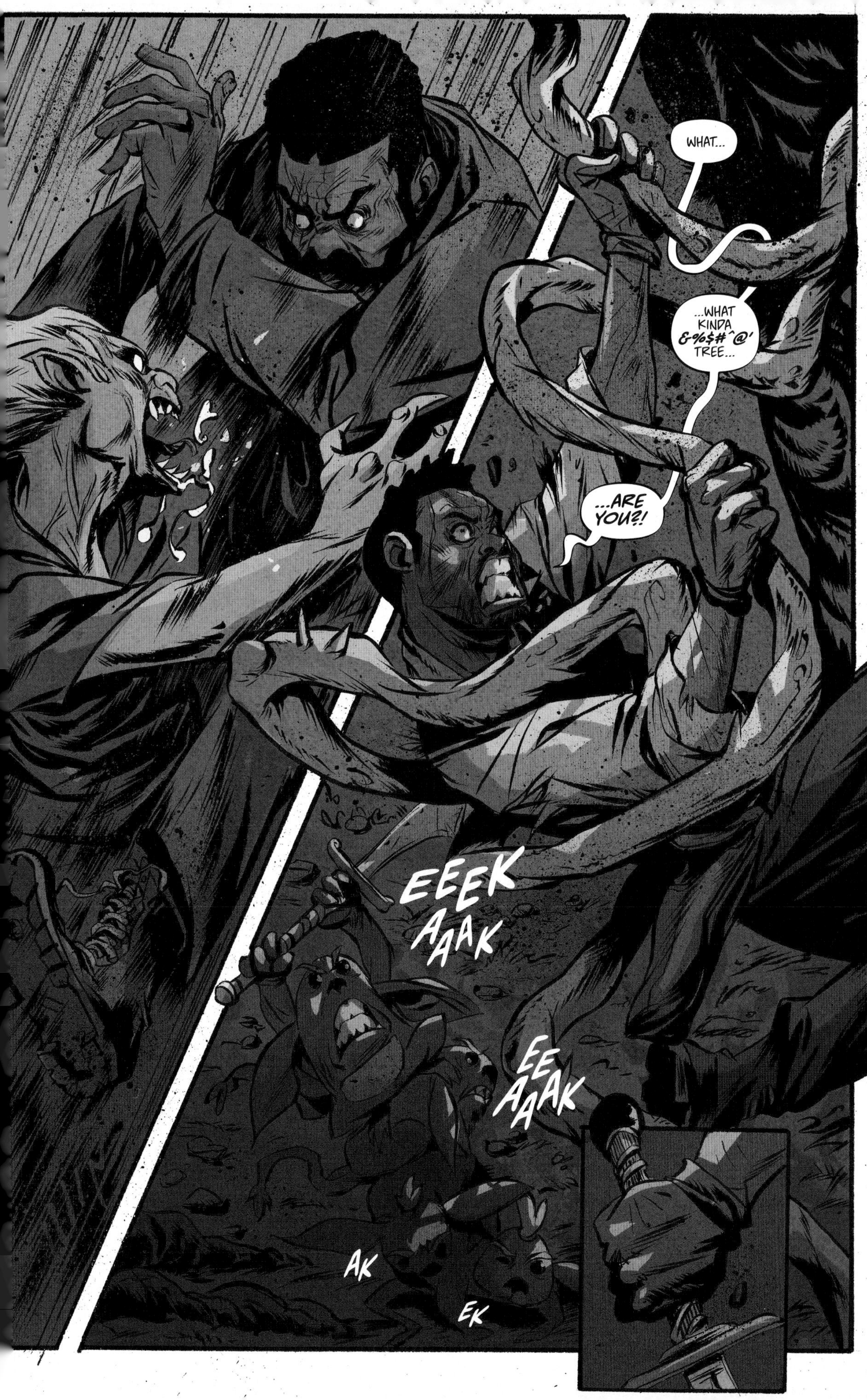
WHAT...
...WHAT KINDA &%$#^@' TREE...
...ARE YOU?!
EEEK AAAK
EE AAAK
AK
EK

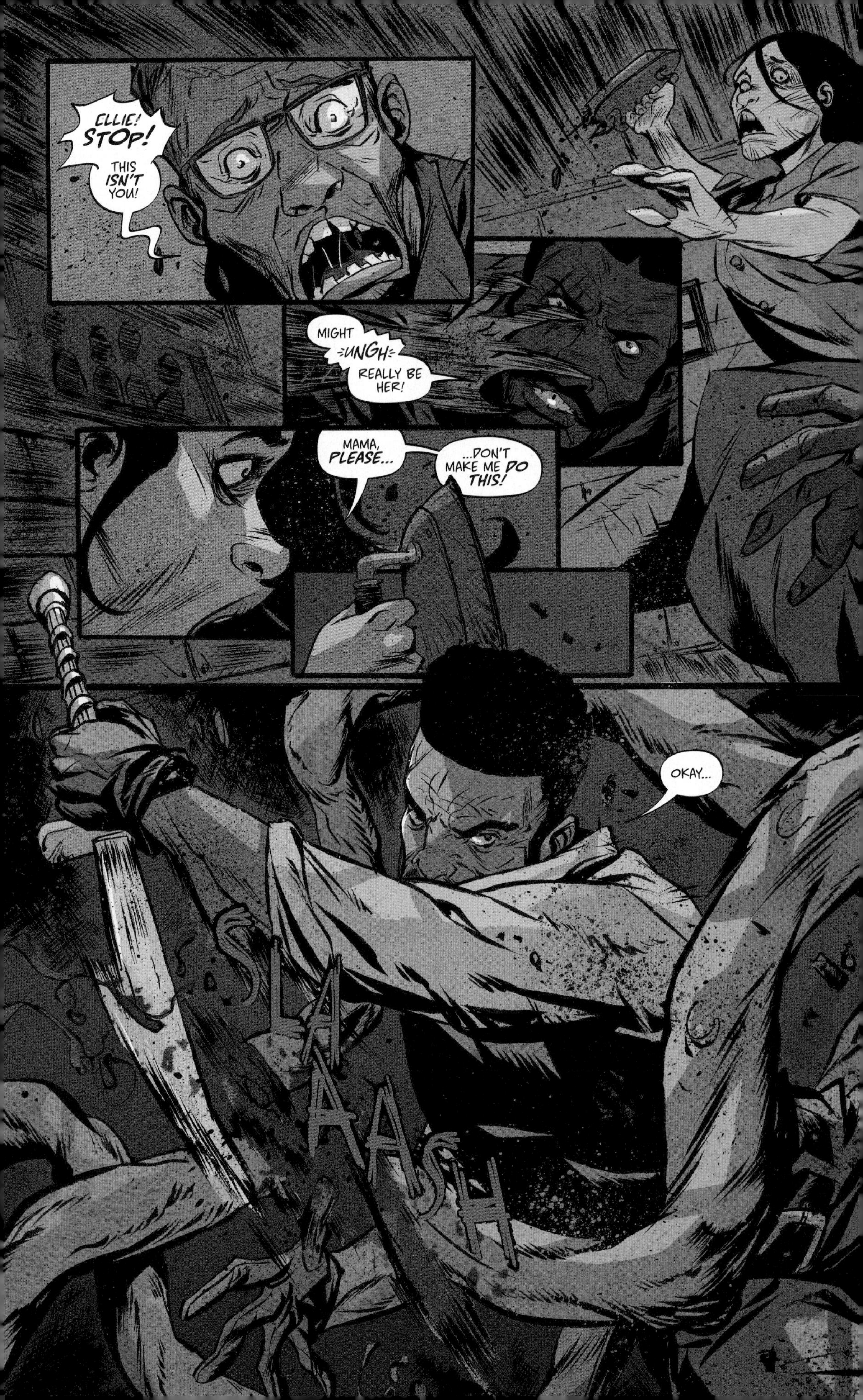
ELLIE! STOP!
THIS ISN'T YOU!
MIGHT -UNGH- REALLY BE HER!
MAMA, PLEASE...
...DON'T MAKE ME DO THIS!
OKAY...
SLAAASH

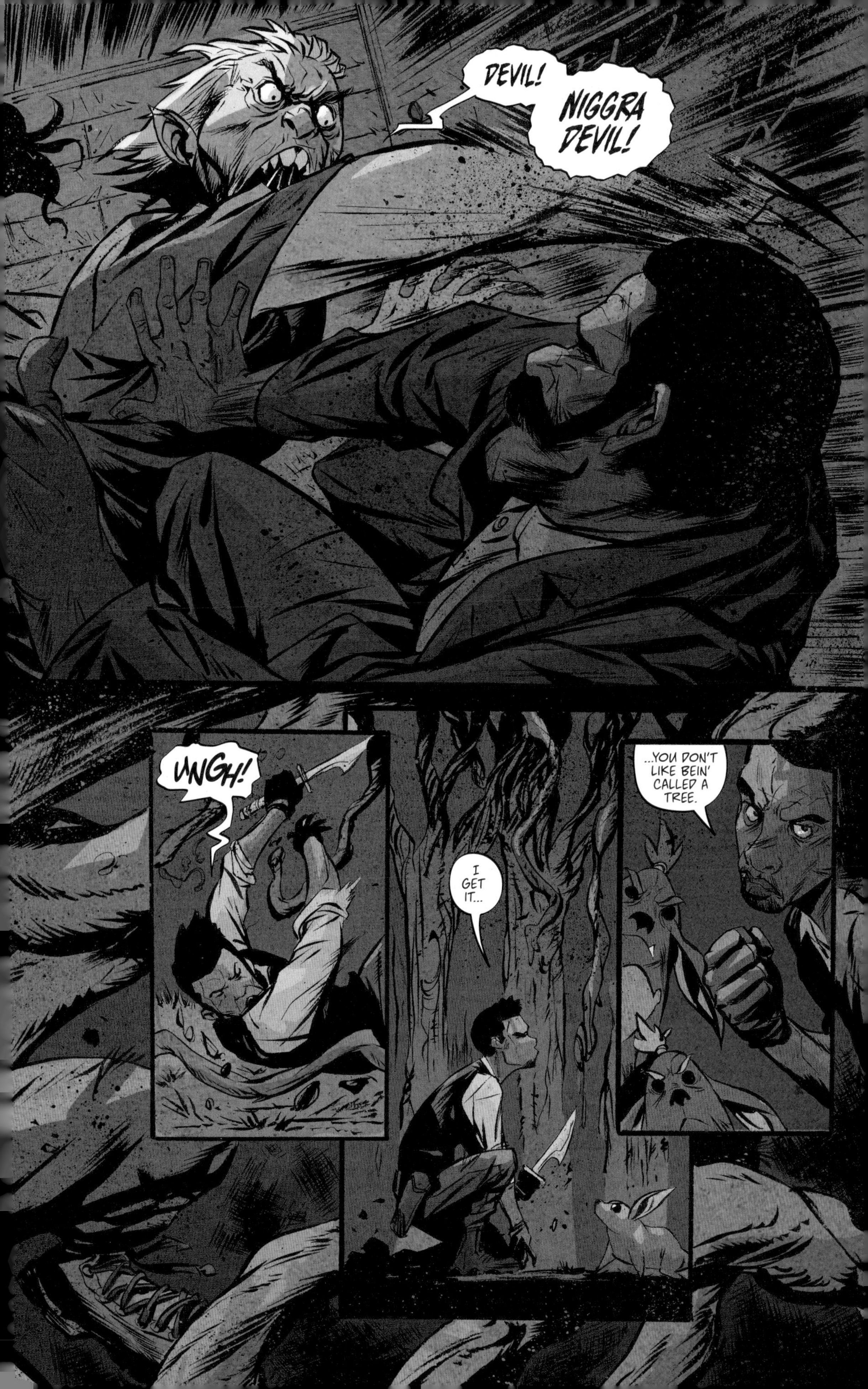
DEVIL!
NIGGRA DEVIL!
UNGH!
I GET IT...
...YOU DON'T LIKE BEIN' CALLED A TREE.

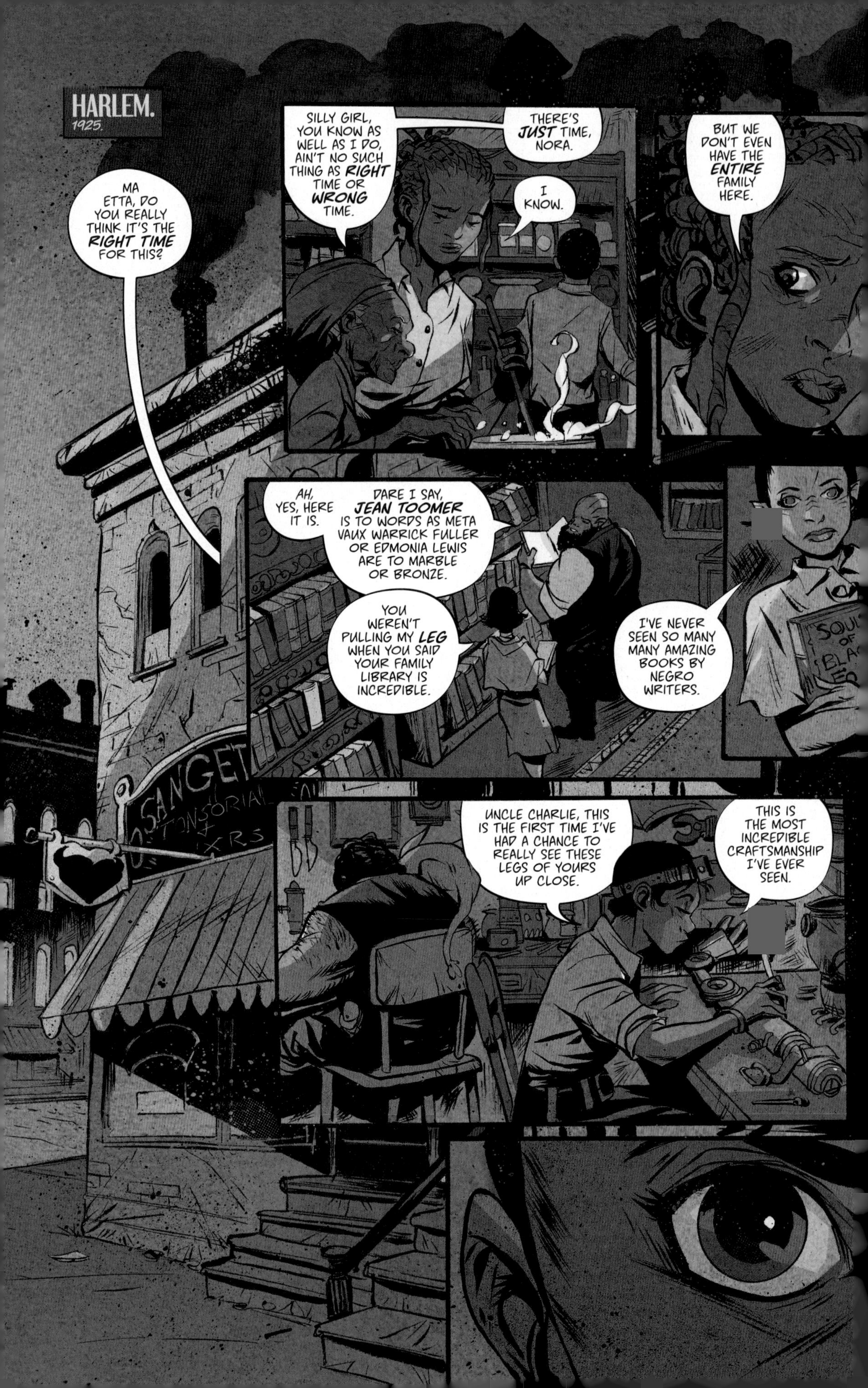
HARLEM.
1925.
MA ETTA, DO YOU REALLY THINK IT'S THE RIGHT TIME FOR THIS?
SILLY GIRL, YOU KNOW AS WELL AS I DO, AIN'T NO SUCH THING AS RIGHT TIME OR WRONG TIME.
THERE'S JUST TIME, NORA.
I KNOW.
BUT WE DON'T EVEN HAVE THE ENTIRE FAMILY HERE.
AH, YES, HERE IT IS.
DARE I SAY, JEAN TOOMER IS TO WORDS AS META VAUX WARRICK FULLER OR EDMONIA LEWIS ARE TO MARBLE OR BRONZE.
YOU WEREN'T PULLING MY LEG WHEN YOU SAID YOUR FAMILY LIBRARY IS INCREDIBLE.
I'VE NEVER SEEN SO MANY MANY AMAZING BOOKS BY NEGRO WRITERS.
UNCLE CHARLIE, THIS IS THE FIRST TIME I'VE HAD A CHANCE TO REALLY SEE THESE LEGS OF YOURS UP CLOSE.
THIS IS THE MOST INCREDIBLE CRAFTSMANSHIP I'VE EVER SEEN.

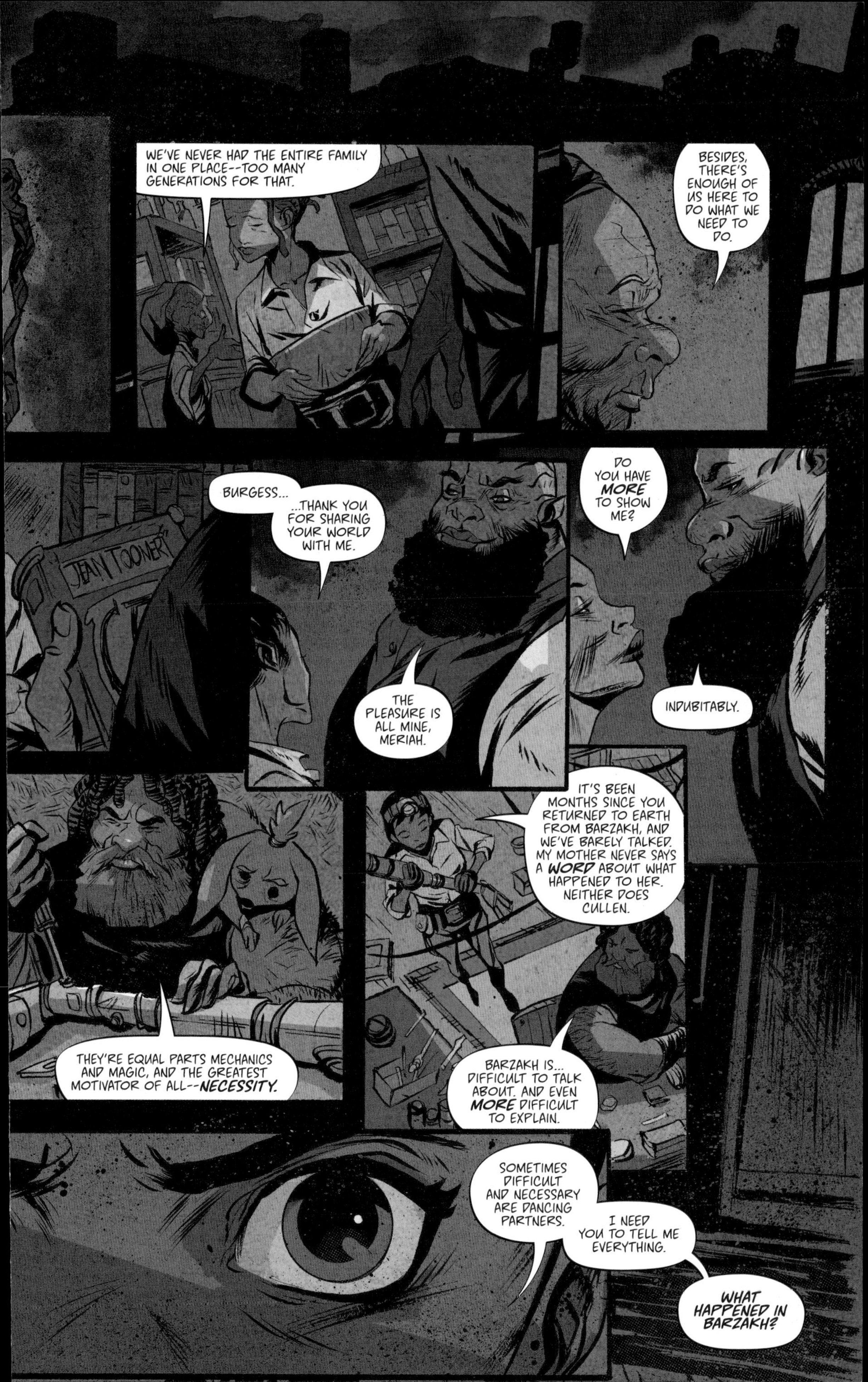
WE'VE NEVER HAD THE ENTIRE FAMILY IN ONE PLACE--TOO MANY GENERATIONS FOR THAT.
BESIDES, THERE'S ENOUGH OF US HERE TO DO WHAT WE NEED TO DO.
JEAN TOONER
BURGESS...
...THANK YOU FOR SHARING YOUR WORLD WITH ME.
THE PLEASURE IS ALL MINE, MERIAH.
DO YOU HAVE MORE TO SHOW ME?
INDUBITABLY.
THEY'RE EQUAL PARTS MECHANICS AND MAGIC, AND THE GREATEST MOTIVATOR OF ALL--NECESSITY.
IT'S BEEN MONTHS SINCE YOU RETURNED TO EARTH FROM BARZAKH, AND WE'VE BARELY TALKED. MY MOTHER NEVER SAYS A WORD ABOUT WHAT HAPPENED TO HER. NEITHER DOES CULLEN.
BARZAKH IS... DIFFICULT TO TALK ABOUT. AND EVEN MORE DIFFICULT TO EXPLAIN.
SOMETIMES DIFFICULT AND NECESSARY ARE DANCING PARTNERS.
I NEED YOU TO TELL ME EVERYTHING.
WHAT HAPPENED IN BARZAKH?

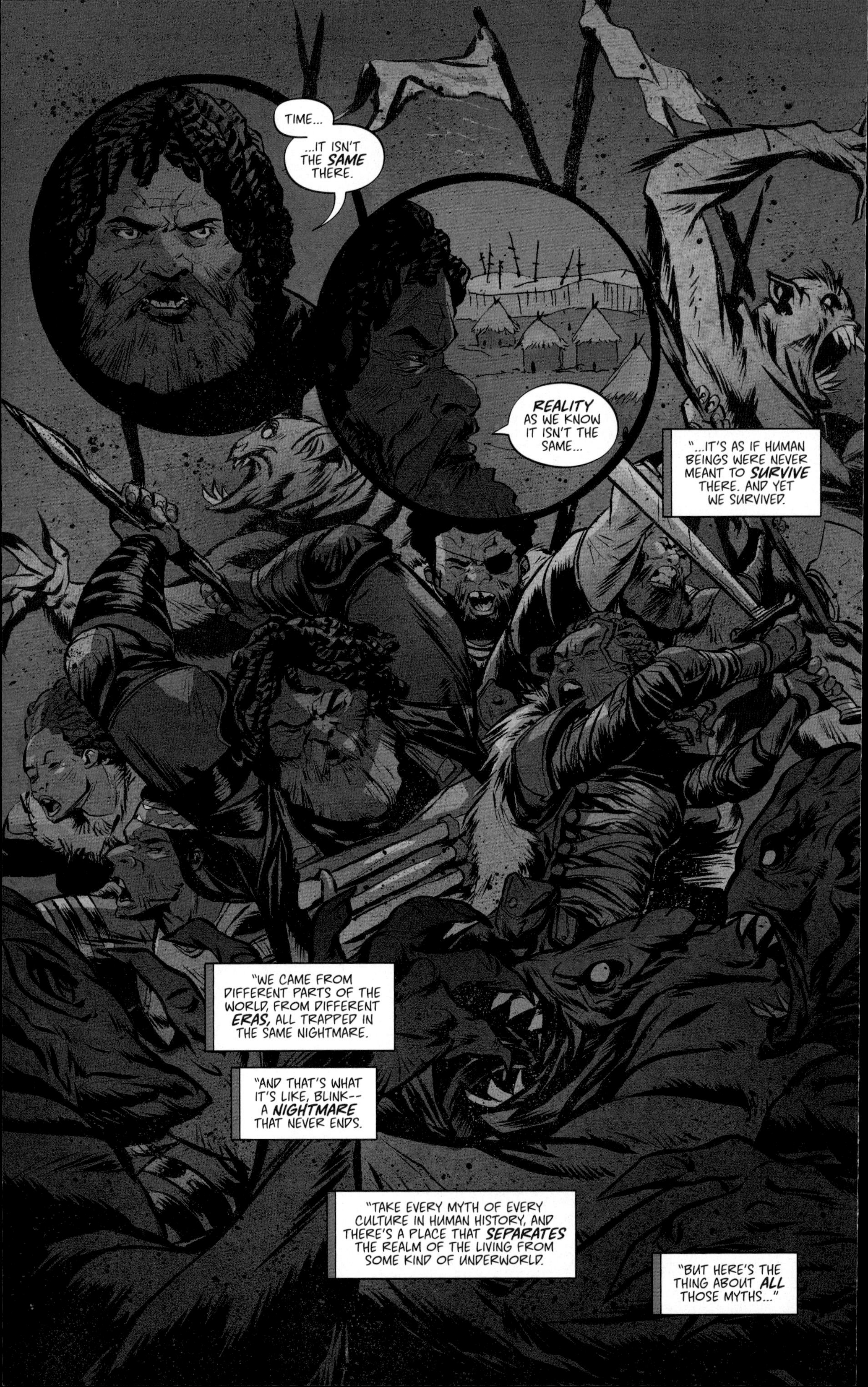
TIME...
...IT ISN'T THE SAME THERE.
REALITY AS WE KNOW IT ISN'T THE SAME...
"...IT'S AS IF HUMAN BEINGS WERE NEVER MEANT TO SURVIVE THERE. AND YET WE SURVIVED.
"WE CAME FROM DIFFERENT PARTS OF THE WORLD, FROM DIFFERENT ERAS, ALL TRAPPED IN THE SAME NIGHTMARE.
"AND THAT'S WHAT IT'S LIKE, BLINK-- A NIGHTMARE THAT NEVER ENDS.
"TAKE EVERY MYTH OF EVERY CULTURE IN HUMAN HISTORY, AND THERE'S A PLACE THAT SEPARATES THE REALM OF THE LIVING FROM SOME KIND OF UNDERWORLD.
"BUT HERE'S THE THING ABOUT ALL THOSE MYTHS..."

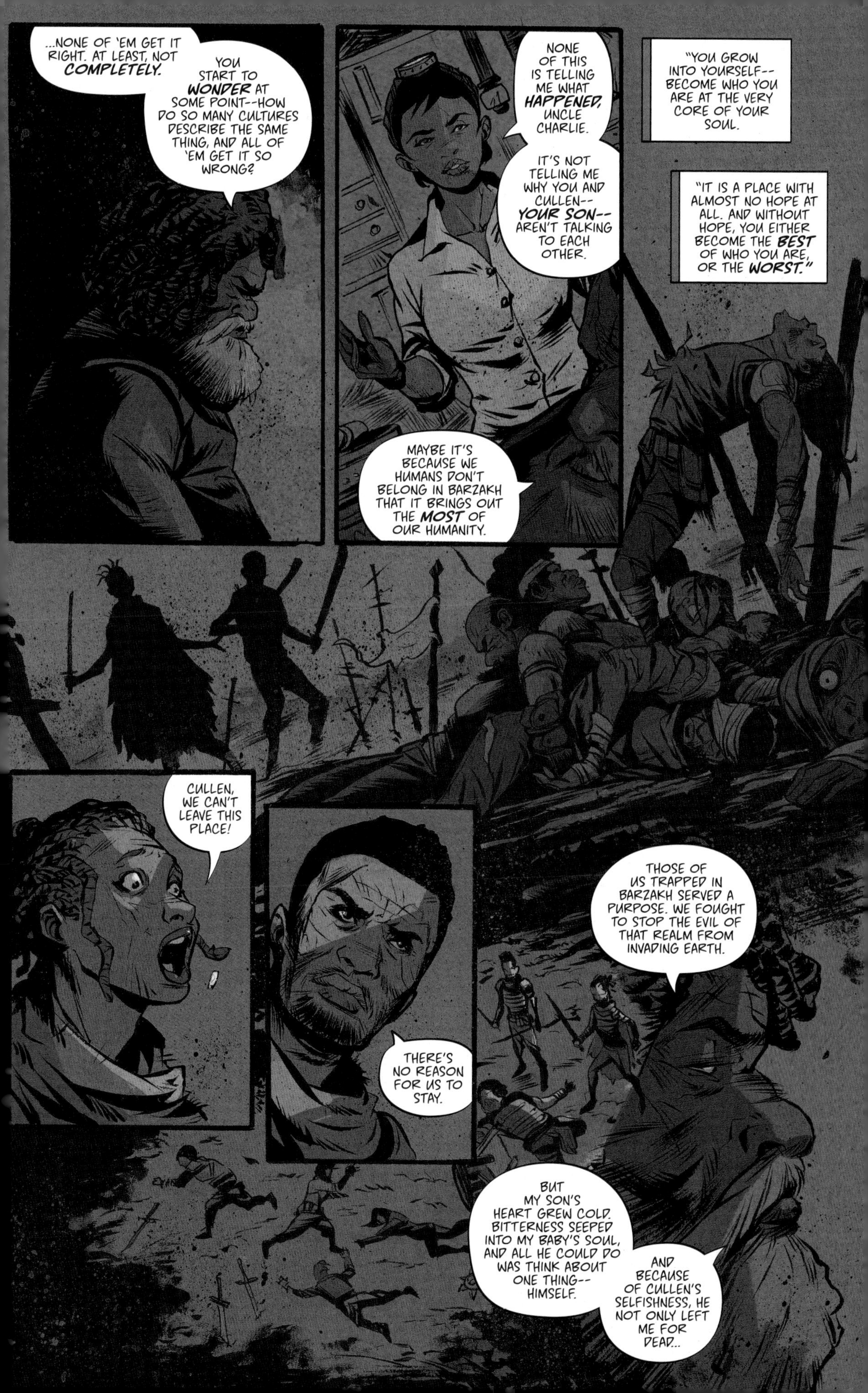
...NONE OF 'EM GET IT RIGHT. AT LEAST, NOT COMPLETELY.
YOU START TO WONDER AT SOME POINT--HOW DO SO MANY CULTURES DESCRIBE THE SAME THING, AND ALL OF 'EM GET IT SO WRONG?
NONE OF THIS IS TELLING ME WHAT HAPPENED, UNCLE CHARLIE.
IT'S NOT TELLING ME WHY YOU AND CULLEN--YOUR SON--AREN'T TALKING TO EACH OTHER.
"YOU GROW INTO YOURSELF--BECOME WHO YOU ARE AT THE VERY CORE OF YOUR SOUL.
"IT IS A PLACE WITH ALMOST NO HOPE AT ALL. AND WITHOUT HOPE, YOU EITHER BECOME THE BEST OF WHO YOU ARE, OR THE WORST."
MAYBE IT'S BECAUSE WE HUMANS DON'T BELONG IN BARZAKH THAT IT BRINGS OUT THE MOST OF OUR HUMANITY.
CULLEN, WE CAN'T LEAVE THIS PLACE!
THERE'S NO REASON FOR US TO STAY.
THOSE OF US TRAPPED IN BARZAKH SERVED A PURPOSE. WE FOUGHT TO STOP THE EVIL OF THAT REALM FROM INVADING EARTH.
BUT MY SON'S HEART GREW COLD. BITTERNESS SEEPED INTO MY BABY'S SOUL, AND ALL HE COULD DO WAS THINK ABOUT ONE THING--HIMSELF.
AND BECAUSE OF CULLEN'S SELFISHNESS, HE NOT ONLY LEFT ME FOR DEAD...

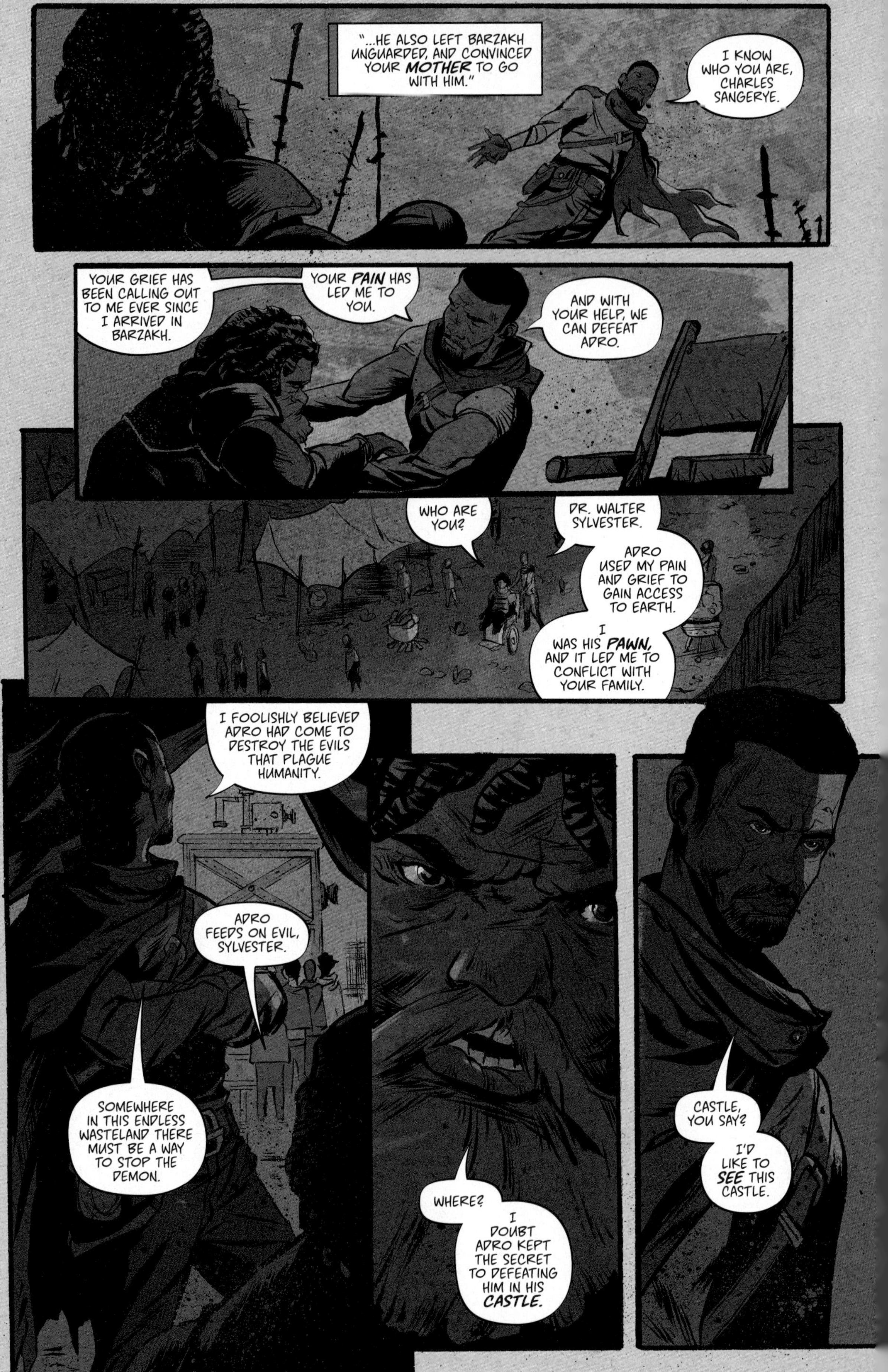
"...HE ALSO LEFT BARZAKH UNGUARDED, AND CONVINCED YOUR MOTHER TO GO WITH HIM."
I KNOW WHO YOU ARE, CHARLES SANGERYE.
YOUR GRIEF HAS BEEN CALLING OUT TO ME EVER SINCE I ARRIVED IN BARZAKH.
YOUR PAIN HAS LED ME TO YOU.
AND WITH YOUR HELP, WE CAN DEFEAT ADRO.
WHO ARE YOU?
DR. WALTER SYLVESTER.
ADRO USED MY PAIN AND GRIEF TO GAIN ACCESS TO EARTH.
I WAS HIS PAWN, AND IT LED ME TO CONFLICT WITH YOUR FAMILY.
I FOOLISHLY BELIEVED ADRO HAD COME TO DESTROY THE EVILS THAT PLAGUE HUMANITY.
ADRO FEEDS ON EVIL, SYLVESTER.
SOMEWHERE IN THIS ENDLESS WASTELAND THERE MUST BE A WAY TO STOP THE DEMON.
WHERE?
I DOUBT ADRO KEPT THE SECRET TO DEFEATING HIM IN HIS CASTLE.
CASTLE, YOU SAY?
I'D LIKE TO SEE THIS CASTLE.

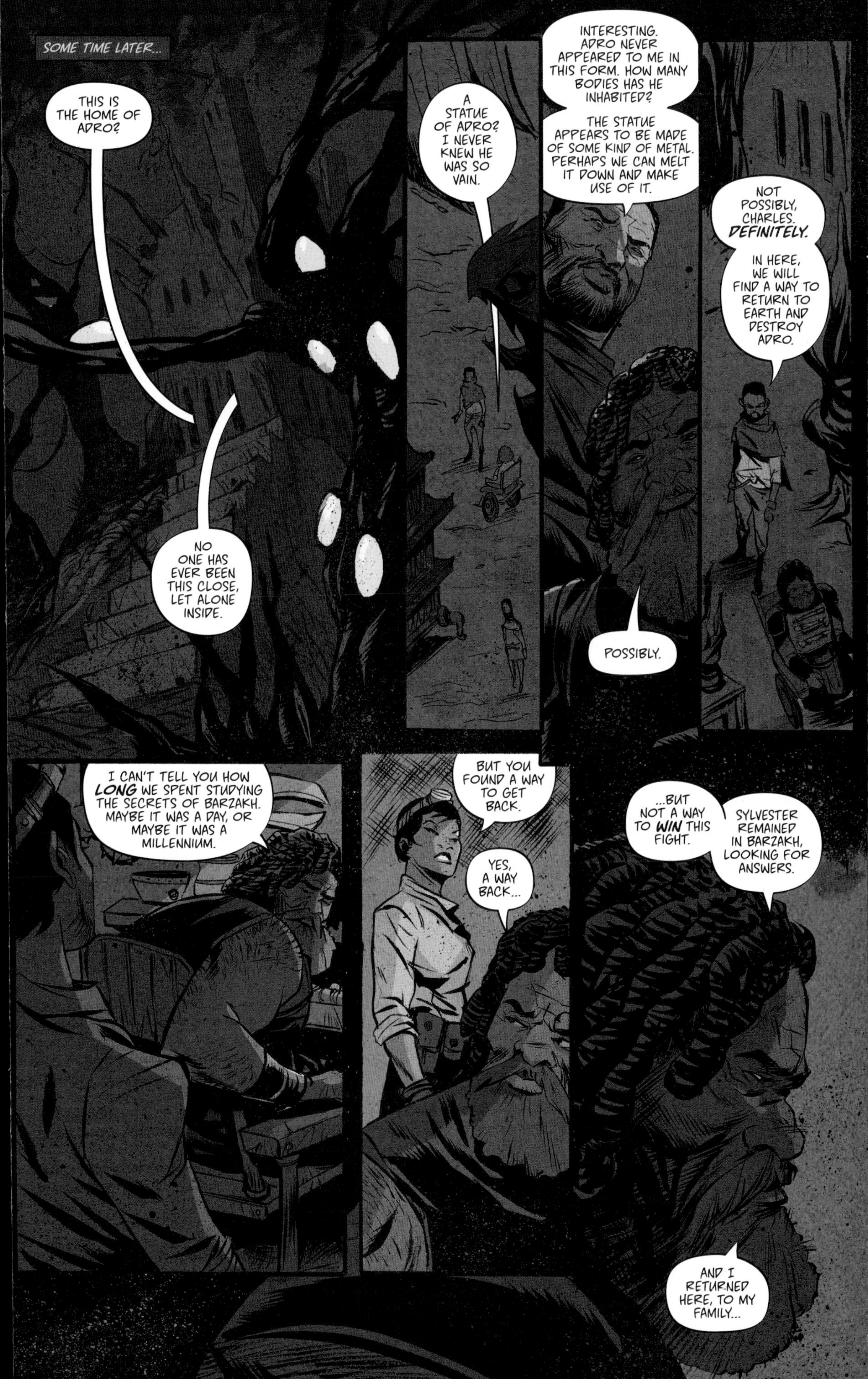
SOME TIME LATER...
THIS IS THE HOME OF ADRO?
NO ONE HAS EVER BEEN THIS CLOSE, LET ALONE INSIDE.
A STATUE OF ADRO? I NEVER KNEW HE WAS SO VAIN.
INTERESTING. ADRO NEVER APPEARED TO ME IN THIS FORM. HOW MANY BODIES HAS HE INHABITED?
THE STATUE APPEARS TO BE MADE OF SOME KIND OF METAL. PERHAPS WE CAN MELT IT DOWN AND MAKE USE OF IT.
POSSIBLY.
NOT POSSIBLY, CHARLES. DEFINITELY.
IN HERE, WE WILL FIND A WAY TO RETURN TO EARTH AND DESTROY ADRO.
I CAN'T TELL YOU HOW LONG WE SPENT STUDYING THE SECRETS OF BARZAKH. MAYBE IT WAS A DAY, OR MAYBE IT WAS A MILLENNIUM.
BUT YOU FOUND A WAY TO GET BACK.
YES, A WAY BACK...
...BUT NOT A WAY TO WIN THIS FIGHT.
SYLVESTER REMAINED IN BARZAKH, LOOKING FOR ANSWERS.
AND I RETURNED HERE, TO MY FAMILY...

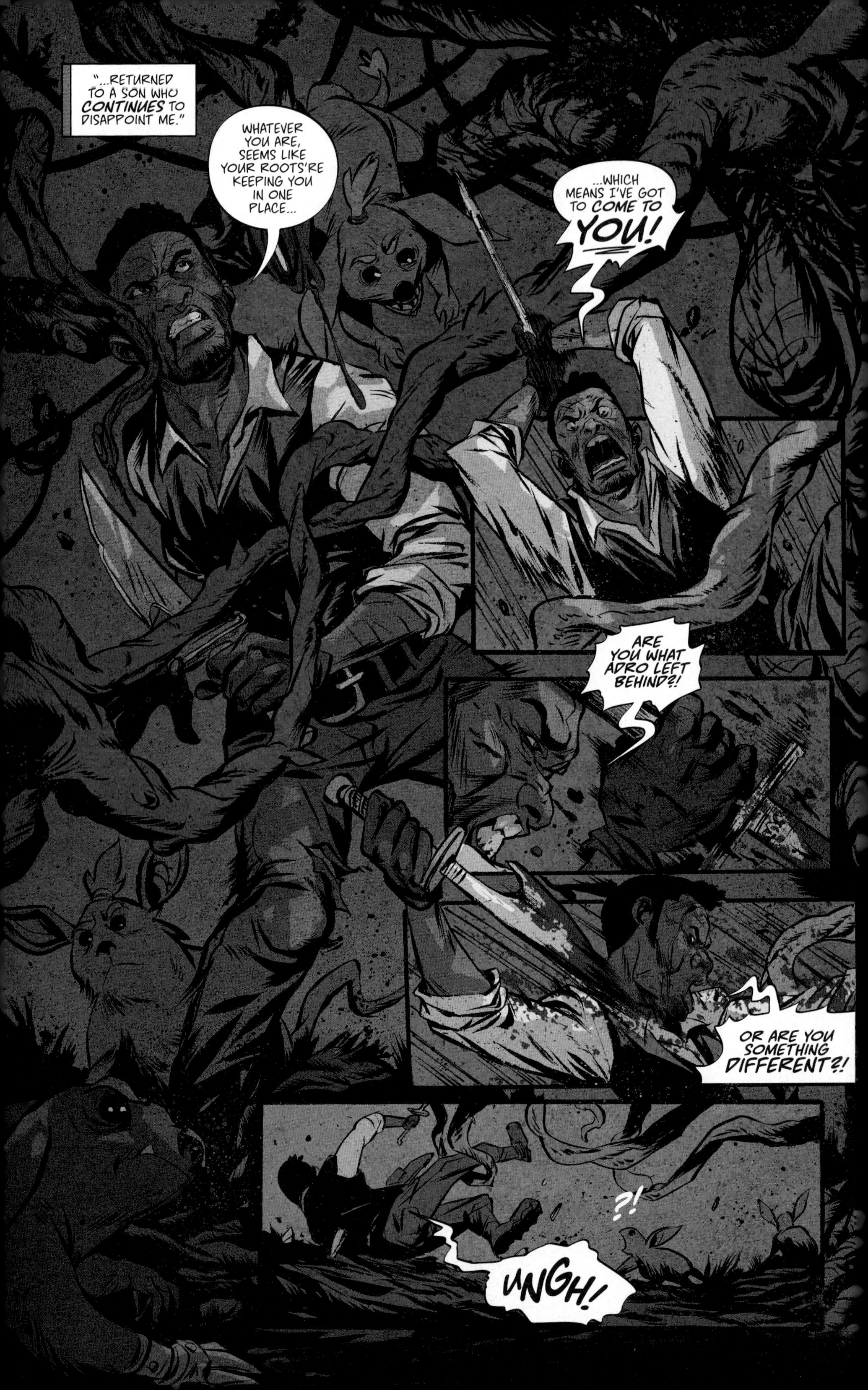
"...RETURNED TO A SON WHO CONTINUES TO DISAPPOINT ME."
WHATEVER YOU ARE, SEEMS LIKE YOUR ROOTS'RE KEEPING YOU IN ONE PLACE...
...WHICH MEANS I'VE GOT TO COME TO YOU!
ARE YOU WHAT ADRO LEFT BEHIND?!
OR ARE YOU SOMETHING DIFFERENT?!
?!
UNGH!

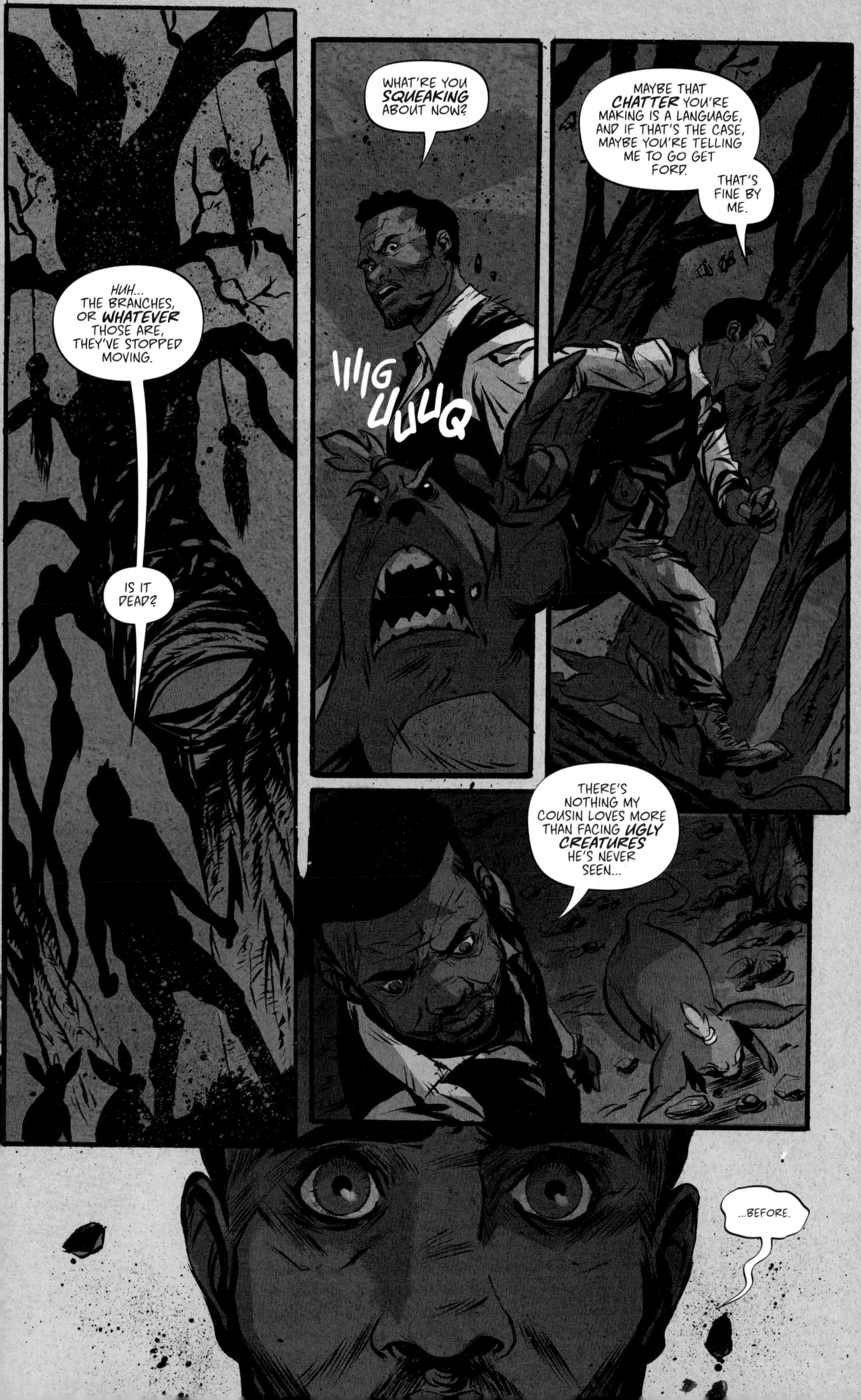
HUH... THE BRANCHES, OR WHATEVER THOSE ARE, THEY'VE STOPPED MOVING.
IS IT DEAD?
WHAT'RE YOU SQUEAKING ABOUT NOW?
IIIIG UUUQ
MAYBE THAT CHATTER YOU'RE MAKING IS A LANGUAGE, AND IF THAT'S THE CASE, MAYBE YOU'RE TELLING ME TO GO GET FORD.
THAT'S FINE BY ME.
THERE'S NOTHING MY COUSIN LOVES MORE THAN FACING UGLY CREATURES HE'S NEVER SEEN...
...BEFORE.

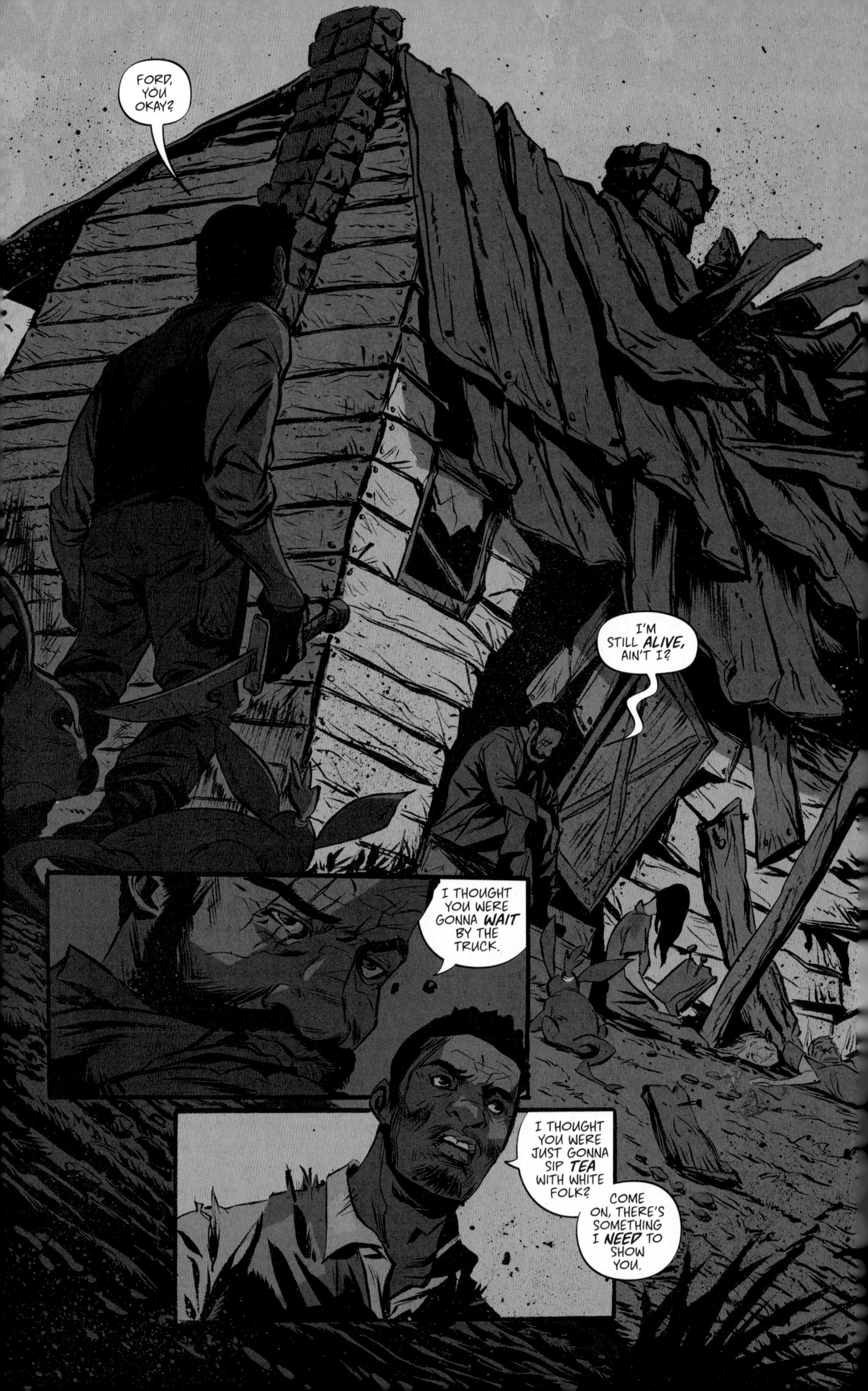
FORD, YOU OKAY?
I'M STILL ALIVE, AIN'T I?
I THOUGHT YOU WERE GONNA WAIT BY THE TRUCK.
I THOUGHT YOU WERE JUST GONNA SIP TEA WITH WHITE FOLK?
COME ON, THERE'S SOMETHING I NEED TO SHOW YOU.

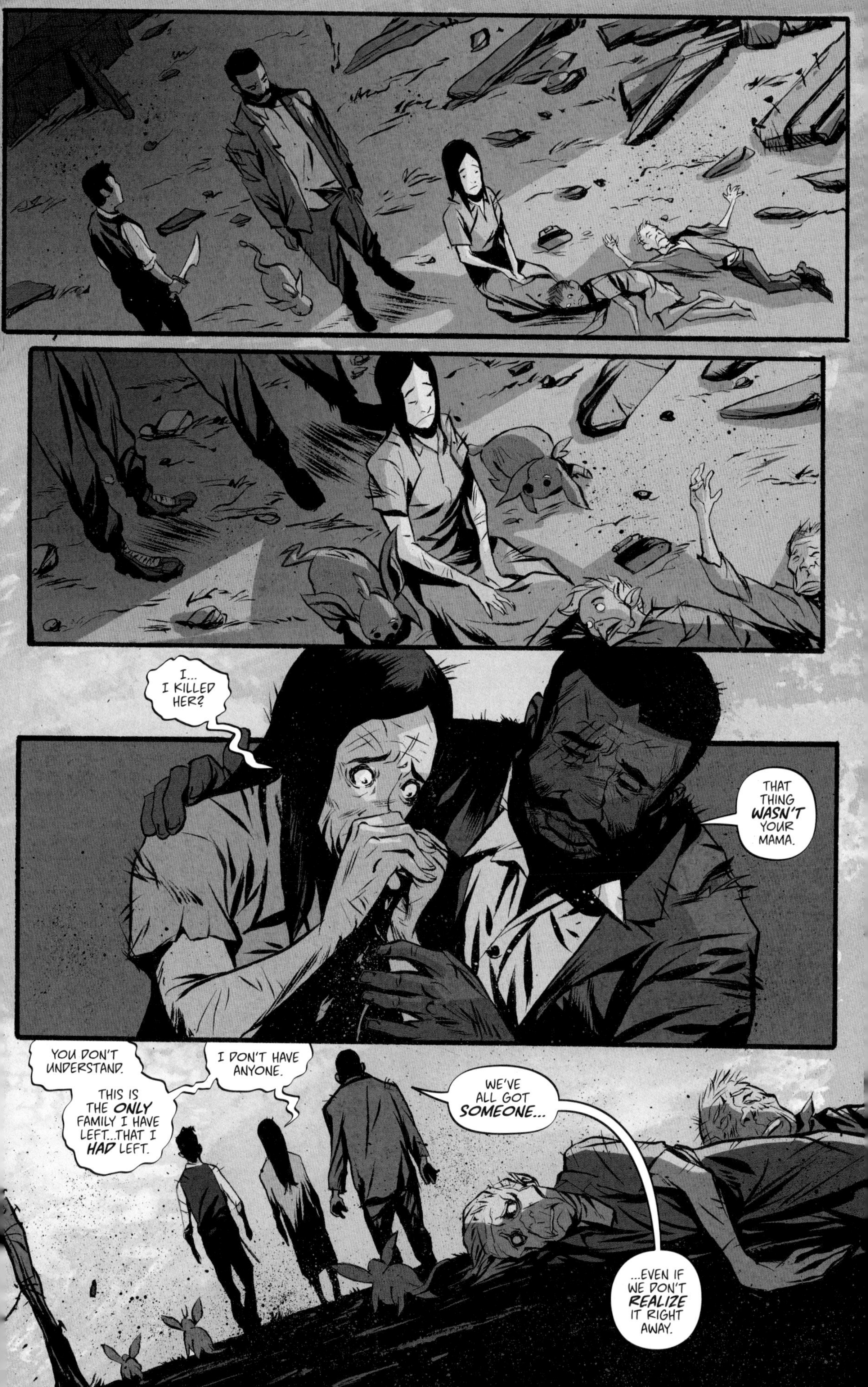
I... I KILLED HER?
THAT THING WASN'T YOUR MAMA.
YOU DON'T UNDERSTAND.
THIS IS THE ONLY FAMILY I HAVE LEFT...THAT I HAD LEFT.
I DON'T HAVE ANYONE.
WE'VE ALL GOT SOMEONE...
...EVEN IF WE DON'T REALIZE IT RIGHT AWAY.

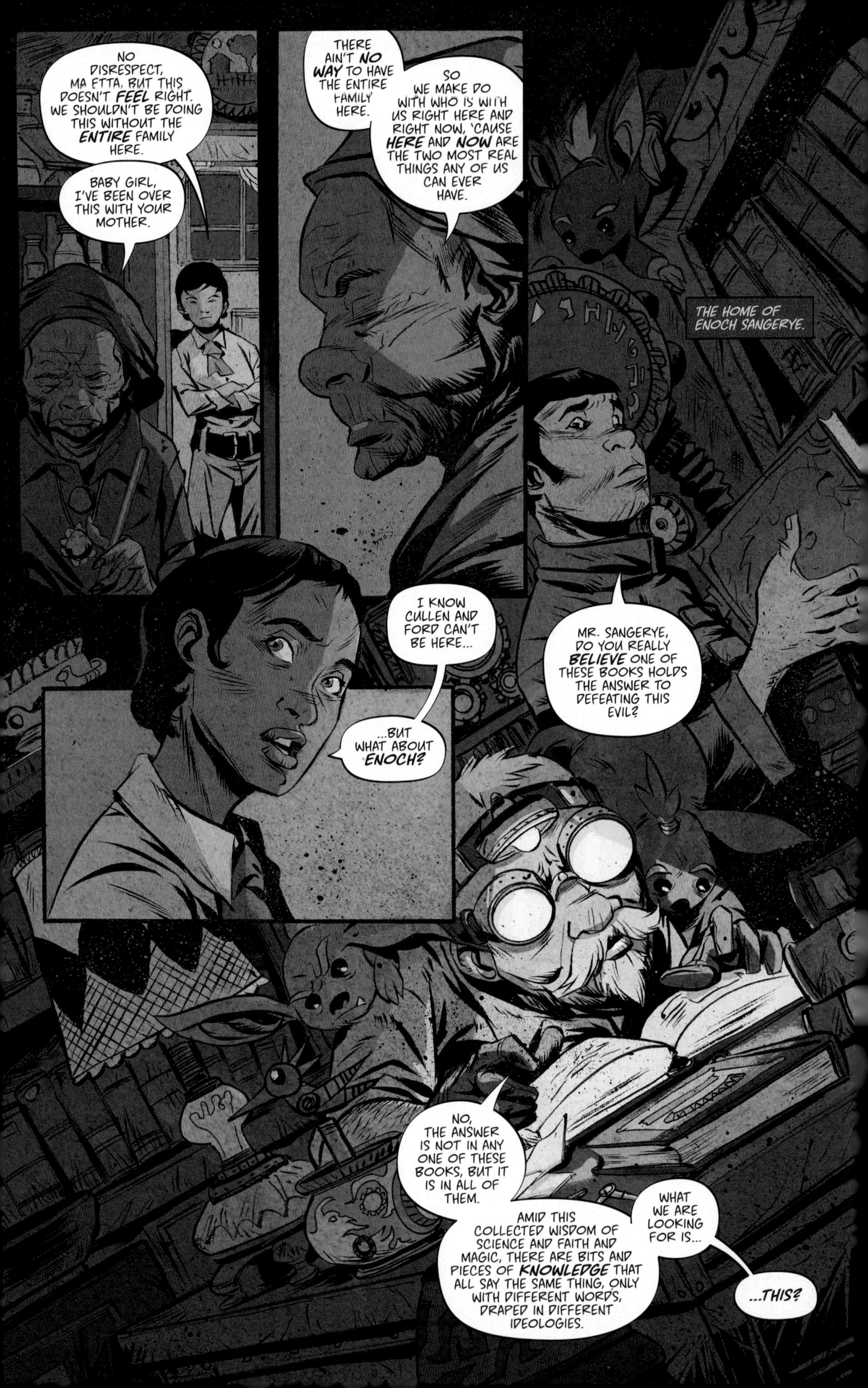
NO DISRESPECT, MA ETTA, BUT THIS DOESN'T FEEL RIGHT. WE SHOULDN'T BE DOING THIS WITHOUT THE ENTIRE FAMILY HERE.
BABY GIRL, I'VE BEEN OVER THIS WITH YOUR MOTHER.
THERE AIN'T NO WAY TO HAVE THE ENTIRE FAMILY HERE.
SO WE MAKE DO WITH WHO IS WITH US RIGHT HERE AND RIGHT NOW, 'CAUSE HERE AND NOW ARE THE TWO MOST REAL THINGS ANY OF US CAN EVER HAVE.
THE HOME OF ENOCH SANGERYE.
I KNOW CULLEN AND FORD CAN'T BE HERE...
...BUT WHAT ABOUT ENOCH?
MR. SANGERYE, DO YOU REALLY BELIEVE ONE OF THESE BOOKS HOLDS THE ANSWER TO DEFEATING THIS EVIL?
NO, THE ANSWER IS NOT IN ANY ONE OF THESE BOOKS, BUT IT IS IN ALL OF THEM.
AMID THIS COLLECTED WISDOM OF SCIENCE AND FAITH AND MAGIC, THERE ARE BITS AND PIECES OF KNOWLEDGE THAT ALL SAY THE SAME THING, ONLY WITH DIFFERENT WORDS, DRAPED IN DIFFERENT IDEOLOGIES.
WHAT WE ARE LOOKING FOR IS...
...THIS?

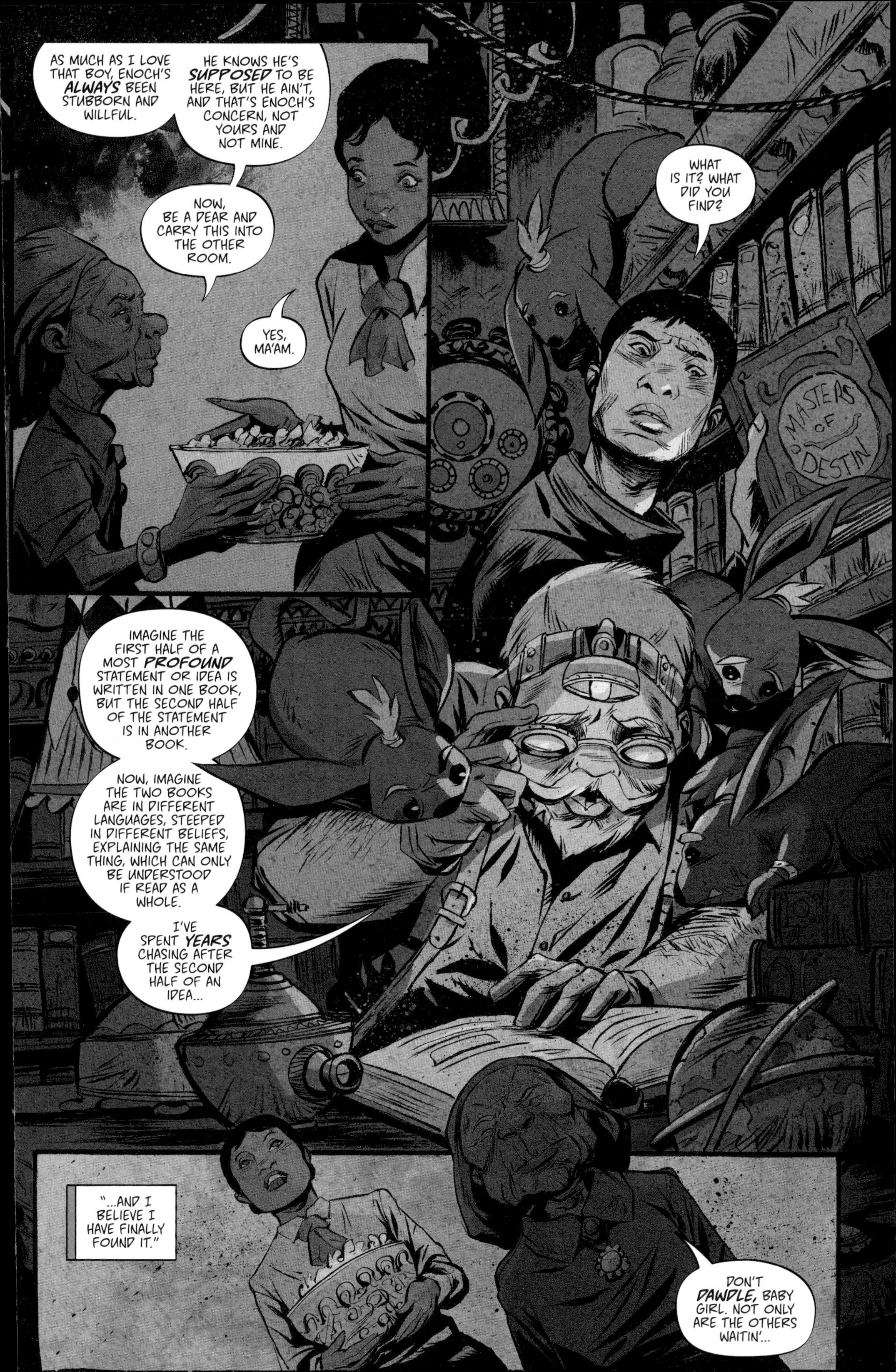
AS MUCH AS I LOVE THAT BOY, ENOCH'S ALWAYS BEEN STUBBORN AND WILLFUL.
HE KNOWS HE'S SUPPOSED TO BE HERE, BUT HE AIN'T, AND THAT'S ENOCH'S CONCERN, NOT YOURS AND NOT MINE.
NOW, BE A DEAR AND CARRY THIS INTO THE OTHER ROOM.
YES, MA'AM.
WHAT IS IT? WHAT DID YOU FIND?
MASTERS OF DESTIN
IMAGINE THE FIRST HALF OF A MOST PROFOUND STATEMENT OR IDEA IS WRITTEN IN ONE BOOK, BUT THE SECOND HALF OF THE STATEMENT IS IN ANOTHER BOOK.
NOW, IMAGINE THE TWO BOOKS ARE IN DIFFERENT LANGUAGES, STEEPED IN DIFFERENT BELIEFS, EXPLAINING THE SAME THING, WHICH CAN ONLY BE UNDERSTOOD IF READ AS A WHOLE.
I'VE SPENT YEARS CHASING AFTER THE SECOND HALF OF AN IDEA...
"...AND I BELIEVE I HAVE FINALLY FOUND IT."
DON'T DAWDLE, BABY GIRL. NOT ONLY ARE THE OTHERS WAITIN'...

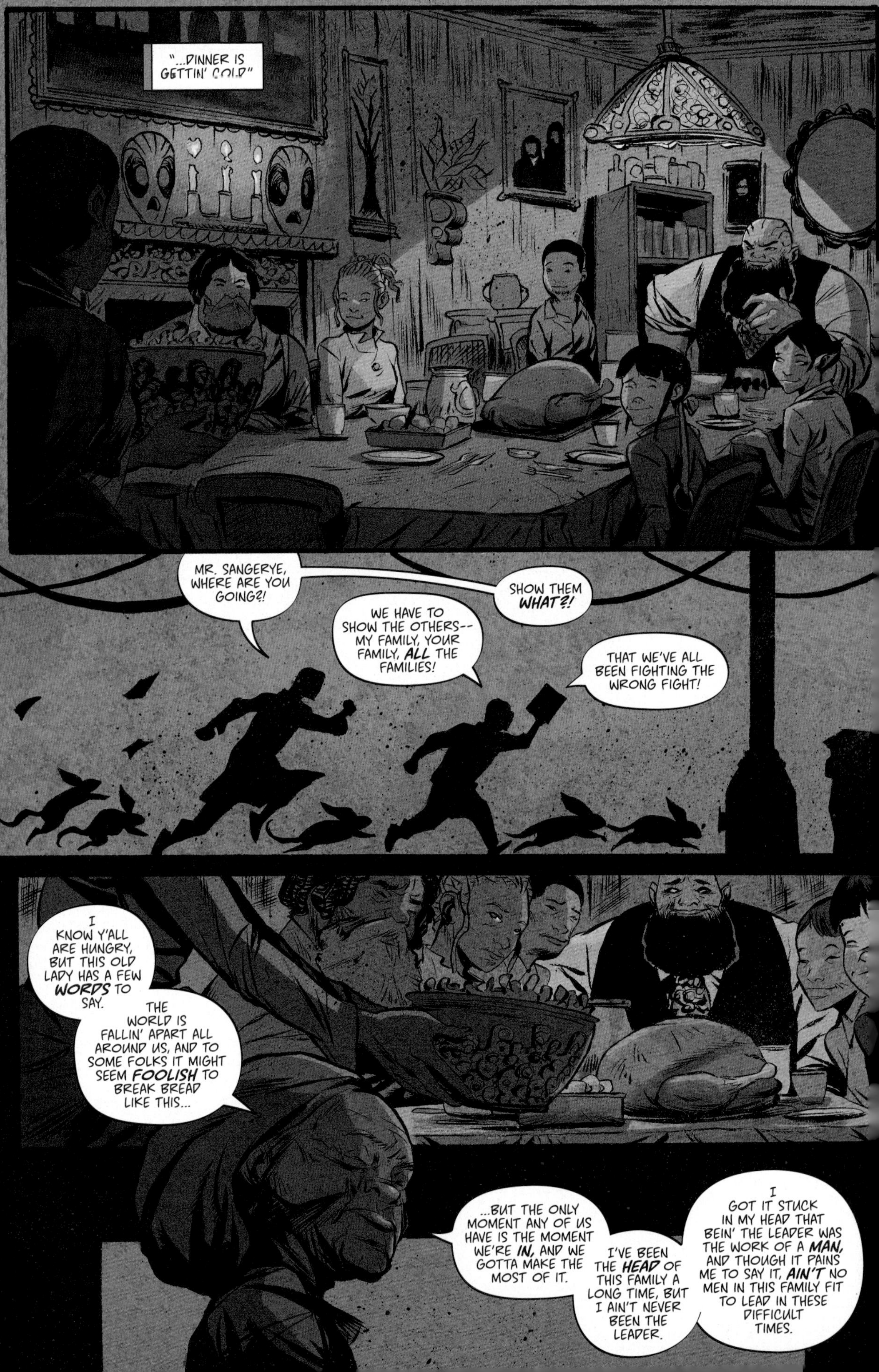
"...DINNER IS GETTIN' COLD"
MR. SANGERYE, WHERE ARE YOU GOING?!
WE HAVE TO SHOW THE OTHERS-- MY FAMILY, YOUR FAMILY, ALL THE FAMILIES!
SHOW THEM WHAT?!
THAT WE'VE ALL BEEN FIGHTING THE WRONG FIGHT!
I KNOW Y'ALL ARE HUNGRY, BUT THIS OLD LADY HAS A FEW WORDS TO SAY.
THE WORLD IS FALLIN' APART ALL AROUND US, AND TO SOME FOLKS IT MIGHT SEEM FOOLISH TO BREAK BREAD LIKE THIS...
...BUT THE ONLY MOMENT ANY OF US HAVE IS THE MOMENT WE'RE IN, AND WE GOTTA MAKE THE MOST OF IT.
I'VE BEEN THE HEAD OF THIS FAMILY A LONG TIME, BUT I AIN'T NEVER BEEN THE LEADER.
I GOT IT STUCK IN MY HEAD THAT BEIN' THE LEADER WAS THE WORK OF A MAN, AND THOUGH IT PAINS ME TO SAY IT, AIN'T NO MEN IN THIS FAMILY FIT TO LEAD IN THESE DIFFICULT TIMES.

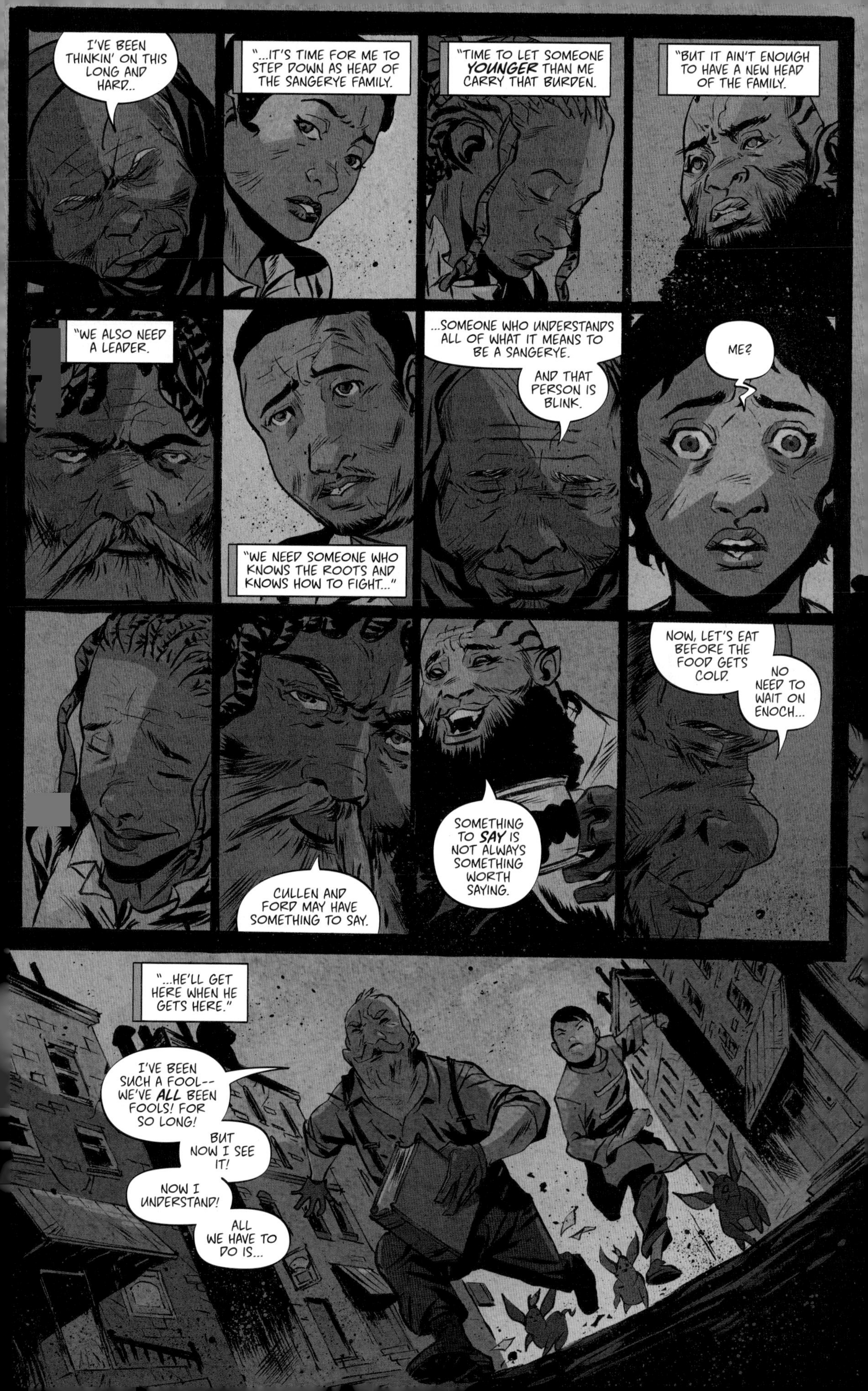
I'VE BEEN THINKIN' ON THIS LONG AND HARD...
"...IT'S TIME FOR ME TO STEP DOWN AS HEAD OF THE SANGERYE FAMILY.
"TIME TO LET SOMEONE YOUNGER THAN ME CARRY THAT BURDEN.
"BUT IT AIN'T ENOUGH TO HAVE A NEW HEAD OF THE FAMILY.
"WE ALSO NEED A LEADER.
"WE NEED SOMEONE WHO KNOWS THE ROOTS AND KNOWS HOW TO FIGHT..."
...SOMEONE WHO UNDERSTANDS ALL OF WHAT IT MEANS TO BE A SANGERYE.
AND THAT PERSON IS BLINK.
ME?
CULLEN AND FORD MAY HAVE SOMETHING TO SAY.
SOMETHING TO SAY IS NOT ALWAYS SOMETHING WORTH SAYING.
NOW, LET'S EAT BEFORE THE FOOD GETS COLD.
NO NEED TO WAIT ON ENOCH...
"...HE'LL GET HERE WHEN HE GETS HERE."
I'VE BEEN SUCH A FOOL-- WE'VE ALL BEEN FOOLS! FOR SO LONG!
BUT NOW I SEE IT!
NOW I UNDERSTAND!
ALL WE HAVE TO DO IS...

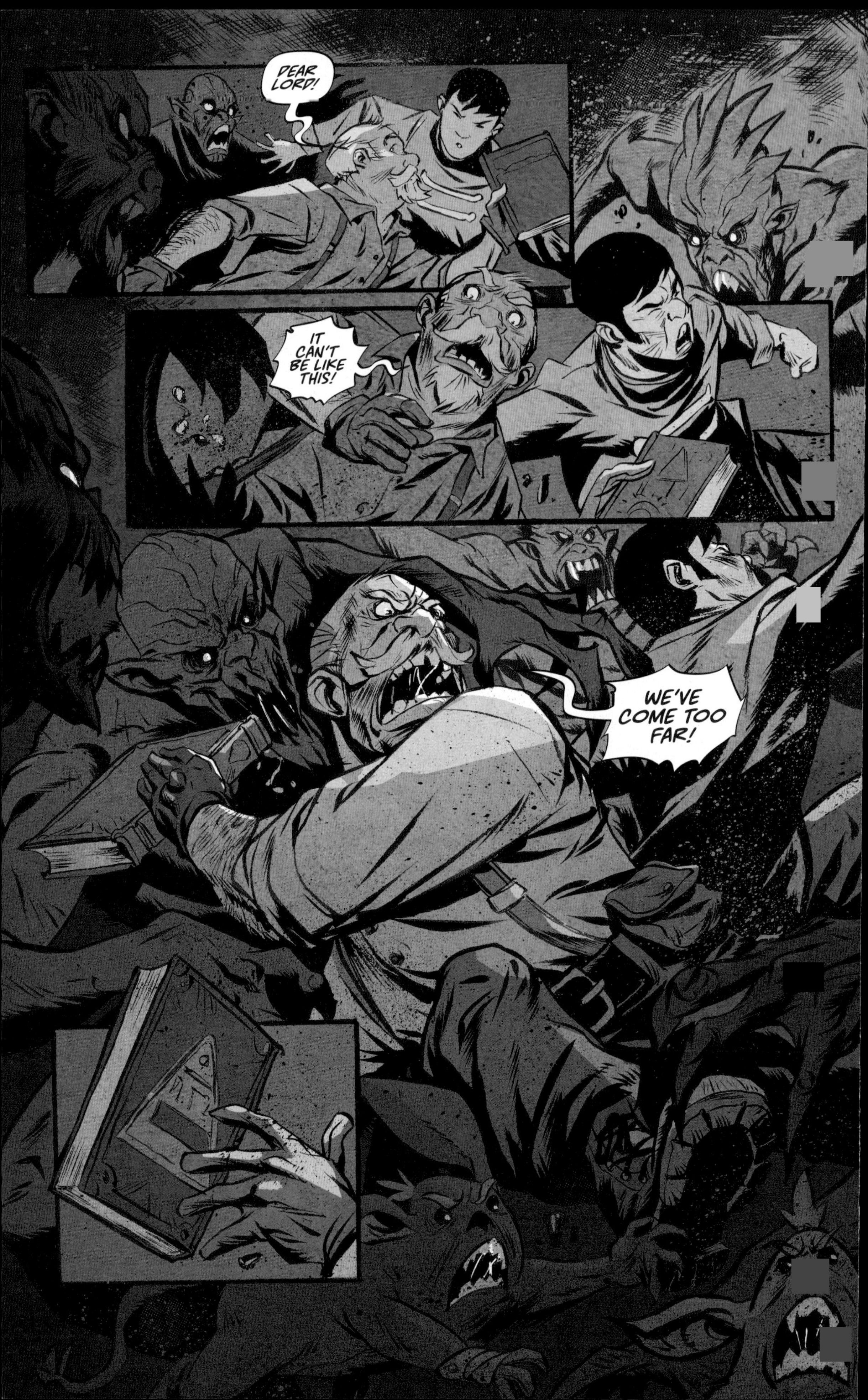
DEAR LORD!
IT CAN'T BE LIKE THIS!
WE'VE COME TOO FAR!

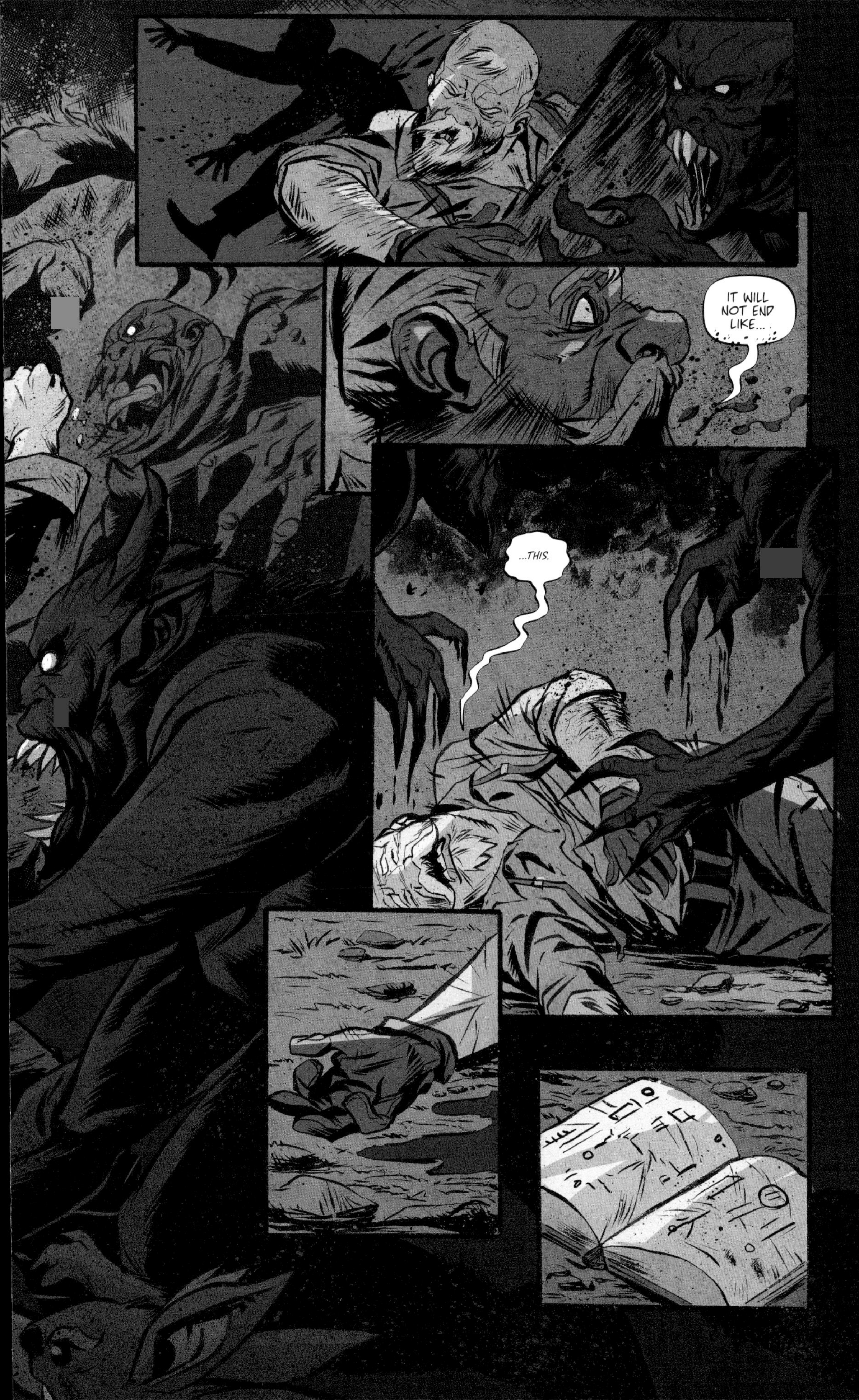
IT WILL NOT END LIKE...
...THIS.

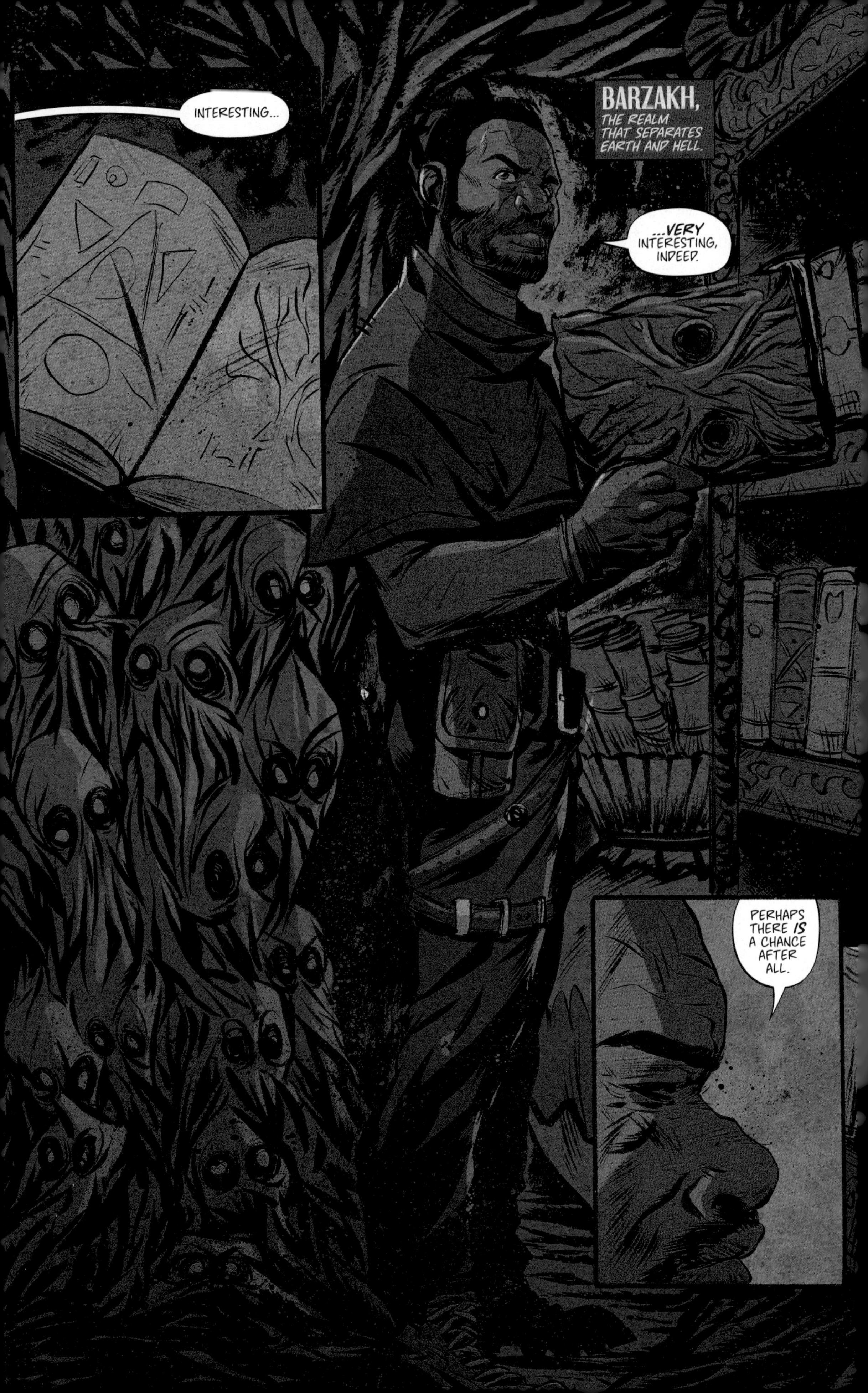
INTERESTING...
BARZAKH, THE REALM THAT SEPARATES EARTH AND HELL.
...VERY INTERESTING, INDEED.
PERHAPS THERE IS A CHANCE AFTER ALL.

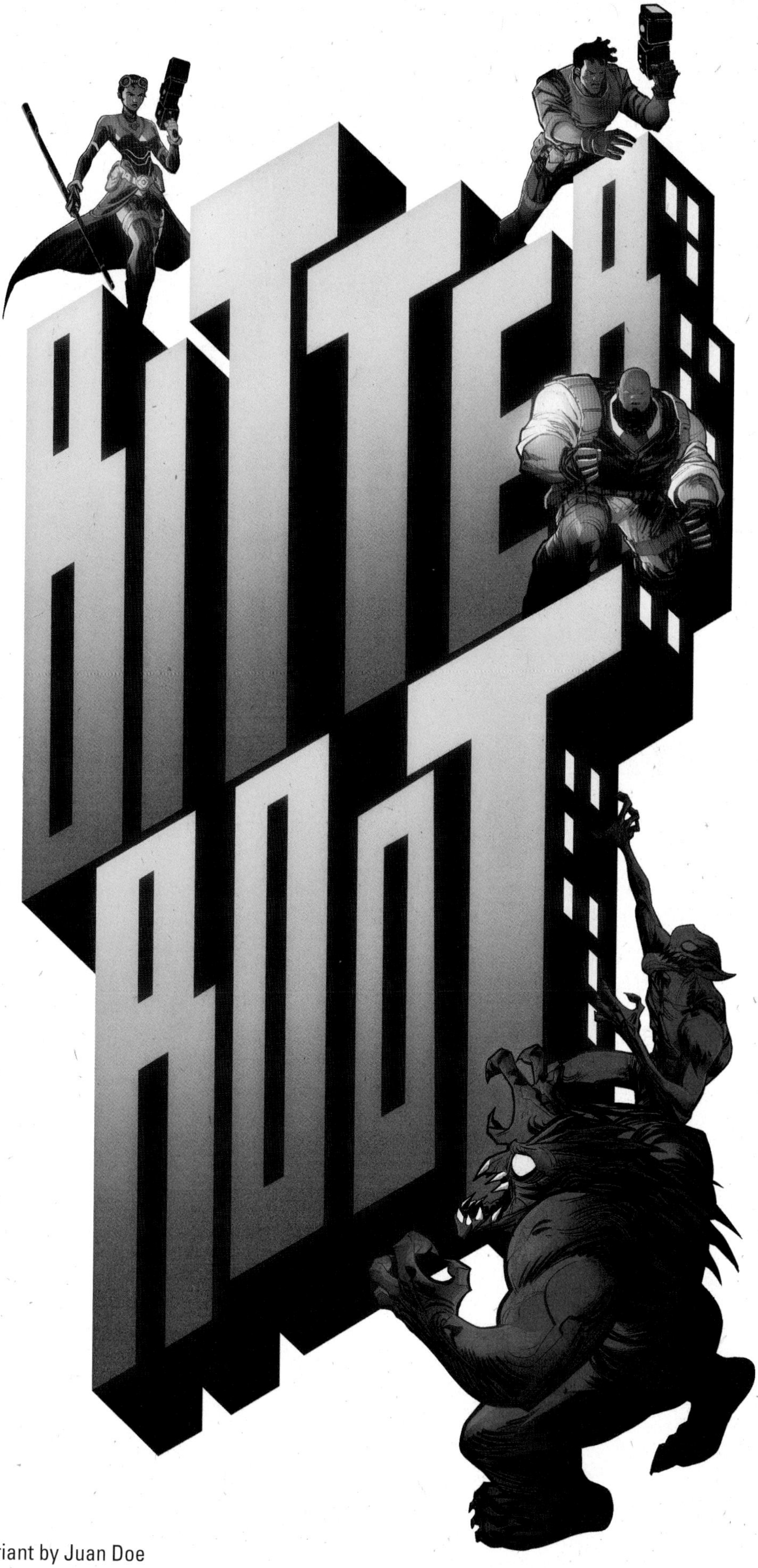
BITTER
ROOT

Issue #13 variant by Juan Doe

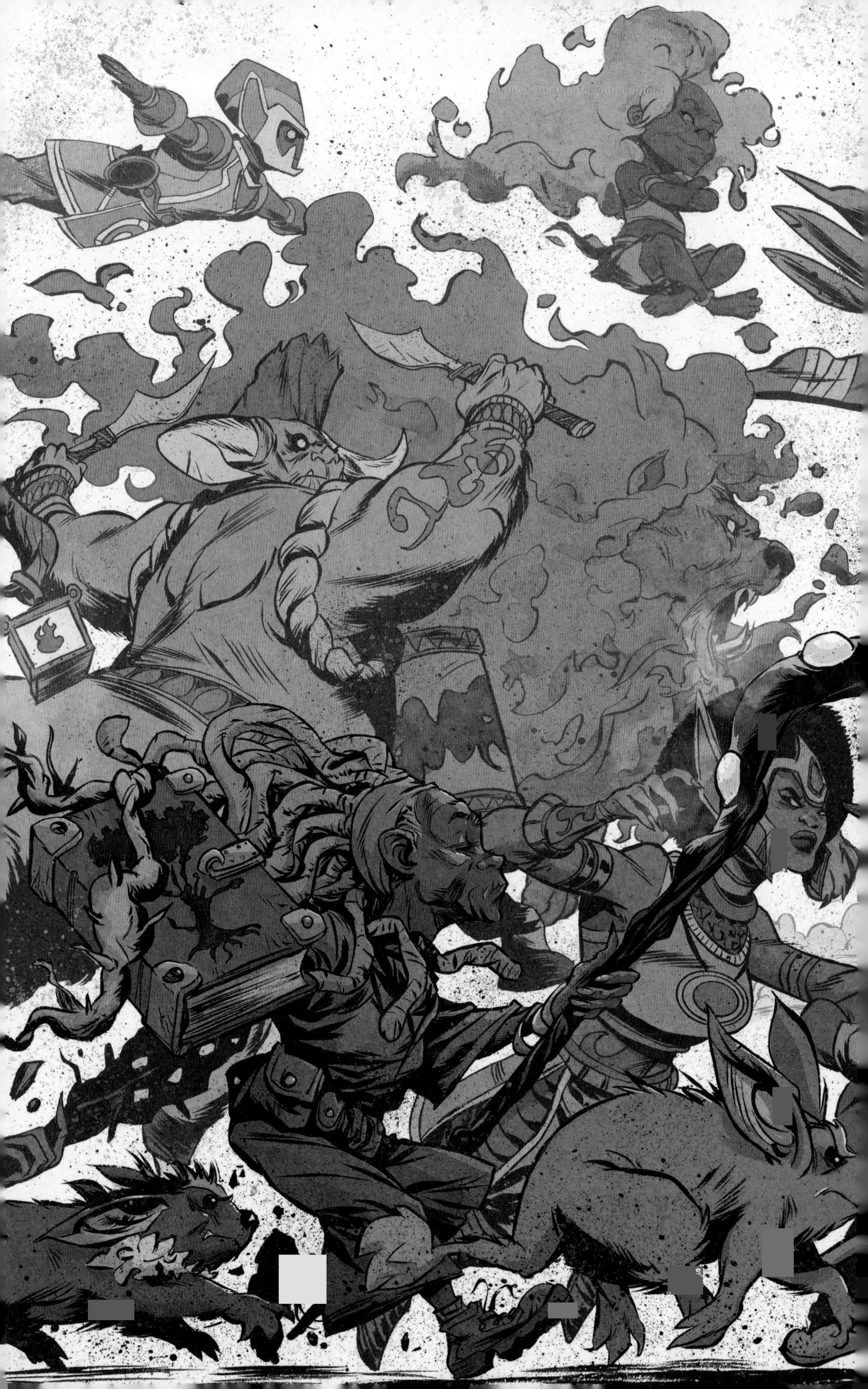

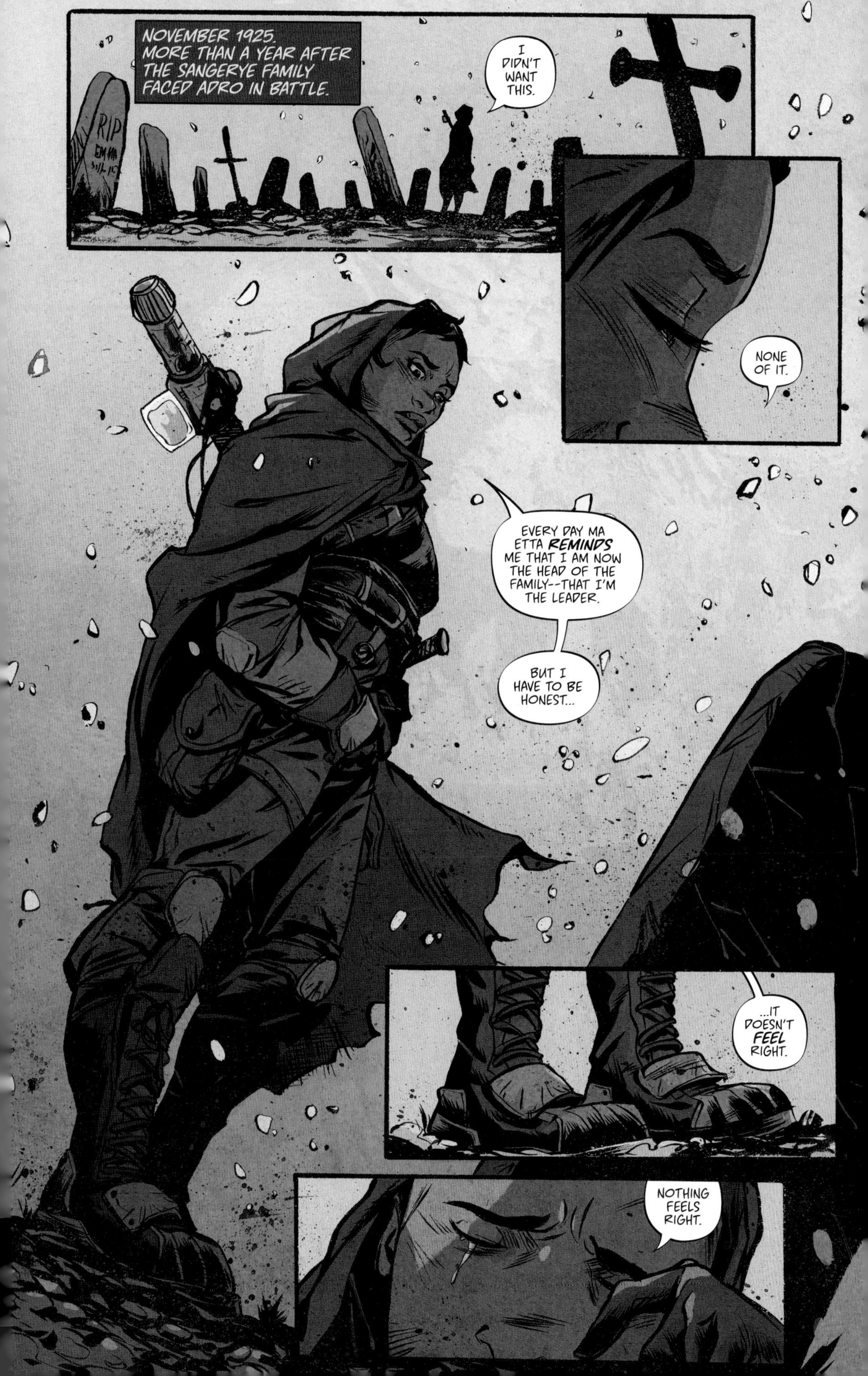

NOVEMBER 1925. MORE THAN A YEAR AFTER THE SANGERYE FAMILY FACED ADRO IN BATTLE.
RIP
I DIDN'T WANT THIS.
NONE OF IT.
EVERY DAY MA ETTA REMINDS ME THAT I AM NOW THE HEAD OF THE FAMILY--THAT I'M THE LEADER.
BUT I HAVE TO BE HONEST...
...IT DOESN'T FEEL RIGHT.
NOTHING FEELS RIGHT.

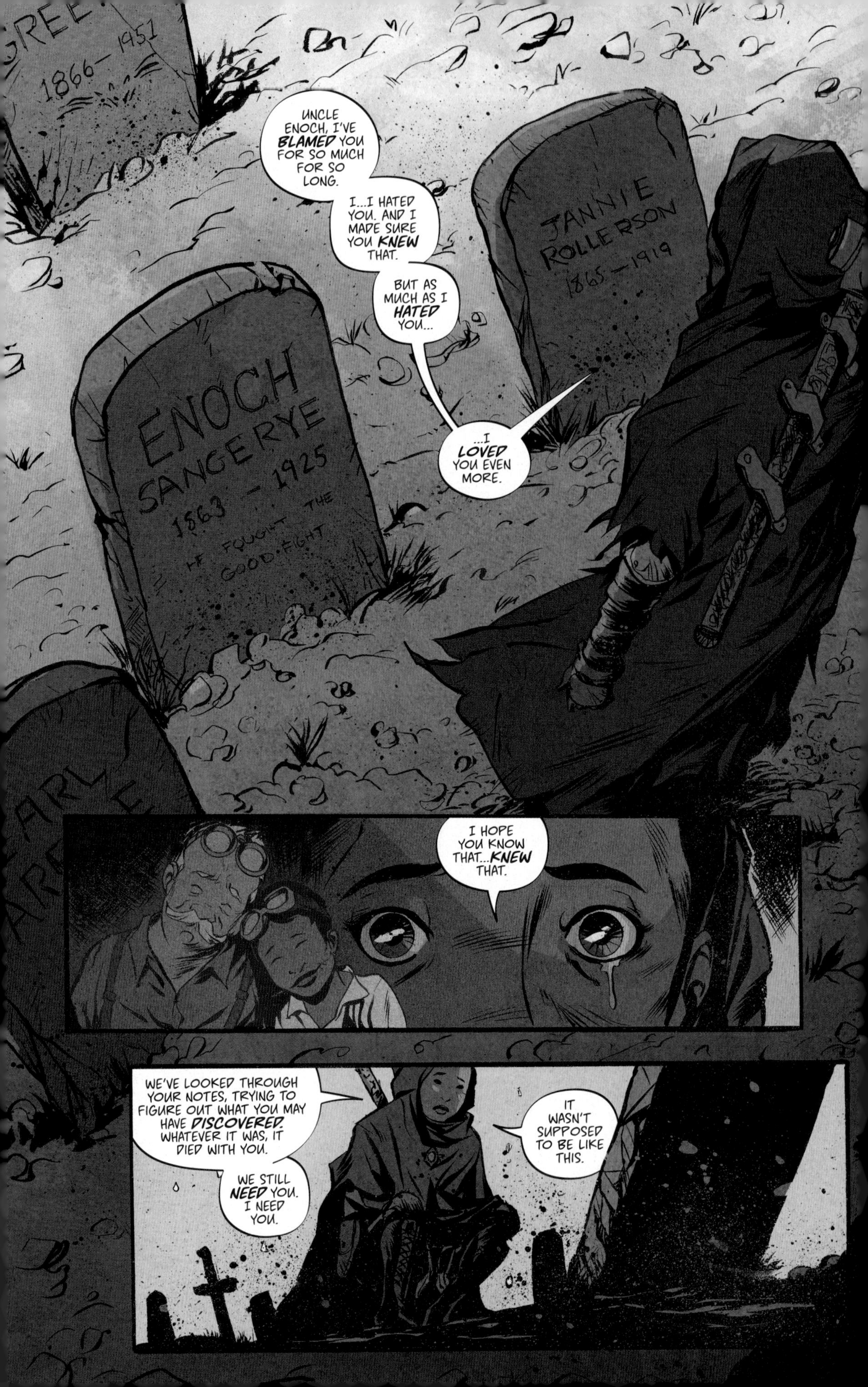
GREE
1866 – 1951
UNCLE ENOCH, I'VE BLAMED YOU FOR SO MUCH FOR SO LONG.
I...I HATED YOU. AND I MADE SURE YOU KNEW THAT.
BUT AS MUCH AS I HATED YOU...
...I LOVED YOU EVEN MORE.
JANNIE ROLLERSON 1865 – 1919
ENOCH SANGERYE 1863 – 1925 HE FOUGHT THE GOOD FIGHT
I HOPE YOU KNOW THAT...KNEW THAT.
WE'VE LOOKED THROUGH YOUR NOTES, TRYING TO FIGURE OUT WHAT YOU MAY HAVE DISCOVERED. WHATEVER IT WAS, IT DIED WITH YOU.
WE STILL NEED YOU. I NEED YOU.
IT WASN'T SUPPOSED TO BE LIKE THIS.

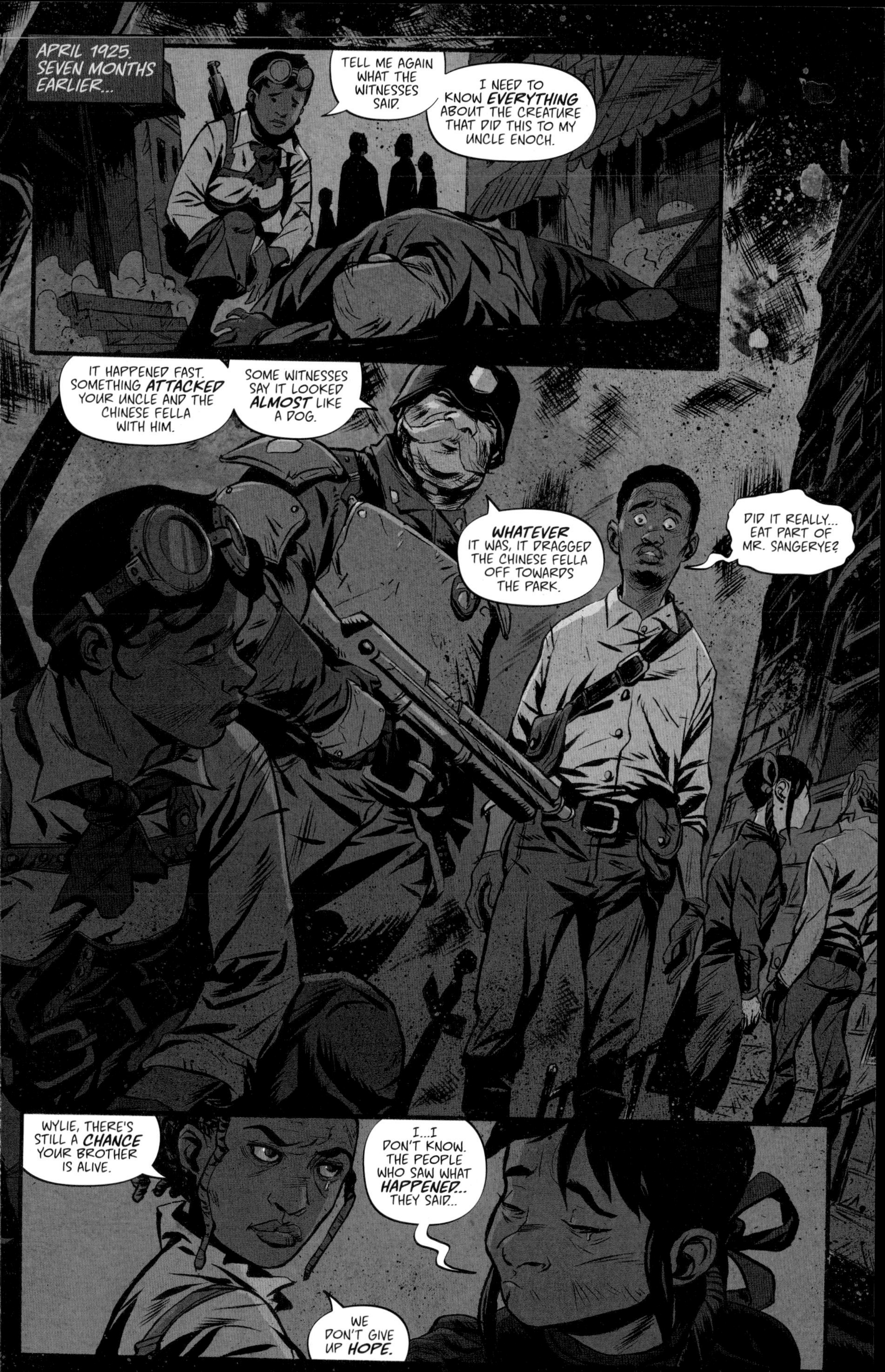
APRIL 1925. SEVEN MONTHS EARLIER...
TELL ME AGAIN WHAT THE WITNESSES SAID.
I NEED TO KNOW EVERYTHING ABOUT THE CREATURE THAT DID THIS TO MY UNCLE ENOCH.
IT HAPPENED FAST. SOMETHING ATTACKED YOUR UNCLE AND THE CHINESE FELLA WITH HIM.
SOME WITNESSES SAY IT LOOKED ALMOST LIKE A DOG.
WHATEVER IT WAS, IT DRAGGED THE CHINESE FELLA OFF TOWARDS THE PARK.
DID IT REALLY... EAT PART OF MR. SANGERYE?
WYLIE, THERE'S STILL A CHANCE YOUR BROTHER IS ALIVE.
I...I DON'T KNOW. THE PEOPLE WHO SAW WHAT HAPPENED... THEY SAID...
WE DON'T GIVE UP HOPE.

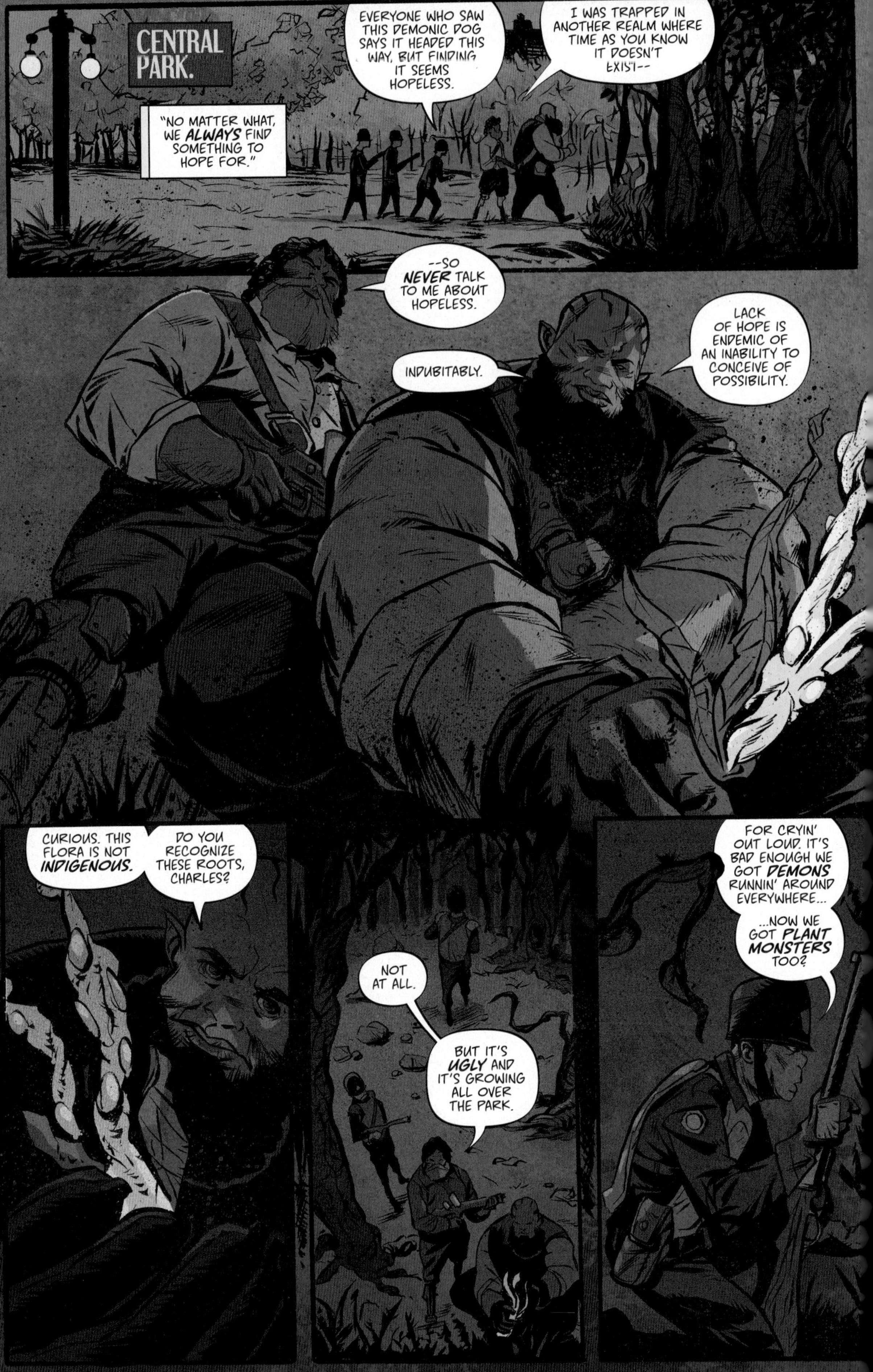
CENTRAL PARK.
"NO MATTER WHAT, WE ALWAYS FIND SOMETHING TO HOPE FOR."
EVERYONE WHO SAW THIS DEMONIC DOG SAYS IT HEADED THIS WAY, BUT FINDING IT SEEMS HOPELESS.
I WAS TRAPPED IN ANOTHER REALM WHERE TIME AS YOU KNOW IT DOESN'T EXIST--
--SO NEVER TALK TO ME ABOUT HOPELESS.
INDUBITABLY.
LACK OF HOPE IS ENDEMIC OF AN INABILITY TO CONCEIVE OF POSSIBILITY.
CURIOUS. THIS FLORA IS NOT INDIGENOUS.
DO YOU RECOGNIZE THESE ROOTS, CHARLES?
NOT AT ALL.
BUT IT'S UGLY AND IT'S GROWING ALL OVER THE PARK.
FOR CRYIN' OUT LOUD. IT'S BAD ENOUGH WE GOT DEMONS RUNNIN' AROUND EVERYWHERE...
...NOW WE GOT PLANT MONSTERS TOO?

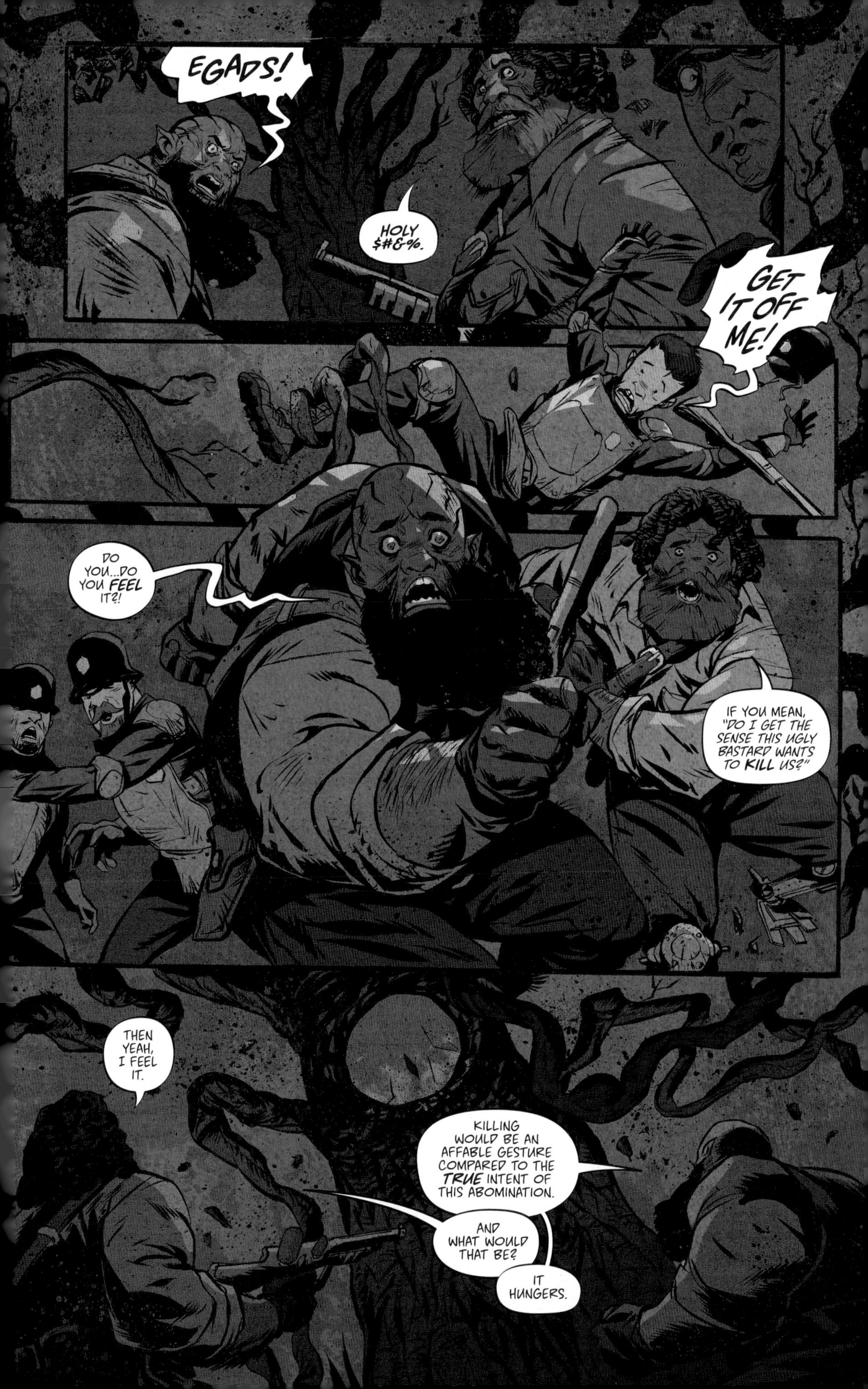

EGADS!
HOLY $#&%.
GET IT OFF ME!
DO YOU...DO YOU FEEL IT?!
IF YOU MEAN, "DO I GET THE SENSE THIS UGLY BASTARD WANTS TO KILL US?"
THEN YEAH, I FEEL IT.
KILLING WOULD BE AN AFFABLE GESTURE COMPARED TO THE TRUE INTENT OF THIS ABOMINATION.
AND WHAT WOULD THAT BE?
IT HUNGERS.

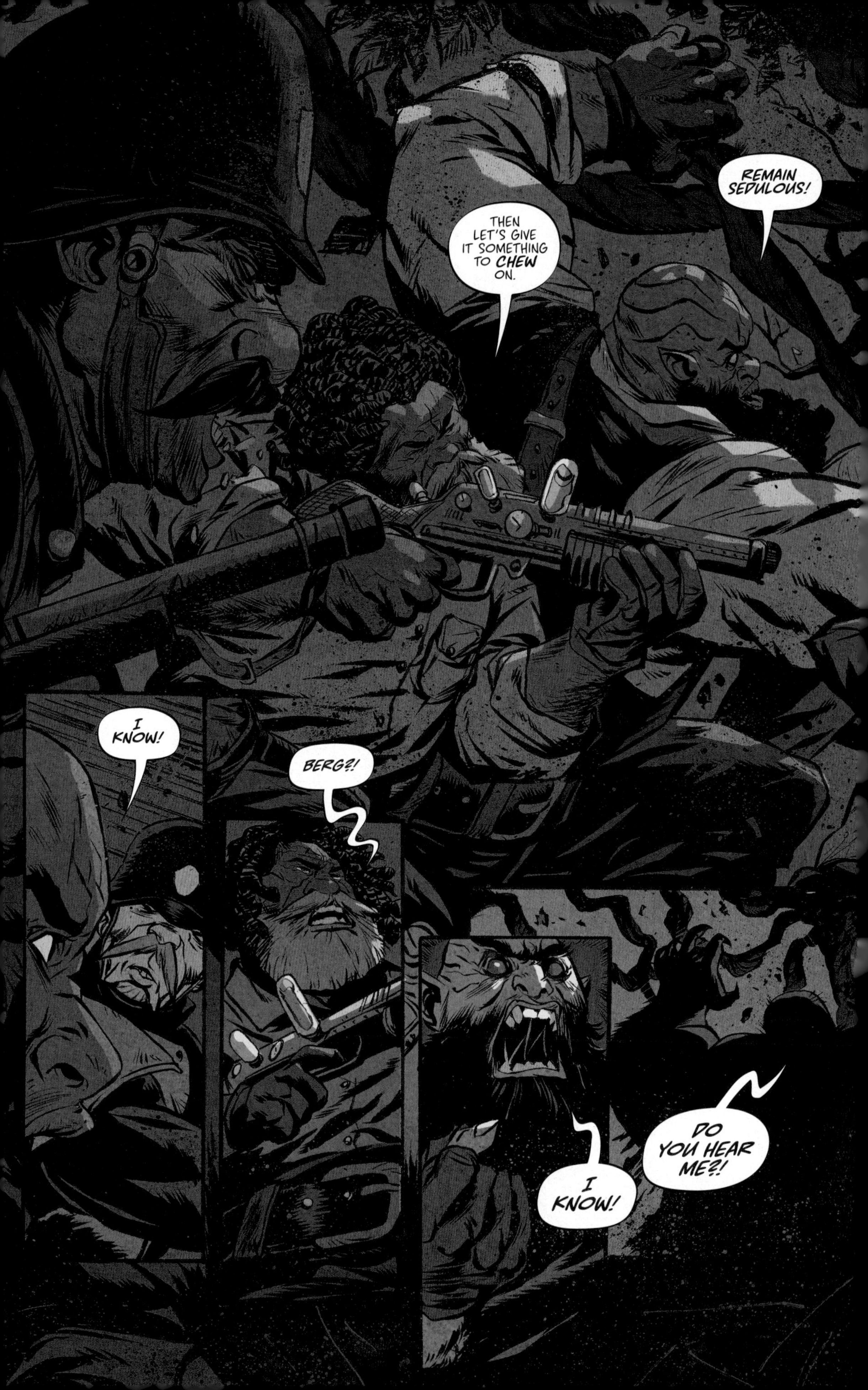
REMAIN SEDULOUS!
THEN LET'S GIVE IT SOMETHING TO CHEW ON.
I KNOW!
BERG?!
DO YOU HEAR ME?!
I KNOW!

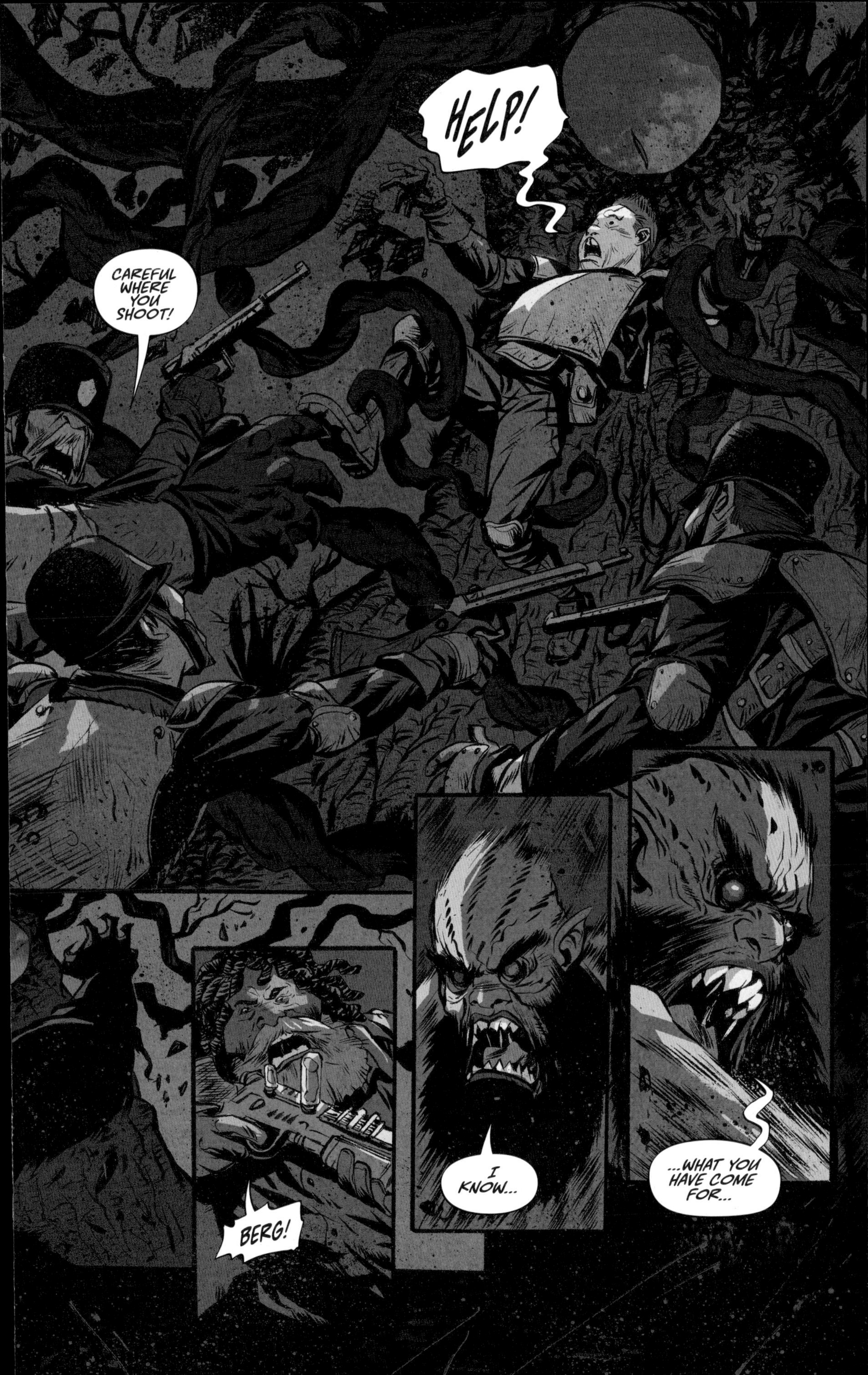
HELP!
CAREFUL WHERE YOU SHOOT!
BERG!
I KNOW...
...WHAT YOU HAVE COME FOR...

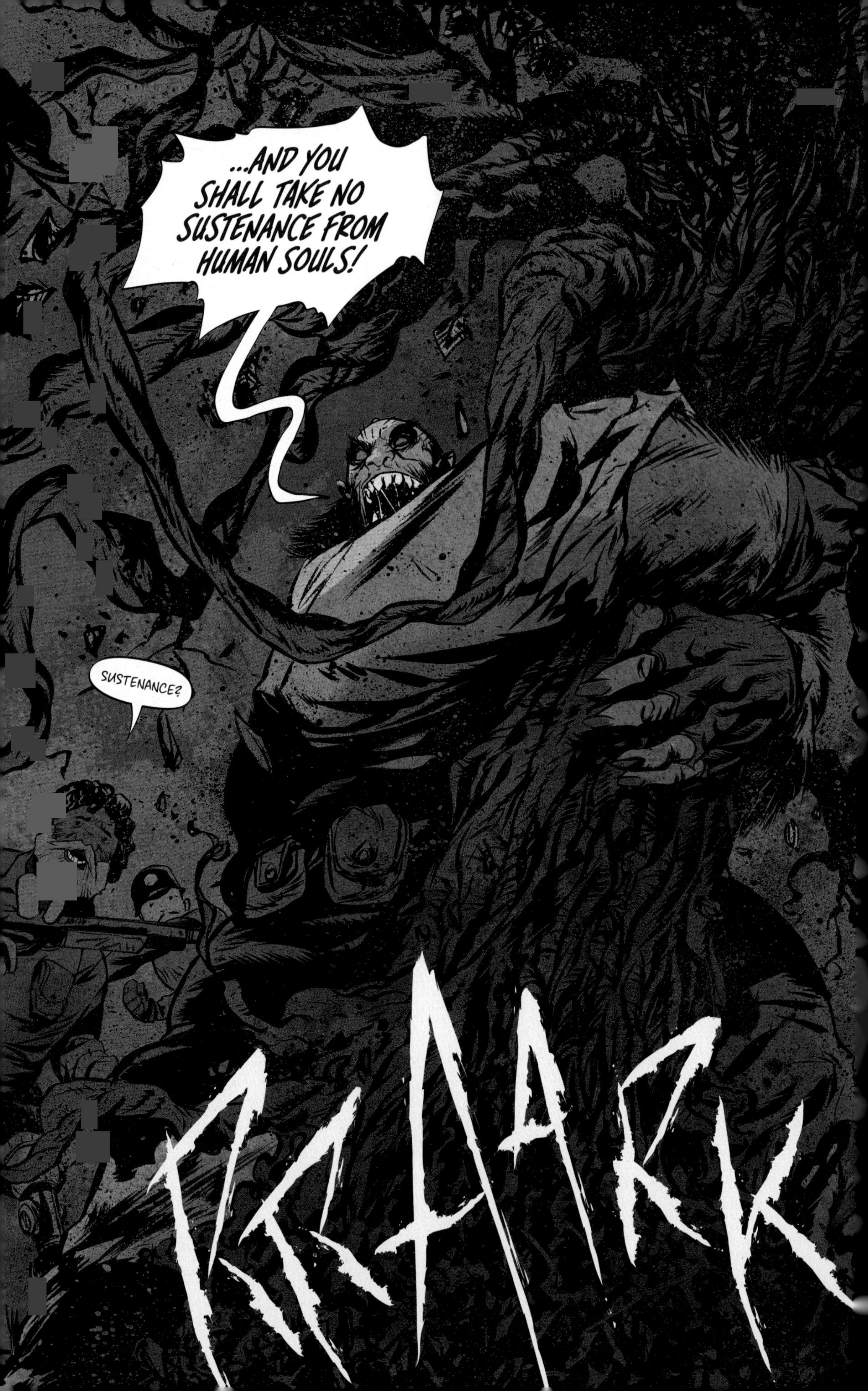
...AND YOU SHALL TAKE NO SUSTENANCE FROM HUMAN SOULS!
SUSTENANCE?
RAARK

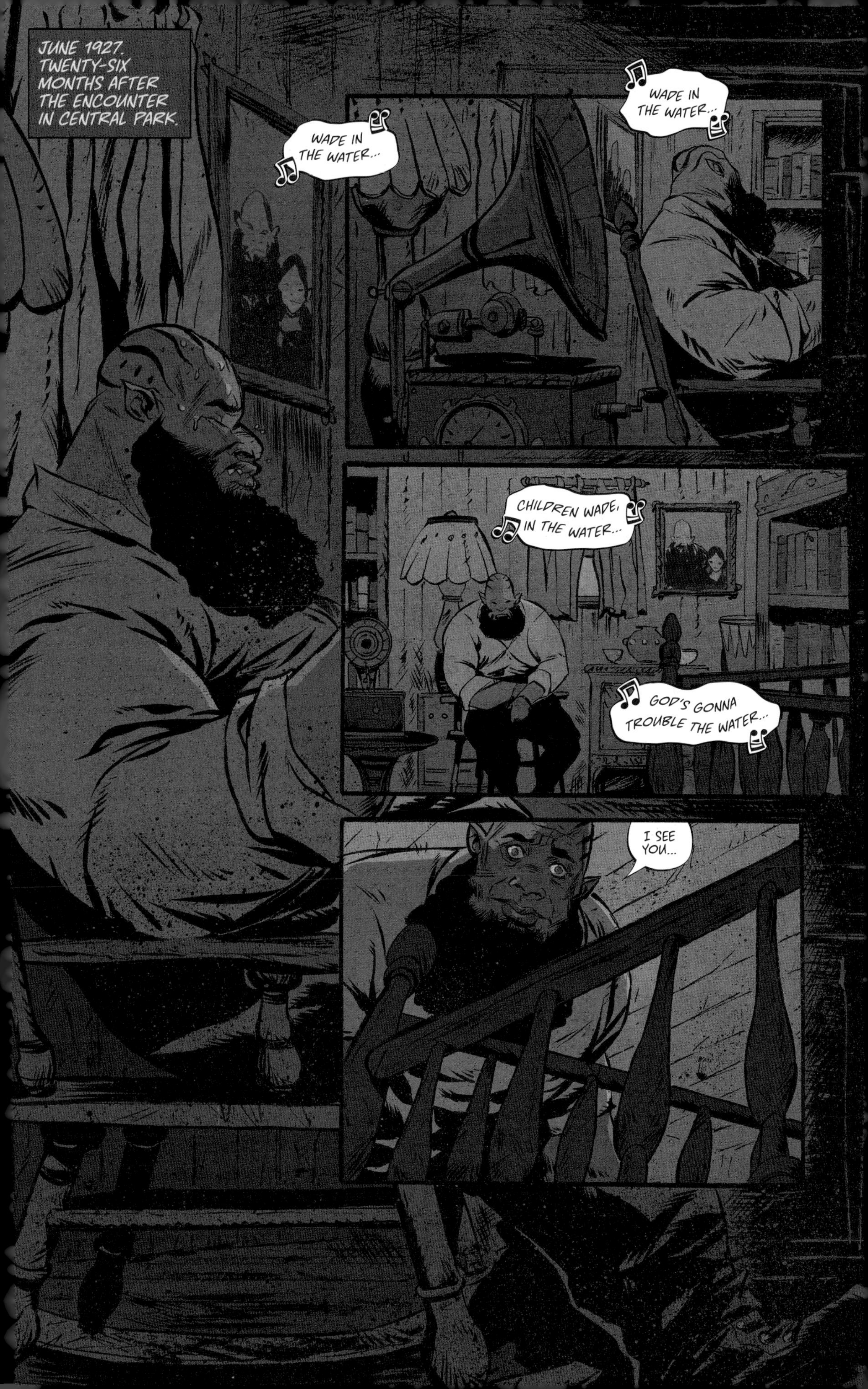
JUNE 1927. TWENTY-SIX MONTHS AFTER THE ENCOUNTER IN CENTRAL PARK.
WADE IN THE WATER...
WADE IN THE WATER...
CHILDREN WADE, IN THE WATER...
GOD'S GONNA TROUBLE THE WATER...
I SEE YOU...

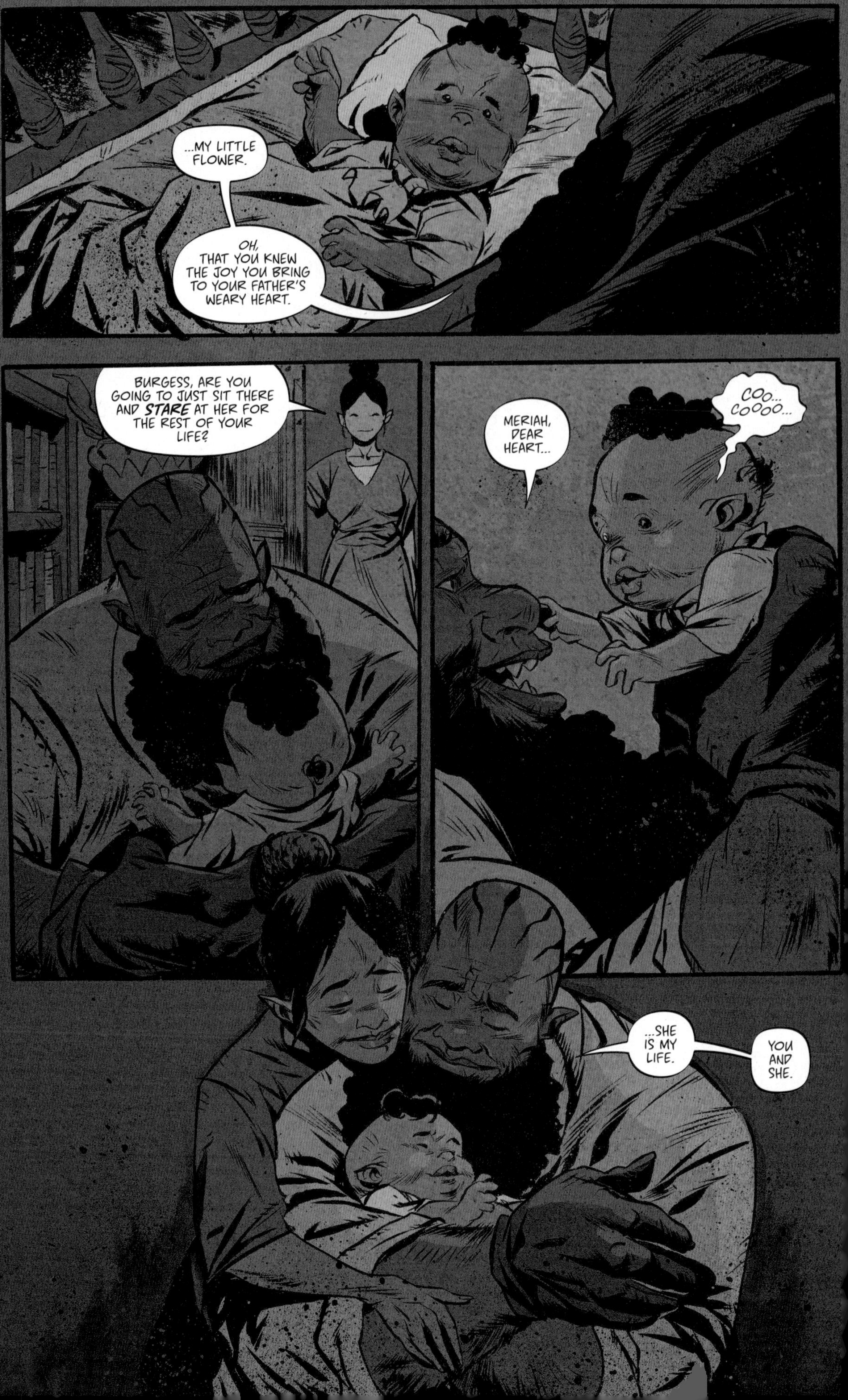
...MY LITTLE FLOWER.
OH, THAT YOU KNEW THE JOY YOU BRING TO YOUR FATHER'S WEARY HEART.
BURGESS, ARE YOU GOING TO JUST SIT THERE AND STARE AT HER FOR THE REST OF YOUR LIFE?
MERIAH, DEAR HEART...
COO... COOOO...
...SHE IS MY LIFE.
YOU AND SHE.

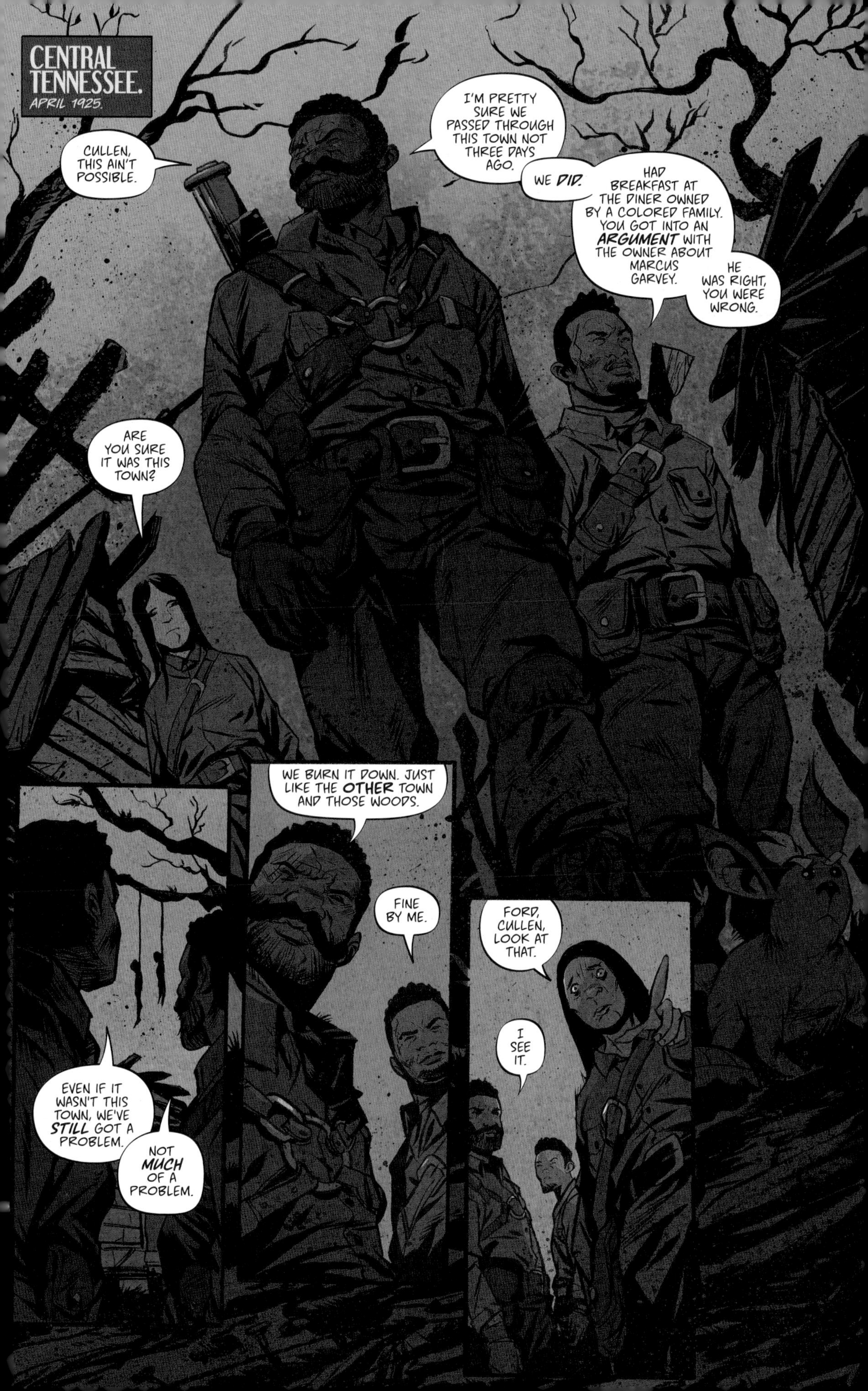
CENTRAL TENNESSEE.
APRIL 1925.
CULLEN, THIS AIN'T POSSIBLE.
I'M PRETTY SURE WE PASSED THROUGH THIS TOWN NOT THREE DAYS AGO.
WE DID.
HAD BREAKFAST AT THE DINER OWNED BY A COLORED FAMILY. YOU GOT INTO AN ARGUMENT WITH THE OWNER ABOUT MARCUS GARVEY.
HE WAS RIGHT, YOU WERE WRONG.
ARE YOU SURE IT WAS THIS TOWN?
EVEN IF IT WASN'T THIS TOWN, WE'VE STILL GOT A PROBLEM.
NOT MUCH OF A PROBLEM.
WE BURN IT DOWN. JUST LIKE THE OTHER TOWN AND THOSE WOODS.
FINE BY ME.
FORD, CULLEN, LOOK AT THAT.
I SEE IT.

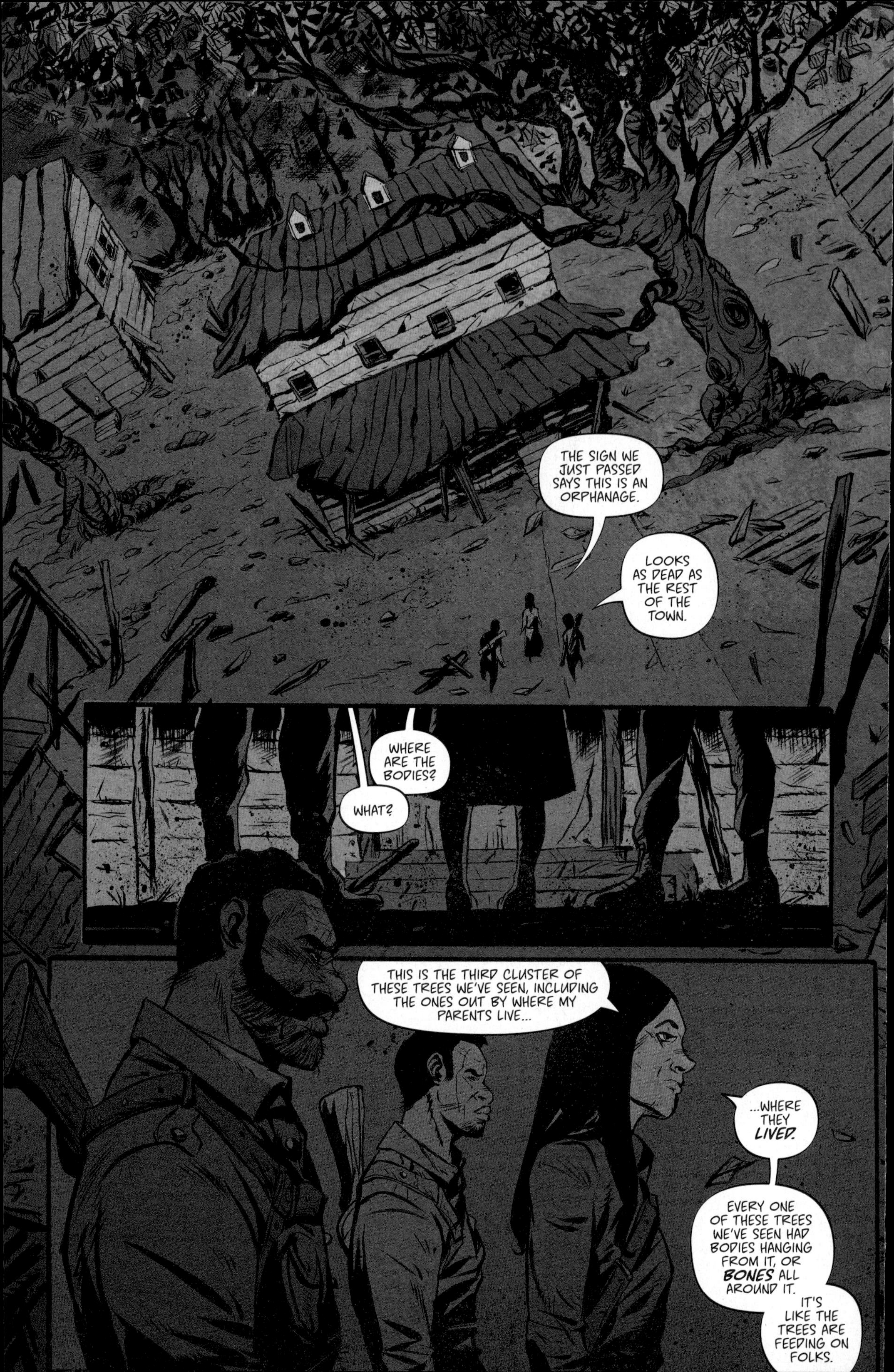
THE SIGN WE JUST PASSED SAYS THIS IS AN ORPHANAGE.
LOOKS AS DEAD AS THE REST OF THE TOWN.
WHERE ARE THE BODIES?
WHAT?
THIS IS THE THIRD CLUSTER OF THESE TREES WE'VE SEEN, INCLUDING THE ONES OUT BY WHERE MY PARENTS LIVE...
...WHERE THEY *LIVED.*
EVERY ONE OF THESE TREES WE'VE SEEN HAD BODIES HANGING FROM IT, OR **BONES** ALL AROUND IT.
IT'S LIKE THE TREES ARE FEEDING ON FOLKS.

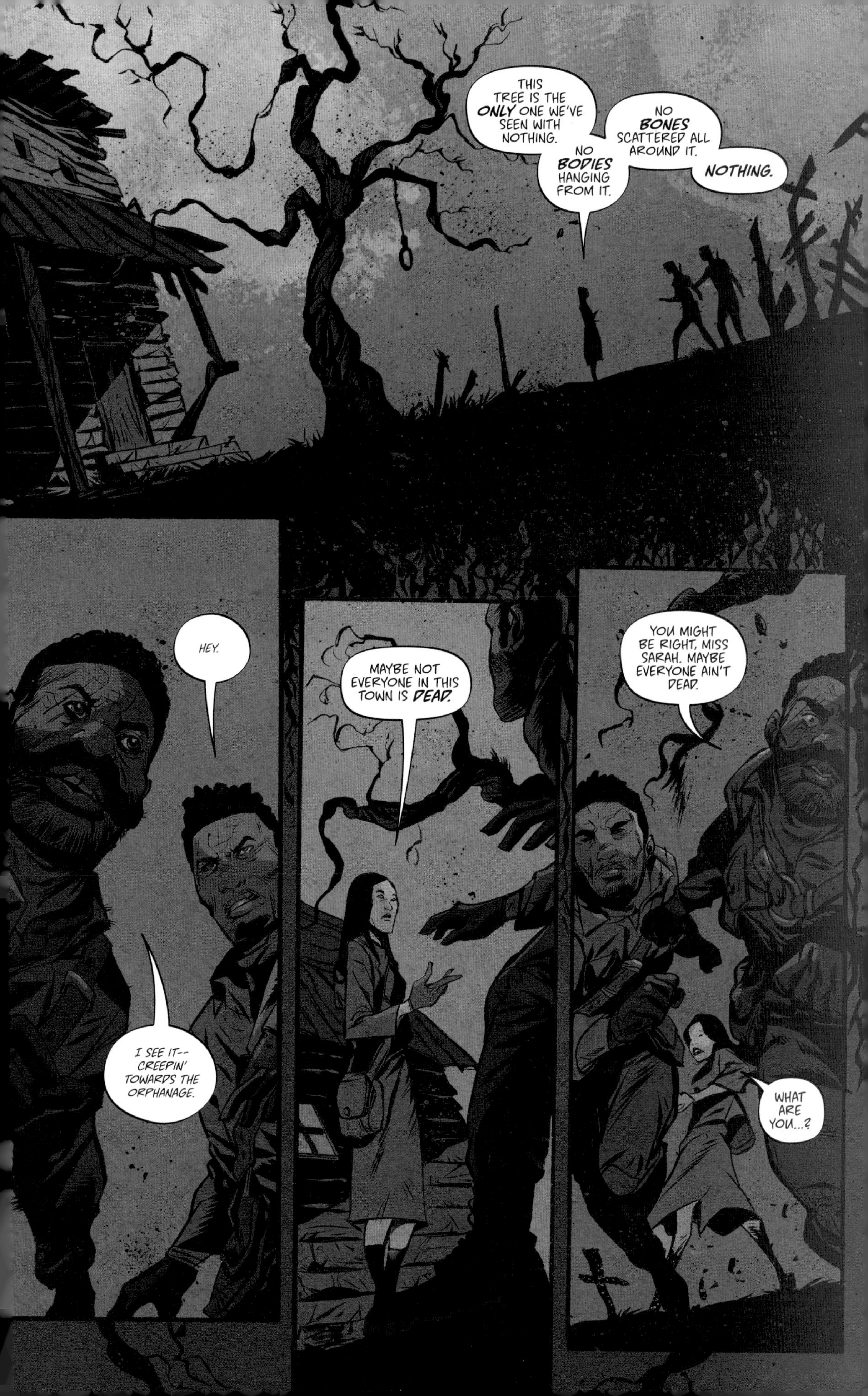
THIS TREE IS THE ONLY ONE WE'VE SEEN WITH NOTHING.
NO BODIES HANGING FROM IT.
NO BONES SCATTERED ALL AROUND IT.
NOTHING.
HEY.
I SEE IT-- CREEPIN' TOWARDS THE ORPHANAGE.
MAYBE NOT EVERYONE IN THIS TOWN IS DEAD.
YOU MIGHT BE RIGHT, MISS SARAH. MAYBE EVERYONE AIN'T DEAD.
WHAT ARE YOU...?

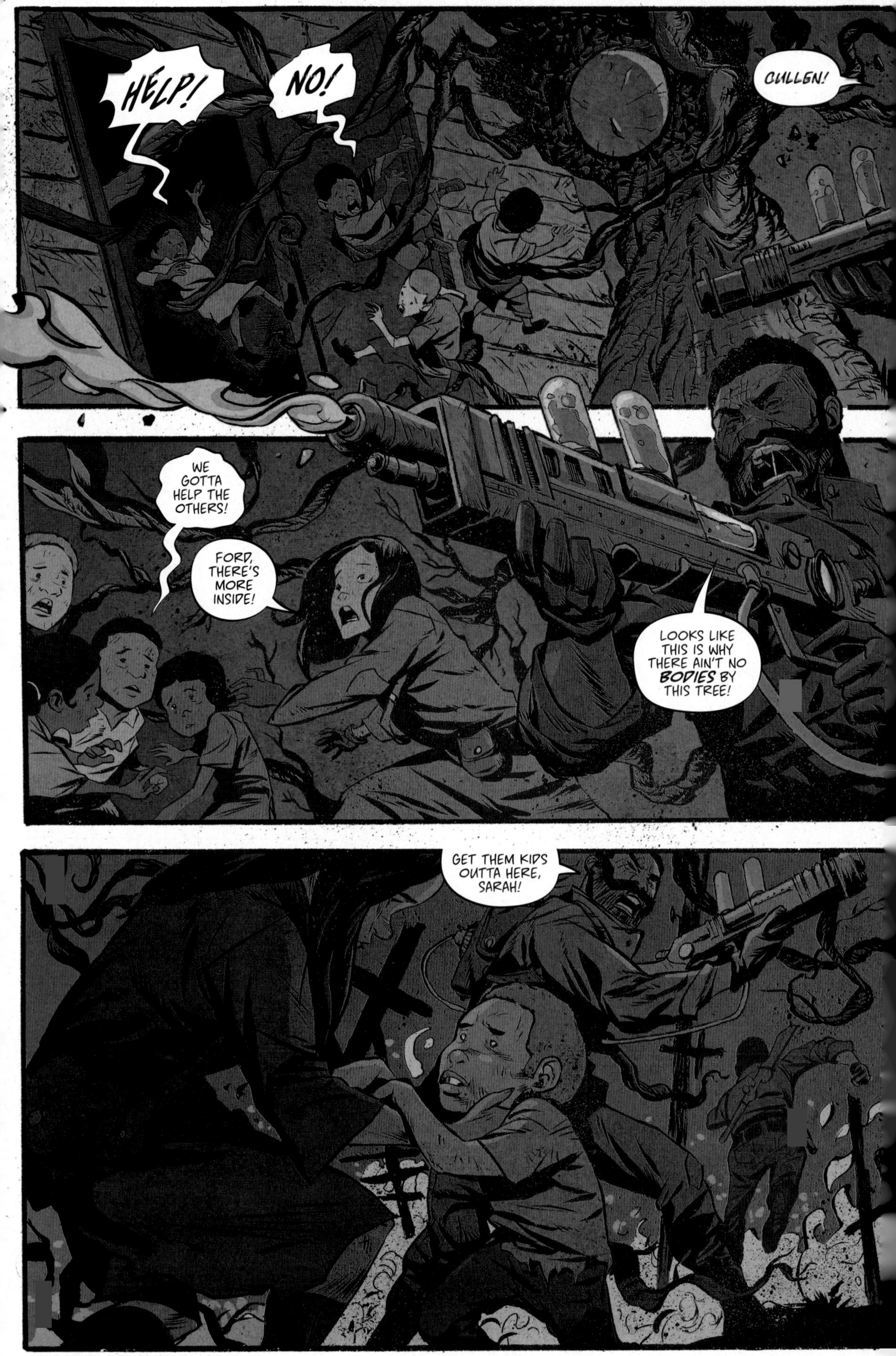
HELP!
NO!
CULLEN!
WE GOTTA HELP THE OTHERS!
FORD, THERE'S MORE INSIDE!
LOOKS LIKE THIS IS WHY THERE AIN'T NO BODIES BY THIS TREE!
GET THEM KIDS OUTTA HERE, SARAH!

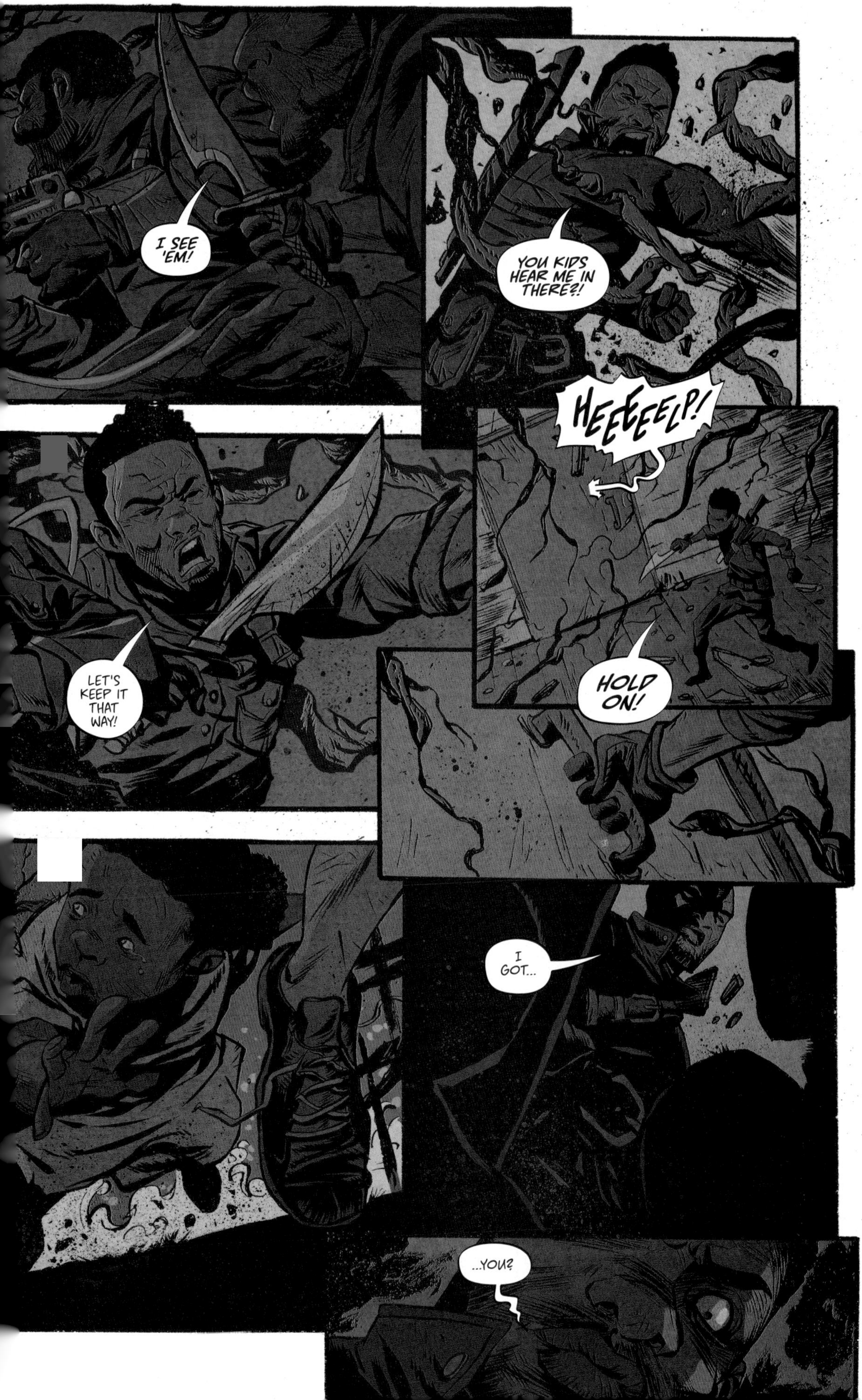
I SEE 'EM!
YOU KIDS HEAR ME IN THERE?!
LET'S KEEP IT THAT WAY!
HEEEEELP!
HOLD ON!
I GOT...
...YOU?

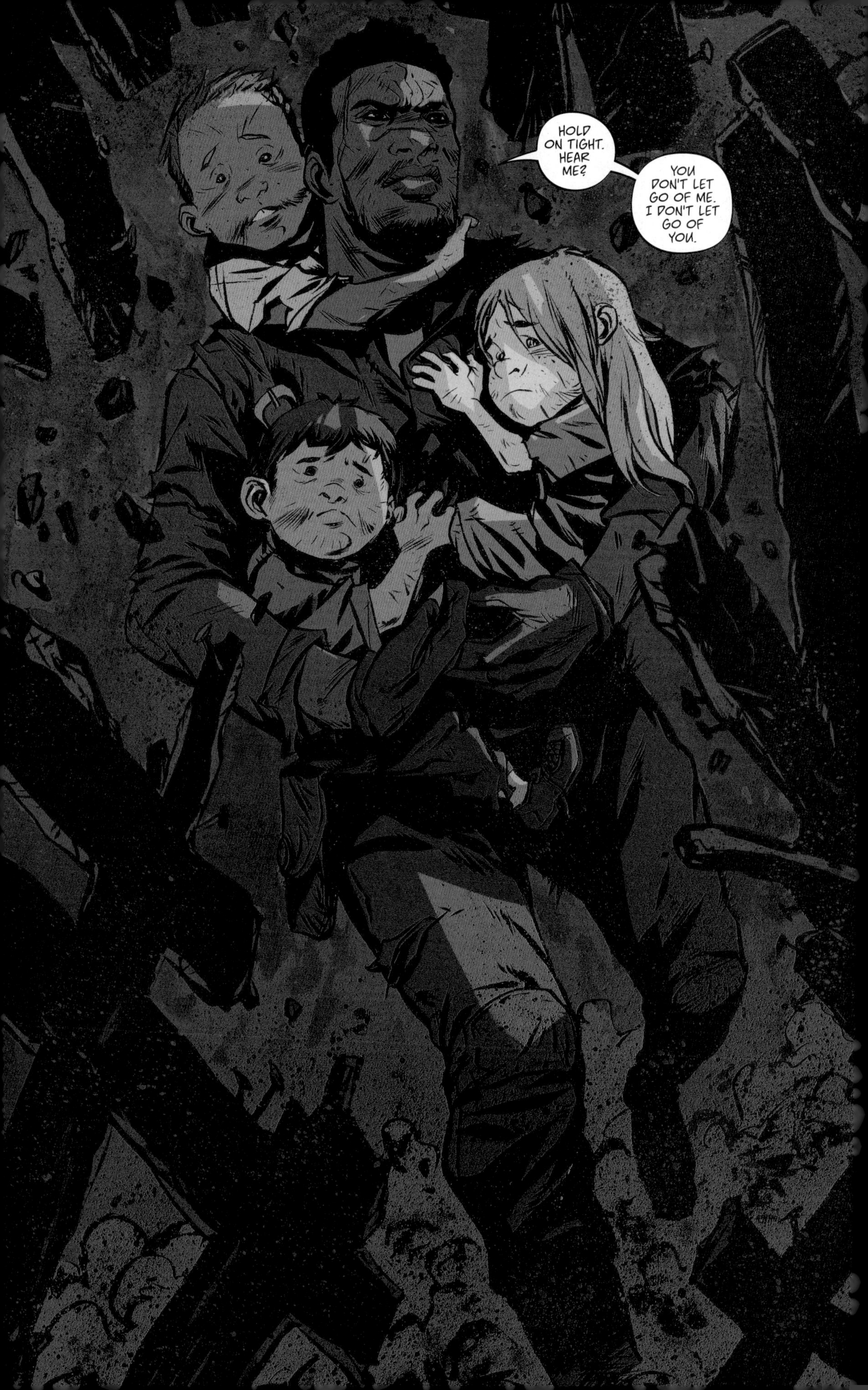
HOLD ON TIGHT. HEAR ME?
YOU DON'T LET GO OF ME. I DON'T LET GO OF YOU.

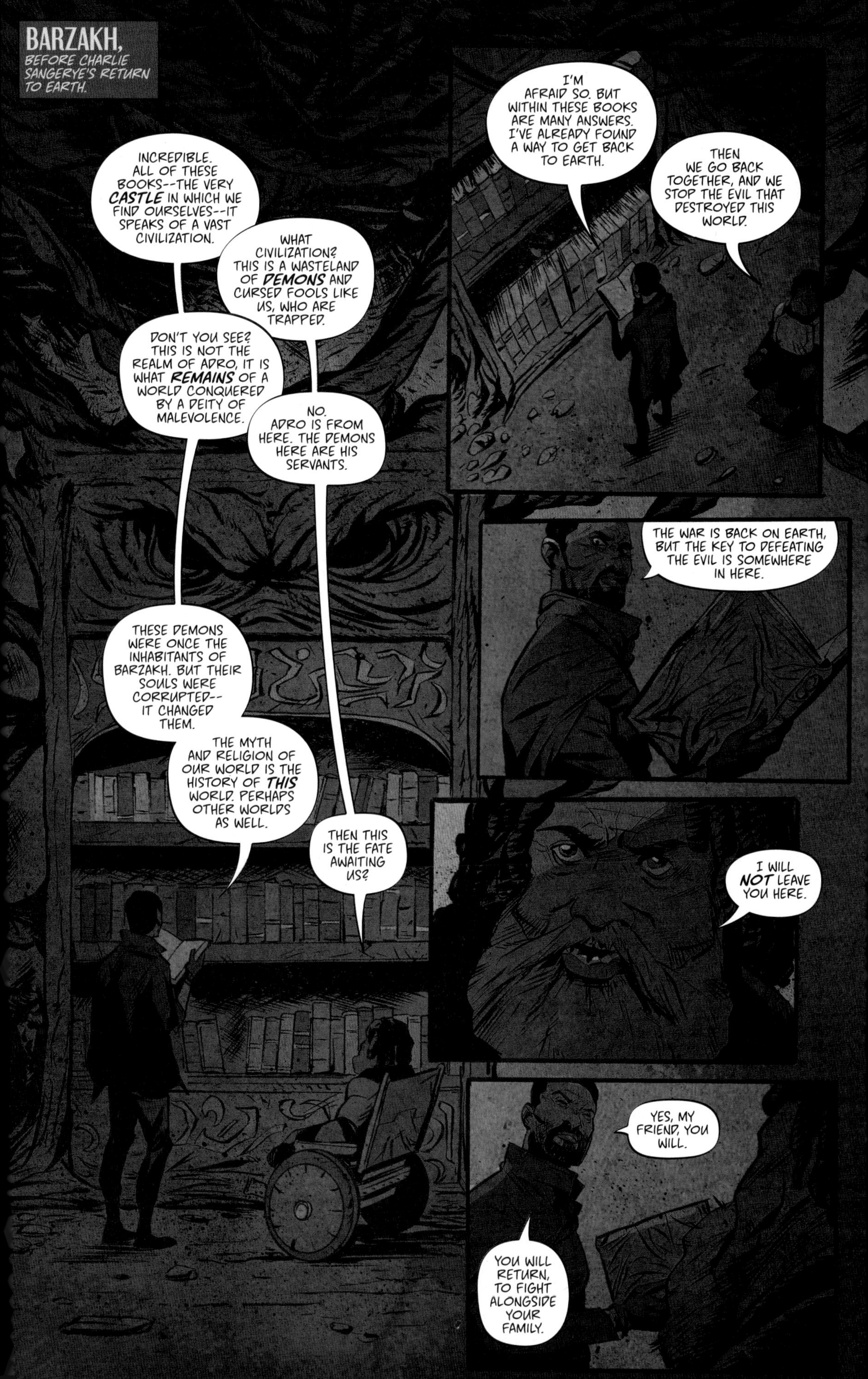
BARZAKH,
BEFORE CHARLIE SANGERYE'S RETURN TO EARTH.
INCREDIBLE. ALL OF THESE BOOKS--THE VERY CASTLE IN WHICH WE FIND OURSELVES--IT SPEAKS OF A VAST CIVILIZATION.
WHAT CIVILIZATION? THIS IS A WASTELAND OF DEMONS AND CURSED FOOLS LIKE US, WHO ARE TRAPPED.
DON'T YOU SEE? THIS IS NOT THE REALM OF ADRO, IT IS WHAT REMAINS OF A WORLD CONQUERED BY A DEITY OF MALEVOLENCE.
NO. ADRO IS FROM HERE. THE DEMONS HERE ARE HIS SERVANTS.
THESE DEMONS WERE ONCE THE INHABITANTS OF BARZAKH. BUT THEIR SOULS WERE CORRUPTED-- IT CHANGED THEM.
THE MYTH AND RELIGION OF OUR WORLD IS THE HISTORY OF THIS WORLD. PERHAPS OTHER WORLDS AS WELL.
THEN THIS IS THE FATE AWAITING US?
I'M AFRAID SO. BUT WITHIN THESE BOOKS ARE MANY ANSWERS. I'VE ALREADY FOUND A WAY TO GET BACK TO EARTH.
THEN WE GO BACK TOGETHER, AND WE STOP THE EVIL THAT DESTROYED THIS WORLD.
THE WAR IS BACK ON EARTH, BUT THE KEY TO DEFEATING THE EVIL IS SOMEWHERE IN HERE.
I WILL NOT LEAVE YOU HERE.
YES, MY FRIEND, YOU WILL.
YOU WILL RETURN, TO FIGHT ALONGSIDE YOUR FAMILY.

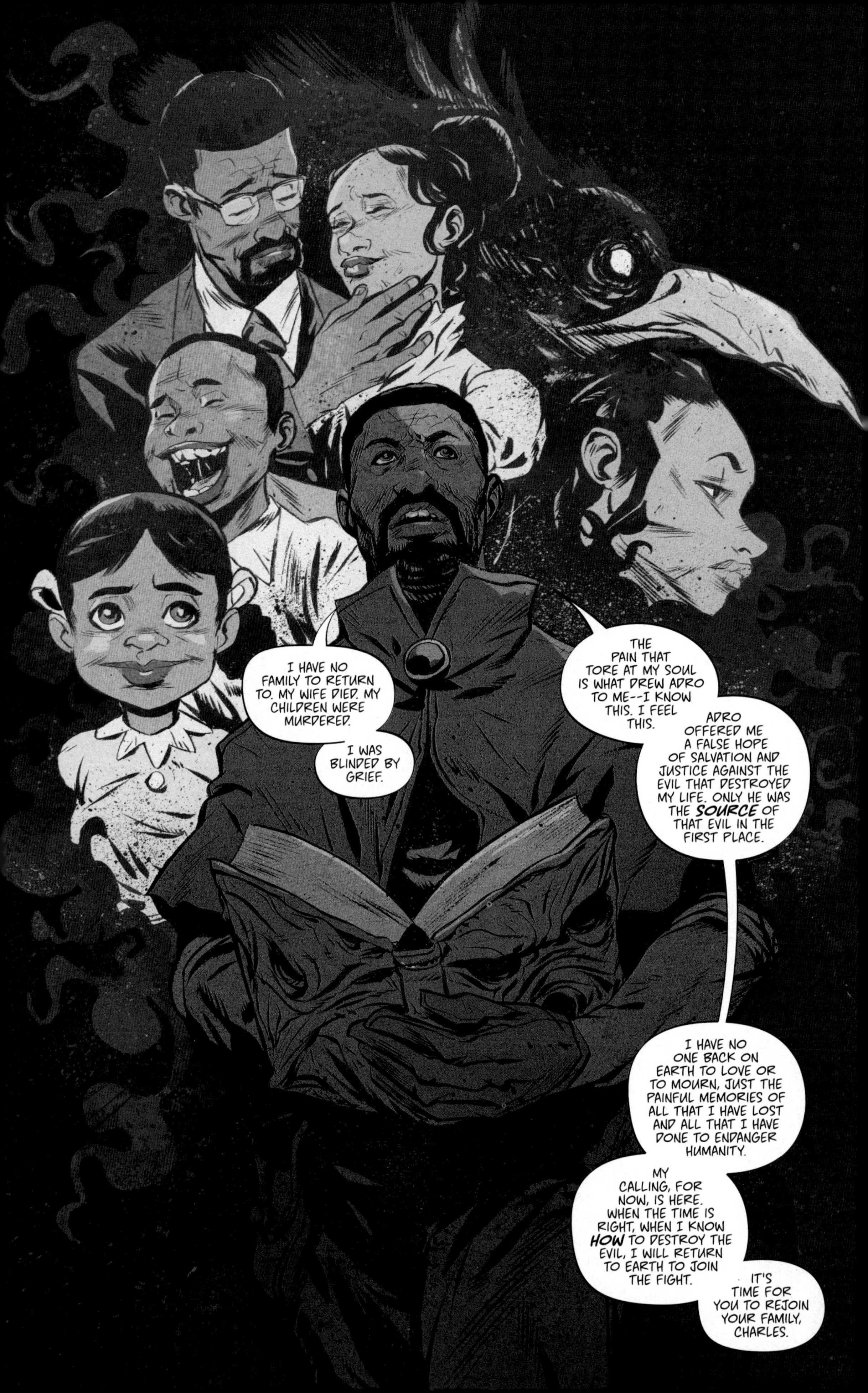
I HAVE NO FAMILY TO RETURN TO. MY WIFE DIED. MY CHILDREN WERE MURDERED.
I WAS BLINDED BY GRIEF.
THE PAIN THAT TORE AT MY SOUL IS WHAT DREW ADRO TO ME--I KNOW THIS. I FEEL THIS.
ADRO OFFERED ME A FALSE HOPE OF SALVATION AND JUSTICE AGAINST THE EVIL THAT DESTROYED MY LIFE. ONLY HE WAS THE SOURCE OF THAT EVIL IN THE FIRST PLACE.
I HAVE NO ONE BACK ON EARTH TO LOVE OR TO MOURN, JUST THE PAINFUL MEMORIES OF ALL THAT I HAVE LOST AND ALL THAT I HAVE DONE TO ENDANGER HUMANITY.
MY CALLING, FOR NOW, IS HERE. WHEN THE TIME IS RIGHT, WHEN I KNOW HOW TO DESTROY THE EVIL, I WILL RETURN TO EARTH TO JOIN THE FIGHT.
IT'S TIME FOR YOU TO REJOIN YOUR FAMILY, CHARLES.

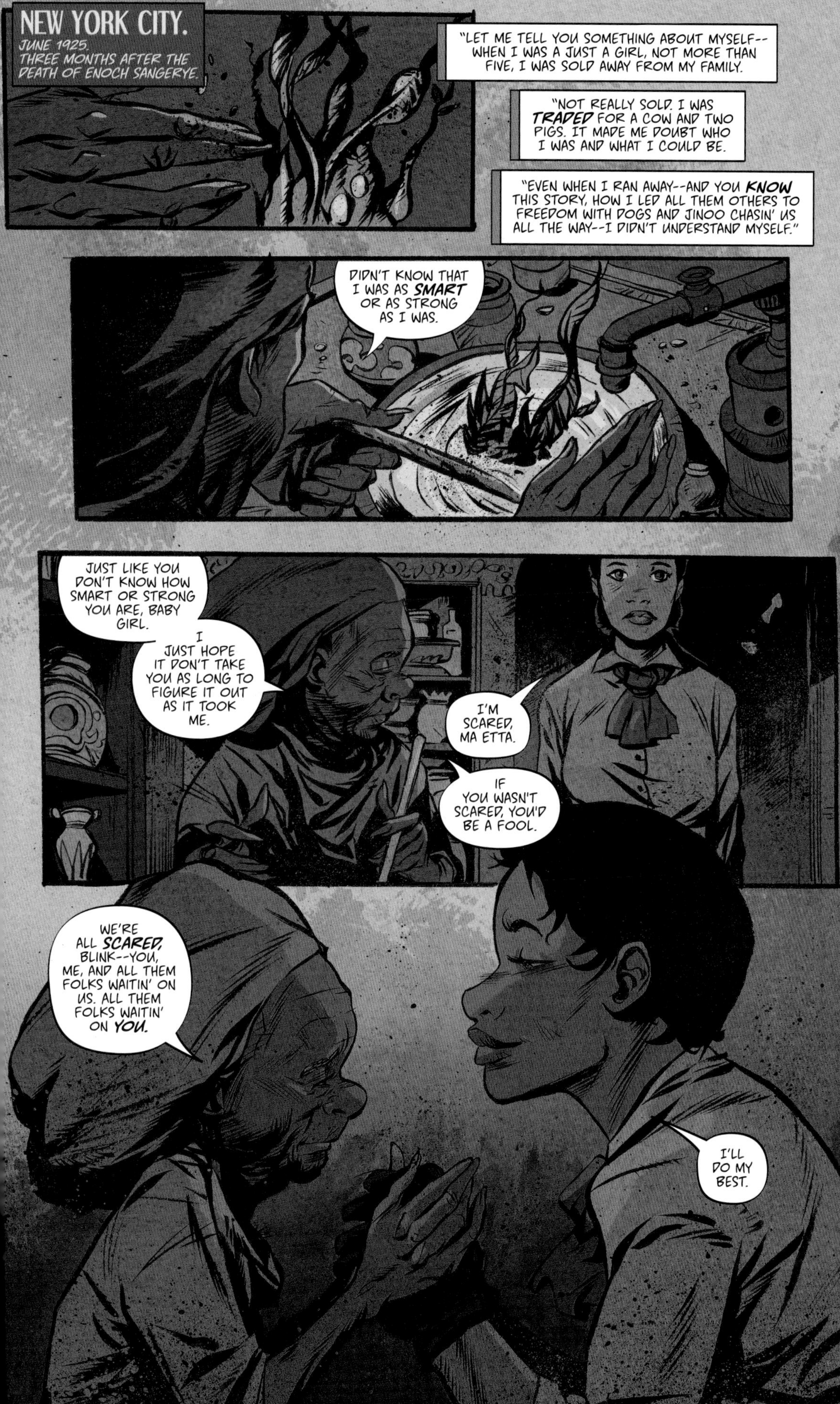
NEW YORK CITY.
JUNE 1925. THREE MONTHS AFTER THE DEATH OF ENOCH SANGERYE.
"LET ME TELL YOU SOMETHING ABOUT MYSELF-- WHEN I WAS A JUST A GIRL, NOT MORE THAN FIVE, I WAS SOLD AWAY FROM MY FAMILY.
"NOT REALLY SOLD. I WAS TRADED FOR A COW AND TWO PIGS. IT MADE ME DOUBT WHO I WAS AND WHAT I COULD BE.
"EVEN WHEN I RAN AWAY--AND YOU KNOW THIS STORY, HOW I LED ALL THEM OTHERS TO FREEDOM WITH DOGS AND JINOO CHASIN' US ALL THE WAY--I DIDN'T UNDERSTAND MYSELF."
DIDN'T KNOW THAT I WAS AS SMART OR AS STRONG AS I WAS.
JUST LIKE YOU DON'T KNOW HOW SMART OR STRONG YOU ARE, BABY GIRL.
I JUST HOPE IT DON'T TAKE YOU AS LONG TO FIGURE IT OUT AS IT TOOK ME.
I'M SCARED, MA ETTA.
IF YOU WASN'T SCARED, YOU'D BE A FOOL.
WE'RE ALL SCARED, BLINK--YOU, ME, AND ALL THEM FOLKS WAITIN' ON US. ALL THEM FOLKS WAITIN' ON YOU.
I'LL DO MY BEST.

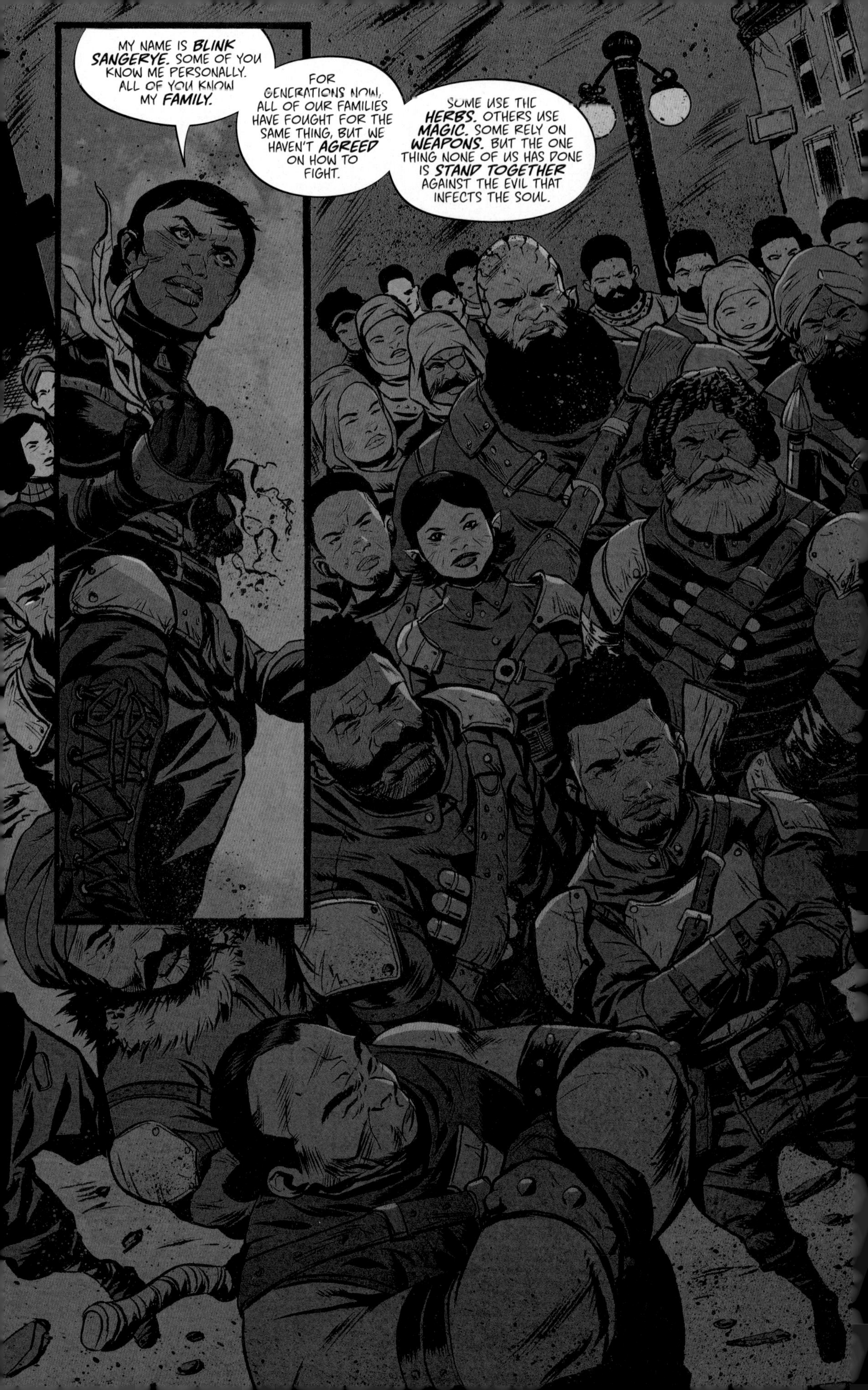
MY NAME IS **BLINK SANGERYE.** SOME OF YOU KNOW ME PERSONALLY. ALL OF YOU KNOW MY **FAMILY.**
FOR GENERATIONS NOW, ALL OF OUR FAMILIES HAVE FOUGHT FOR THE SAME THING, BUT WE HAVEN'T **AGREED** ON HOW TO FIGHT.
SOME USE THE **HERBS.** OTHERS USE **MAGIC.** SOME RELY ON **WEAPONS.** BUT THE ONE THING NONE OF US HAS DONE IS **STAND TOGETHER** AGAINST THE EVIL THAT INFECTS THE SOUL.

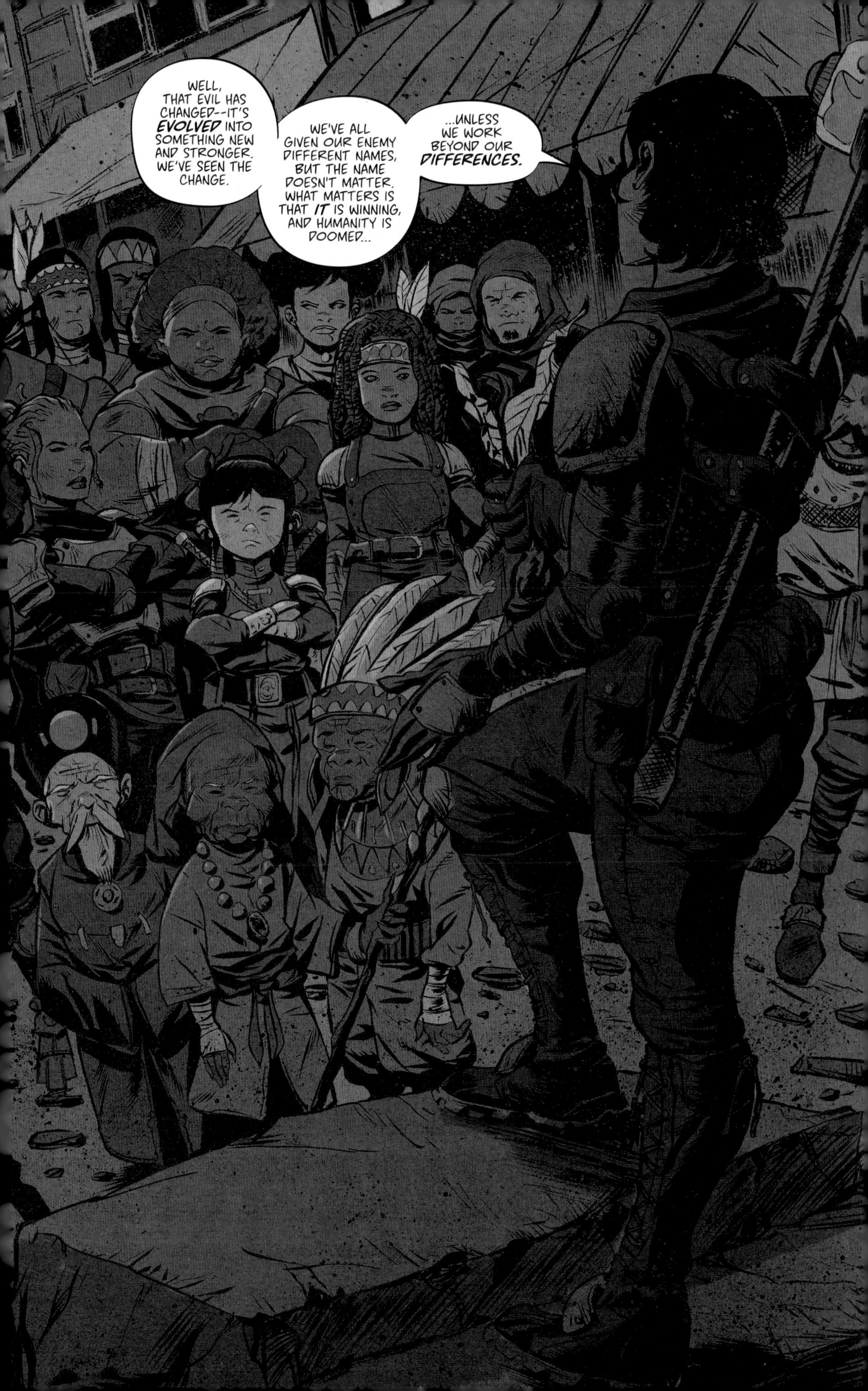
WELL, THAT EVIL HAS CHANGED--IT'S EVOLVED INTO SOMETHING NEW AND STRONGER. WE'VE SEEN THE CHANGE.
WE'VE ALL GIVEN OUR ENEMY DIFFERENT NAMES, BUT THE NAME DOESN'T MATTER. WHAT MATTERS IS THAT IT IS WINNING, AND HUMANITY IS DOOMED...
...UNLESS WE WORK BEYOND OUR DIFFERENCES.

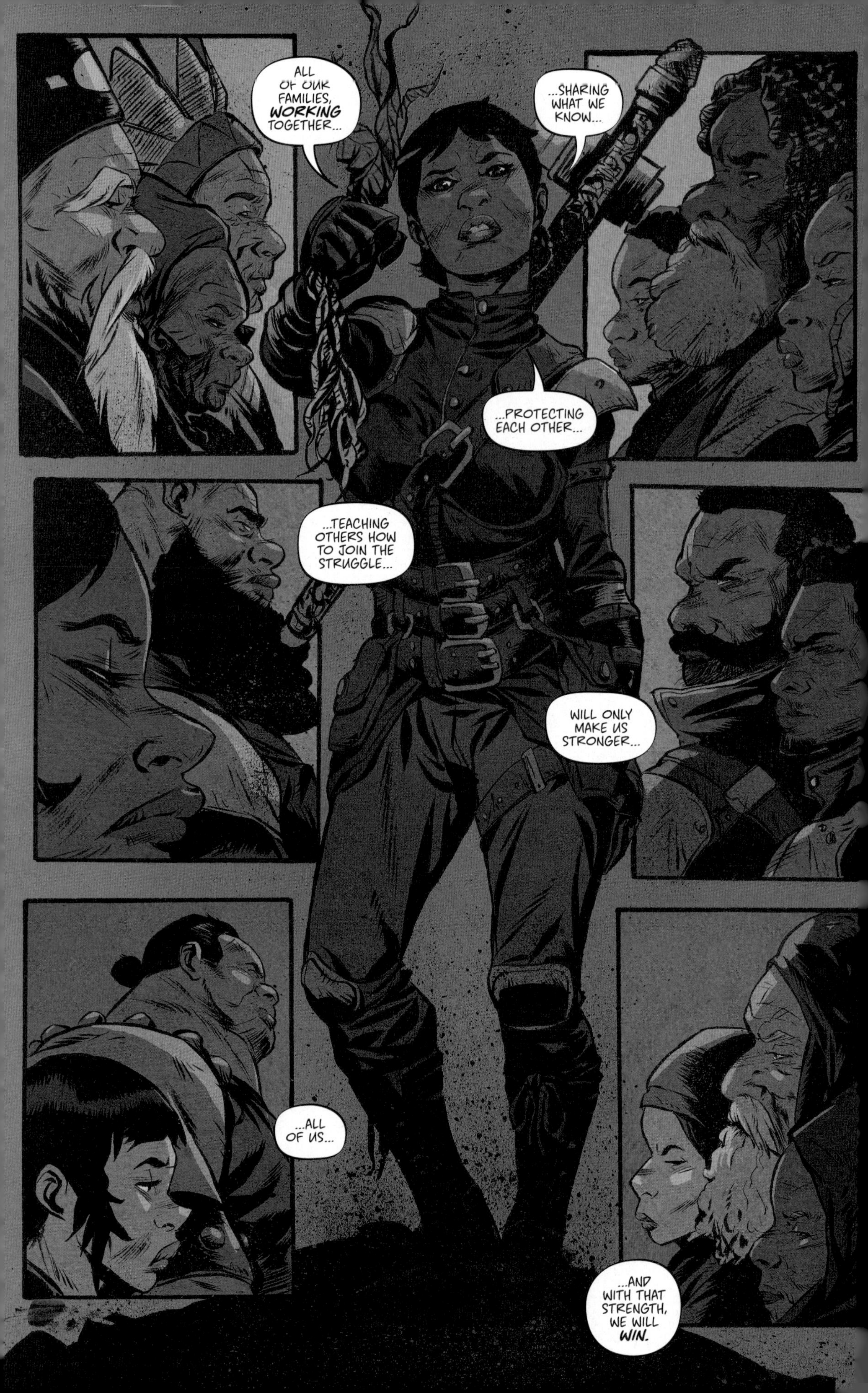
ALL OF OUR FAMILIES, **WORKING** TOGETHER...
...SHARING WHAT WE KNOW...
...PROTECTING EACH OTHER...
...TEACHING OTHERS HOW TO JOIN THE STRUGGLE...
WILL ONLY MAKE US STRONGER...
...ALL OF US...
...AND WITH THAT STRENGTH, WE WILL **WIN.**

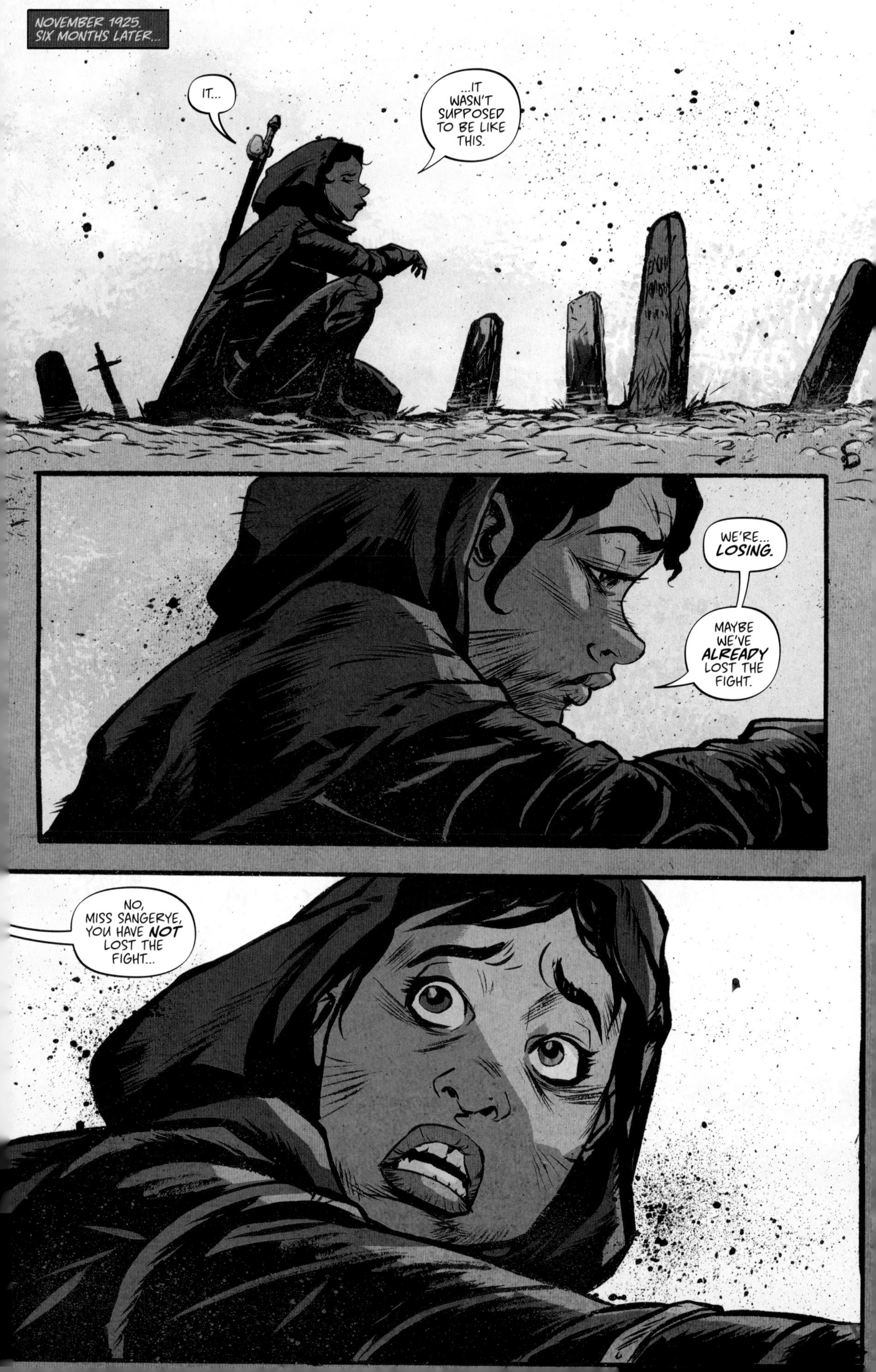
NOVEMBER 1925.
SIX MONTHS LATER...
IT...
...IT WASN'T SUPPOSED TO BE LIKE THIS.
WE'RE... **LOSING.**
MAYBE WE'VE **ALREADY** LOST THE FIGHT.
NO, MISS SANGERYE, YOU HAVE **NOT** LOST THE FIGHT...

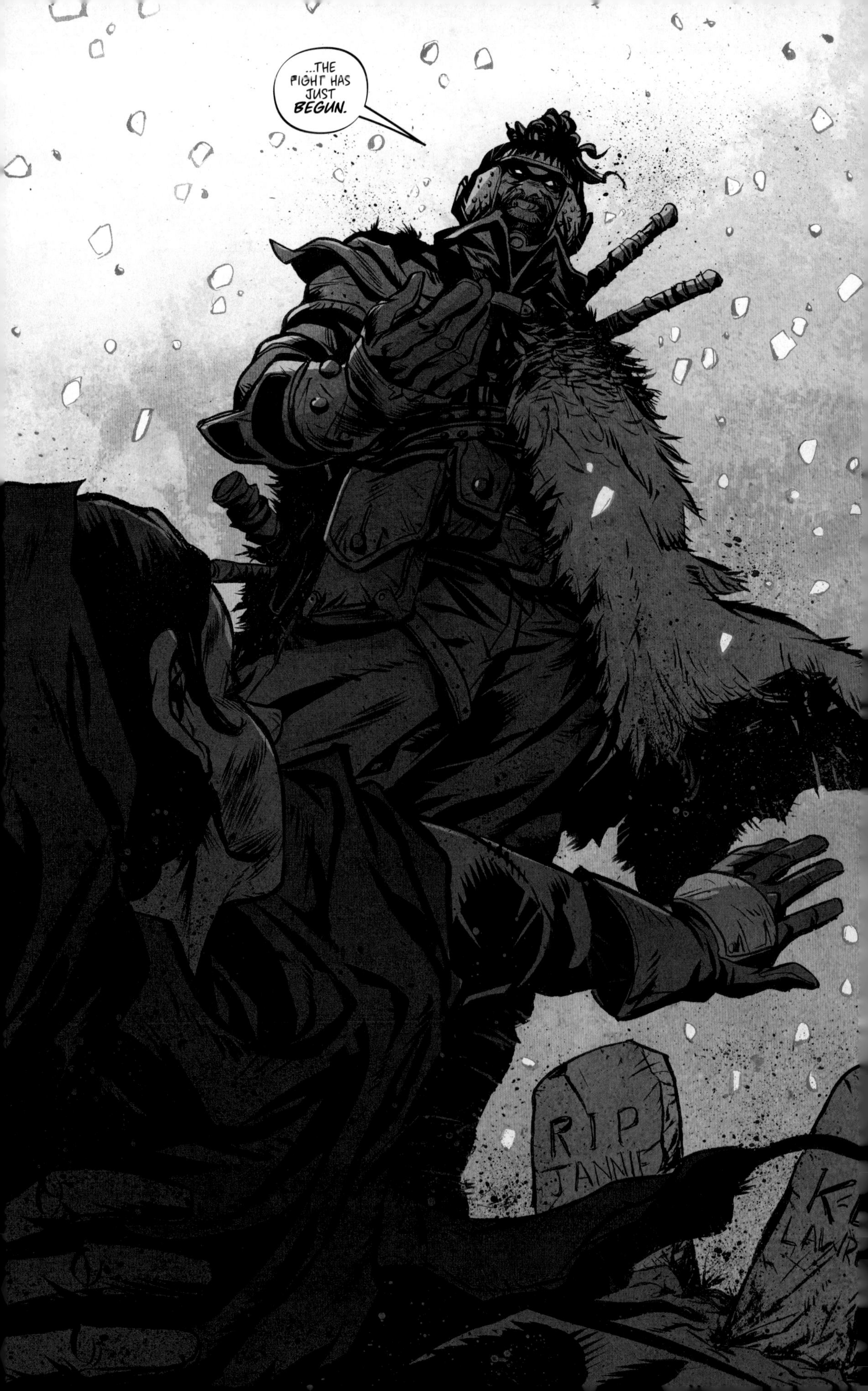
...THE FIGHT HAS JUST BEGUN.
RIP JANNIE

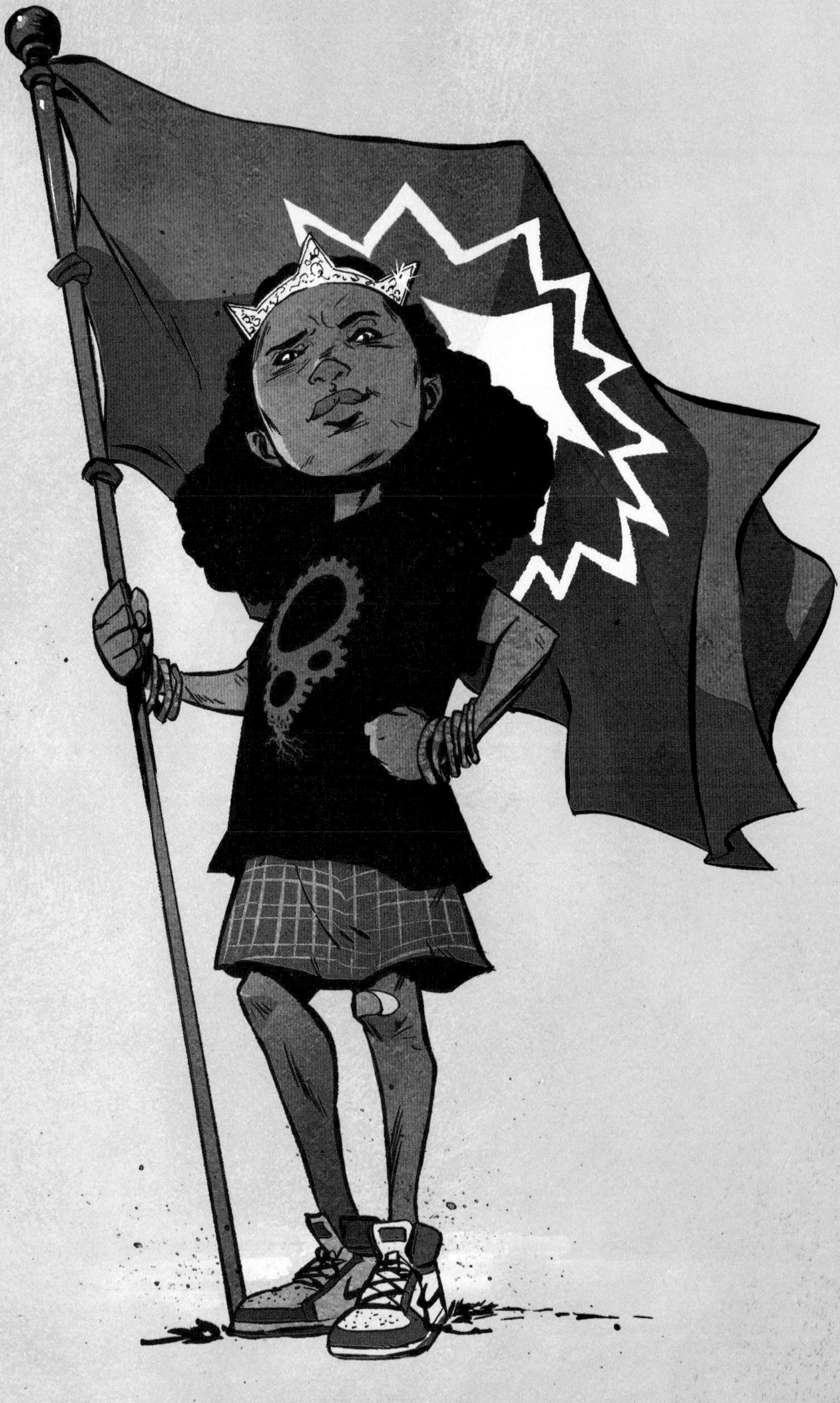

Issue #14 Juneteenth variant by Sanford Greene

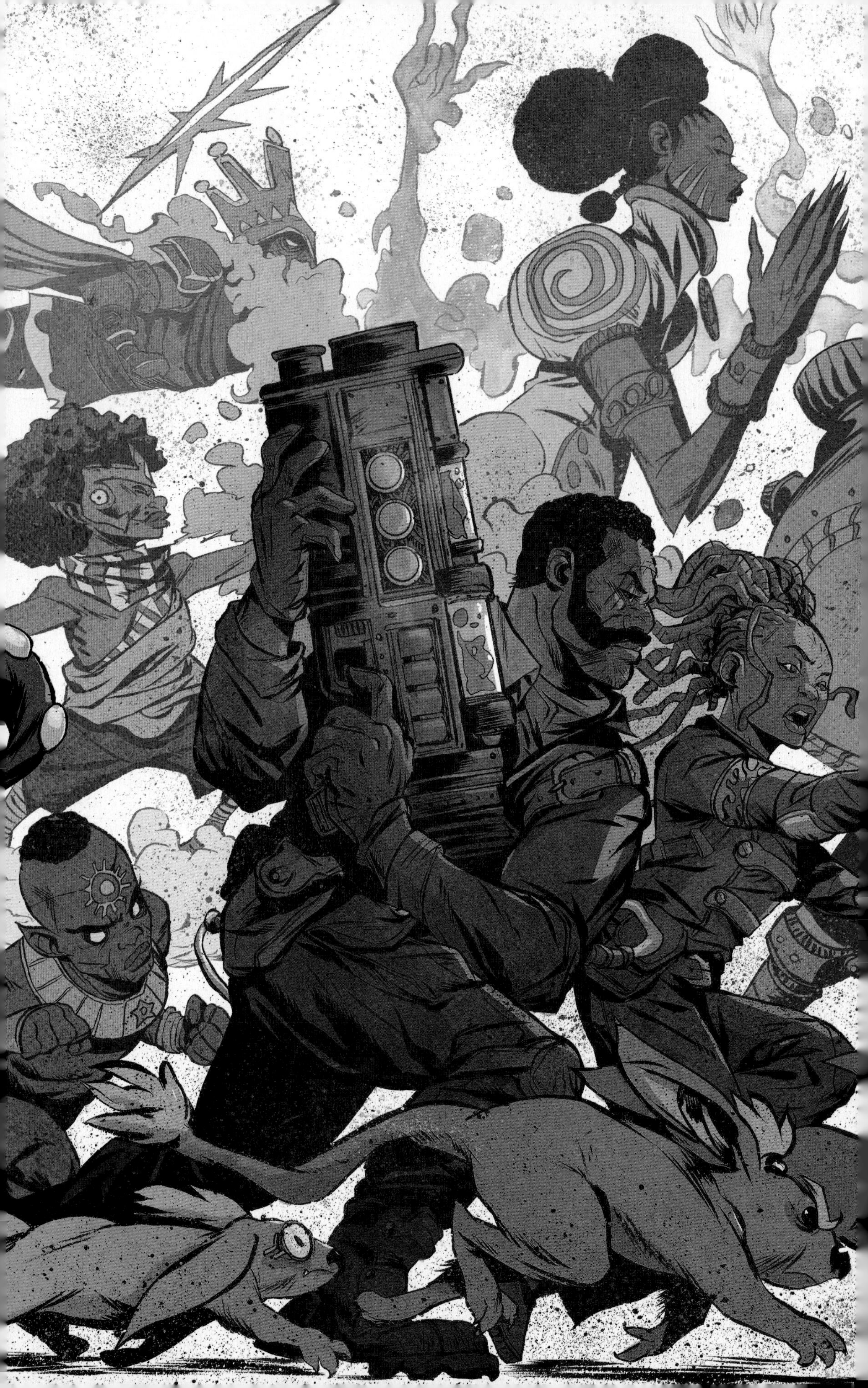

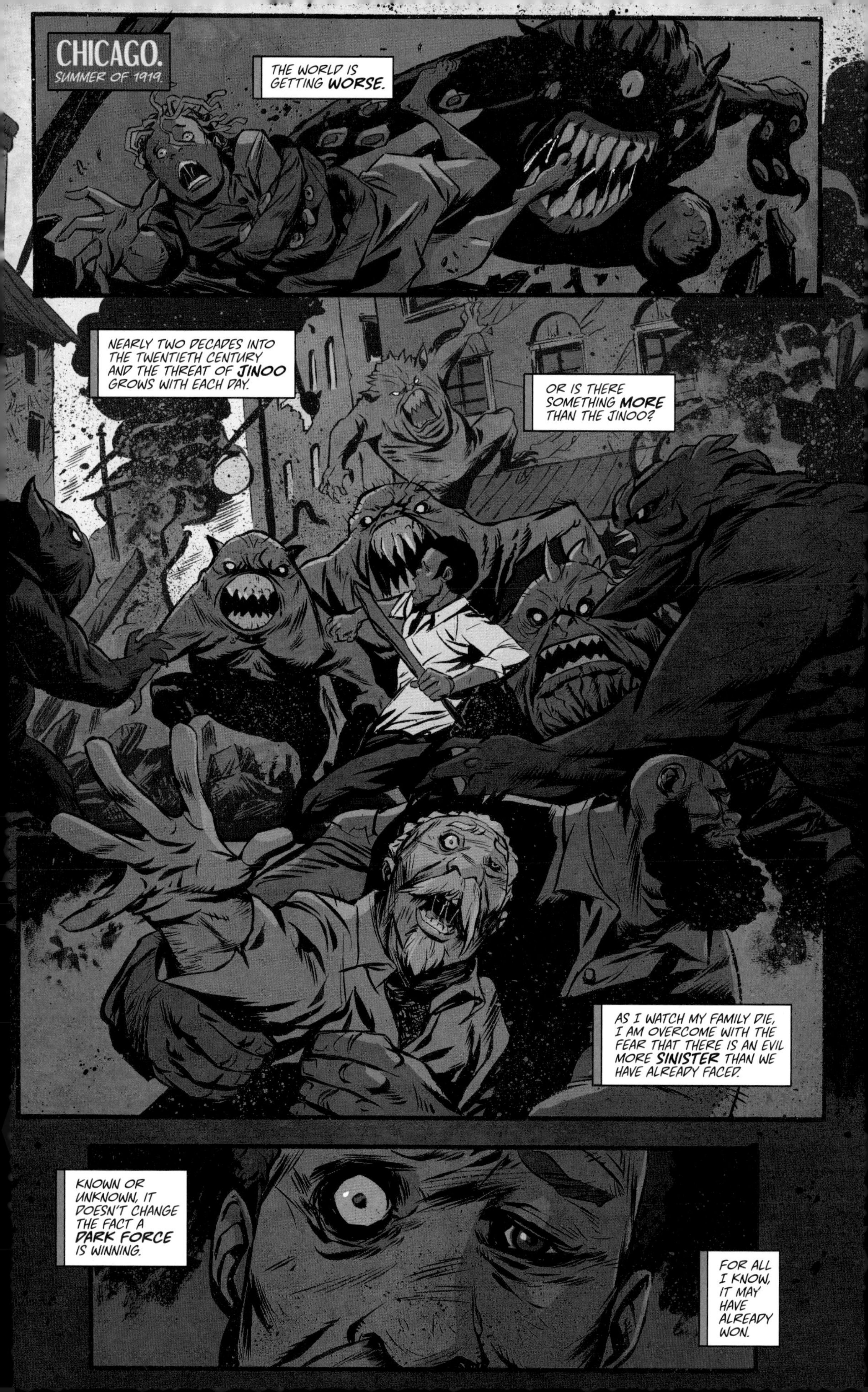
CHICAGO.
SUMMER OF 1919.
THE WORLD IS GETTING WORSE.
NEARLY TWO DECADES INTO THE TWENTIETH CENTURY AND THE THREAT OF JINOO GROWS WITH EACH DAY.
OR IS THERE SOMETHING MORE THAN THE JINOO?
AS I WATCH MY FAMILY DIE, I AM OVERCOME WITH THE FEAR THAT THERE IS AN EVIL MORE SINISTER THAN WE HAVE ALREADY FACED.
KNOWN OR UNKNOWN, IT DOESN'T CHANGE THE FACT A DARK FORCE IS WINNING.
FOR ALL I KNOW, IT MAY HAVE ALREADY WON.

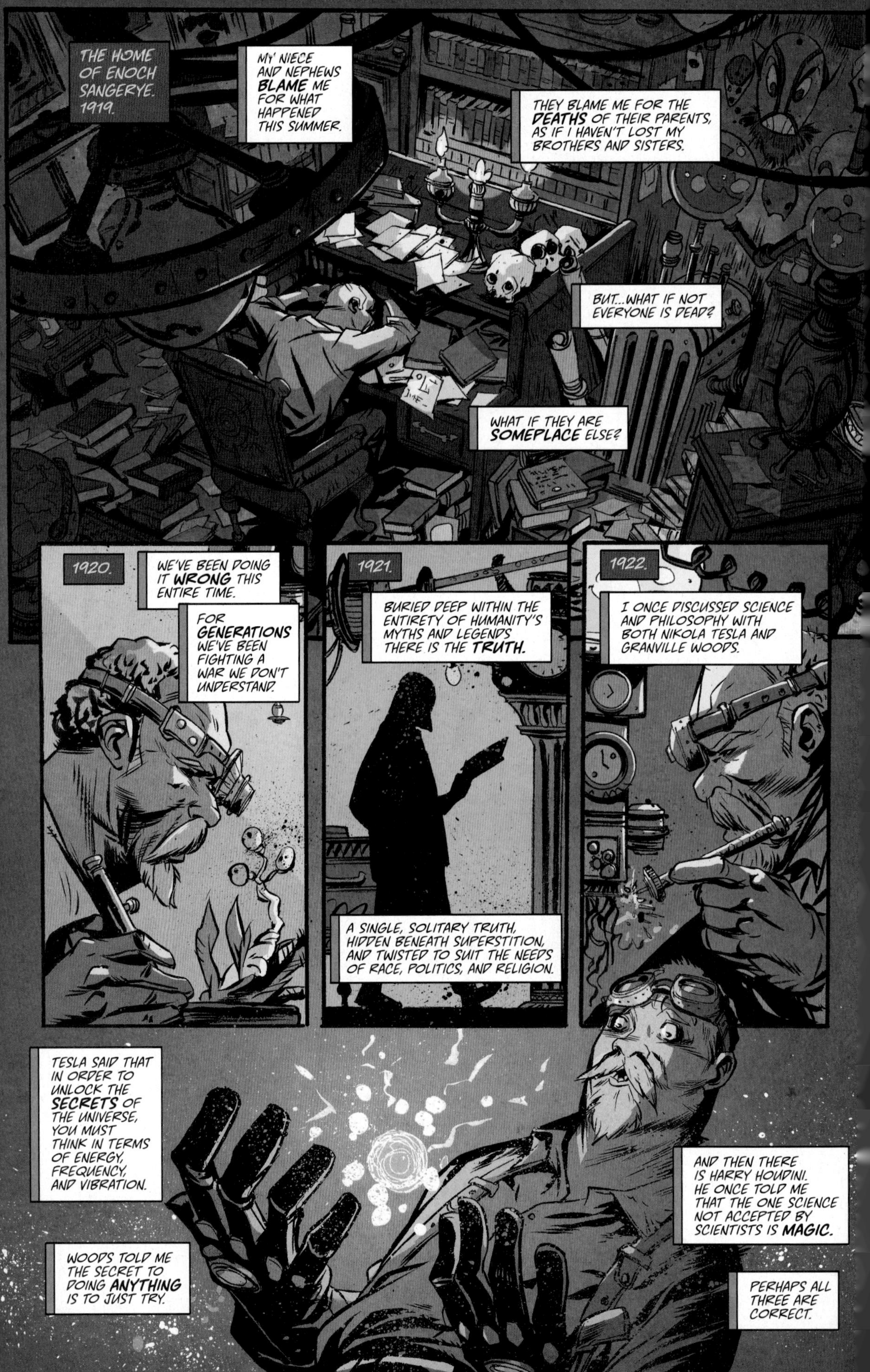
THE HOME OF ENOCH SANGERYE. 1919.
MY NIECE AND NEPHEWS BLAME ME FOR WHAT HAPPENED THIS SUMMER.
THEY BLAME ME FOR THE DEATHS OF THEIR PARENTS, AS IF I HAVEN'T LOST MY BROTHERS AND SISTERS.
BUT...WHAT IF NOT EVERYONE IS DEAD?
WHAT IF THEY ARE SOMEPLACE ELSE?
1920.
WE'VE BEEN DOING IT WRONG THIS ENTIRE TIME.
FOR GENERATIONS WE'VE BEEN FIGHTING A WAR WE DON'T UNDERSTAND.
1921.
BURIED DEEP WITHIN THE ENTIRETY OF HUMANITY'S MYTHS AND LEGENDS THERE IS THE TRUTH.
A SINGLE, SOLITARY TRUTH, HIDDEN BENEATH SUPERSTITION, AND TWISTED TO SUIT THE NEEDS OF RACE, POLITICS, AND RELIGION.
1922.
I ONCE DISCUSSED SCIENCE AND PHILOSOPHY WITH BOTH NIKOLA TESLA AND GRANVILLE WOODS.
TESLA SAID THAT IN ORDER TO UNLOCK THE SECRETS OF THE UNIVERSE, YOU MUST THINK IN TERMS OF ENERGY, FREQUENCY, AND VIBRATION.
WOODS TOLD ME THE SECRET TO DOING ANYTHING IS TO JUST TRY.
AND THEN THERE IS HARRY HOUDINI. HE ONCE TOLD ME THAT THE ONE SCIENCE NOT ACCEPTED BY SCIENTISTS IS MAGIC.
PERHAPS ALL THREE ARE CORRECT.

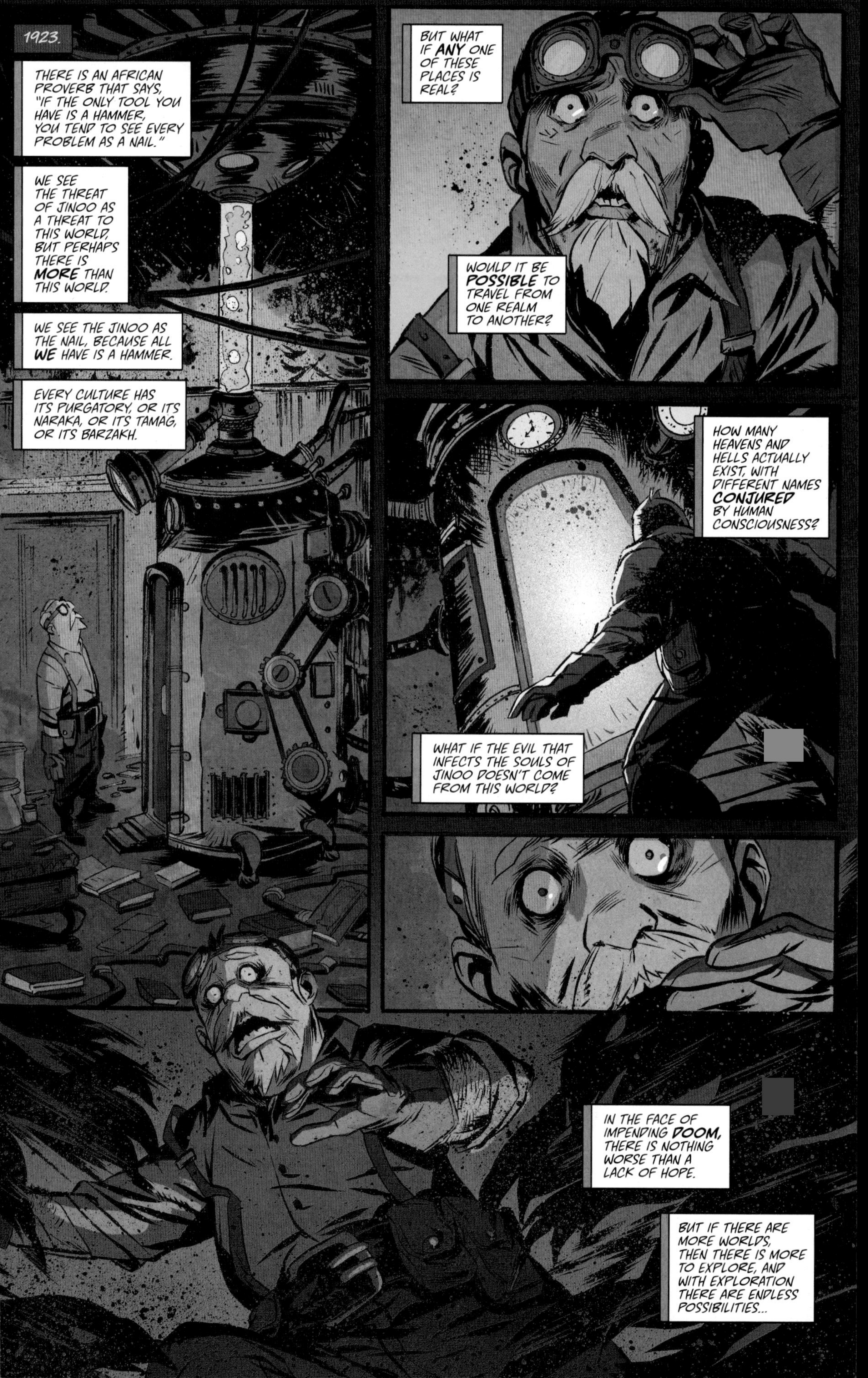
1923.
THERE IS AN AFRICAN PROVERB THAT SAYS, "IF THE ONLY TOOL YOU HAVE IS A HAMMER, YOU TEND TO SEE EVERY PROBLEM AS A NAIL."
WE SEE THE THREAT OF JINOO AS A THREAT TO THIS WORLD, BUT PERHAPS THERE IS MORE THAN THIS WORLD.
WE SEE THE JINOO AS THE NAIL, BECAUSE ALL WE HAVE IS A HAMMER.
EVERY CULTURE HAS ITS PURGATORY, OR ITS NARAKA, OR ITS TAMAG, OR ITS BARZAKH.
BUT WHAT IF ANY ONE OF THESE PLACES IS REAL?
WOULD IT BE POSSIBLE TO TRAVEL FROM ONE REALM TO ANOTHER?
HOW MANY HEAVENS AND HELLS ACTUALLY EXIST, WITH DIFFERENT NAMES CONJURED BY HUMAN CONSCIOUSNESS?
WHAT IF THE EVIL THAT INFECTS THE SOULS OF JINOO DOESN'T COME FROM THIS WORLD?
IN THE FACE OF IMPENDING DOOM, THERE IS NOTHING WORSE THAN A LACK OF HOPE.
BUT IF THERE ARE MORE WORLDS, THEN THERE IS MORE TO EXPLORE, AND WITH EXPLORATION THERE ARE ENDLESS POSSIBILITIES...

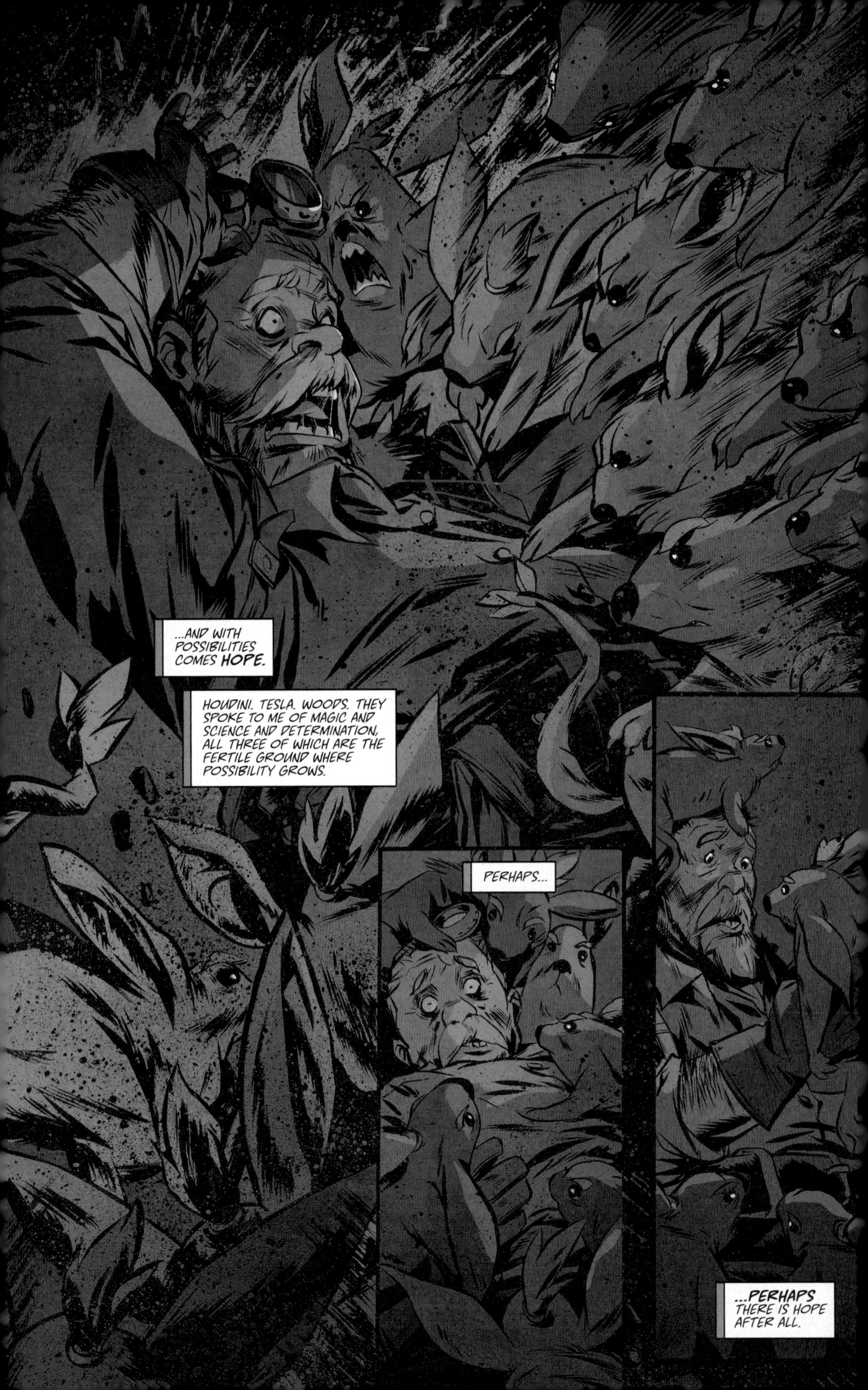
...AND WITH POSSIBILITIES COMES HOPE.
HOUDINI. TESLA. WOODS. THEY SPOKE TO ME OF MAGIC AND SCIENCE AND DETERMINATION, ALL THREE OF WHICH ARE THE FERTILE GROUND WHERE POSSIBILITY GROWS.
PERHAPS...
...PERHAPS THERE IS HOPE AFTER ALL.

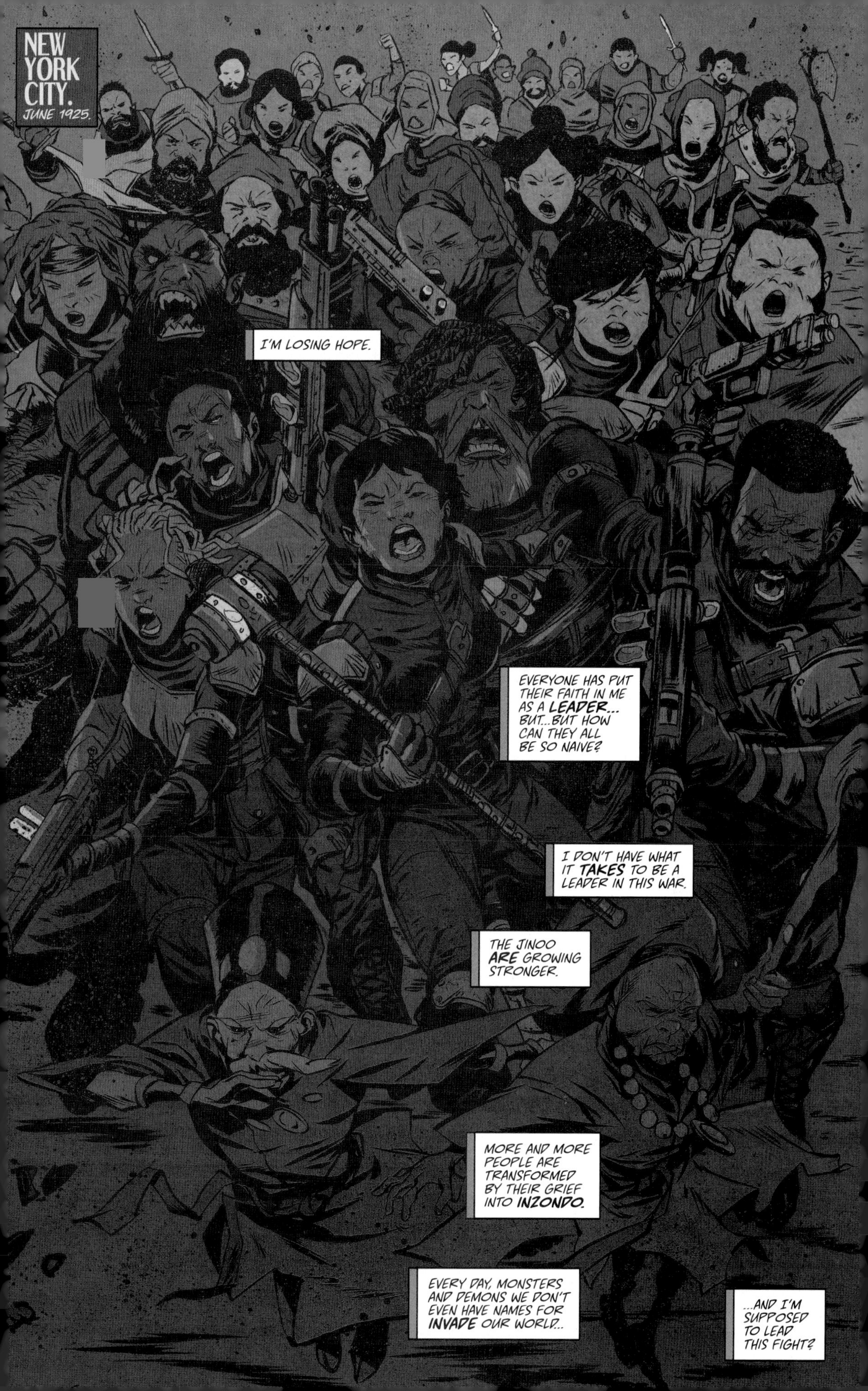
NEW YORK CITY.
JUNE 1925.
I'M LOSING HOPE.
EVERYONE HAS PUT THEIR FAITH IN ME AS A LEADER... BUT...BUT HOW CAN THEY ALL BE SO NAIVE?
I DON'T HAVE WHAT IT TAKES TO BE A LEADER IN THIS WAR.
THE JINOO ARE GROWING STRONGER.
MORE AND MORE PEOPLE ARE TRANSFORMED BY THEIR GRIEF INTO INZONDO.
EVERY DAY, MONSTERS AND DEMONS WE DON'T EVEN HAVE NAMES FOR INVADE OUR WORLD...
...AND I'M SUPPOSED TO LEAD THIS FIGHT?

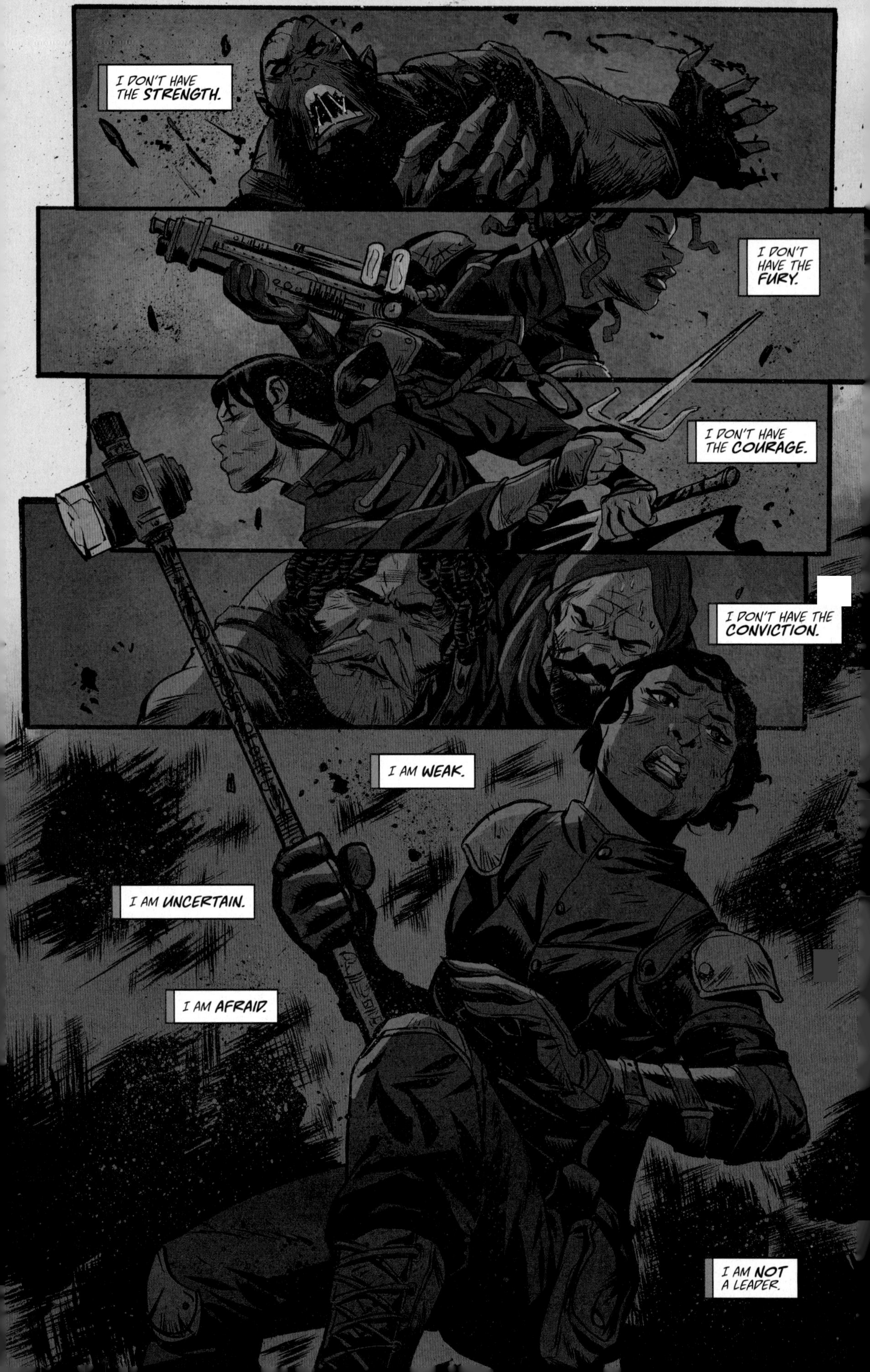
I DON'T HAVE THE STRENGTH.
I DON'T HAVE THE FURY.
I DON'T HAVE THE COURAGE.
I DON'T HAVE THE CONVICTION.
I AM WEAK.
I AM UNCERTAIN.
I AM AFRAID.
I AM NOT A LEADER.

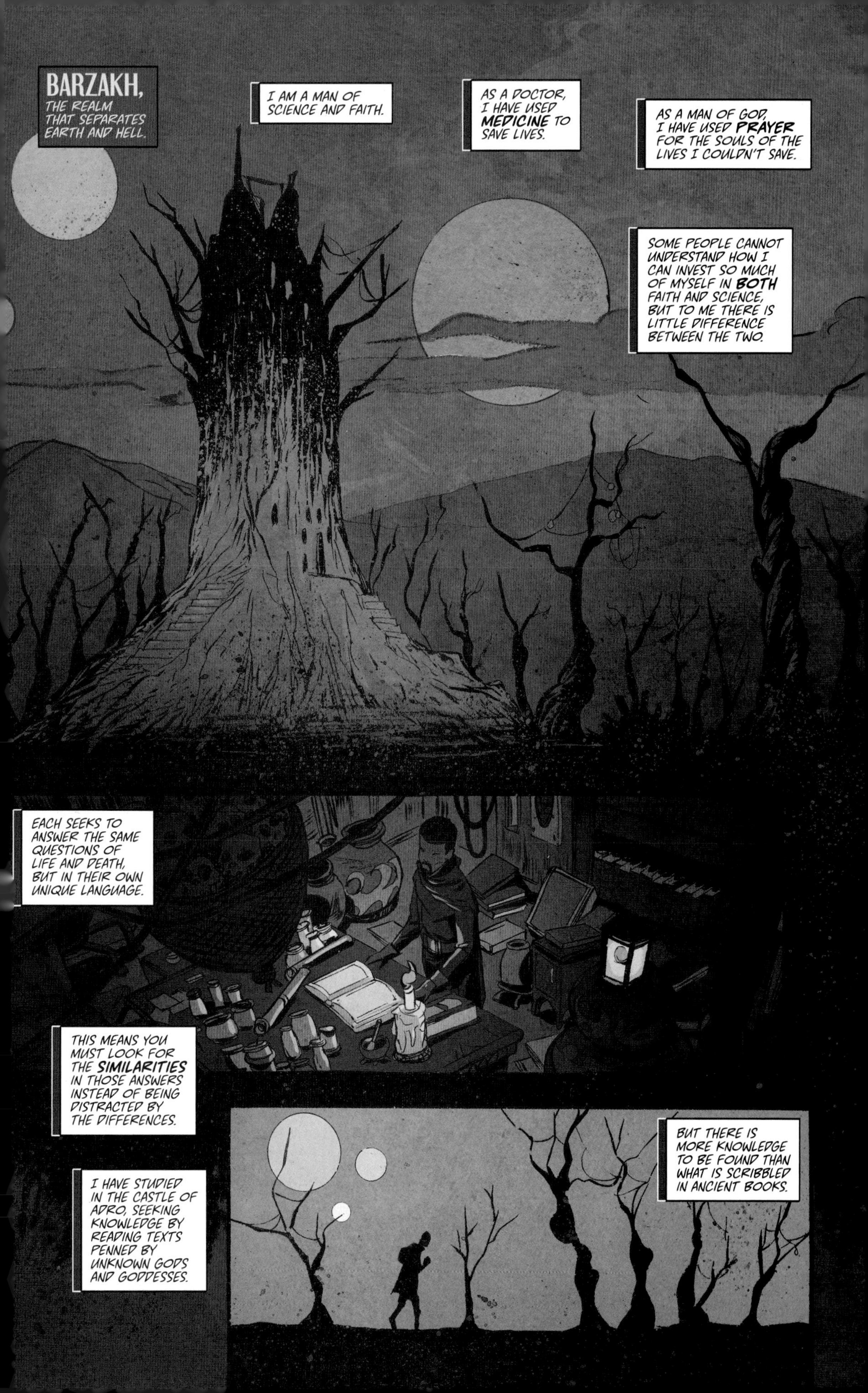
BARZAKH,
THE REALM THAT SEPARATES EARTH AND HELL.
I AM A MAN OF SCIENCE AND FAITH.
AS A DOCTOR, I HAVE USED **MEDICINE** TO SAVE LIVES.
AS A MAN OF GOD, I HAVE USED **PRAYER** FOR THE SOULS OF THE LIVES I COULDN'T SAVE.
SOME PEOPLE CANNOT UNDERSTAND HOW I CAN INVEST SO MUCH OF MYSELF IN **BOTH** FAITH AND SCIENCE, BUT TO ME THERE IS LITTLE DIFFERENCE BETWEEN THE TWO.
EACH SEEKS TO ANSWER THE SAME QUESTIONS OF LIFE AND DEATH, BUT IN THEIR OWN UNIQUE LANGUAGE.
THIS MEANS YOU MUST LOOK FOR THE **SIMILARITIES** IN THOSE ANSWERS INSTEAD OF BEING DISTRACTED BY THE DIFFERENCES.
I HAVE STUDIED IN THE CASTLE OF ADRO, SEEKING KNOWLEDGE BY READING TEXTS PENNED BY UNKNOWN GODS AND GODDESSES.
BUT THERE IS MORE KNOWLEDGE TO BE FOUND THAN WHAT IS SCRIBBLED IN ANCIENT BOOKS.

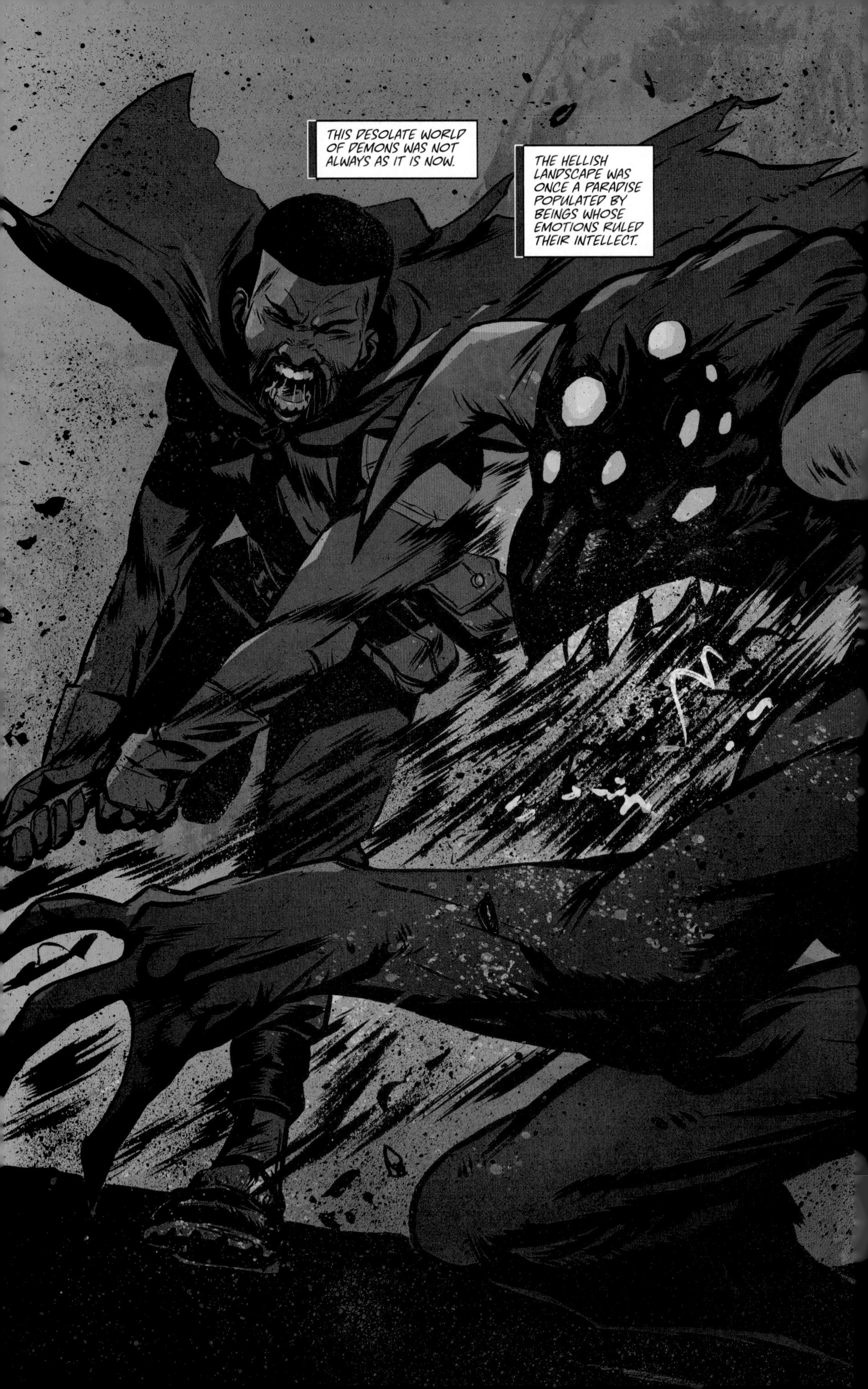
THIS DESOLATE WORLD OF DEMONS WAS NOT ALWAYS AS IT IS NOW.
THE HELLISH LANDSCAPE WAS ONCE A PARADISE POPULATED BY BEINGS WHOSE EMOTIONS RULED THEIR INTELLECT.

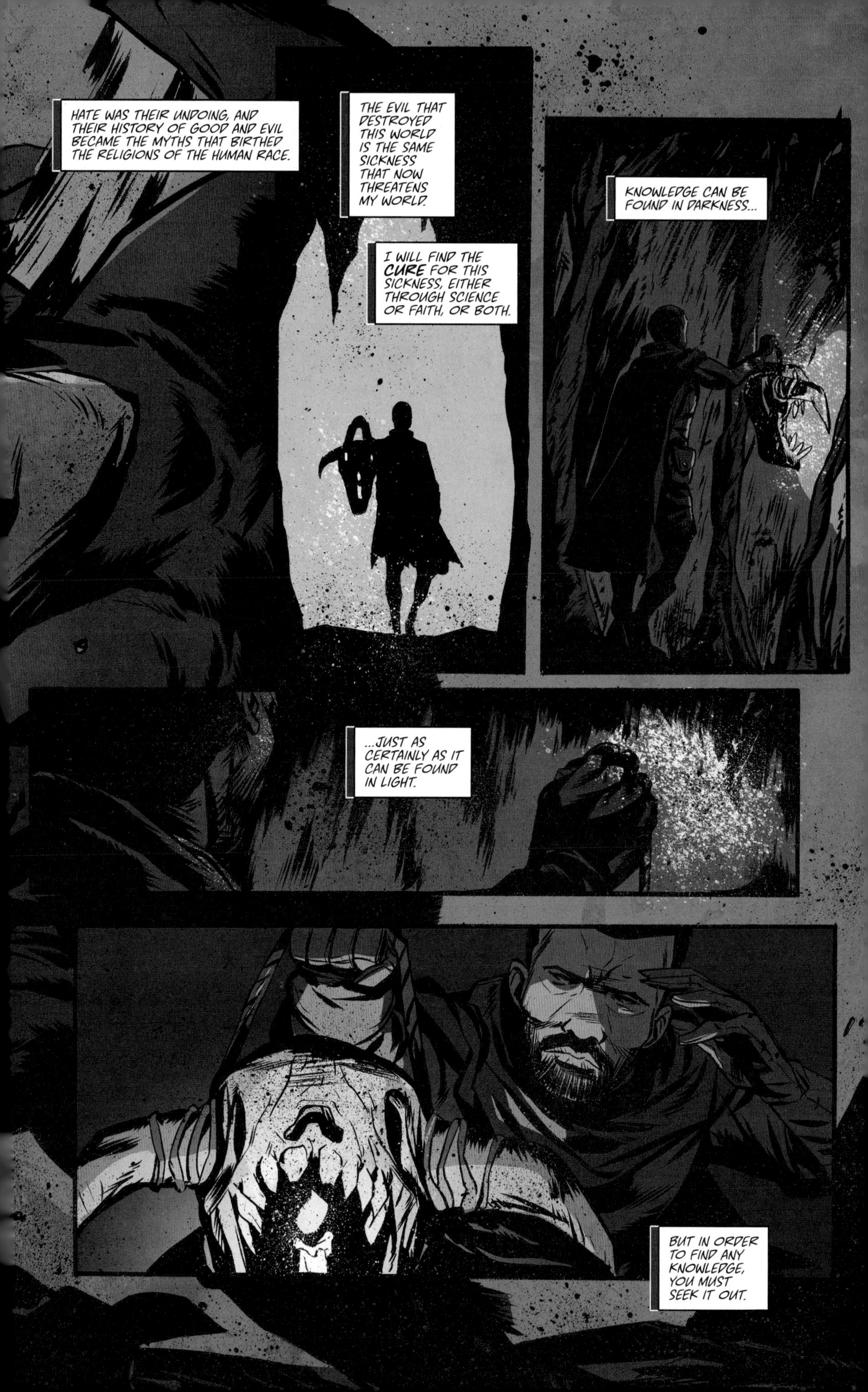
HATE WAS THEIR UNDOING, AND THEIR HISTORY OF GOOD AND EVIL BECAME THE MYTHS THAT BIRTHED THE RELIGIONS OF THE HUMAN RACE.
THE EVIL THAT DESTROYED THIS WORLD IS THE SAME SICKNESS THAT NOW THREATENS MY WORLD.
I WILL FIND THE CURE FOR THIS SICKNESS, EITHER THROUGH SCIENCE OR FAITH, OR BOTH.
KNOWLEDGE CAN BE FOUND IN DARKNESS...
...JUST AS CERTAINLY AS IT CAN BE FOUND IN LIGHT.
BUT IN ORDER TO FIND ANY KNOWLEDGE, YOU MUST SEEK IT OUT.

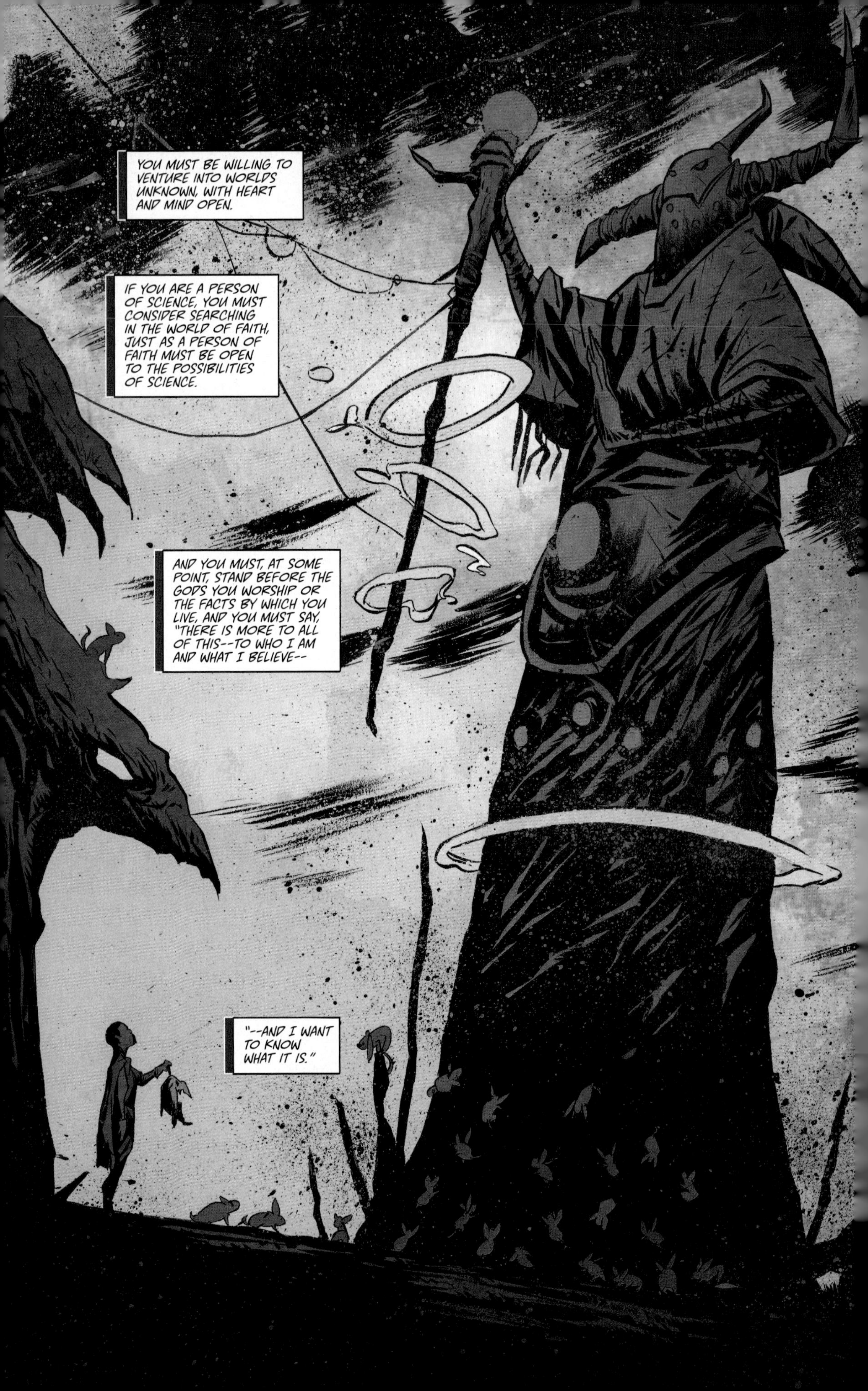
YOU MUST BE WILLING TO VENTURE INTO WORLDS UNKNOWN, WITH HEART AND MIND OPEN.
IF YOU ARE A PERSON OF SCIENCE, YOU MUST CONSIDER SEARCHING IN THE WORLD OF FAITH, JUST AS A PERSON OF FAITH MUST BE OPEN TO THE POSSIBILITIES OF SCIENCE.
AND YOU MUST, AT SOME POINT, STAND BEFORE THE GODS YOU WORSHIP OR THE FACTS BY WHICH YOU LIVE, AND YOU MUST SAY, "THERE IS MORE TO ALL OF THIS--TO WHO I AM AND WHAT I BELIEVE--
"--AND I WANT TO KNOW WHAT IT IS."

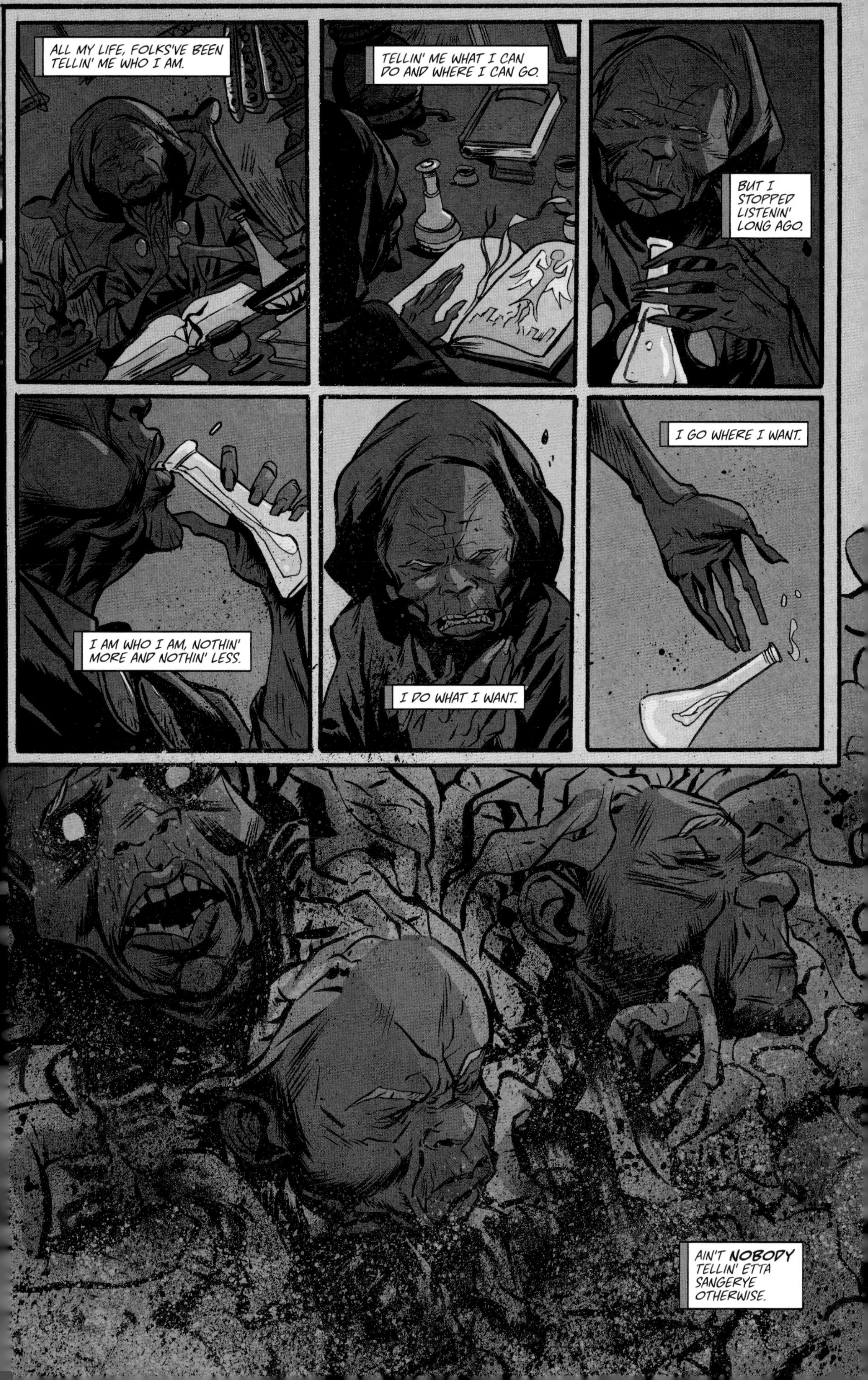
ALL MY LIFE, FOLKS'VE BEEN TELLIN' ME WHO I AM.
TELLIN' ME WHAT I CAN DO AND WHERE I CAN GO.
BUT I STOPPED LISTENIN' LONG AGO.
I AM WHO I AM, NOTHIN' MORE AND NOTHIN' LESS.
I DO WHAT I WANT.
I GO WHERE I WANT.
AIN'T **NOBODY** TELLIN' ETTA SANGERYE OTHERWISE.

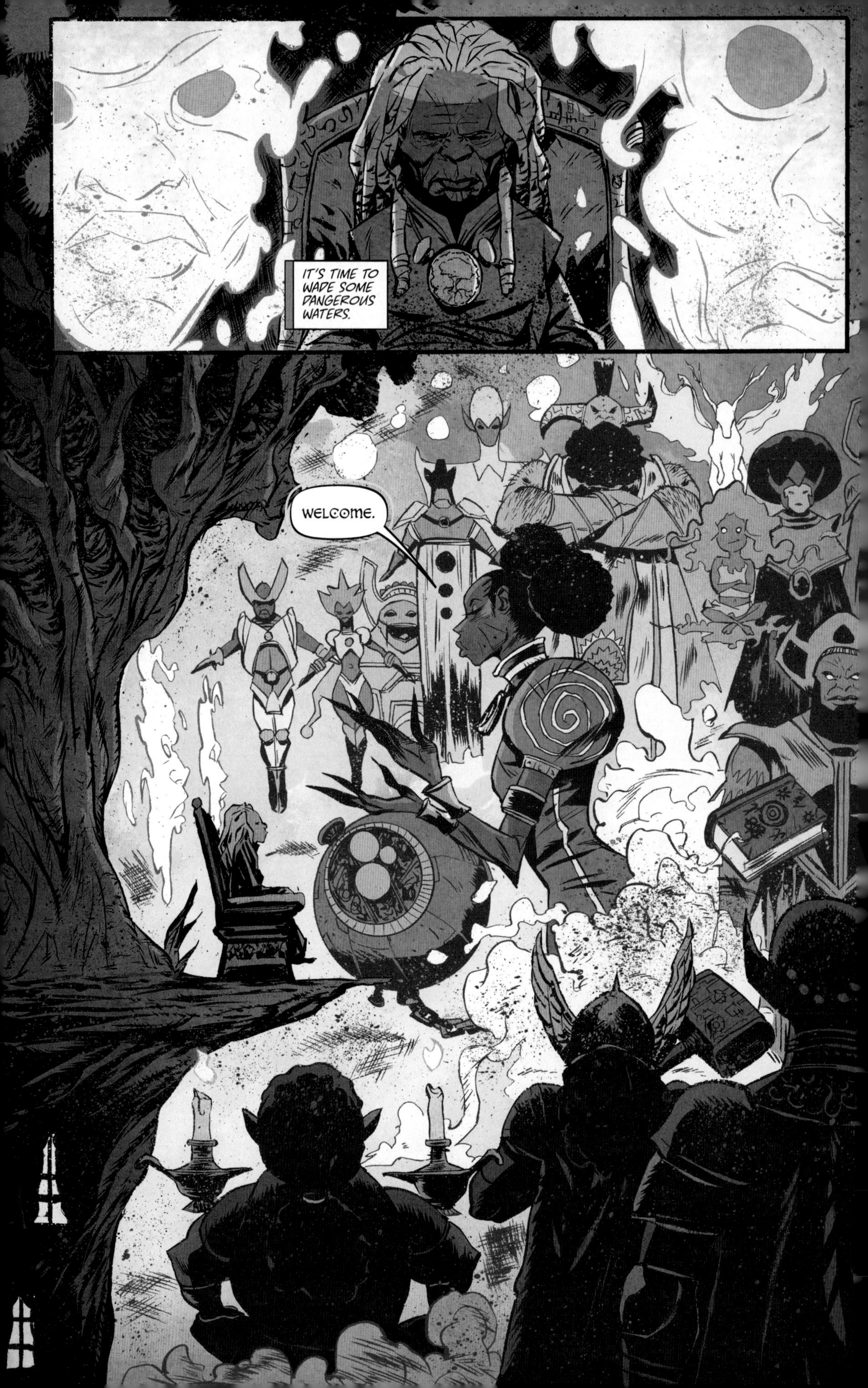
IT'S TIME TO WADE SOME DANGEROUS WATERS.
WELCOME.

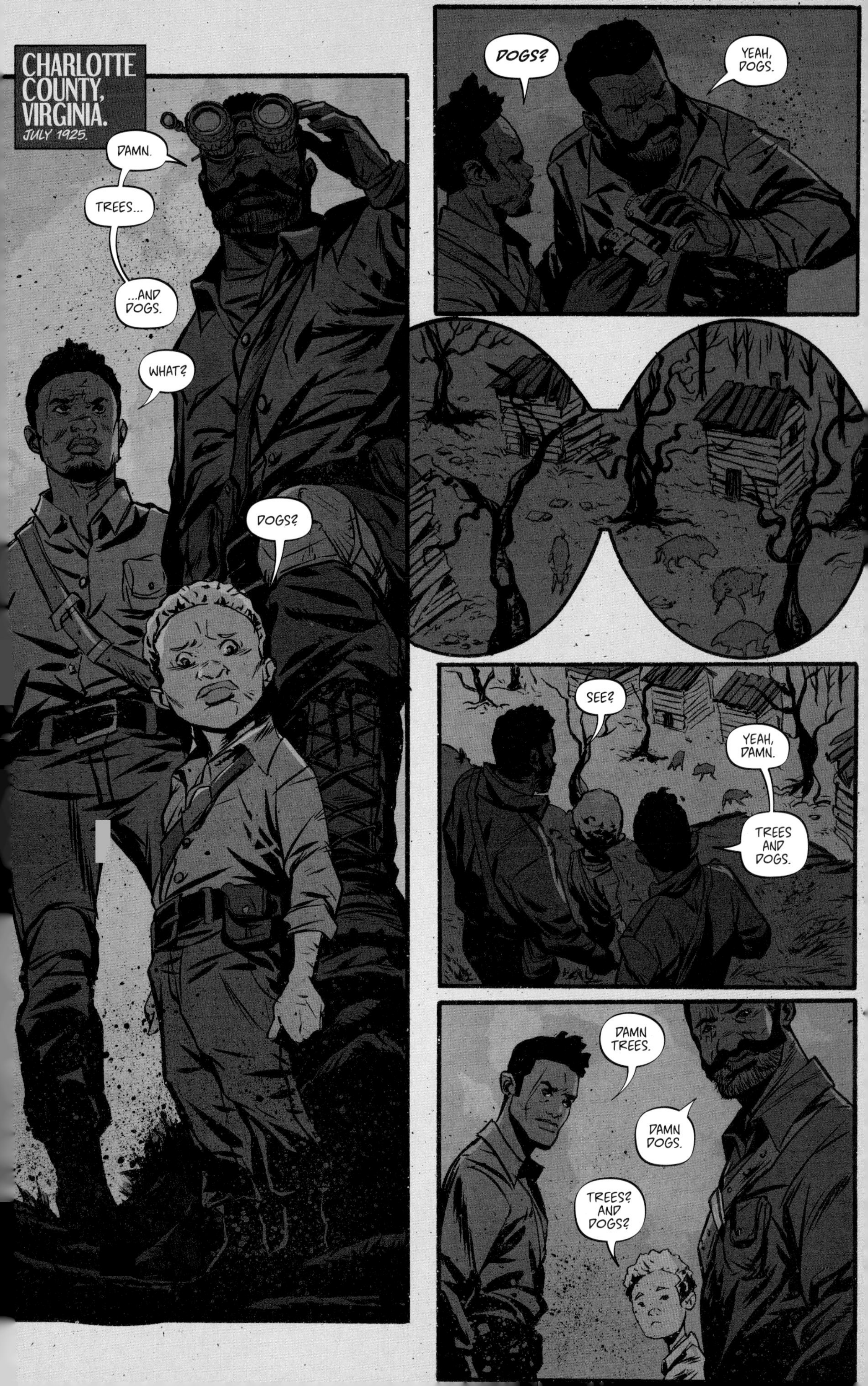
CHARLOTTE COUNTY, VIRGINIA.
JULY 1925.
DAMN.
TREES...
...AND DOGS.
WHAT?
DOGS?
DOGS?
YEAH, DOGS.
SEE?
YEAH, DAMN.
TREES AND DOGS.
DAMN TREES.
DAMN DOGS.
TREES? AND DOGS?

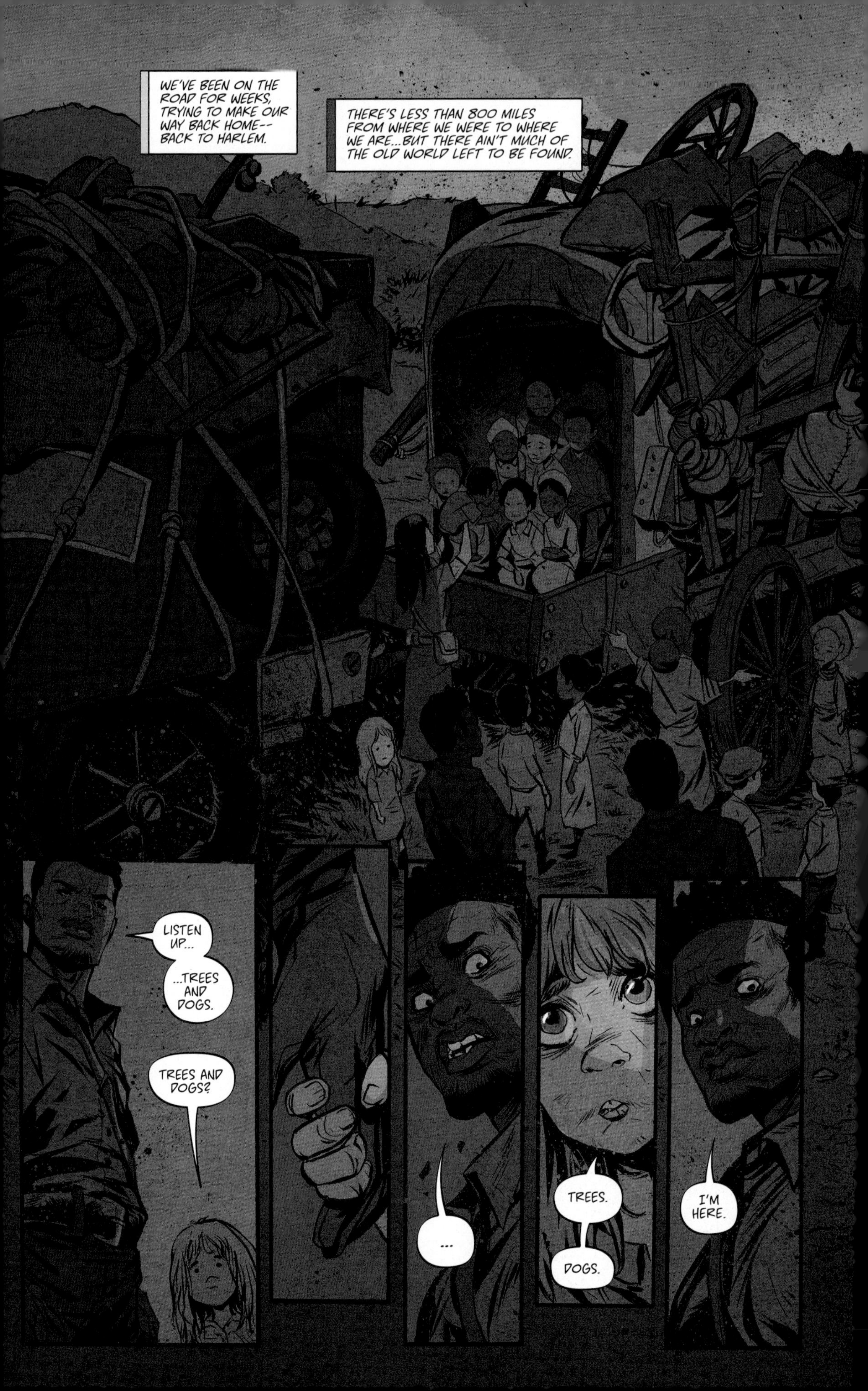
WE'VE BEEN ON THE ROAD FOR WEEKS, TRYING TO MAKE OUR WAY BACK HOME-- BACK TO HARLEM.
THERE'S LESS THAN 800 MILES FROM WHERE WE WERE TO WHERE WE ARE...BUT THERE AIN'T MUCH OF THE OLD WORLD LEFT TO BE FOUND.
LISTEN UP...
...TREES AND DOGS.
TREES AND DOGS?
...
TREES.
DOGS.
I'M HERE.

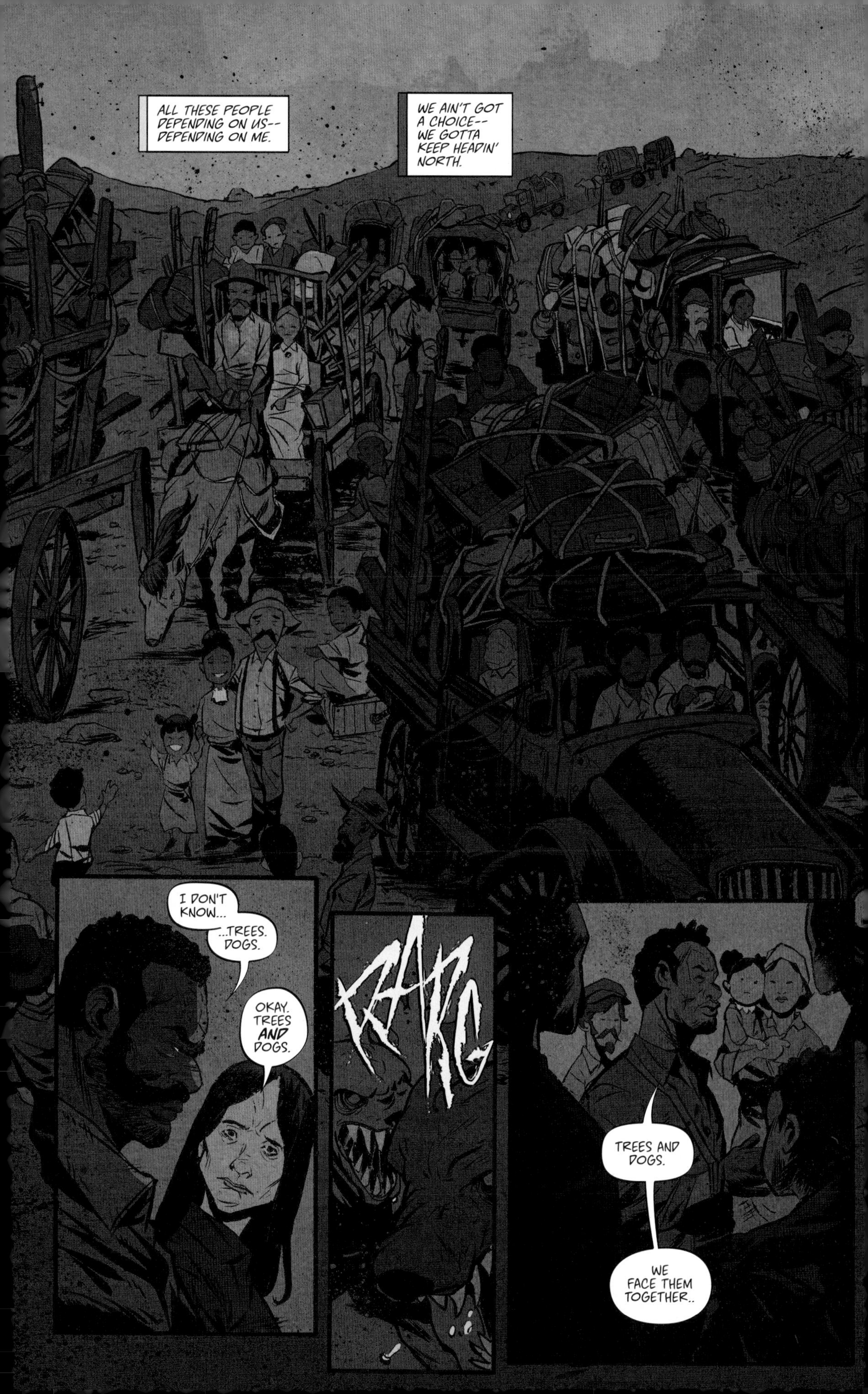
ALL THESE PEOPLE DEPENDING ON US-- DEPENDING ON ME.
WE AIN'T GOT A CHOICE-- WE GOTTA KEEP HEADIN' NORTH.
I DON'T KNOW...
...TREES. DOGS.
OKAY. TREES AND DOGS.
RAARG
TREES AND DOGS.
WE FACE THEM TOGETHER..

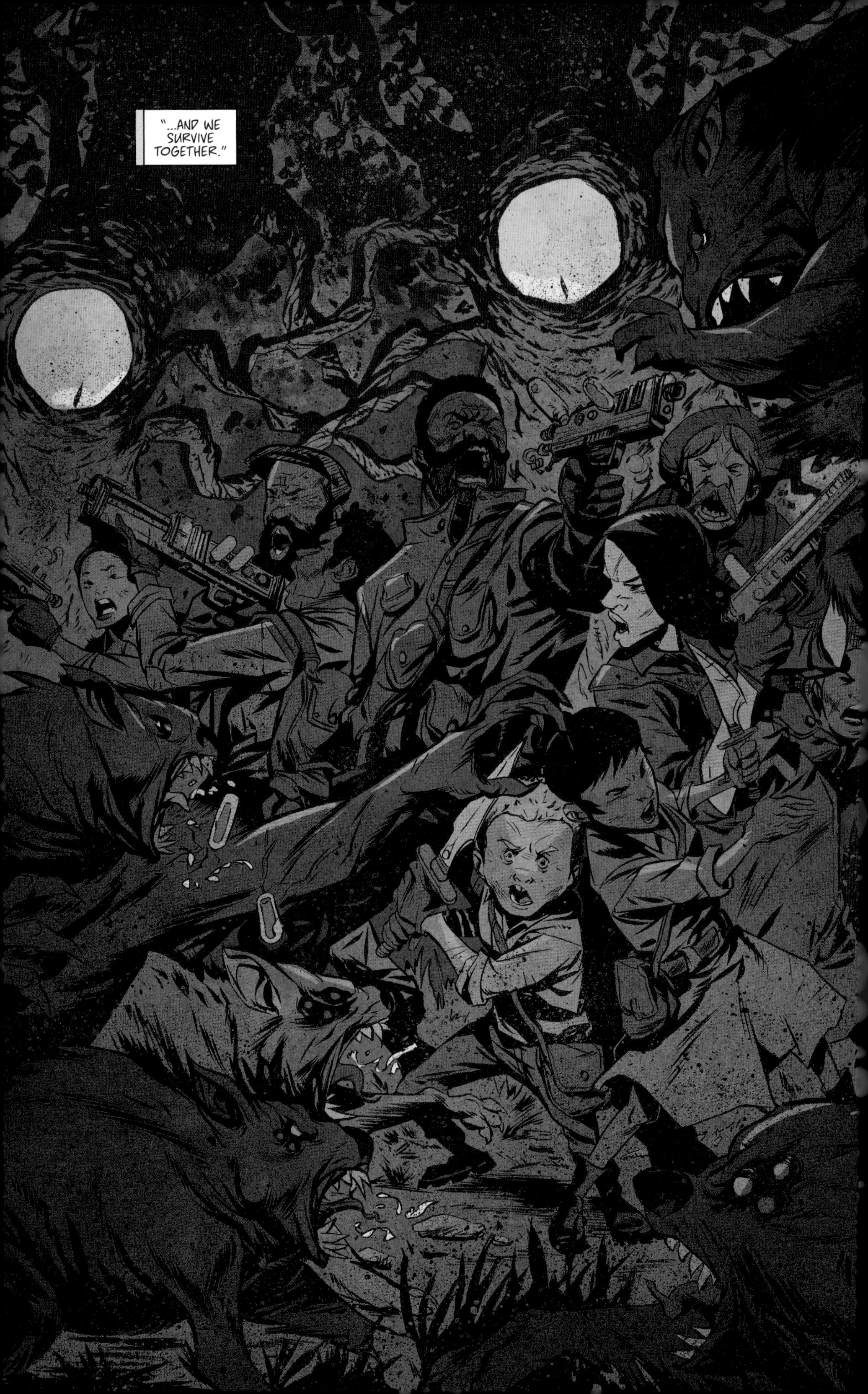
"...AND WE SURVIVE TOGETHER."

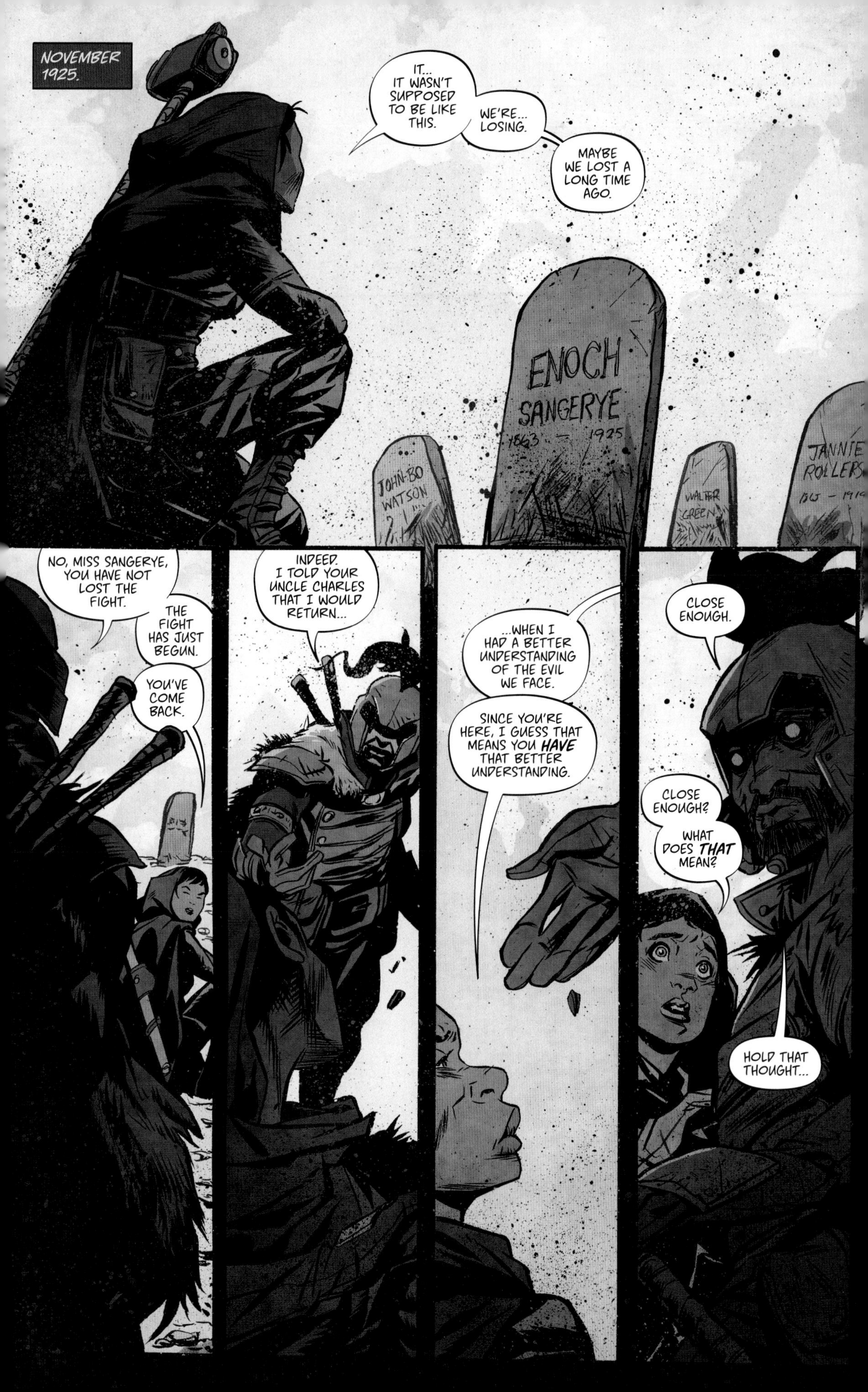
NOVEMBER 1925.
IT... IT WASN'T SUPPOSED TO BE LIKE THIS.
WE'RE... LOSING.
MAYBE WE LOST A LONG TIME AGO.
ENOCH SANGERYE 1863 — 1925
JOHN-BO WATSON
WALTER GREEN
JANNIE ROLLERS
NO, MISS SANGERYE, YOU HAVE NOT LOST THE FIGHT.
THE FIGHT HAS JUST BEGUN.
YOU'VE COME BACK.
INDEED. I TOLD YOUR UNCLE CHARLES THAT I WOULD RETURN...
...WHEN I HAD A BETTER UNDERSTANDING OF THE EVIL WE FACE.
SINCE YOU'RE HERE, I GUESS THAT MEANS YOU **HAVE** THAT BETTER UNDERSTANDING.
CLOSE ENOUGH.
CLOSE ENOUGH?
WHAT DOES **THAT** MEAN?
HOLD THAT THOUGHT...

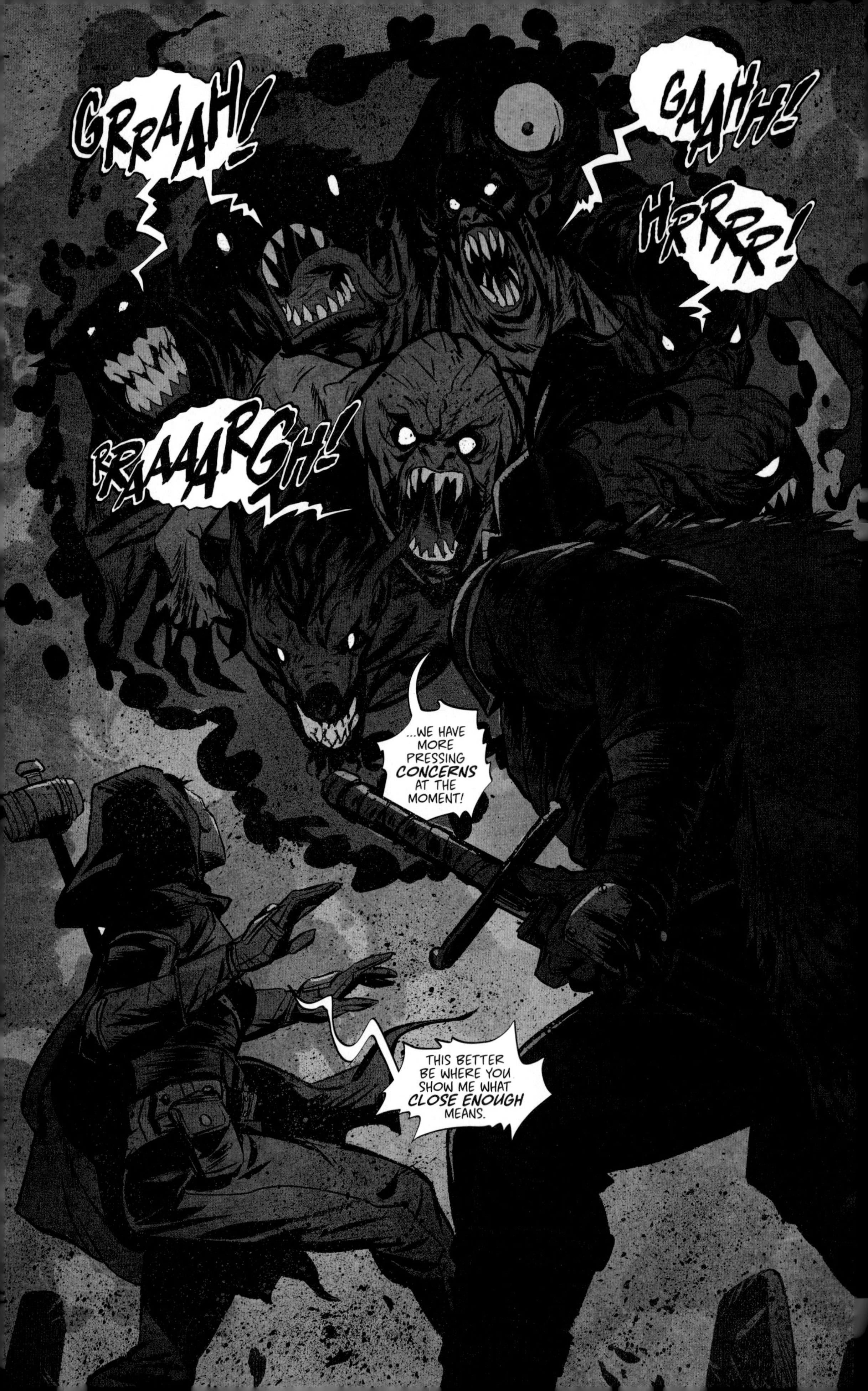
GRRAAH!
GAAHH!
HRRRR!
RRAAAARGH!
...WE HAVE MORE PRESSING CONCERNS AT THE MOMENT!
THIS BETTER BE WHERE YOU SHOW ME WHAT CLOSE ENOUGH MEANS.

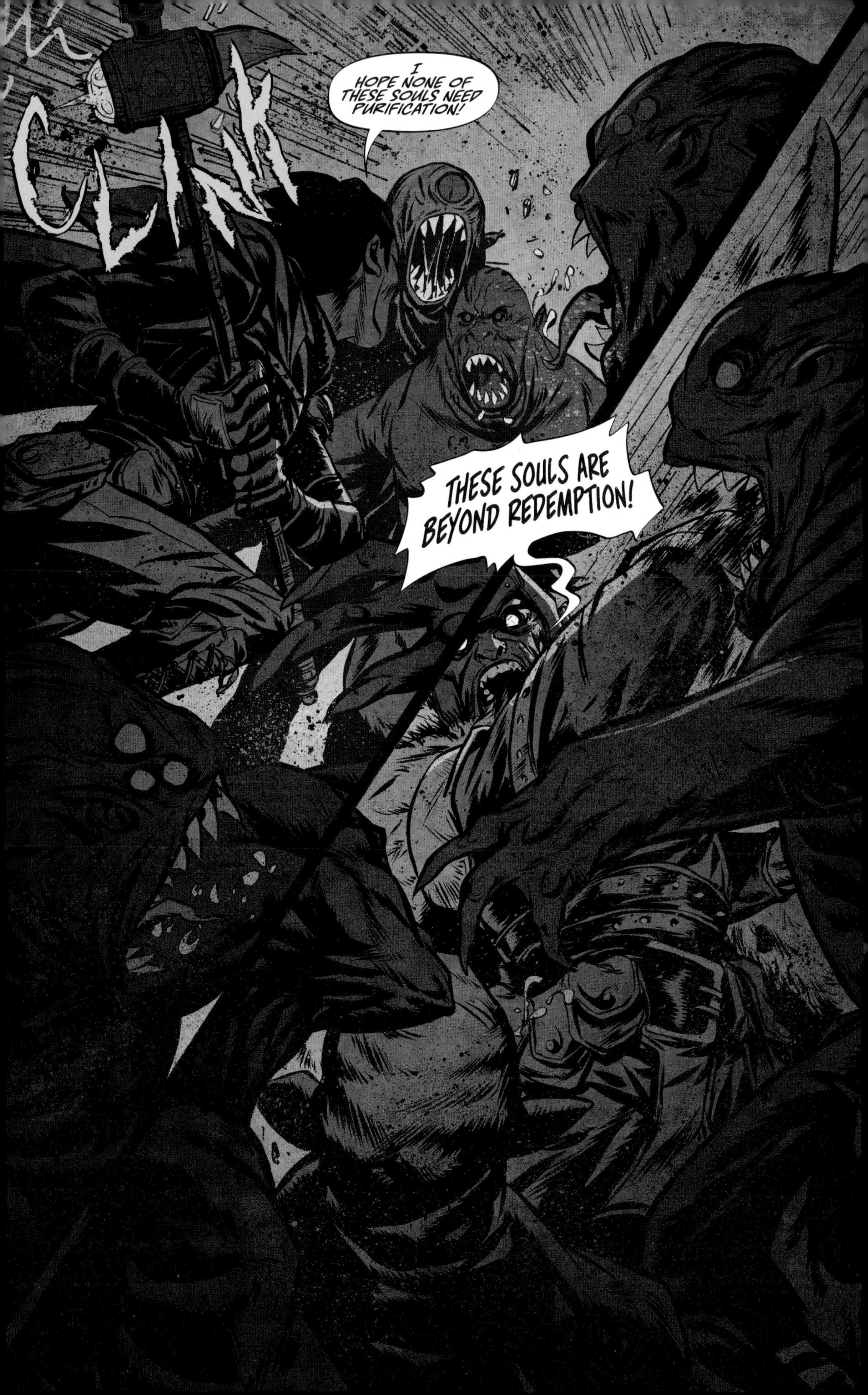
CLINK
I HOPE NONE OF THESE SOULS NEED PURIFICATION!
THESE SOULS ARE BEYOND REDEMPTION!

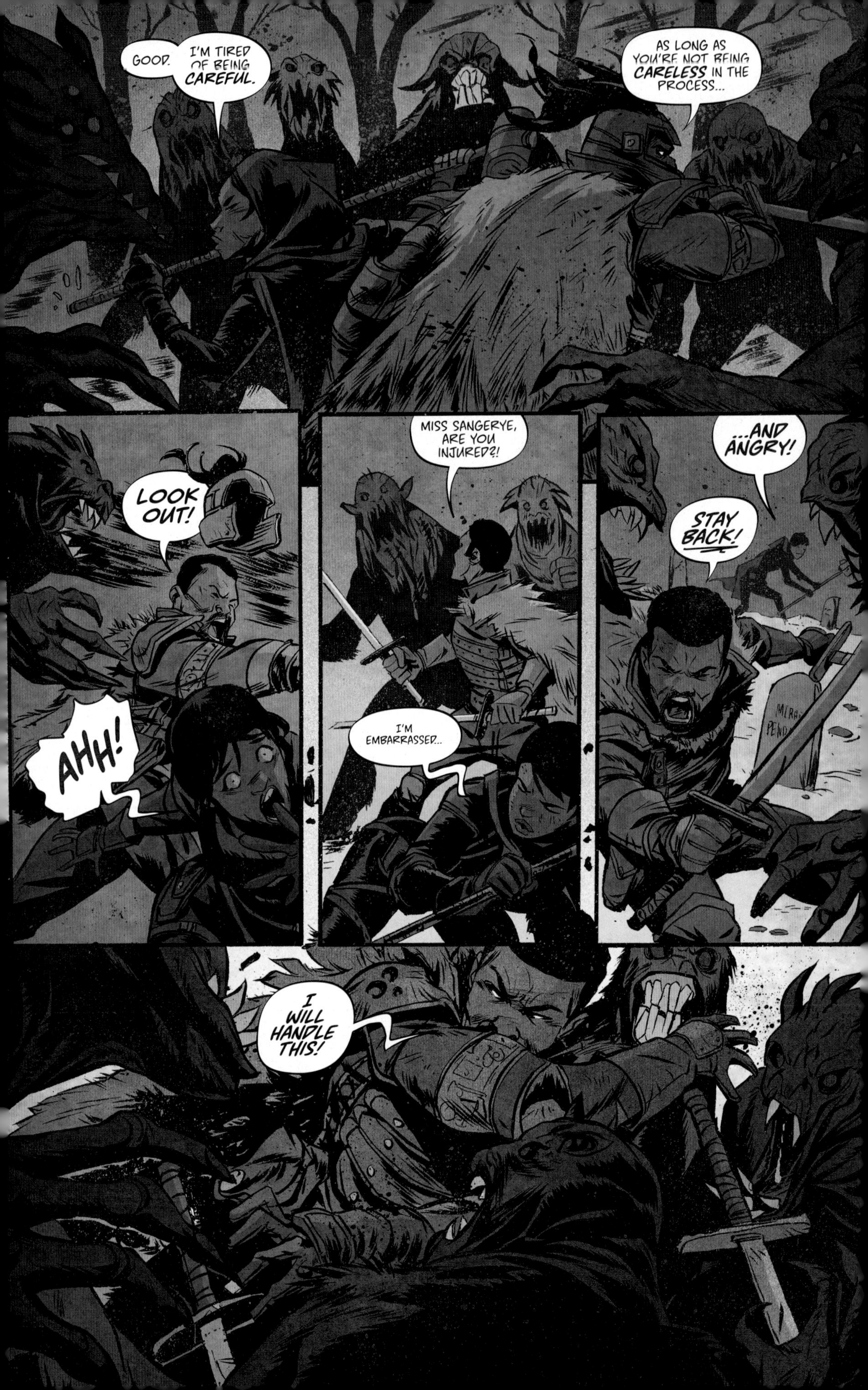
GOOD.
I'M TIRED OF BEING CAREFUL.
AS LONG AS YOU'RE NOT BEING CARELESS IN THE PROCESS...
LOOK OUT!
AHH!
MISS SANGERYE, ARE YOU INJURED?!
I'M EMBARRASSED...
...AND ANGRY!
STAY BACK!
I WILL HANDLE THIS!

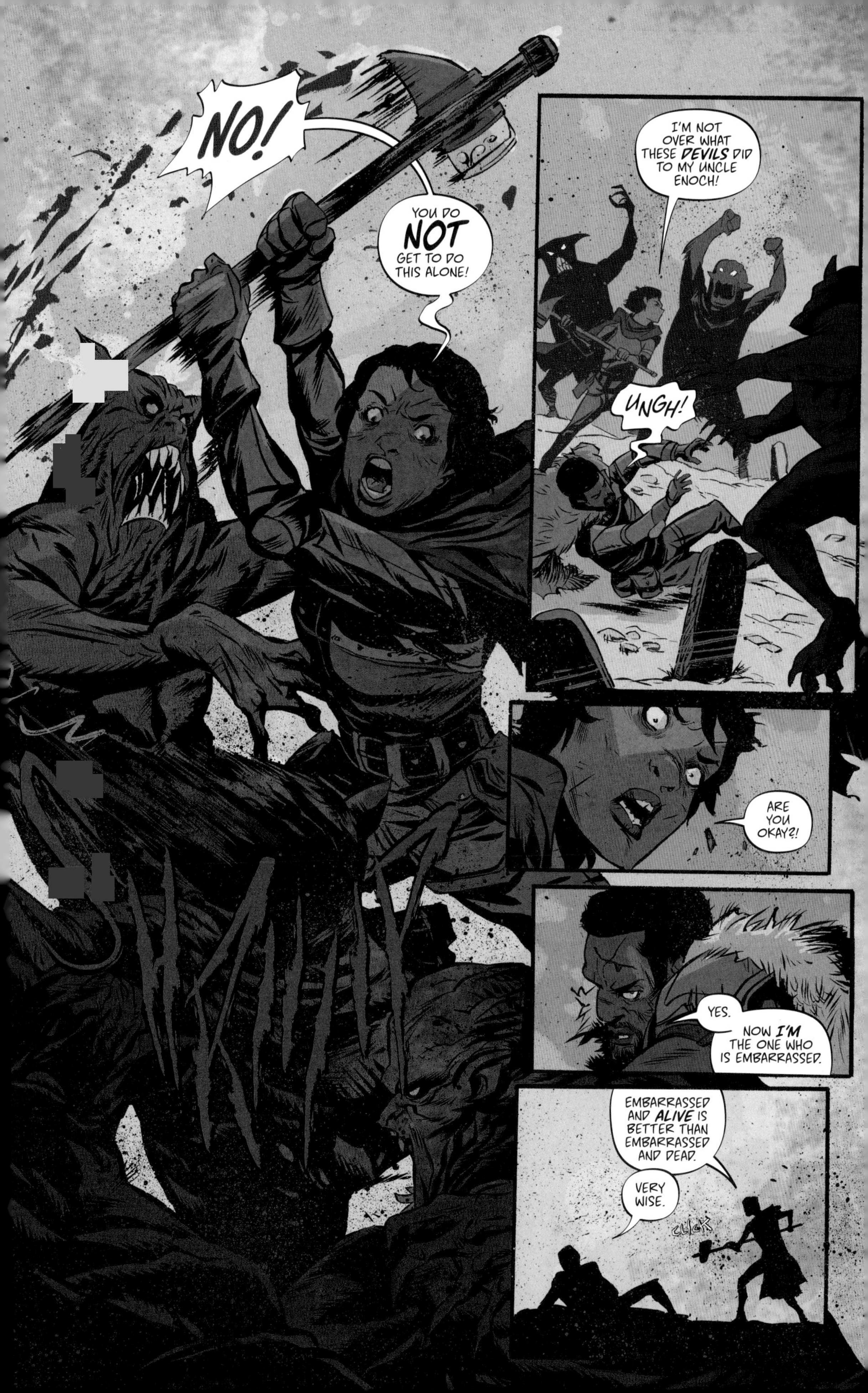
NO!
YOU DO NOT GET TO DO THIS ALONE!
I'M NOT OVER WHAT THESE DEVILS DID TO MY UNCLE ENOCH!
UNGH!
ARE YOU OKAY?!
YES.
NOW I'M THE ONE WHO IS EMBARRASSED.
EMBARRASSED AND ALIVE IS BETTER THAN EMBARRASSED AND DEAD.
VERY WISE.
CLICK

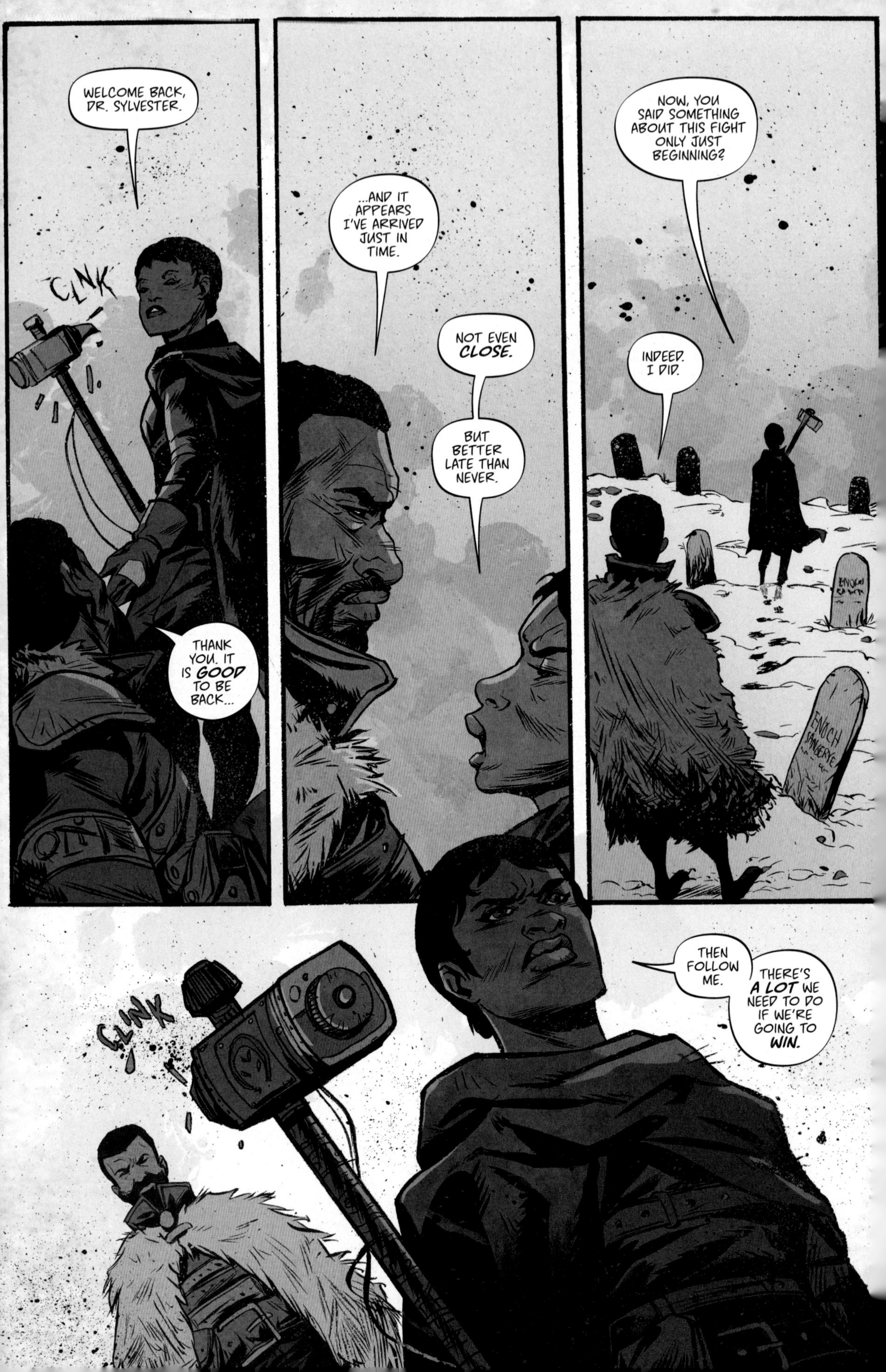
WELCOME BACK, DR. SYLVESTER.
CLNK
THANK YOU. IT IS GOOD TO BE BACK...
...AND IT APPEARS I'VE ARRIVED JUST IN TIME.
NOT EVEN CLOSE.
BUT BETTER LATE THAN NEVER.
NOW, YOU SAID SOMETHING ABOUT THIS FIGHT ONLY JUST BEGINNING?
INDEED. I DID.
CLINK
THEN FOLLOW ME.
THERE'S A LOT WE NEED TO DO IF WE'RE GOING TO WIN.

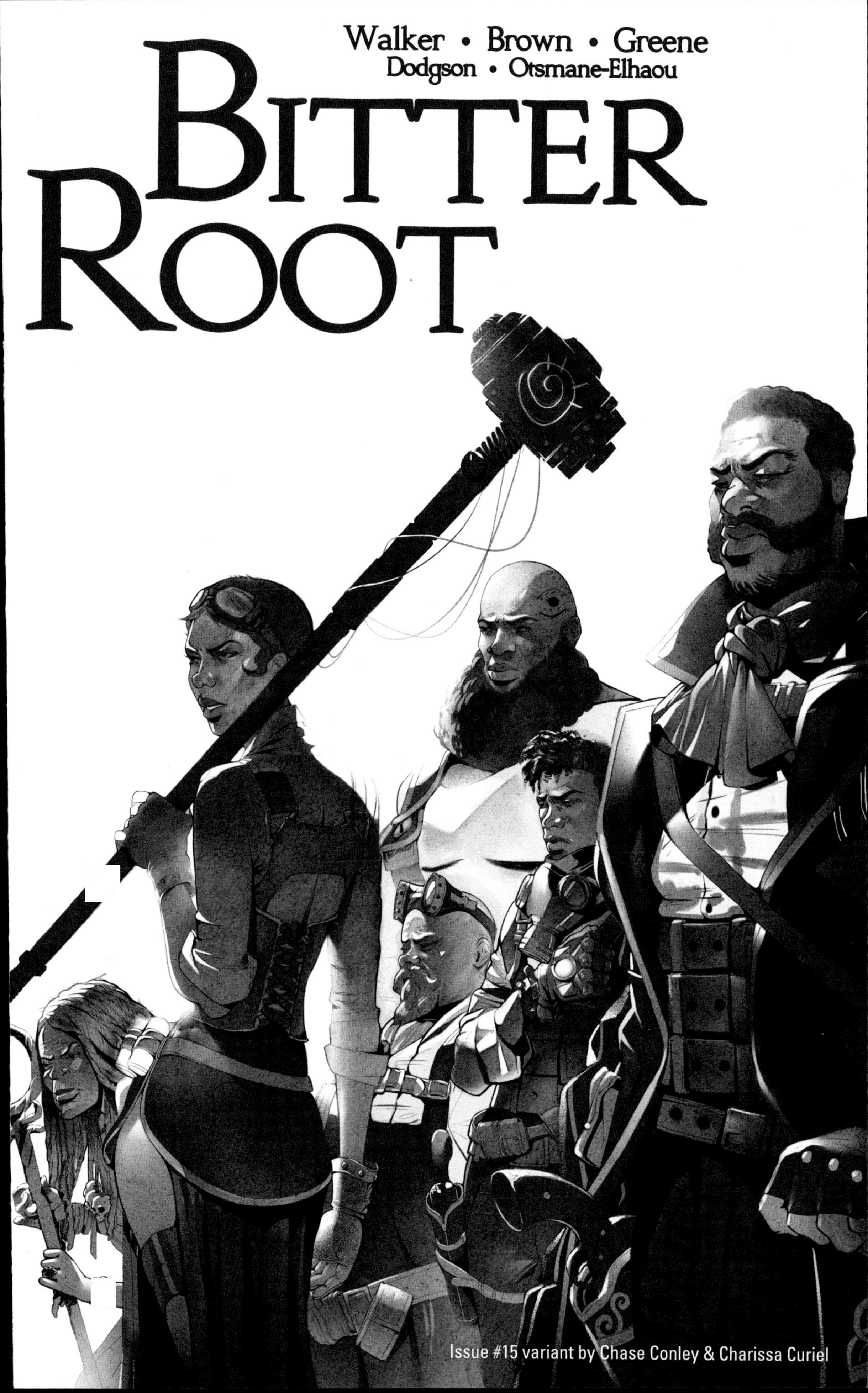
Walker • Brown • Greene
Dodgson • Otsmane-Elhaou
BITTER ROOT

Issue #15 variant by Chase Conley & Charissa Curiel

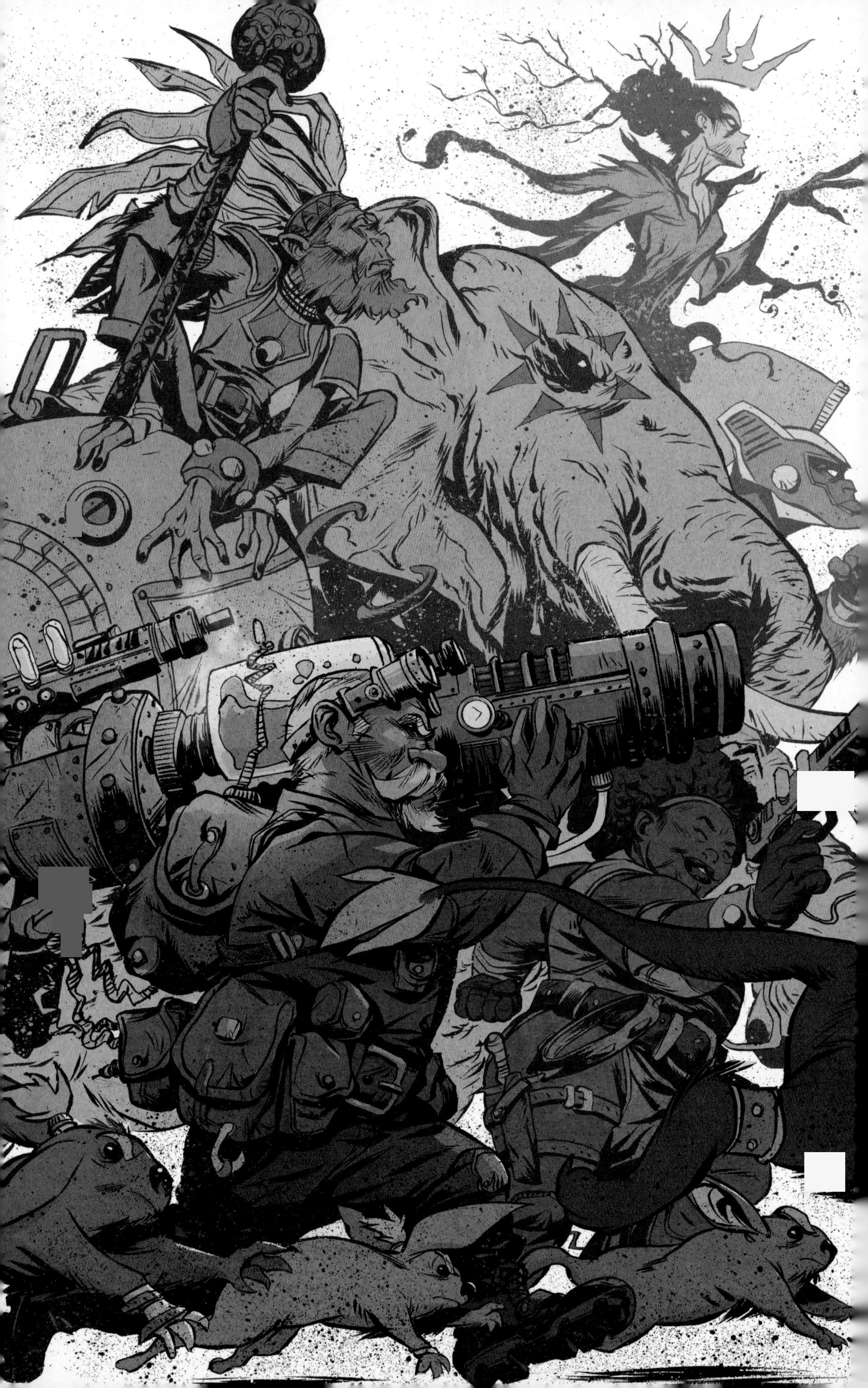

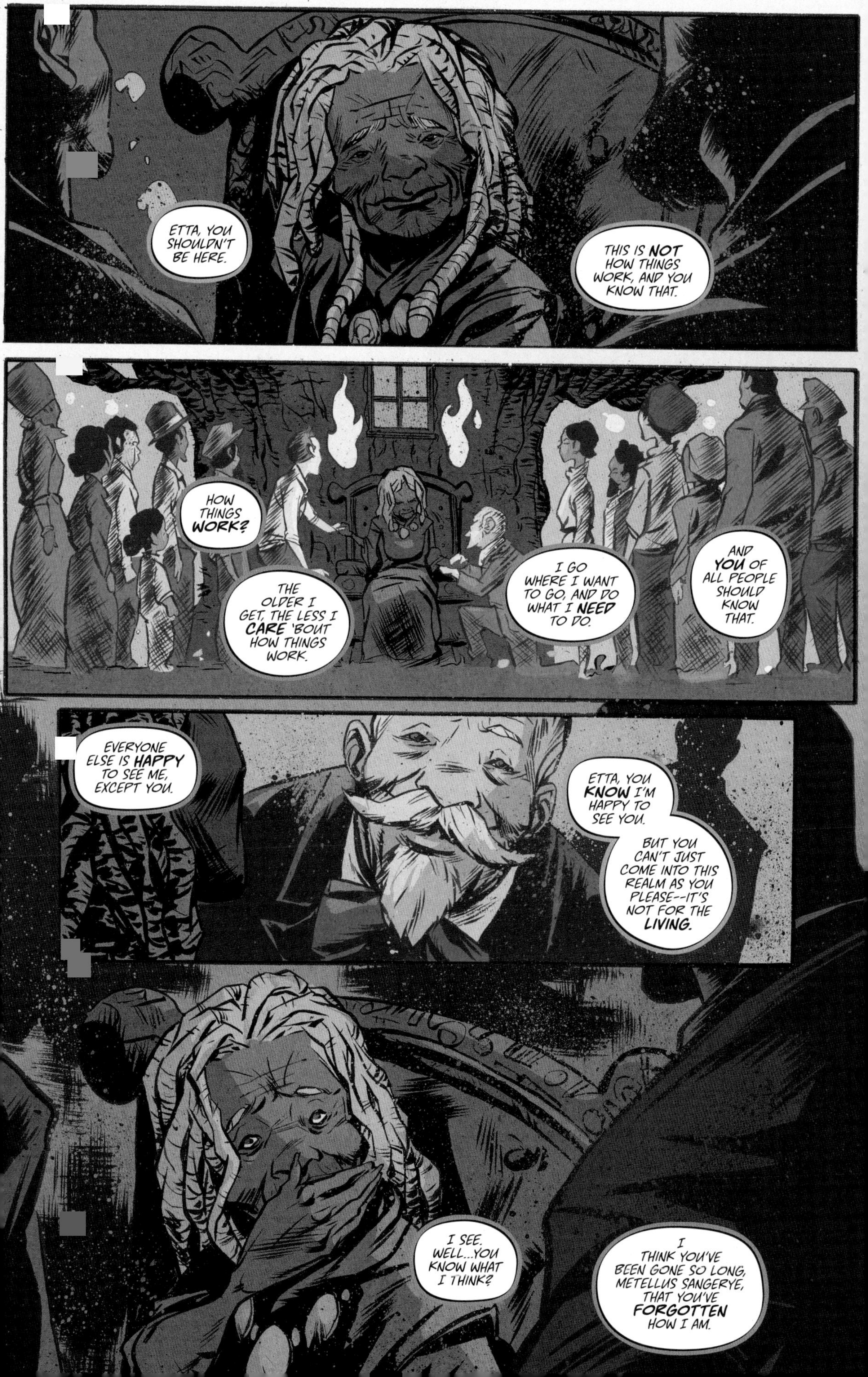

ETTA, YOU SHOULDN'T BE HERE.
THIS IS **NOT** HOW THINGS WORK, AND YOU KNOW THAT.
HOW THINGS **WORK?**
THE OLDER I GET, THE LESS I **CARE** 'BOUT HOW THINGS WORK.
I GO WHERE I WANT TO GO, AND DO WHAT I **NEED** TO DO.
AND **YOU** OF ALL PEOPLE SHOULD KNOW THAT.
EVERYONE ELSE IS **HAPPY** TO SEE ME, EXCEPT YOU.
ETTA, YOU **KNOW** I'M HAPPY TO SEE YOU.
BUT YOU CAN'T JUST COME INTO THIS REALM AS YOU PLEASE--IT'S NOT FOR THE **LIVING.**
I SEE. WELL...YOU KNOW WHAT I THINK?
I THINK YOU'VE BEEN GONE SO LONG, METELLUS SANGERYE, THAT YOU'VE **FORGOTTEN** HOW I AM.

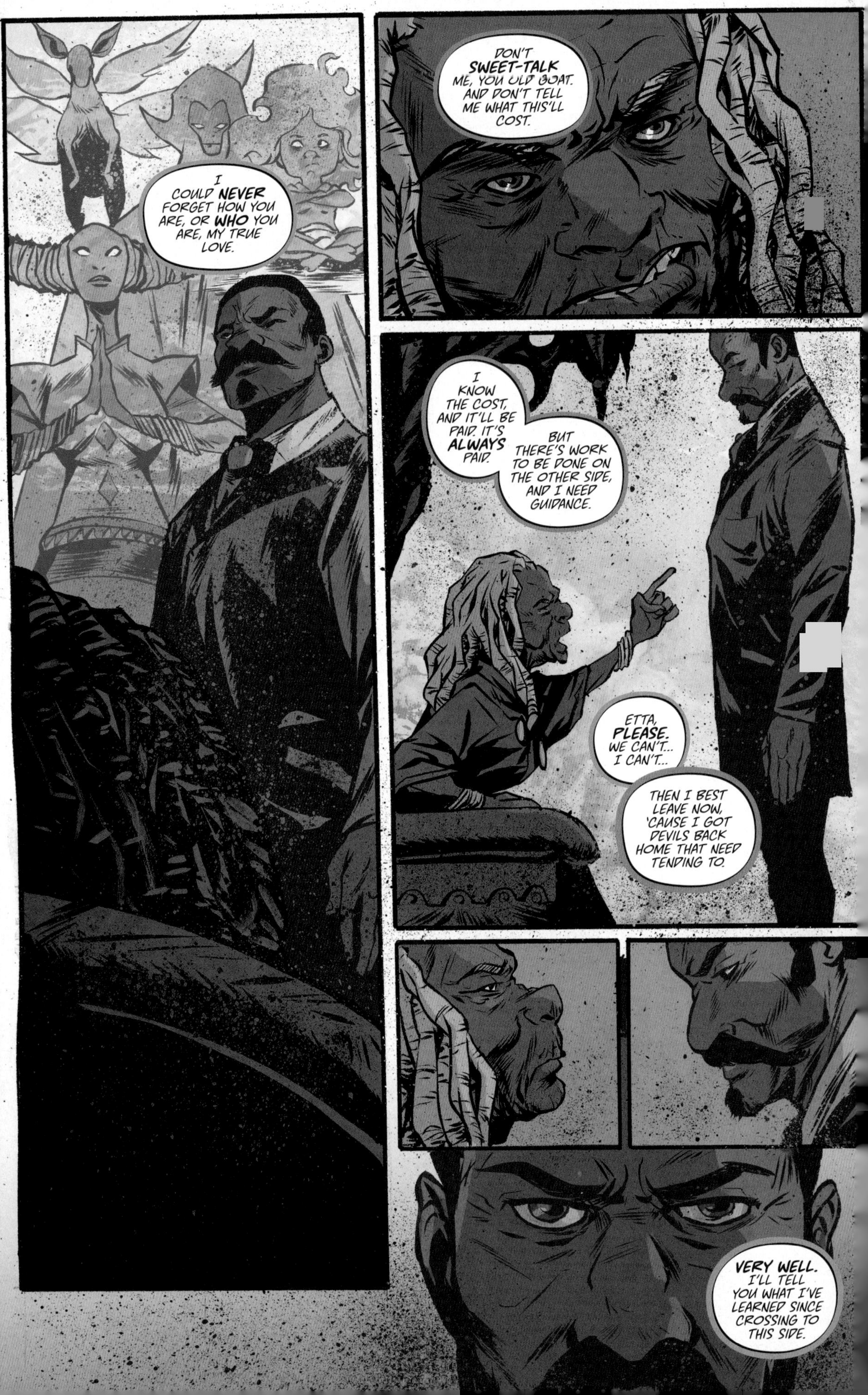
I COULD NEVER FORGET HOW YOU ARE, OR WHO YOU ARE, MY TRUE LOVE.
DON'T SWEET-TALK ME, YOU OLD GOAT. AND DON'T TELL ME WHAT THIS'LL COST.
I KNOW THE COST, AND IT'LL BE PAID. IT'S ALWAYS PAID.
BUT THERE'S WORK TO BE DONE ON THE OTHER SIDE, AND I NEED GUIDANCE.
ETTA, PLEASE. WE CAN'T... I CAN'T...
THEN I BEST LEAVE NOW, 'CAUSE I GOT DEVILS BACK HOME THAT NEED TENDING TO.
VERY WELL. I'LL TELL YOU WHAT I'VE LEARNED SINCE CROSSING TO THIS SIDE.

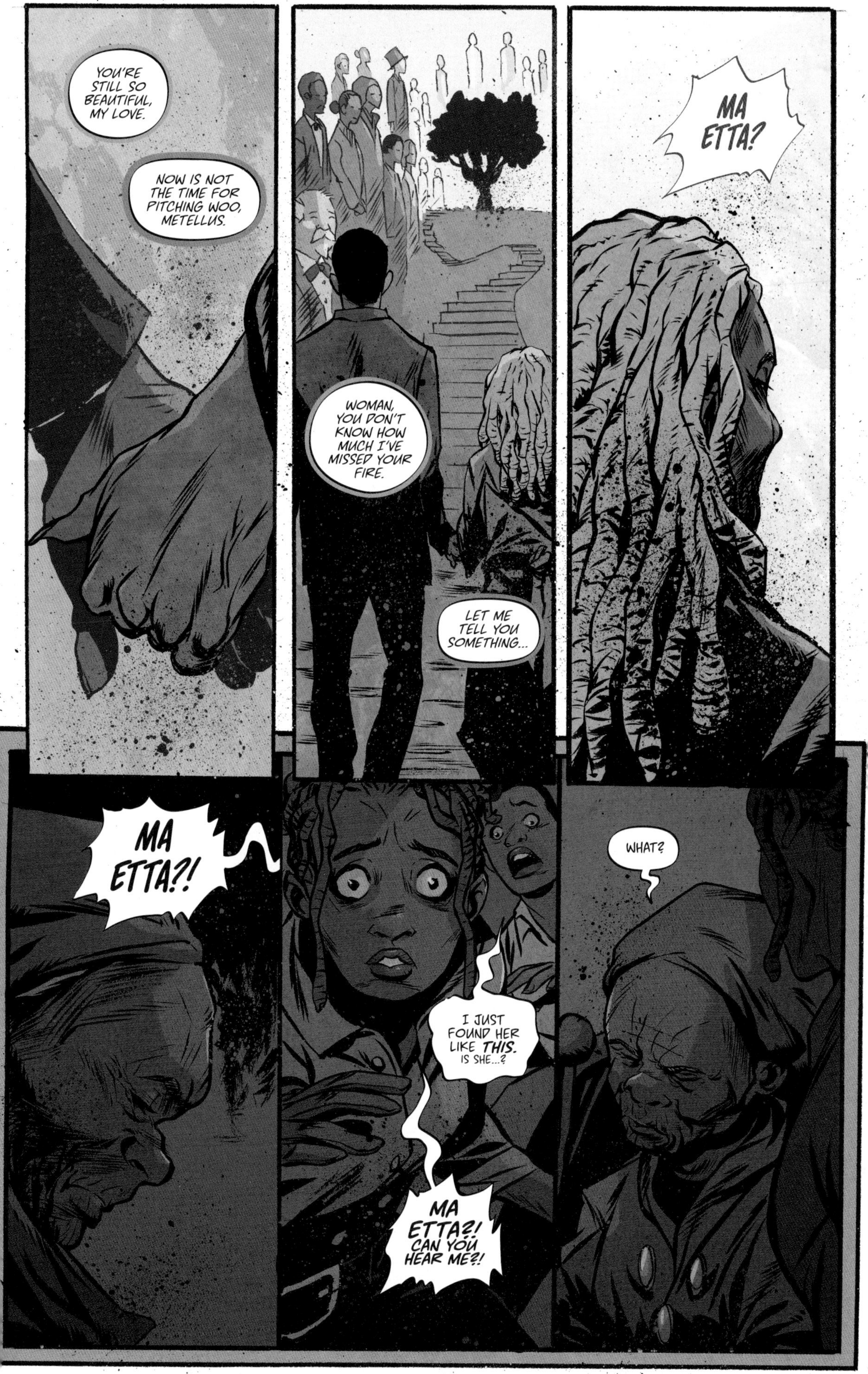
YOU'RE STILL SO BEAUTIFUL, MY LOVE.
NOW IS NOT THE TIME FOR PITCHING WOO, METELLUS.
WOMAN, YOU DON'T KNOW HOW MUCH I'VE MISSED YOUR FIRE.
LET ME TELL YOU SOMETHING...
MA ETTA?
MA ETTA?!
I JUST FOUND HER LIKE THIS. IS SHE...?
MA ETTA?! CAN YOU HEAR ME?!
WHAT?

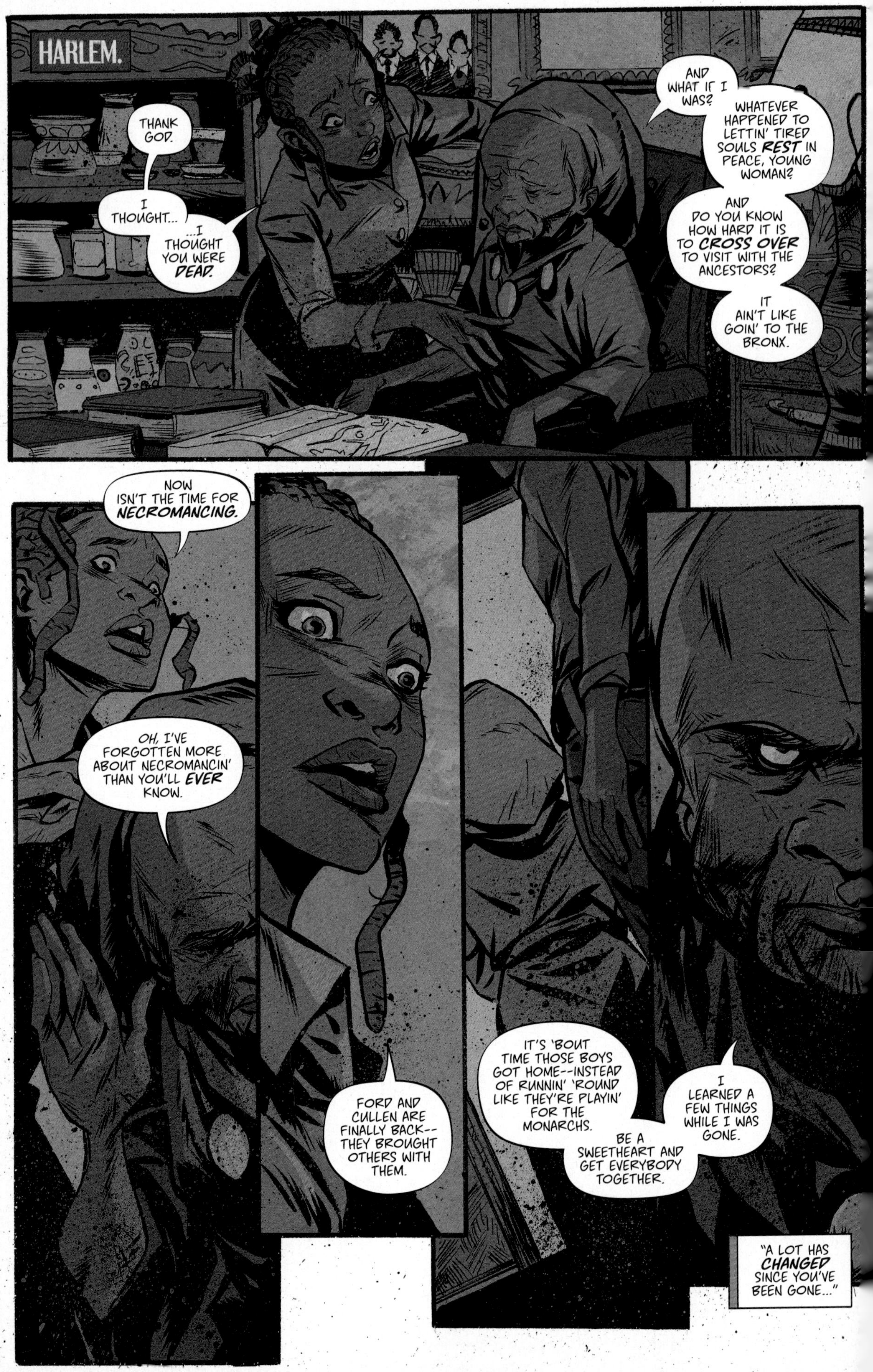
HARLEM.
THANK GOD.
I THOUGHT...
...I THOUGHT YOU WERE **DEAD.**
AND WHAT IF I WAS?
WHATEVER HAPPENED TO LETTIN' TIRED SOULS **REST** IN PEACE, YOUNG WOMAN?
AND DO YOU KNOW HOW HARD IT IS TO **CROSS OVER** TO VISIT WITH THE ANCESTORS?
IT AIN'T LIKE GOIN' TO THE BRONX.
NOW ISN'T THE TIME FOR **NECROMANCING.**
OH, I'VE FORGOTTEN MORE ABOUT NECROMANCIN' THAN YOU'LL **EVER** KNOW.
FORD AND CULLEN ARE FINALLY BACK--THEY BROUGHT OTHERS WITH THEM.
IT'S 'BOUT TIME THOSE BOYS GOT HOME--INSTEAD OF RUNNIN' 'ROUND LIKE THEY'RE PLAYIN' FOR THE MONARCHS.
I LEARNED A FEW THINGS WHILE I WAS GONE.
BE A SWEETHEART AND GET EVERYBODY TOGETHER.
"A LOT HAS **CHANGED** SINCE YOU'VE BEEN GONE..."

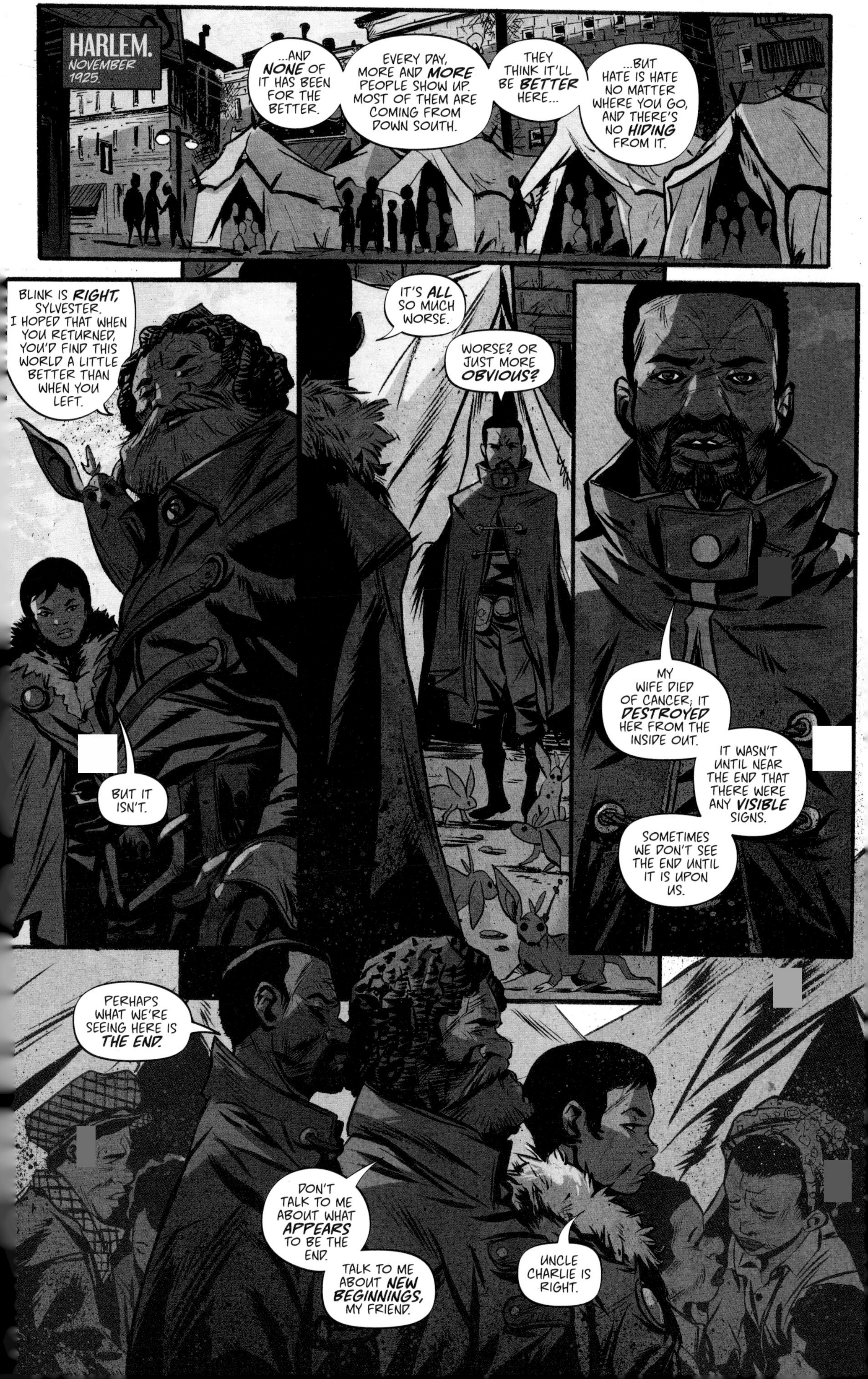
HARLEM. NOVEMBER 1925.
...AND NONE OF IT HAS BEEN FOR THE BETTER.
EVERY DAY, MORE AND MORE PEOPLE SHOW UP. MOST OF THEM ARE COMING FROM DOWN SOUTH.
THEY THINK IT'LL BE BETTER HERE...
...BUT HATE IS HATE NO MATTER WHERE YOU GO, AND THERE'S NO HIDING FROM IT.
BLINK IS RIGHT, SYLVESTER. I HOPED THAT WHEN YOU RETURNED, YOU'D FIND THIS WORLD A LITTLE BETTER THAN WHEN YOU LEFT.
BUT IT ISN'T.
IT'S ALL SO MUCH WORSE.
WORSE? OR JUST MORE OBVIOUS?
MY WIFE DIED OF CANCER; IT DESTROYED HER FROM THE INSIDE OUT.
IT WASN'T UNTIL NEAR THE END THAT THERE WERE ANY VISIBLE SIGNS.
SOMETIMES WE DON'T SEE THE END UNTIL IT IS UPON US.
PERHAPS WHAT WE'RE SEEING HERE IS THE END.
DON'T TALK TO ME ABOUT WHAT APPEARS TO BE THE END.
TALK TO ME ABOUT NEW BEGINNINGS, MY FRIEND.
UNCLE CHARLIE IS RIGHT.

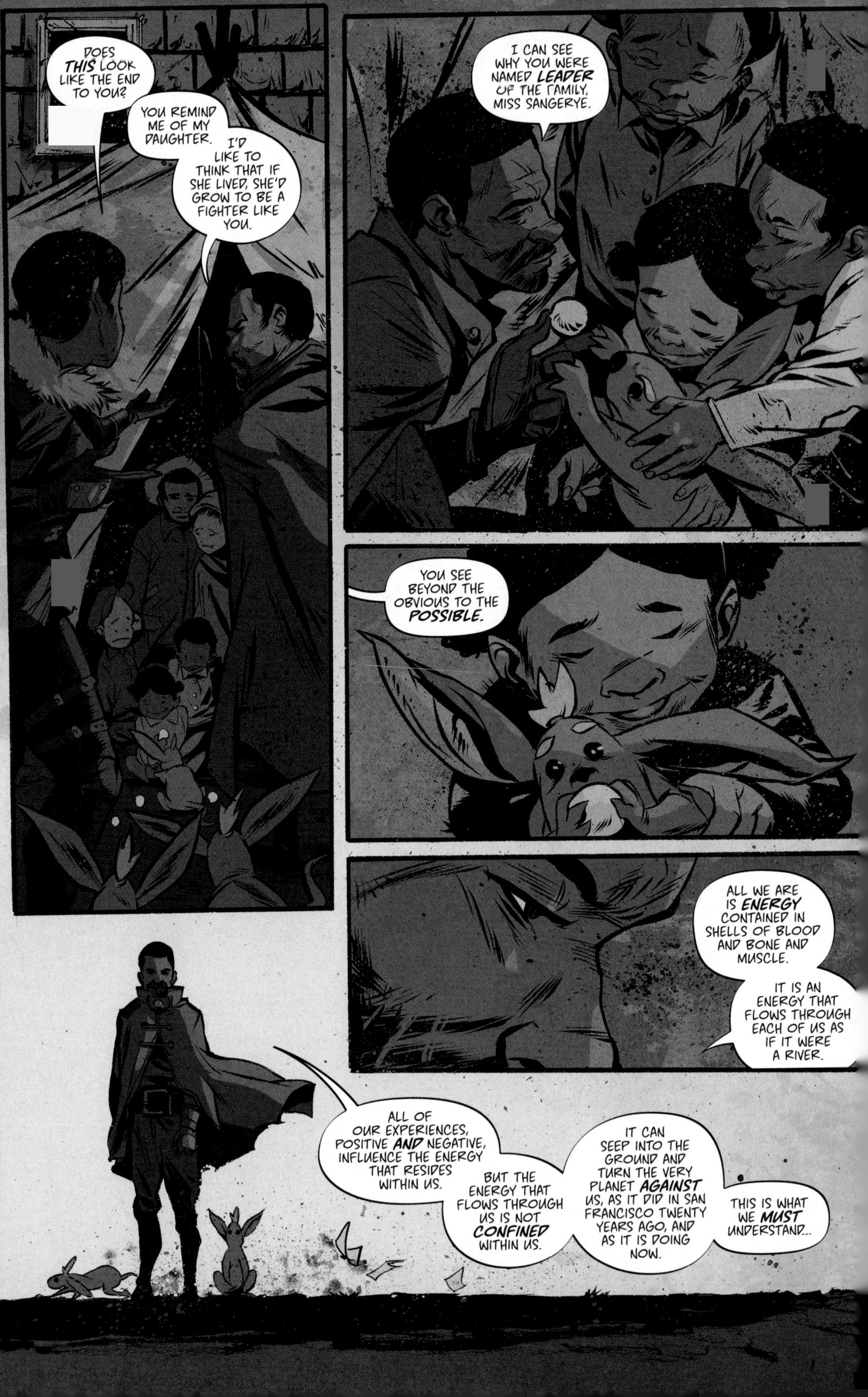
DOES THIS LOOK LIKE THE END TO YOU?
YOU REMIND ME OF MY DAUGHTER.
I'D LIKE TO THINK THAT IF SHE LIVED, SHE'D GROW TO BE A FIGHTER LIKE YOU.
I CAN SEE WHY YOU WERE NAMED LEADER OF THE FAMILY, MISS SANGERYE.
YOU SEE BEYOND THE OBVIOUS TO THE POSSIBLE.
ALL WE ARE IS ENERGY CONTAINED IN SHELLS OF BLOOD AND BONE AND MUSCLE.
IT IS AN ENERGY THAT FLOWS THROUGH EACH OF US AS IF IT WERE A RIVER.
ALL OF OUR EXPERIENCES, POSITIVE AND NEGATIVE, INFLUENCE THE ENERGY THAT RESIDES WITHIN US.
BUT THE ENERGY THAT FLOWS THROUGH US IS NOT CONFINED WITHIN US.
IT CAN SEEP INTO THE GROUND AND TURN THE VERY PLANET AGAINST US, AS IT DID IN SAN FRANCISCO TWENTY YEARS AGO, AND AS IT IS DOING NOW.
THIS IS WHAT WE MUST UNDERSTAND...

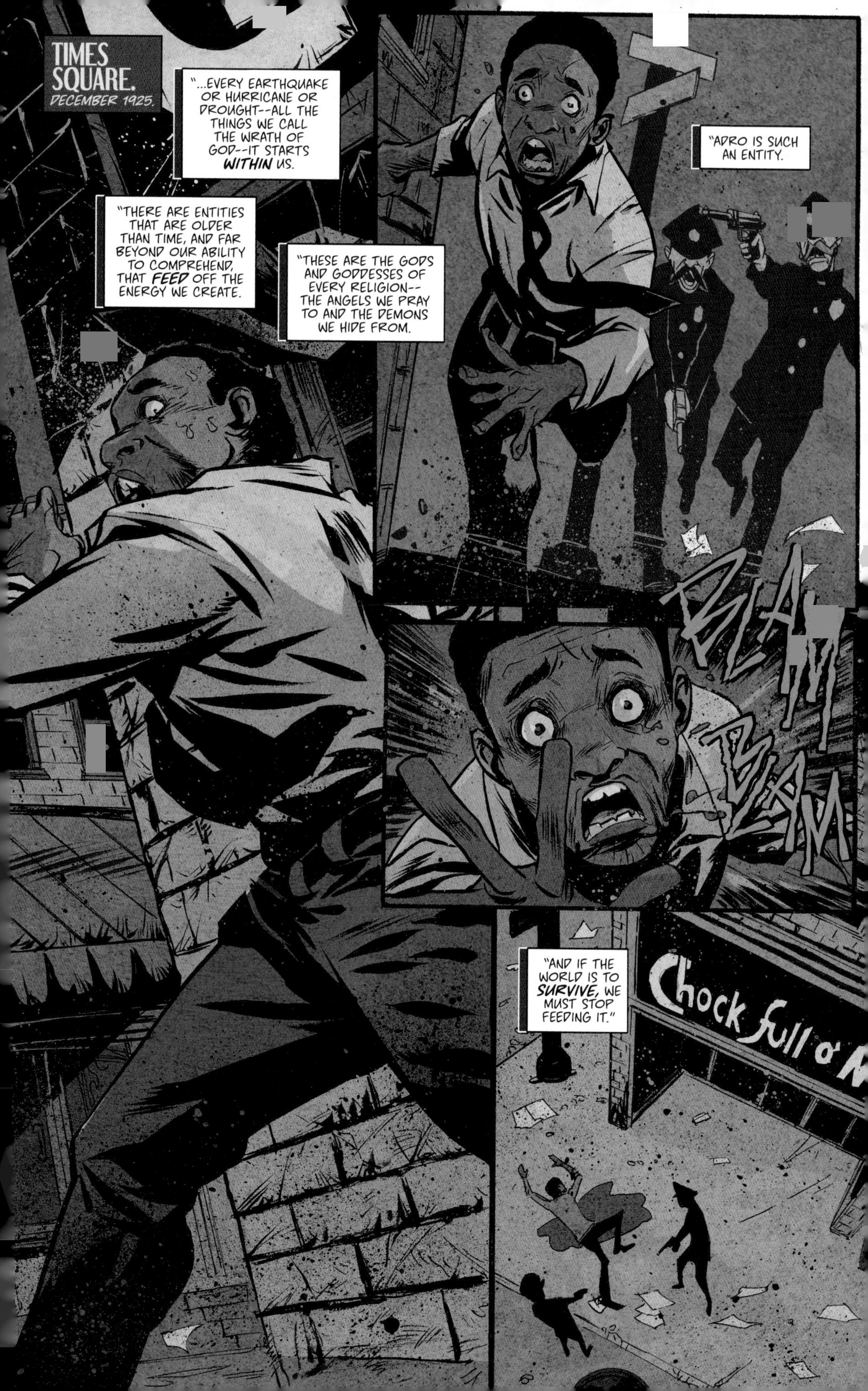
TIMES SQUARE.
DECEMBER 1925.
"...EVERY EARTHQUAKE OR HURRICANE OR DROUGHT--ALL THE THINGS WE CALL THE WRATH OF GOD--IT STARTS *WITHIN* US.
"THERE ARE ENTITIES THAT ARE OLDER THAN TIME, AND FAR BEYOND OUR ABILITY TO COMPREHEND, THAT *FEED* OFF THE ENERGY WE CREATE.
"THESE ARE THE GODS AND GODDESSES OF EVERY RELIGION--THE ANGELS WE PRAY TO AND THE DEMONS WE HIDE FROM.
"ADRO IS SUCH AN ENTITY.
BLAM
BLAM
"AND IF THE WORLD IS TO *SURVIVE*, WE MUST STOP FEEDING IT."
Chock full o'

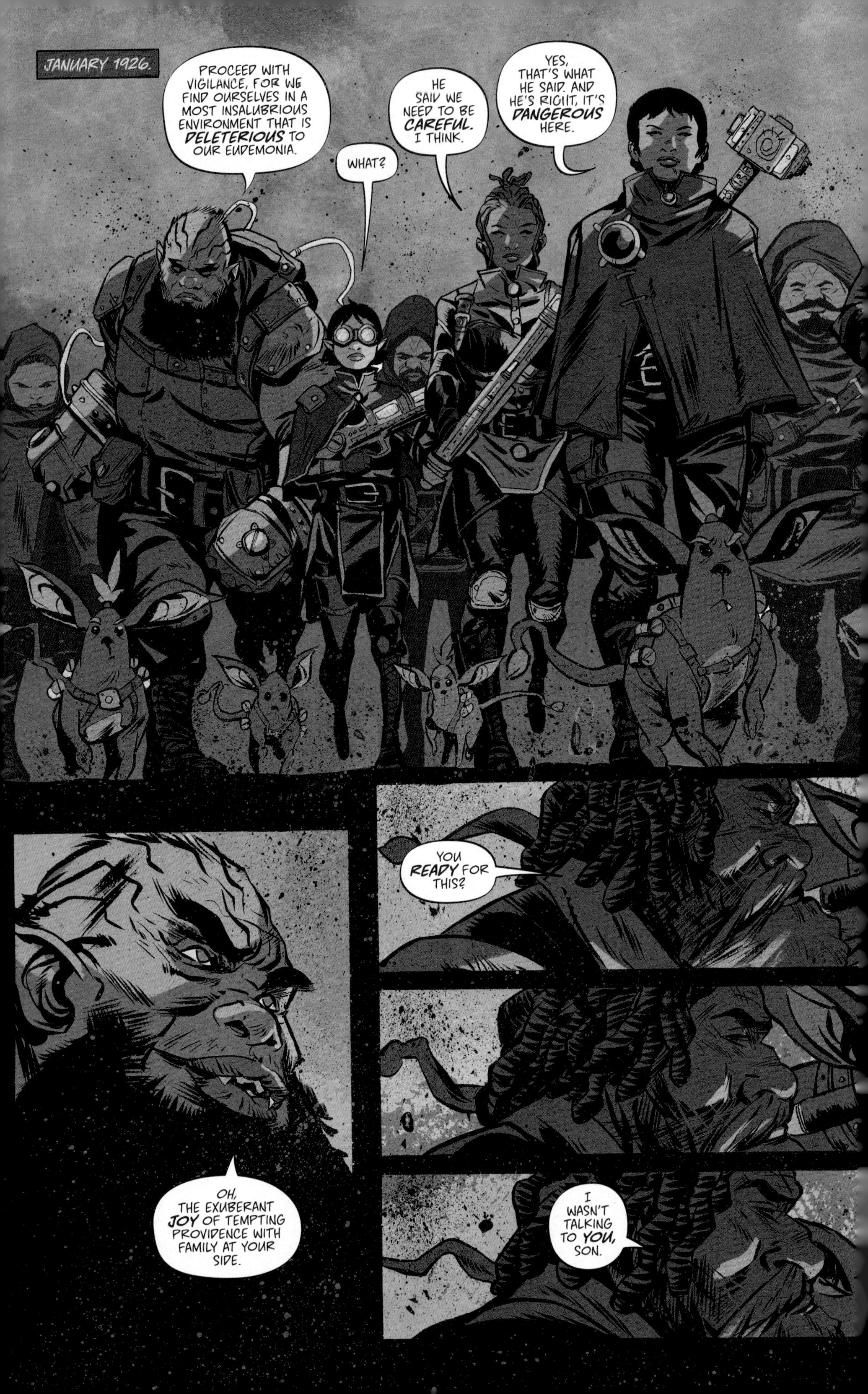
JANUARY 1926.
PROCEED WITH VIGILANCE, FOR WE FIND OURSELVES IN A MOST INSALUBRIOUS ENVIRONMENT THAT IS DELETERIOUS TO OUR EUDEMONIA.
WHAT?
HE SAID WE NEED TO BE CAREFUL. I THINK.
YES, THAT'S WHAT HE SAID. AND HE'S RIGHT, IT'S DANGEROUS HERE.
YOU READY FOR THIS?
OH, THE EXUBERANT JOY OF TEMPTING PROVIDENCE WITH FAMILY AT YOUR SIDE.
I WASN'T TALKING TO YOU, SON.

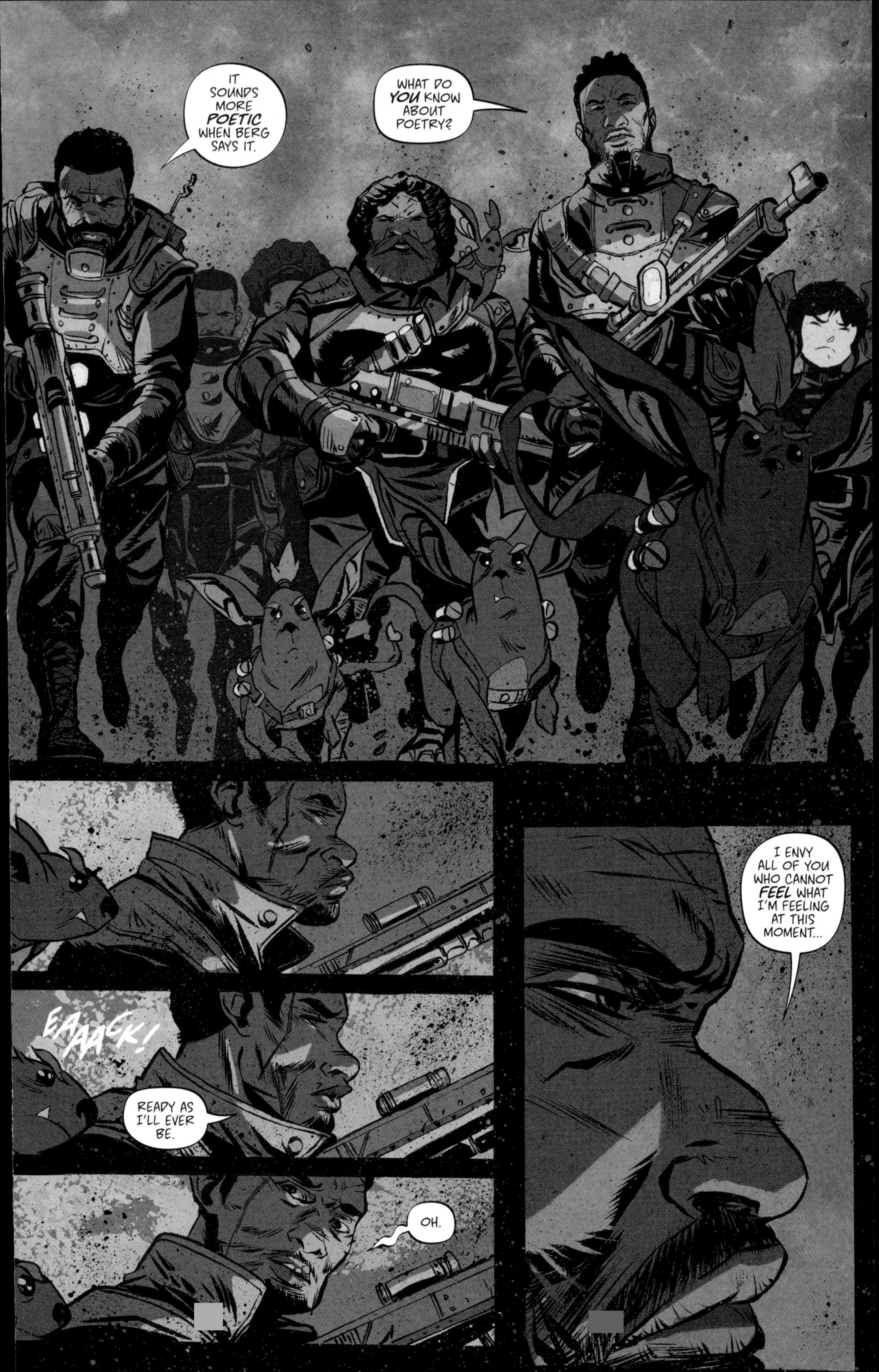
IT SOUNDS MORE POETIC WHEN BERG SAYS IT.
WHAT DO YOU KNOW ABOUT POETRY?
EAAACK!
READY AS I'LL EVER BE.
OH.
I ENVY ALL OF YOU WHO CANNOT FEEL WHAT I'M FEELING AT THIS MOMENT...

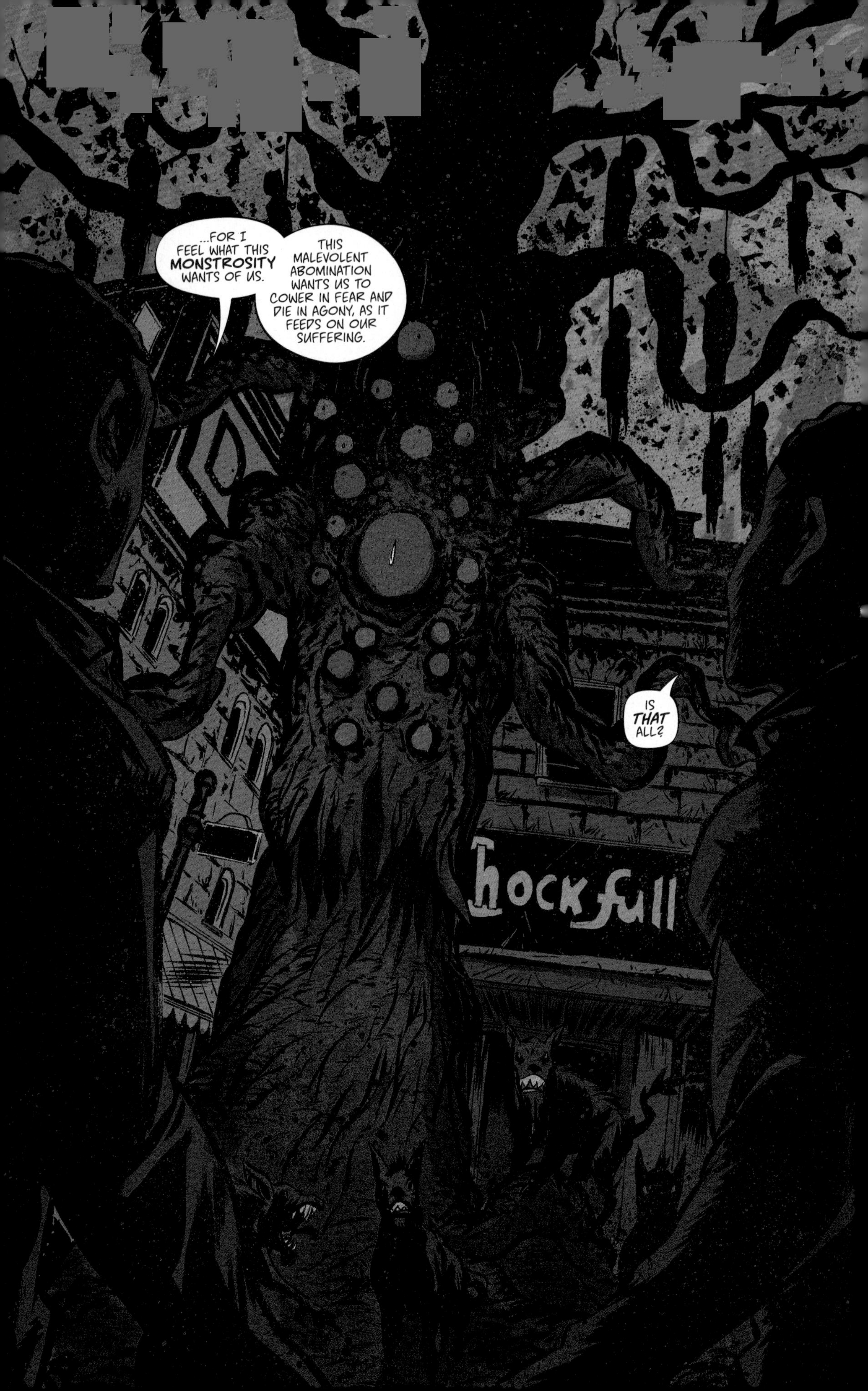
...FOR I FEEL WHAT THIS **MONSTROSITY** WANTS OF US.
THIS MALEVOLENT ABOMINATION WANTS US TO COWER IN FEAR AND DIE IN AGONY, AS IT FEEDS ON OUR SUFFERING.
IS ***THAT*** ALL?
hockfull

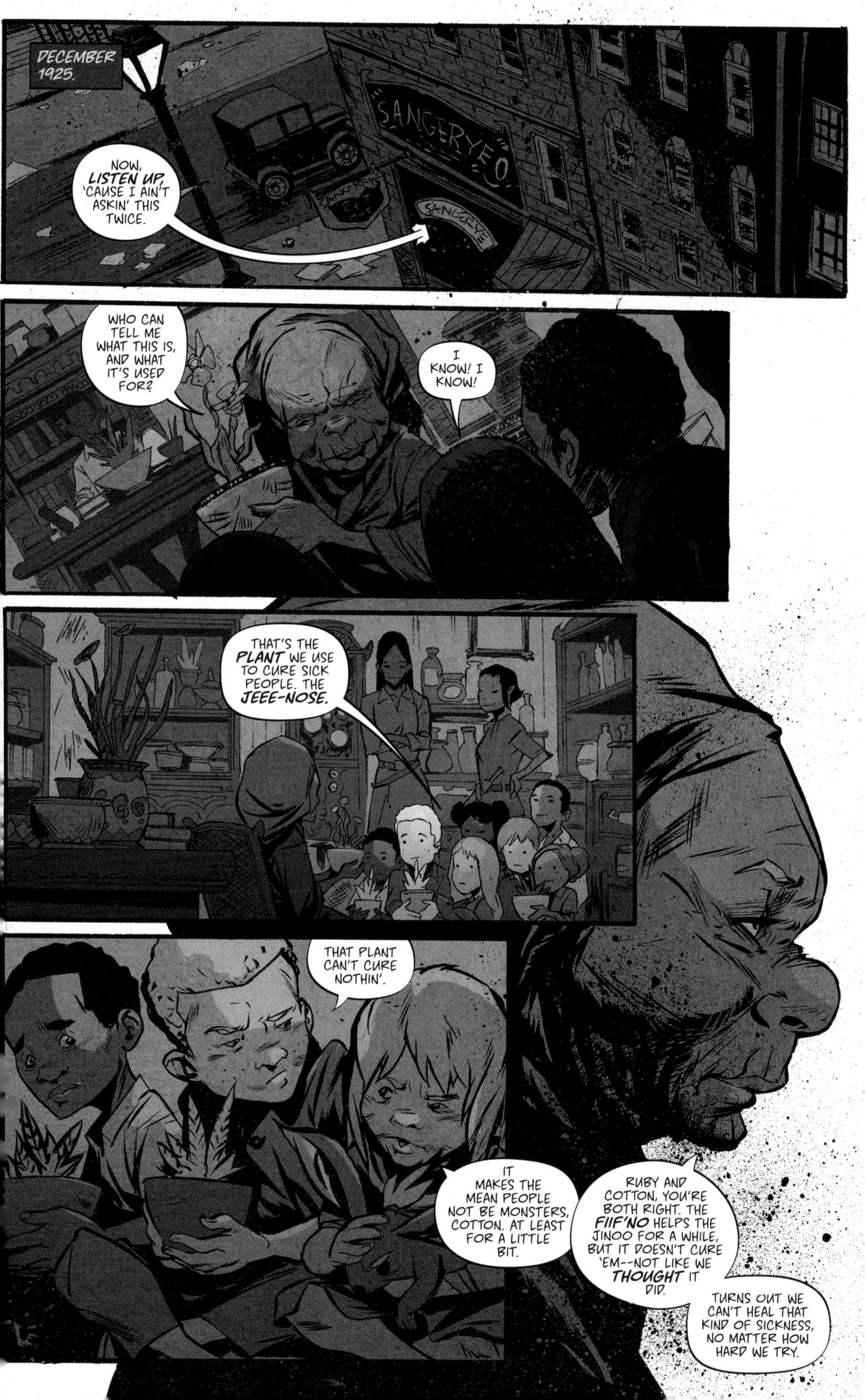
DECEMBER 1925.
SANGERYE
NOW, LISTEN UP, 'CAUSE I AIN'T ASKIN' THIS TWICE.
WHO CAN TELL ME WHAT THIS IS, AND WHAT IT'S USED FOR?
I KNOW! I KNOW!
THAT'S THE PLANT WE USE TO CURE SICK PEOPLE. THE JEEE-NOSE.
THAT PLANT CAN'T CURE NOTHIN'.
IT MAKES THE MEAN PEOPLE NOT BE MONSTERS, COTTON. AT LEAST FOR A LITTLE BIT.
RUBY AND COTTON, YOU'RE BOTH RIGHT. THE FIIF'NO HELPS THE JINOO FOR A WHILE, BUT IT DOESN'T CURE 'EM--NOT LIKE WE THOUGHT IT DID.
TURNS OUT WE CAN'T HEAL THAT KIND OF SICKNESS, NO MATTER HOW HARD WE TRY.

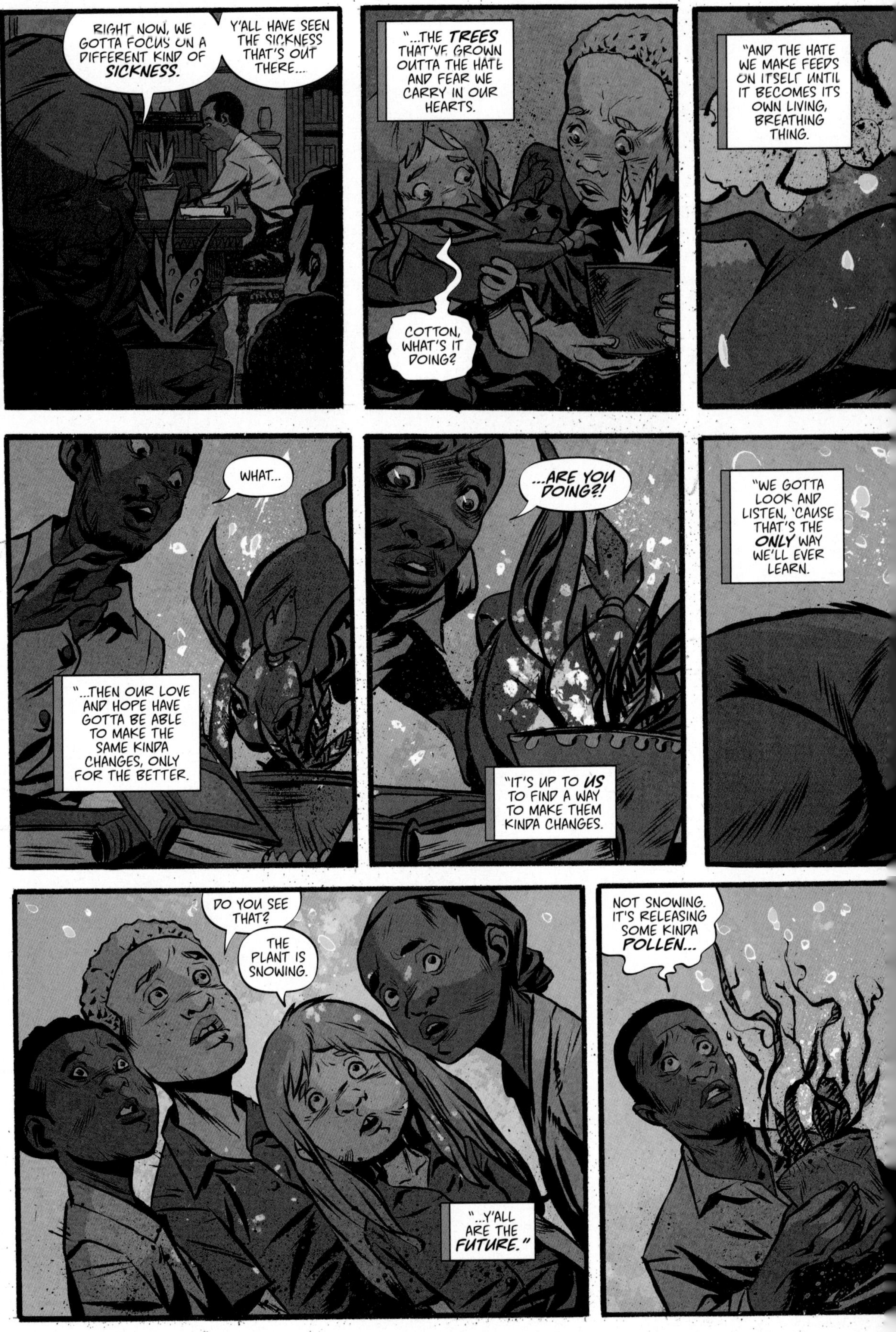
RIGHT NOW, WE GOTTA FOCUS ON A DIFFERENT KIND OF SICKNESS.
Y'ALL HAVE SEEN THE SICKNESS THAT'S OUT THERE...
"...THE TREES THAT'VE GROWN OUTTA THE HATE AND FEAR WE CARRY IN OUR HEARTS.
COTTON, WHAT'S IT DOING?
"AND THE HATE WE MAKE FEEDS ON ITSELF UNTIL IT BECOMES ITS OWN LIVING, BREATHING THING.
WHAT...
"...THEN OUR LOVE AND HOPE HAVE GOTTA BE ABLE TO MAKE THE SAME KINDA CHANGES, ONLY FOR THE BETTER.
...ARE YOU DOING?!
"IT'S UP TO US TO FIND A WAY TO MAKE THEM KINDA CHANGES.
"WE GOTTA LOOK AND LISTEN, 'CAUSE THAT'S THE ONLY WAY WE'LL EVER LEARN.
DO YOU SEE THAT?
THE PLANT IS SNOWING.
"...Y'ALL ARE THE FUTURE."
NOT SNOWING. IT'S RELEASING SOME KINDA POLLEN...

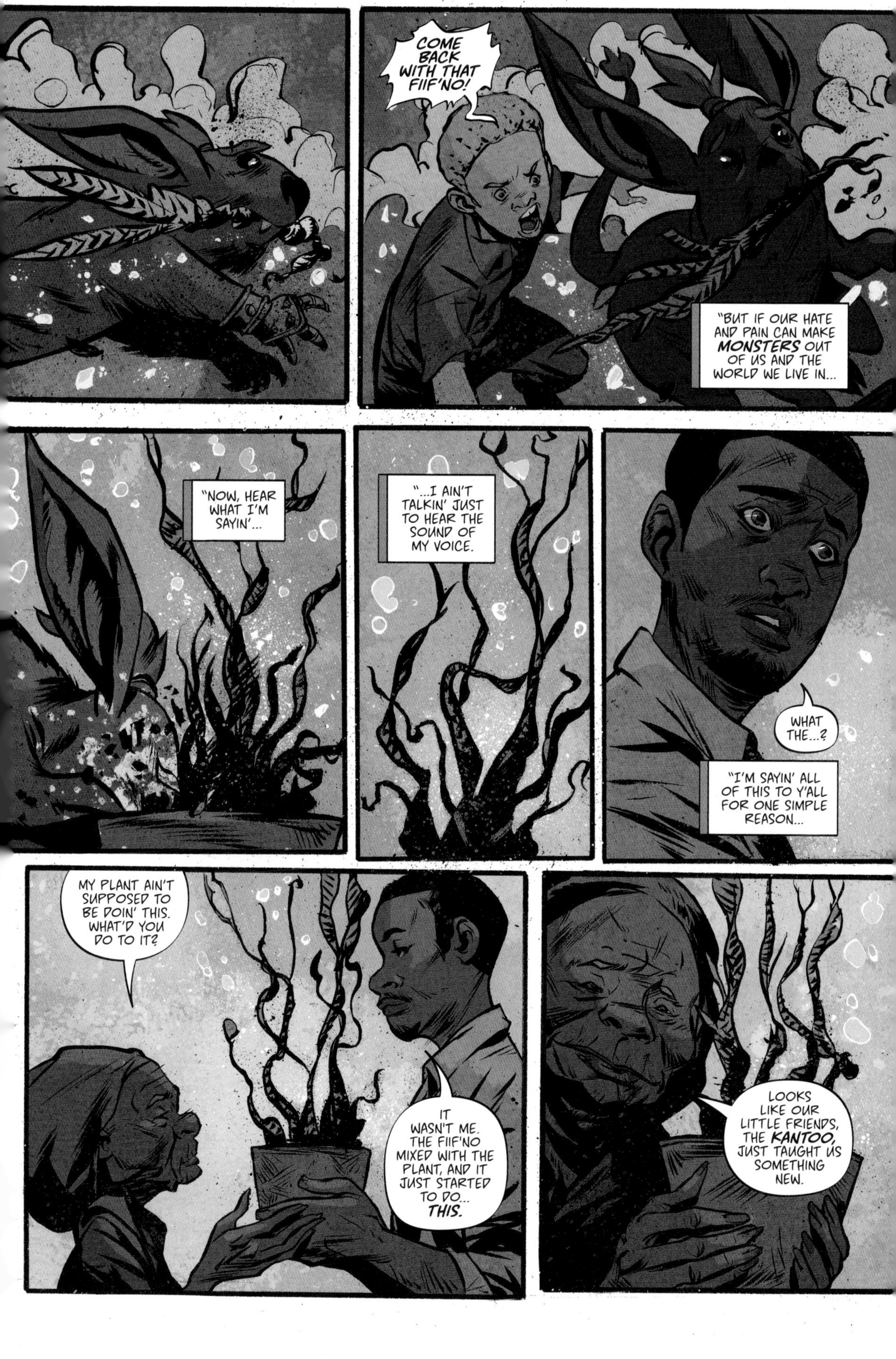
COME BACK WITH THAT FIIF'NO!
"BUT IF OUR HATE AND PAIN CAN MAKE MONSTERS OUT OF US AND THE WORLD WE LIVE IN...
"NOW, HEAR WHAT I'M SAYIN'...
"...I AIN'T TALKIN' JUST TO HEAR THE SOUND OF MY VOICE.
WHAT THE...?
"I'M SAYIN' ALL OF THIS TO Y'ALL FOR ONE SIMPLE REASON...
MY PLANT AIN'T SUPPOSED TO BE DOIN' THIS. WHAT'D YOU DO TO IT?
IT WASN'T ME. THE FIIF'NO MIXED WITH THE PLANT, AND IT JUST STARTED TO DO... THIS.
LOOKS LIKE OUR LITTLE FRIENDS, THE KANTOO, JUST TAUGHT US SOMETHING NEW.

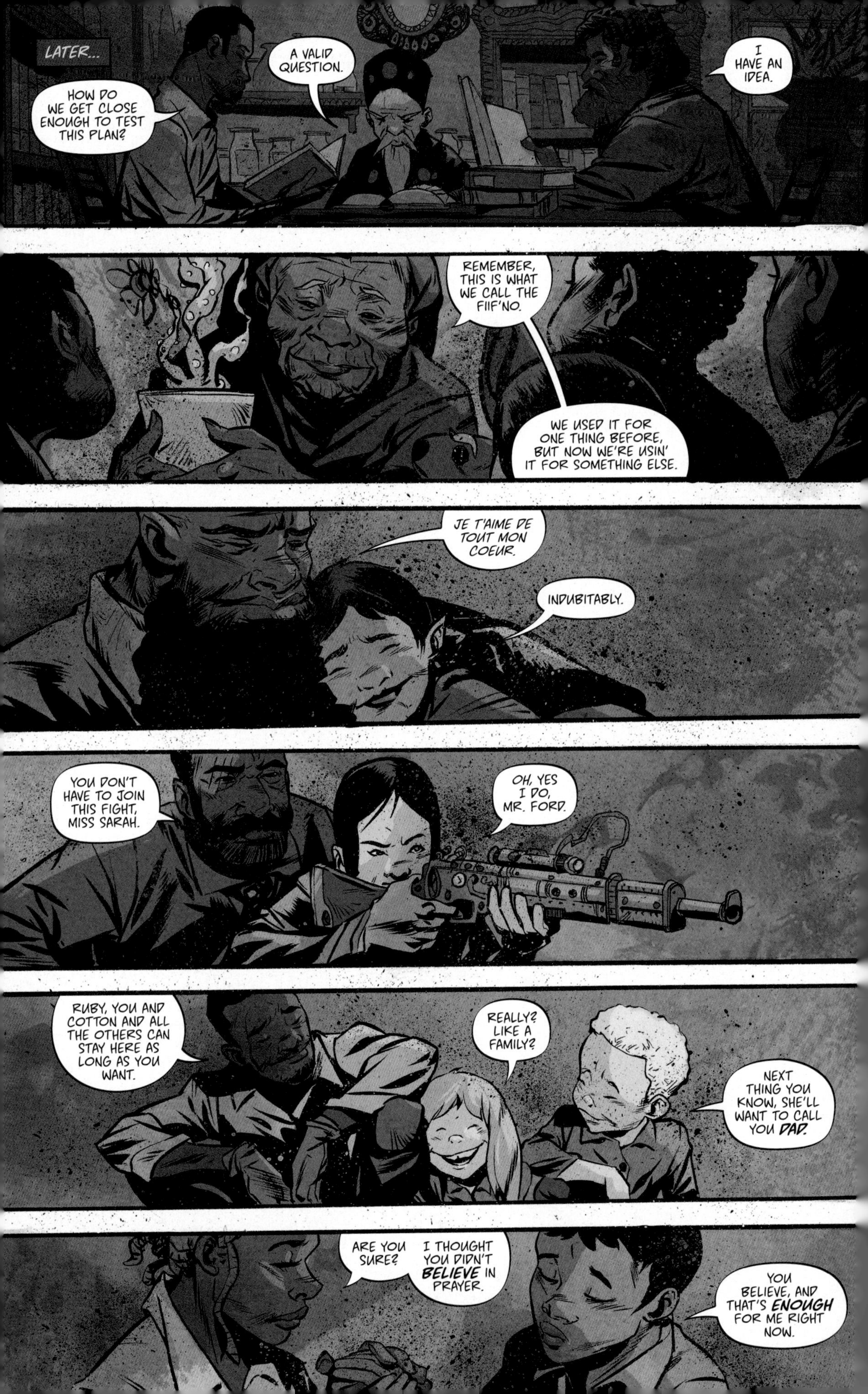
LATER...
HOW DO WE GET CLOSE ENOUGH TO TEST THIS PLAN?
A VALID QUESTION.
I HAVE AN IDEA.
REMEMBER, THIS IS WHAT WE CALL THE FIIF'NO.
WE USED IT FOR ONE THING BEFORE, BUT NOW WE'RE USIN' IT FOR SOMETHING ELSE.
JE T'AIME DE TOUT MON COEUR.
INDUBITABLY.
YOU DON'T HAVE TO JOIN THIS FIGHT, MISS SARAH.
OH, YES I DO, MR. FORD.
RUBY, YOU AND COTTON AND ALL THE OTHERS CAN STAY HERE AS LONG AS YOU WANT.
REALLY? LIKE A FAMILY?
NEXT THING YOU KNOW, SHE'LL WANT TO CALL YOU DAD.
ARE YOU SURE?
I THOUGHT YOU DIDN'T BELIEVE IN PRAYER.
YOU BELIEVE, AND THAT'S ENOUGH FOR ME RIGHT NOW.

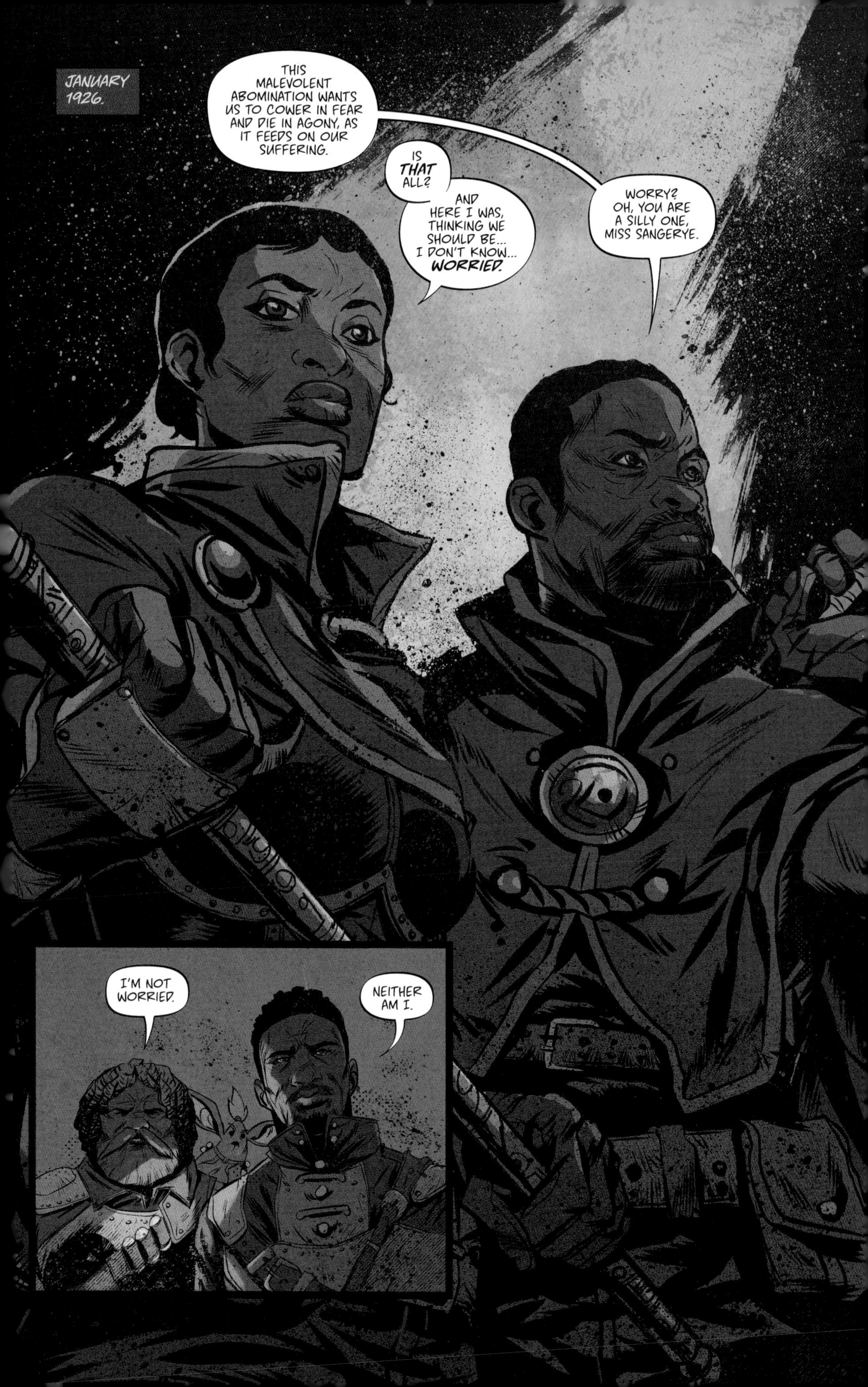
JANUARY 1926.
THIS MALEVOLENT ABOMINATION WANTS US TO COWER IN FEAR AND DIE IN AGONY, AS IT FEEDS ON OUR SUFFERING.
IS THAT ALL?
AND HERE I WAS, THINKING WE SHOULD BE... I DON'T KNOW... WORRIED.
WORRY? OH, YOU ARE A SILLY ONE, MISS SANGERYE.
I'M NOT WORRIED.
NEITHER AM I.

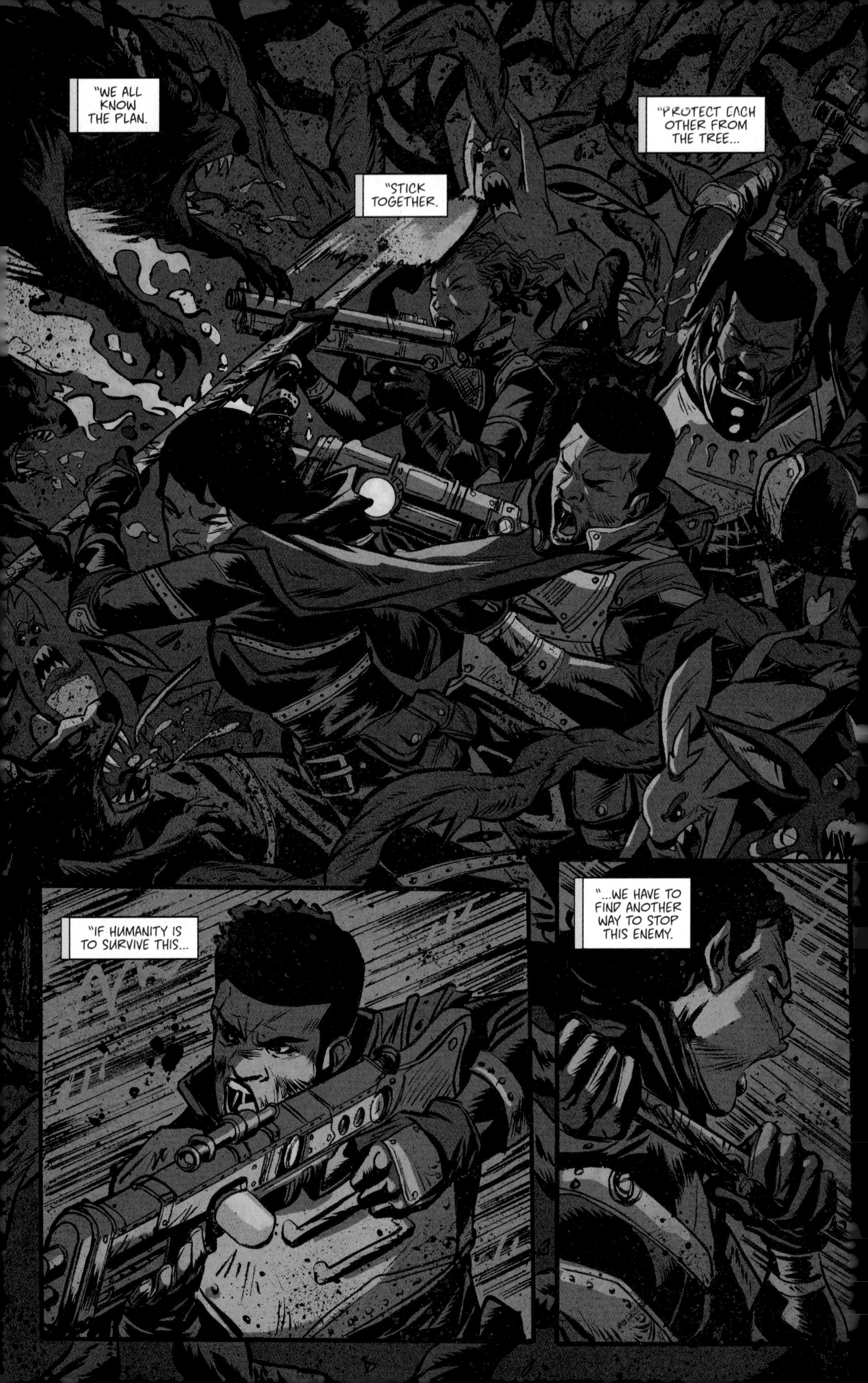
"WE ALL KNOW THE PLAN.
"STICK TOGETHER.
"PROTECT EACH OTHER FROM THE TREE...
"IF HUMANITY IS TO SURVIVE THIS...
"...WE HAVE TO FIND ANOTHER WAY TO STOP THIS ENEMY.

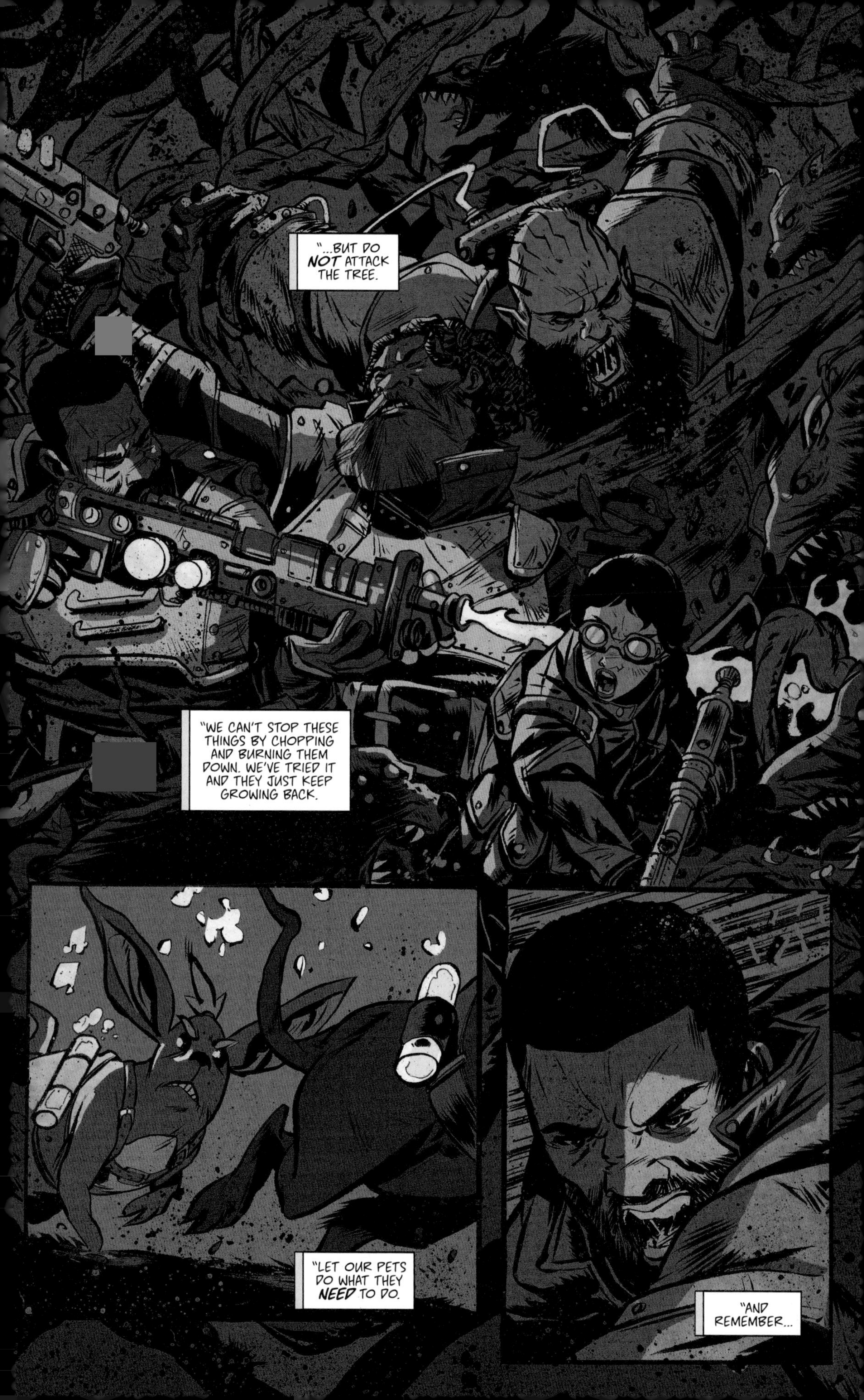
"...BUT DO NOT ATTACK THE TREE.
"WE CAN'T STOP THESE THINGS BY CHOPPING AND BURNING THEM DOWN. WE'VE TRIED IT AND THEY JUST KEEP GROWING BACK.
"LET OUR PETS DO WHAT THEY NEED TO DO.
"AND REMEMBER...

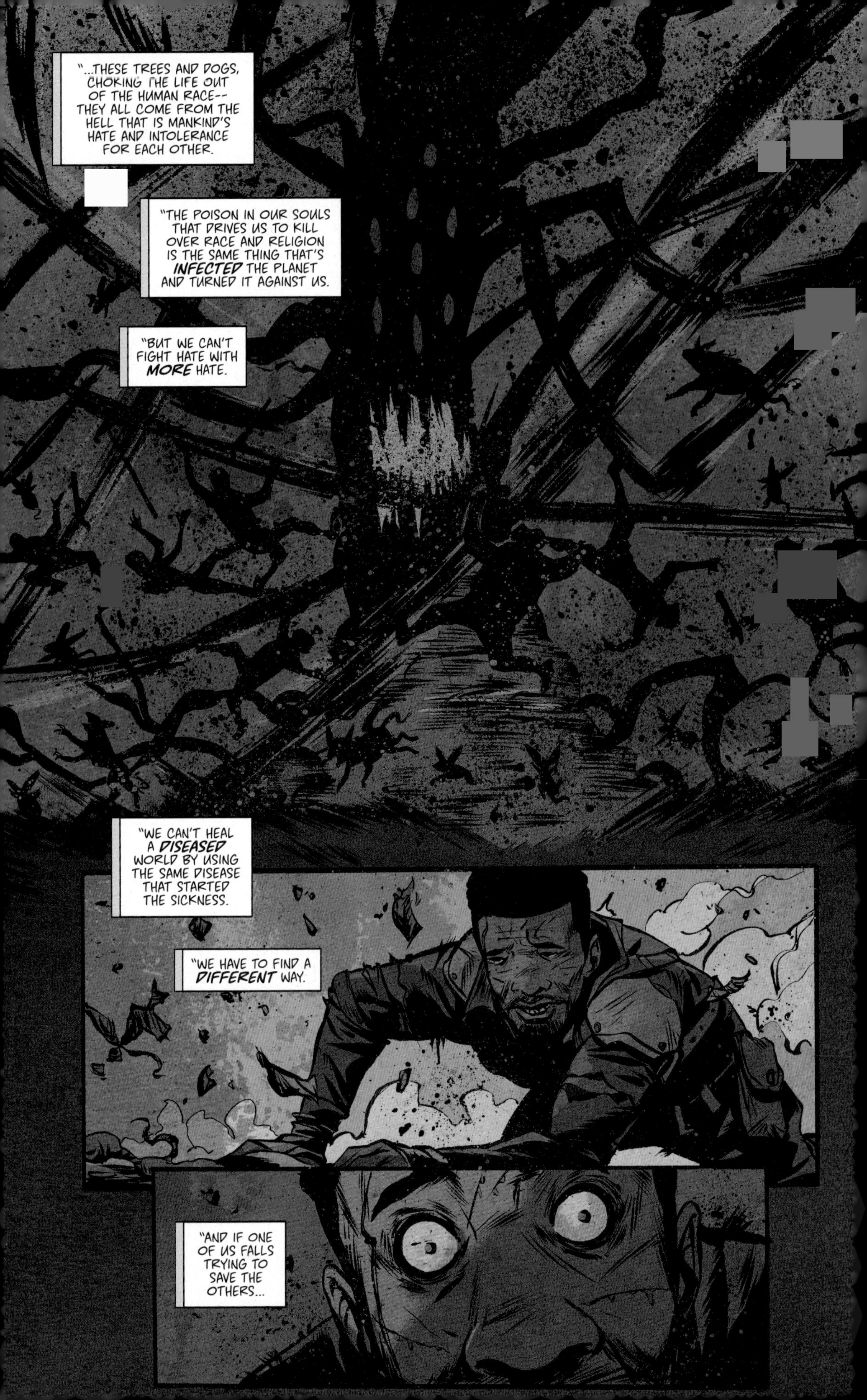
"...THESE TREES AND DOGS, CHOKING THE LIFE OUT OF THE HUMAN RACE-- THEY ALL COME FROM THE HELL THAT IS MANKIND'S HATE AND INTOLERANCE FOR EACH OTHER.
"THE POISON IN OUR SOULS THAT DRIVES US TO KILL OVER RACE AND RELIGION IS THE SAME THING THAT'S INFECTED THE PLANET AND TURNED IT AGAINST US.
"BUT WE CAN'T FIGHT HATE WITH MORE HATE.
"WE CAN'T HEAL A DISEASED WORLD BY USING THE SAME DISEASE THAT STARTED THE SICKNESS.
"WE HAVE TO FIND A DIFFERENT WAY.
"AND IF ONE OF US FALLS TRYING TO SAVE THE OTHERS...

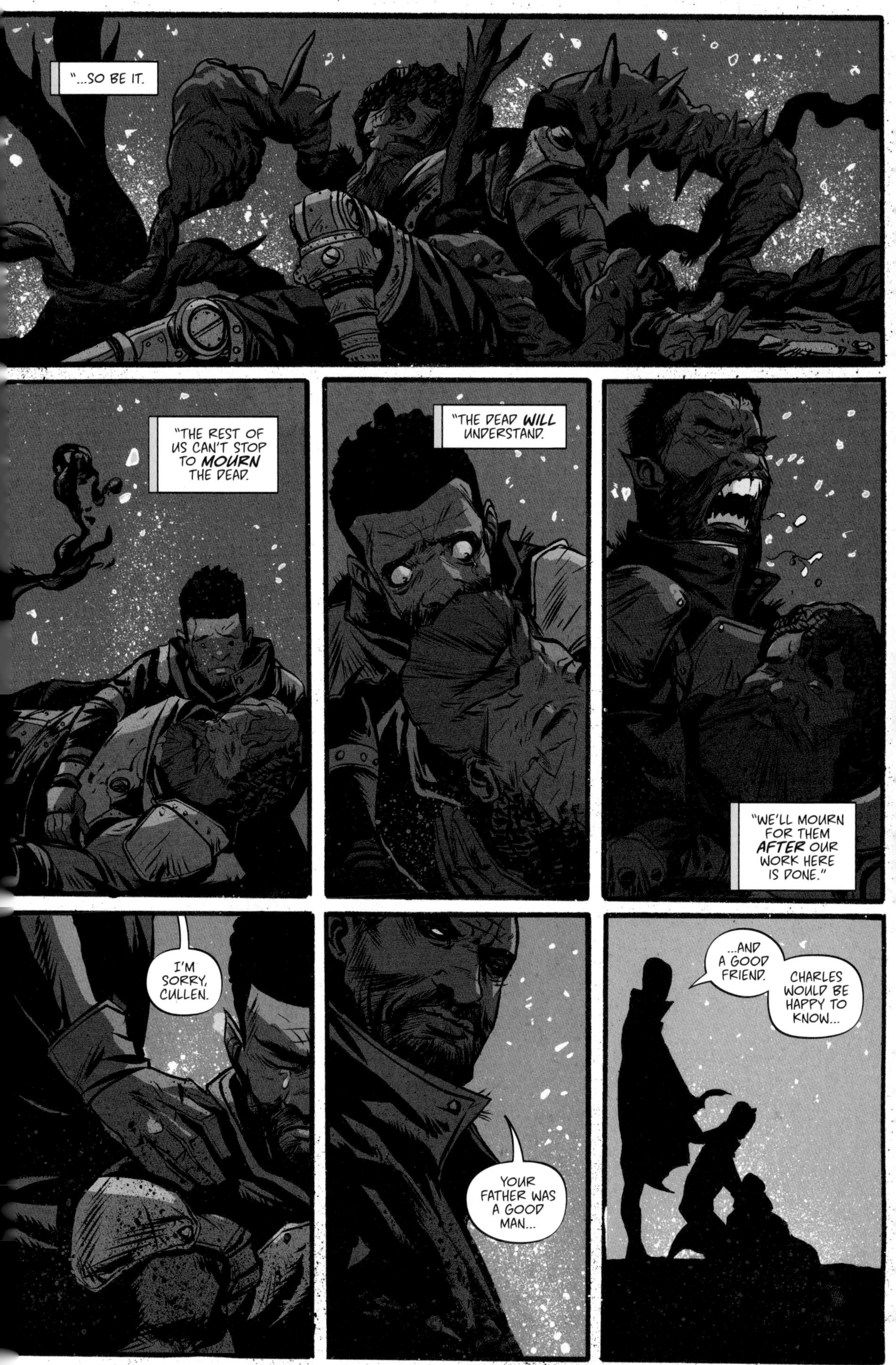
"...SO BE IT.
"THE REST OF US CAN'T STOP TO MOURN THE DEAD.
"THE DEAD WILL UNDERSTAND.
"WE'LL MOURN FOR THEM AFTER OUR WORK HERE IS DONE."
I'M SORRY, CULLEN.
YOUR FATHER WAS A GOOD MAN...
...AND A GOOD FRIEND.
CHARLES WOULD BE HAPPY TO KNOW...

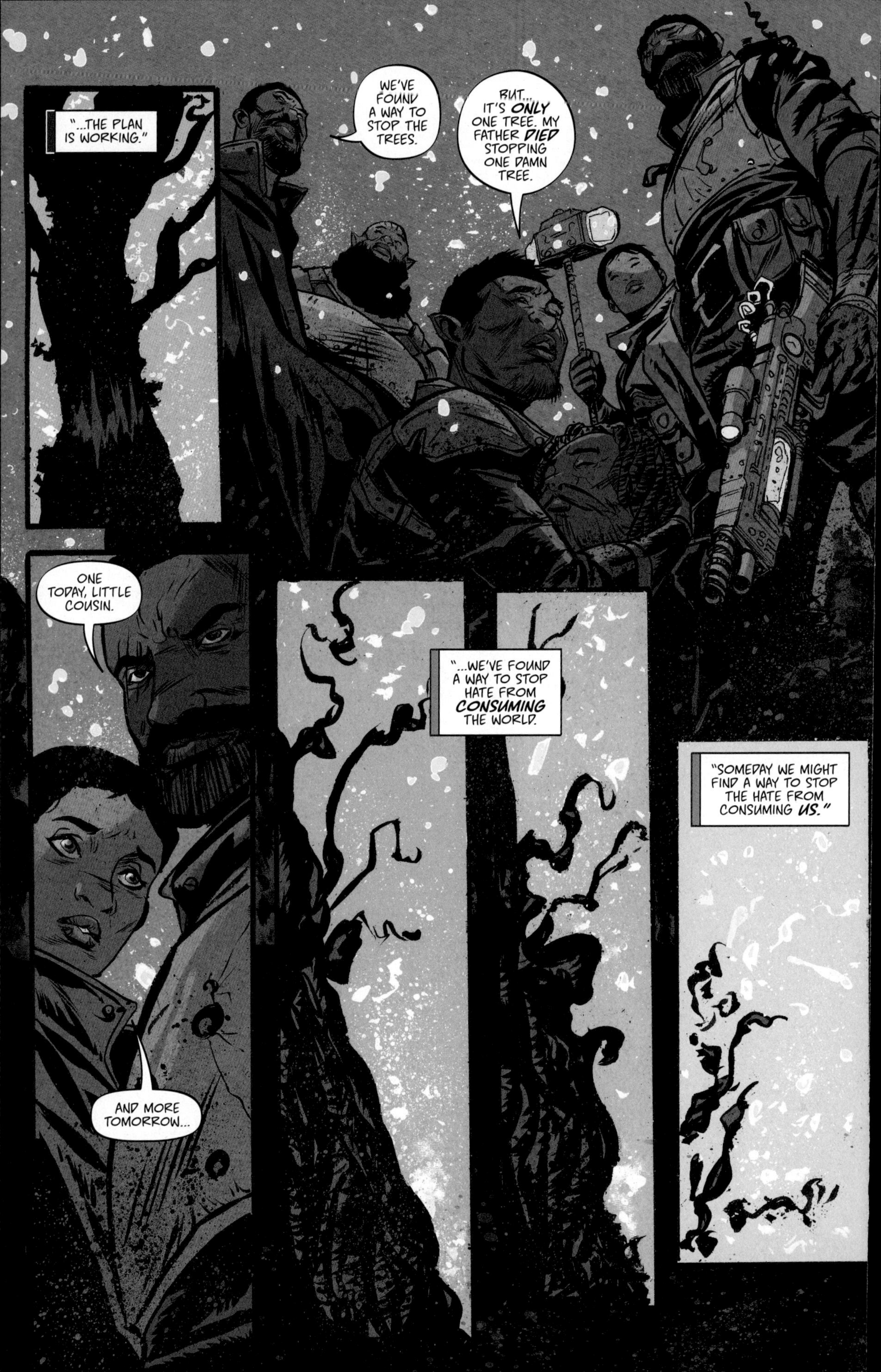
"...THE PLAN IS WORKING."
WE'VE FOUND A WAY TO STOP THE TREES.
BUT... IT'S ONLY ONE TREE. MY FATHER DIED STOPPING ONE DAMN TREE.
ONE TODAY, LITTLE COUSIN.
AND MORE TOMORROW...
"...WE'VE FOUND A WAY TO STOP HATE FROM CONSUMING THE WORLD.
"SOMEDAY WE MIGHT FIND A WAY TO STOP THE HATE FROM CONSUMING US."

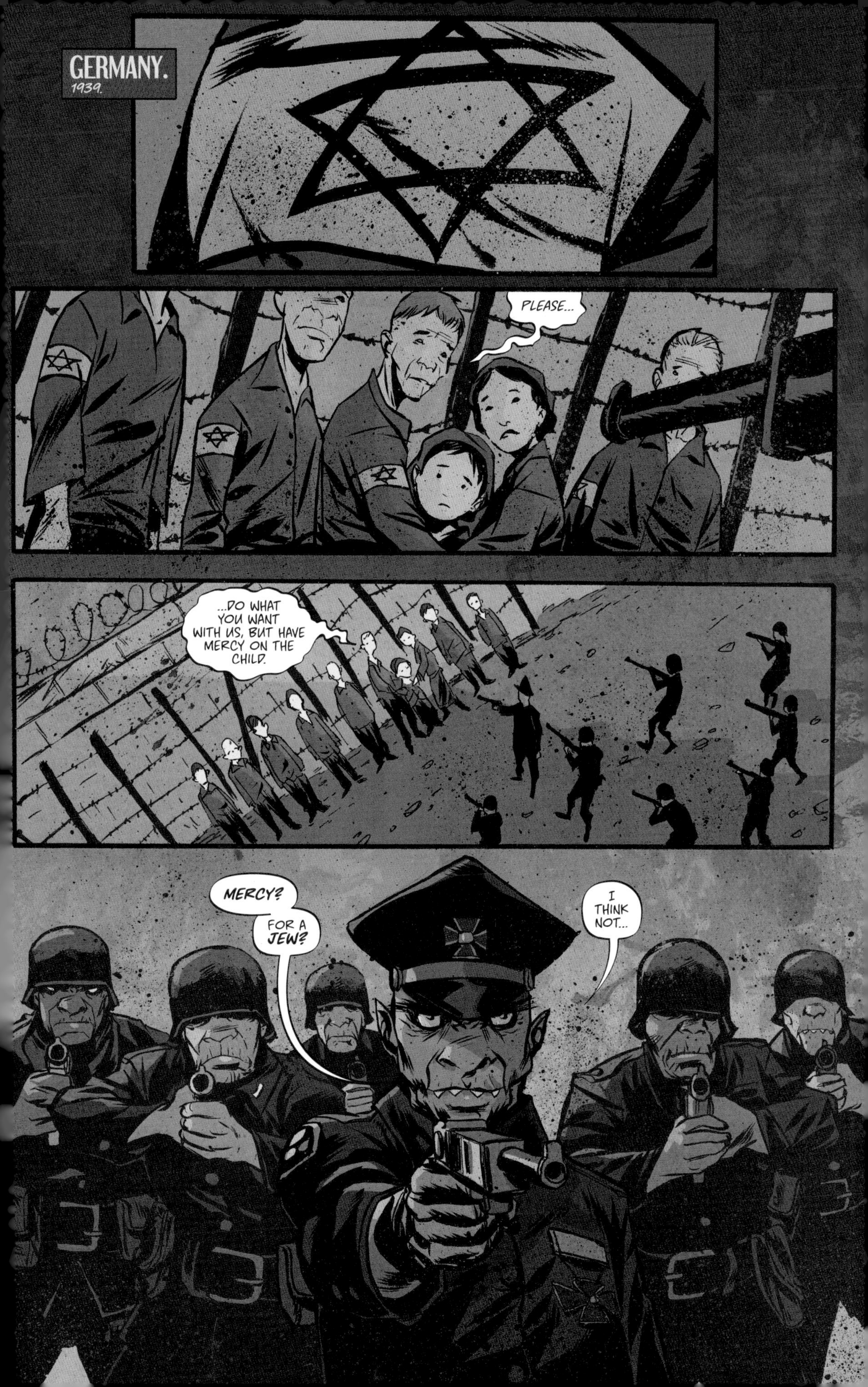
GERMANY.
1939.
PLEASE...
...DO WHAT YOU WANT WITH US, BUT HAVE MERCY ON THE CHILD.
MERCY?
FOR A JEW?
I THINK NOT...

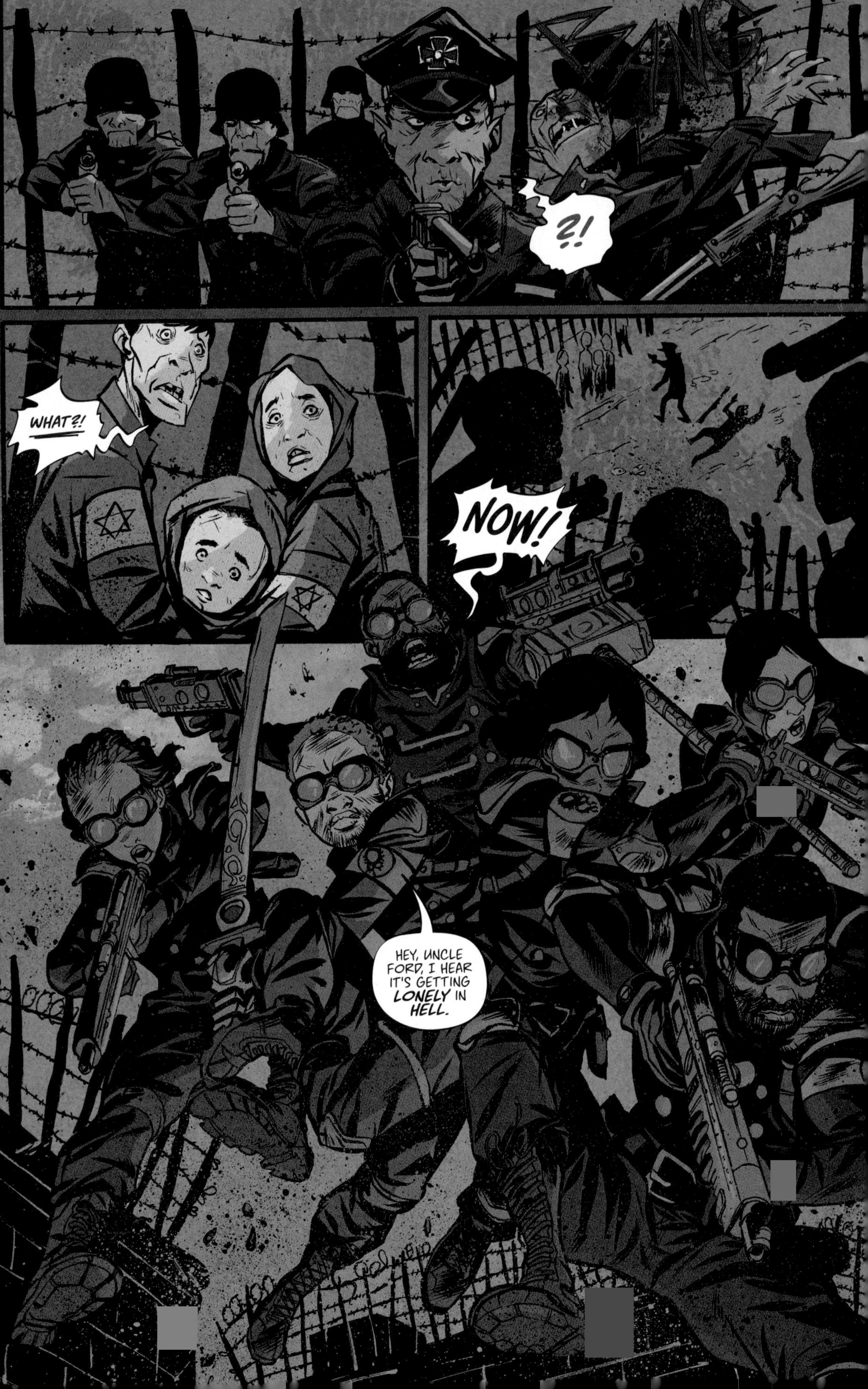

BLAM
?!
WHAT?!
NOW!
HEY, UNCLE FORD, I HEAR IT'S GETTING **LONELY** IN **HELL**.

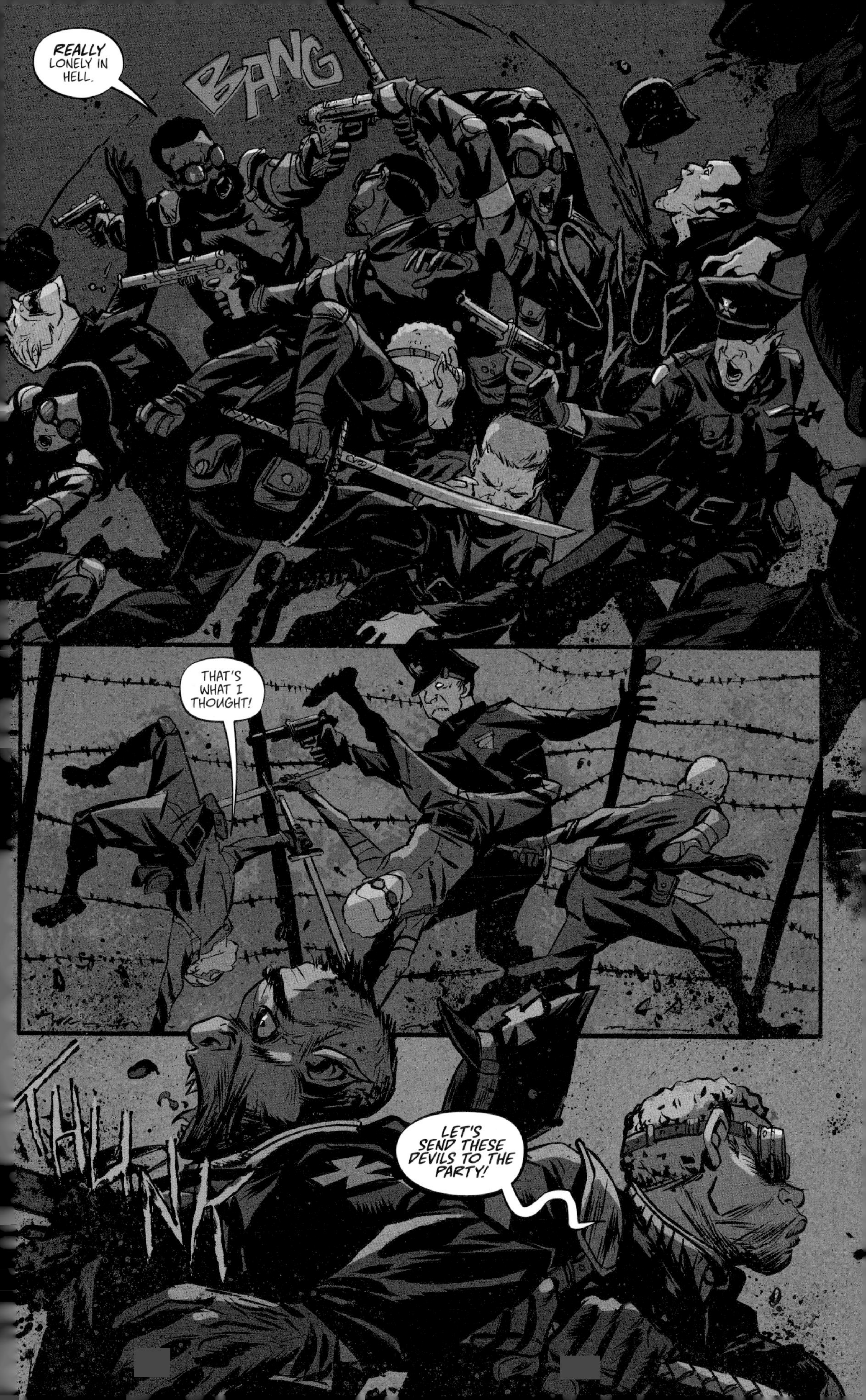
REALLY LONELY IN HELL.
BANG
THAT'S WHAT I THOUGHT!
THUNK
LET'S SEND THESE DEVILS TO THE PARTY!

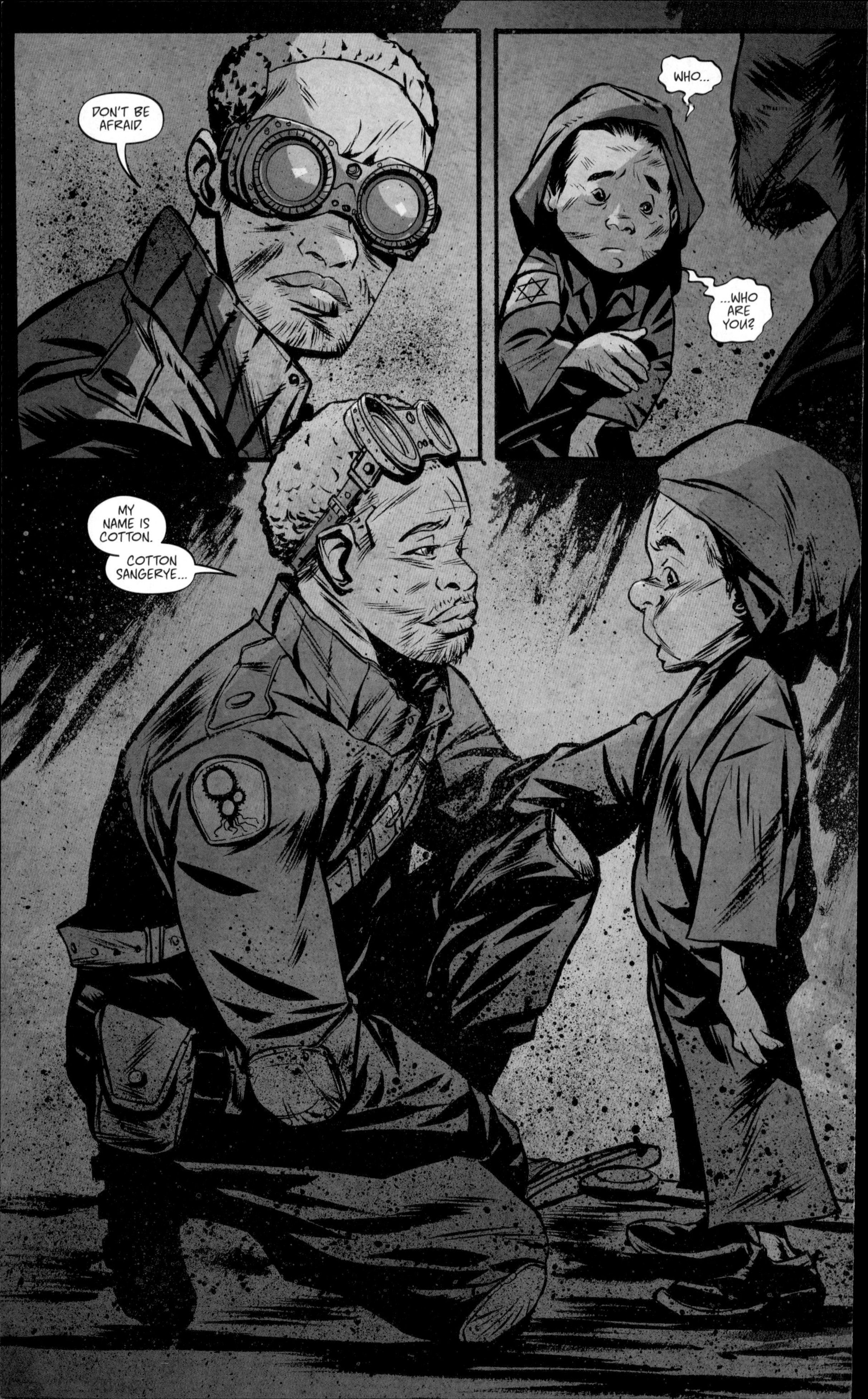
DON'T BE AFRAID.
WHO...
...WHO ARE YOU?
MY NAME IS COTTON.
COTTON SANGERYE...

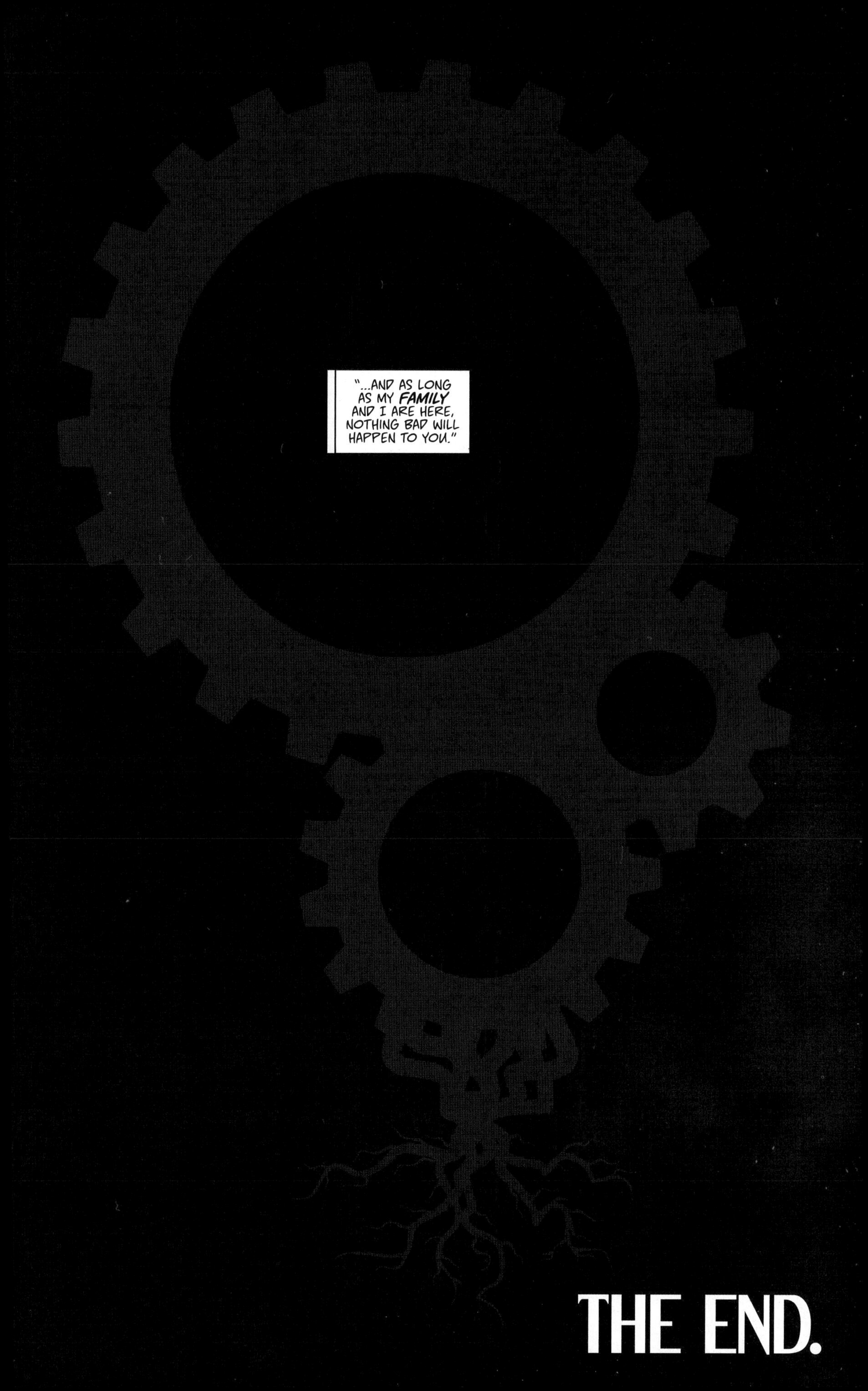
"...AND AS LONG AS MY FAMILY AND I ARE HERE, NOTHING BAD WILL HAPPEN TO YOU."
THE END.

THE SANGERYES

MA ETTA
The matriarch of the Sangerye family, she learned the art of herb mixing and curing Jinoo when she was a runaway slave in the underground railroad.

METELLUS SANGERYE
(deceased)

NORA SANGERYE
Wife of Nelson Sangerye, one of the b̶r̶o̶t̶h̶e̶r̶s̶ presumably killed in 19̶ ̶ ̶ ̶ ̶ ̶ped in the realm of Barzakh for a long time, she makes an escape with Cullen.

BILLY "NOD" SANGERYE
(deceased)

CHARLIE SANGERYE
He's thought to have been killed during the Red Summer of 1919.

SARA SANGERYE
(deceased)

BELINDA "BLINK" SANGERYE
A young woman who excels at fighting, despite it being frowned upon by Ma Etta, who believes Blink's role is mixing herbs and healing the infected.

CULLEN SANGERYE
He lacks the skills of the rest o̶f̶ ̶t̶h̶e̶ ̶f̶a̶m̶i̶l̶y̶, putting lives in danger. During a violent encoun̶t̶e̶r̶ ̶C̶u̶l̶len is presumed to be killed, but is actually d̶r̶a̶w̶n̶ ̶into Barzakh. He eventually escapes, but the experience has turned him into a hardened fighter with a dark secret.

OLIVIA SANGERYE
(deceased)

FRANKFURT SANGERYE
(deceased)

LILLIAN SANGERYE
(deceased)

BURRELL MANIGO
(deceased)

FORD SANGERYE
Injured during the Red Summer, which claimed the life of his parents, Ford is estranged from the rest of the family. He believes there is no curing the Jinoo—only killing them by amputating the soul from the body.

ENOCH SANGERYE
Son of Ma Etta, and the oldest surviving Sangerye brother, he dabbles in dark magic, which many believe is the cause of his siblings' deaths.

BERG MANIGO
Berg is a mountain of a man with a tremendous vocabulary and penchant for using big words. He is infected by a creature that causes him to start transforming into a monster—and there seems to be no cure.

AT THE CROSSROADS OF CONJUREPUNK AND THE AFROFUTURE

SHAWN TAYLOR is a writer, university lecturer, and a pop culture scholar. He is a founding author of **www.thenerdsofcolor.org**, and a founding organizer of the Black and Brown Comix Arts Festival (BCAF). His passion for stories of other worlds led him to an obsession with role-playing games, eventually becoming a paid Dungeon Master for many Dungeons and Dragons campaigns. In high school, he organized a live action D&D battle in his school's cafeteria. He was suspended for two days for orchestrating the battle, but some folks still talk about it as a highlight of their high school experience. Shawn just concluded a Senior Fellowship with the Pop Culture Collaborative where he studied how fandom power could be used for social good. He consults for media and gaming companies as well as provides individual coaching for creatives.

The last two decades have been a vital and fertile time for global Black thought and expression. While I won't be so presumptuous and try to pin down the resurgence point, I will argue for an inspiration point—a point that gave Black artists (Global Citizens of the African Diaspora) a renewed invitation to break with artistic and literary convention, to take more social and cultural risks, and to banish stereotypical creative expectations to the netherworld.

September 29th, 2000 saw the release of the Kevin Powell-edited anthology *Step into a World: A Global Anthology of the New Black Literature*. Like the Harlem Renaissance (a time period that *Bitter Root* showcases so well) and the Black Arts Movement (BAM) that followed, *Step into a World* gave Black artists permission to treat the twenty-six letters of the English alphabet as sigils of infinity. These twenty-six characters were the ingredients of a mass conjuring—infinite affects and results were available with only their deft arrangement and the application of imagination not hindered by the necessity or desire to be intelligible to whiteness. Unlike the wonderful movements before it, this new Black Aesthetic (shout out to Trey Ellis and his phenomenal essay of the same name) seemed to thrive on self-generated power, and not in response to white oppression. In fact, this new drive seemed to disregard (W)hiteness altogether. Not that these new revolutionary literati stuck their heads in the sand while pretending oppression didn't exist, but they didn't prioritize the combating of oppressive, systemic (W)hiteness. They eschewed this in favor of presenting Blackness in all of its multitudinous and global glory—without restriction. They took the past and the present of a globally connected Blackness and crafted an entirely new home, with brand-new tools. While the past and the present were on lock, it took just under two years from the publication of *Step into A World* to propel us into the Afrofuture.

While Afrofuturism, Africanfuturism (Dr. Nnedi Okorafor), Astroblackness (Dr. Reynaldo Anderson) and other phrasing that positions Blackness, technology, and the ethno-speculative in the public sphere are now nigh ubiquitous, it's important that we recognize the seismic shift in thinking that happened in the summer of 2002.

A lot of attention is paid to Mark Dery (1994), a journalist who asked a very important question in his *Black to the Future: Interviews with Samuel R. Delaney, Greg Tate, and Tricia Rose*—I'll paraphrase and remix:

Why don't Black people write science fiction when trans-Atlantic Blackness is science fiction? Aliens came to Africa, abducted our ancestors, stripped them of their language and cosmology, shoved them into vessels, traveled an indescribably long distance, only to deposit them into wholly new lands?

While Dery's essay was concerned with African Americans "in the context of twentieth century technoculture" and "African American signification that appropriates images of technology and a prosthetically enhanced future" this conception is too narrow, too outdated as Afrofuturism (which I'll be using for the rest of this essay) is as expansive as those who contribute to how we conceptualize this idea. And we have Dr. Alondra Nelson to thank for setting the stage to think of Afrofuturism as an open field and not an enclosed sandbox. Dr. Nelson, rightfully called the godmother of Afrofuturism, edited an issue of Duke

University's *SocialText* journal devoted to Afrofuturism. The offerings in this issue (71, Vol 20, No. 2) covered subjects from posthumanism (Alexander Weheliye), to positioning the African Diaspora as a proto internet (Anna Everett), to an interview with author Nalo Hopkinson, who was just coming into her literary prowess (Dr. Alondra Nelson). This slim volume became the passport for so many Black creatives to explore the Afrofuture which had, some would and have argued, its formal debut (out of the realms of scholars and ebony towers) in the late winter of 2018 when the Marvel Cinematic Universe gave us *Black Panther*. *Black Panther*, at the time, was a one-of-a-kind film. It exemplified Jamaican Dub Poet Mutabaruka's words: "Slavery is not African history. Slavery interrupted African history."

Black Panther speculated what an African nation could become if it was never conquered, nor its people enslaved. Granted, the film is a super-hero cum science fiction film, but to see an African nation as the most technologically advanced geography on earth ignited the dream machinery of so many. Many took the fictional concepts presented in the film and found ways for real world application. There are people running for office on Afrofuturist platforms. I coined the word "Oakanda" to connect the real-world revolutionary spirit of Oakland, CA, to the unconquered spirit of Wakanda—linking the historical Black Panther Party for Self-Defense to the Black Panther, king of Wakanda. My cousin summed this up thusly, "It's not a movie. It's a movement, cousin." At first glance, all that I have described here would seem to be at odds. Past/present convergence versus speculative Black futures. I want to disabuse all of this notion.

New Black Aesthetics and Afrofuturism are just facets of a Black cultural diamond, and that diamond is the nearly superhuman ability for Black people to conjure. If there were a universal quality of Global Blackness, it would be the ability to craft world-altering culture despite oppression and lack of resources. Black folks have given the world rock and roll, hip-hop, jazz; Black folks have elevated the mundanity of everyday athletics into nearly divine spectacle. The conjure impulse has produced several schools of artistic and socio-cultural thought that reverberate atemporally—we invented the remix. We swirl the present, past, and future in our cookpots, the herbs of our imaginations season it, and then we share. And the entire world is better, more elevated, more enlightened, frankly, more fly for us having shared. What we do is Black Magick at its more Platonic level. We've taken all that we've been given (or deprived of) and made a way for ourselves, and the world, that is nothing short of miraculous. And we've done this with a simple conjure formula: Imagination x Will + Focus = Result.

I'm excited for what's conjured next.

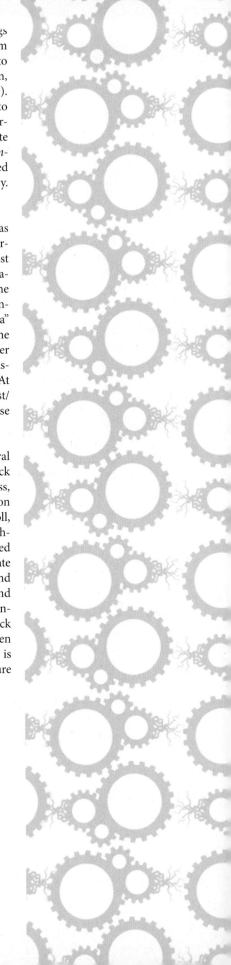

"Call them from their houses and teach them to dream."
– Jean Toomer

FORD SANGERYE AND THE CLEANSING POWER OF BLACK ANGER

ASLUM KHAN is a published and prize-winning freelance writer, blogger, and amateur comics historian and scholar. He currently resides in Chicago where he runs EmEyeSee, a Facebook group dedicated to promoting the participation of people of color in the arts, entertainment, and popular culture.

For every Booker T. Washington, there is a W.E.B. DuBois. For every Martin Luther King, there is a Malcolm X, and for every Ma Etta Sangerye, there is a Ford, ready to drive the struggle forward to victory.

As philosophy Professor Myisha Cherry explained in a 2020 *Atlantic Monthly* article, **"Fear…motivates us to run away. Anger, however, motivates us to run toward a target."** In the universe of *Bitter Root*, no one runs toward his targets faster than Ford, the Sangerye family's southern, Black-clad, gun-toting slayer of evil Jinoo monsters. As he explains in his first appearance, "I don't purify. I amputate," in direct contrast to his northern cousins' desire to simply cleanse the scourge of hatred that has invaded their community. While his family saves the infected, Ford declares that the "[d]ays of purifying are over. Ain't enough rootwork in the world to purify 'em all. All we can do is kill 'em." To those realizing that David F. Walker, Chuck Brown and Sanford Greene's *Bitter Root* is a parable for the battle against racism, this statement might read like a threat. "What about nonviolent resistance?" they might ask. "Can't we all just get along?" Ford Sangerye was likely just getting along before his war against evil began. Like the Black Panther Party though, rather than waiting for the trickle-down social policy of appeasement to get around to him, Ford has decided to uproot the whole tree so the evil can never grow back and harm him or his family again.

To understand the Ford Sangerye mentality, it is useful to understand the world he inhabits, as presented in *Bitter Root*. A historical fiction, *Bitter Root* is explicitly set in 1924, five years after the Red Summer of 1919, and three years after the Tulsa Race Massacre of 1921. Both dates are directly mentioned in its story, as both represent specific outbreaks of hate against Black people, the kind of outbreaks that creates *Bitter Root's* Jinoo. The Jinoo are an outward manifestation of that hate, consuming the hater until s/he becomes a literal monster, violently consuming all who incur its wrath. In 1919, Black veterans who returned from fighting World War I were the objects of a kind of pure hatred. Spurred on both by President Woodrow Wilson's plea to make the world "safe for democracy" and W.E.B DuBois's belief that military service would finally earn Black people the respect and human dignity they had long been denied, they believed that, as DuBois put it, "[w]e of the colored race have no ordinary interest in the outcome [of the war]. That which the German power represents today spells death to the aspirations of Negroes and all darker races for equality, freedom and democracy." Instead of that equality and freedom however, Black World War I veterans met harsh resistance from their own country as Ku Klux Klan membership skyrocketed during the period of unprecedented racial violence that we now call "The Red Summer." In just the months of April through November 1919, historians recorded 27 riots and 97 lynchings, forcing the Black war vets to utilize their newly acquired military training to defend their own homes and businesses. When Black sharecroppers in Elaine, Arkansas tried to organize for rights, they ultimately lost over 200 men, women and children to Klan violence. W.E.B DuBois's tune changed accordingly, reacting to a violent clash at a church in Georgia by saying, "by the God of Heaven, we are cowards and jackasses if now that that [the] war is over, we do not marshal every ounce of our brain and brawn to fight a sterner, longer, more unbending battle against the forces of hell in our own land." Ford Sangerye is no such coward or jackass. He's just angry.

He has plenty of reason to be. Ford Sangerye's 1924 is also three years after the Tulsa Race Massacre that wiped out the prosperous Greenwood district of Tulsa, Oklahoma. This now-famous African American community was then commonly known as "The Black Wall Street" with its 35 square blocks of Black businesses, including lawyers, doctors, dentists, two Black newspapers, several grocery stores, movie theaters and even a hospital. Founded by Booker T. Washington himself, it was the wealthiest Black neighborhood in the country before it was not only destroyed by Jinoo-style hatred but that hatred's memory then suppressed, not to be officially acknowledged and rediscovered until the early 21st century. In Ford's time however, that hatred was widely celebrated, with its accompanying violence presaged in D.W. Griffith's 1915 commercially successful film *The Birth of a Nation*, where the Klan are the heroes and free, voting Blacks are depicted as usurpers. Though never directly stated, Ford's handiness with weaponry suggests that me may very well be one of these disenfranchised World War I veterans, watching as his people's political power and wealth was stripped away despite their sacrifice. The supernatural nature of *Bitter Root's* Jinoo just gives him something to release that sense of disenfranchisement on.

With the events of 1919 and 1921 still fresh in his mind, it's almost as if Ford knew that Black people would one day have to take back their own freedom, and decided to get to the bullet first because the ballot wouldn't help them anymore. Today, Black people have to prove that they matter in a society that only measures value in dollars and cents – it's more profitable to lock away people of color and get paid in corporate welfare than to purify society by getting at the roots of their bondage. It seems that the modern-day Ford Sangeryes of the world also strive to take their freedom by force, if not with violence then through economic empowerment, favoring the ownership represented by business people like Tyler Perry over the noble but ultimately long-awaited freedoms won by marching heroes like John Lewis. If the Jinoo truly do represent the effects of racism, Ford Sangerye represents a determination to force that change. By any means necessary.

"Ford" by Sanford Greene

"*The truth is...everything counts. Everything. Everything we do and everything we say. Everything helps or hurts; everything adds to or takes away from someone else.*"

– *Countee Cullen*

BITTER TWITTER:

@BITTERROOT18 | @Cbrown803 | @sanfordgreene | @DavidWalker1201

BITTER TRUTHS curated and designed and edited by **John Jennings** / tw @JIJennings
Research Assistant: **Edgardo Delgadillo-Aguilera**

DESIGNING MONSTERS

LEILA TAYLOR author of *Darkly: Black History and America's Gothic Soul* is a writer and designer whose work is focused on the gothic in Black culture, horror, and the aesthetics of melancholy. Her work has been published in *The Journal of Horror Studies, The New Urban Gothic,* and *The Repeater Book of the Occult*. She has given talks for the International Gothic Association in Mexico and the U.K. and Morbid Anatomy in New York. She received an MFA from Yale University and an MA in Liberal Studies at The New School for Social Research. She lives in Brooklyn, New York where she is Creative Director for Brooklyn Public Library.

At the 1900 Exposition Universelle in Paris, W. E. B. Du Bois exhibited a series of graphs, charts, and diagrams illustrating Black Americans' social and economic growth since emancipation. The goal of "The Exhibit of American Negroes" was to show the world the accomplishments of Black people in America and to counter the false narrative that the descendants of enslaved people were ignorant, incapable of growth or creativity, and unable to thrive. Du Bois displayed 60 illustrations with the somewhat wordy title *A Series of Statistical Charts Illustrating the Condition of the Descendants of Former African Slaves Now in Residence in the United States of America*. With data collected from students and alumni from Atlanta University, Du Bois centered the Black experience in this sociological study countering the pseudo-scientific propaganda of biological determinism, interpreting the data in techniques designed to inform and uplift. Long before the term "data visualization" was coined, Du Bois knew that a story could be told with pictures, that statistics are more than dots and lines on a page. He knew that those numbers represented people worth counting and lives worth documenting. These weren't dry, black and white tables. These were creative interpretations that spoke to Black modernity, abstract, colorful, and inventive images that would fit comfortably on the walls of the Museum of Modern Art. It's not only about showing the data. It's about how you draw the story.

It may seem incongruous to compare a gothic comic book to a series of information graphics, but Du Bois' work was made right at the cusp of the Harlem Renaissance when *Bitter Root* takes place, a boom of Black creativity and intellectual expansion. Also, the study's idea came from a work of speculative fiction called "The Princess Steel." In the story, Du Bois imagined a **megascope**, a tool for sociological study with which the viewer could see the past, the future, and "The Great Near" his term for the systemic machinations of the "Over-men." These were the people "guiding the world events and dominating the lives of men." The megascope allowed for a view across the color line, revealing the cost of colonialism and capitalist exploitation.

Bitter Root and *A Series of Statistical Charts* are two sides of the same coin to me. They are both visualizations of the impact of racism. What does racism look like? I don't mean how it's performed, how it's enacted, or enabled. I mean, what does the **feeling**, the rage and the madness, look like? I imagine if the Sangerye family were to look through Du Bois megascope, they'd see something resembling a Jinoo.

The brilliantly visceral art in *Bitter Root* depicts white supremacy for the ugly, scary, and grotesque thing that it is. The Jinoo are massive ogres with bulging muscles, blackened claws, yellow eyes, horns, and gaping mouths with sharp fangs and long pointed tongues. Underneath Klan robes are goblin looking creatures with orange eyes, green skin, and pointy ears. The sickness, the corruption that is white supremacy looks on the outside what it is on the inside. Black folks aren't immune to the curse. "Souls tainted by hate" and "ravaged by great sorrow and pain" become Inzondo. The visual difference is clear. Having survived the Tulsa massacre of 1921, Dr. Sylvester's fury and driving need for retribution transforms him into a different looking monster. It is massive in scale, ears pointed, red-eyed with sharp teeth, but the Inzondo is still vaguely human. It's the embodiment of fury but he retains something of its previous self. You can see a bit of the man inside the monster. It's an important distinction; the oppressor's rage is not the same as the oppressed.

You need images to make white supremacy work. Race, as an invention, had to be made manifest. It had to be visible; it had to look like something to keep the engine running. It needed (for lack of a better word) branding. In the episode "Jig-A-Bobo" of the HBO series *Lovecraft Country*, director Misha Green brings to life the stereotypical Topsy image from *Uncle Tom's Cabin*. The illustration on the book cover is the marketing image; Topsy is smiling sweetly with her arm around Eva, the pair standing in front of a mirror. Diana "Dee" Freeman (played by Jada Harris), is cursed by the police on her way home from the funeral of her friend Emmett Till. Two grotesque Topsys pursue and torment her, and the image on the book cover changes. The happy smile is stretched and distorted in a horrific grin, her haphazard braids with the red ribbons are a chaotic matted mess, and her elongated fingers become claws. The illustrated Topsy's eyes bulge as she gleefully smashes Eva's head into the mirror. The happy-go-lucky picaninny from the book cover is how racism is represented. The demonic Topsy is how it feels. But as frightening as these creatures may be, the ability to see the monster comes with the power to fight it.

One of my favorite charts of Du Bois' series is titled "Proportion of freemen and slaves among American Negroes." The line graph shows the percentage of Black people in slavery between 1790 and 1870. A large field of deep rich black represents the number of enslaved people topped with a sliver of vibrant green representing the free. Like a sharp drop off a cliff, the black plunges from 89% to 0%, the green filling in the gap. It is striking and dramatic. It looks like progress.

In *Bitter Root*, racism isn't just a practice or ideology. It is a snarling, slobbering grotesque beast, but like *A Series of Statistical Charts*, the real story isn't about the diagrams or the monsters. It's about the people and what they do about it. It's about the folks mixing the cures, fighting the battles, honoring the ancestors, and teaching the youth. We see the scientists, the inventors, the intellectuals, and the warriors. If Du Bois' megascope reveals the injustice, Ma Etta's serum is going to cure it.

Notes

1 University., Atlanta, and W. E. B. (William Edward Burghardt) Du Bois. "[A Series of Statistical Charts Illustrating the Condition of the Descendants of Former African Slaves Now in Residence in the United States of America] Proportion of Freemen and Slaves among American Negroes." Library of Congress, January 1, 1970. https://www.loc.gov/pictures/item/2014645356/.

2 Du Bois, W.E.B. "The Princess Steel, 1905?" Credo, credo.library.umass.edu/view/full/mums312-b236-i001.

3 B., Du Bois W. E., Whitney Battle-Baptiste, and Britt Rusert. W.E.B Du Bois's Data Portraits: Visualizing Black America. The W.E.B. Du Bois Center At the University of Massachusetts Amherst, 2018.

4 Green, Misha. "Jig-A-Bobo." Lovecraft Country, season 1, episode 8, 4 Oct. 2020. HBO.

5 Public domain, Library of Congress

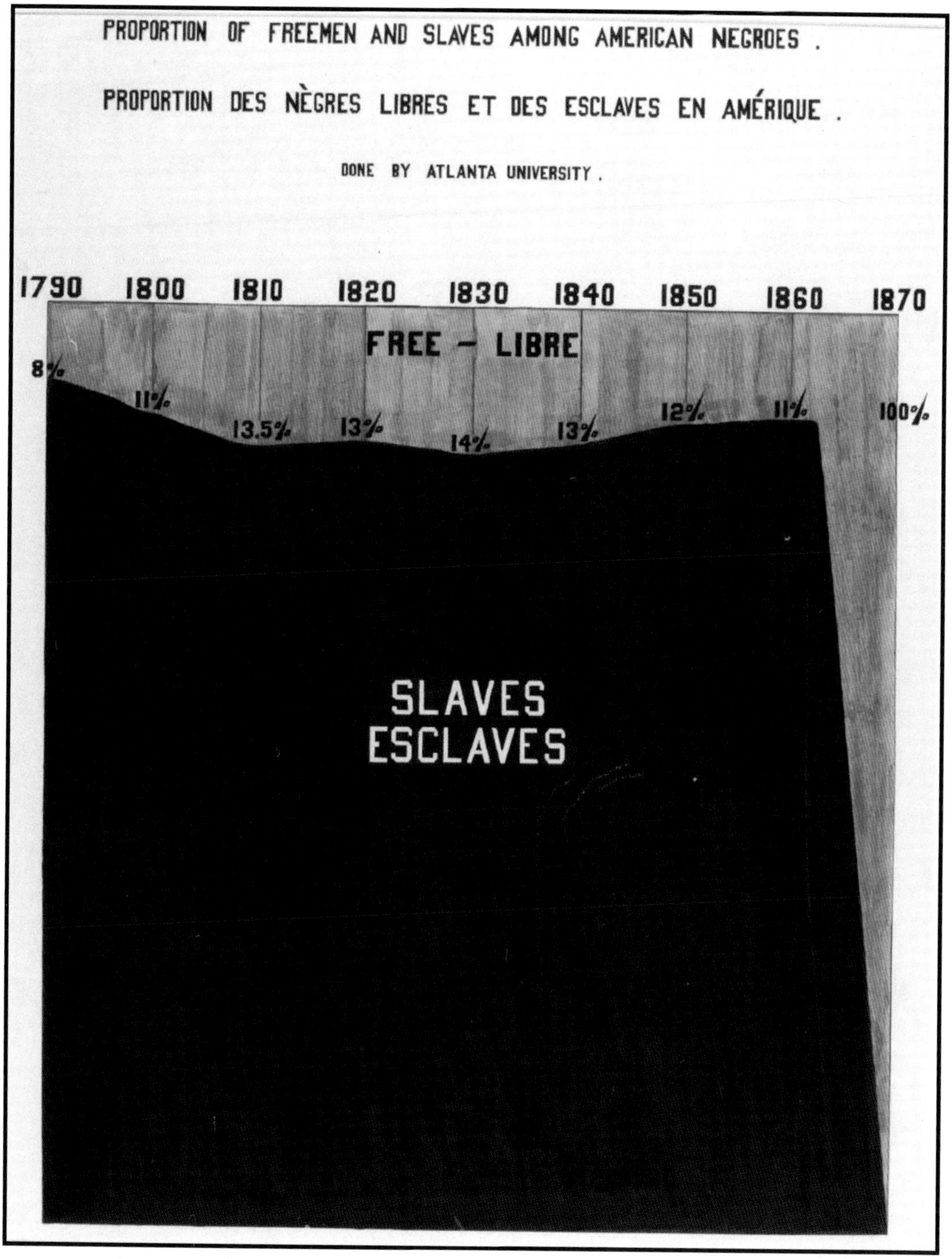
PROPORTION OF FREEMEN AND SLAVES AMONG AMERICAN NEGROES .
PROPORTION DES NÈGRES LIBRES ET DES ESCLAVES EN AMÉRIQUE .
DONE BY ATLANTA UNIVERSITY .
1790
1800
1810
1820
1830
1840
1850
1860
1870
FREE – LIBRE
8%
11%
13.5%
13%
14%
13%
12%
11%
100%
SLAVES
ESCLAVES

"A system cannot fail those
it was never meant to protect."

– W.E.B. DuBois

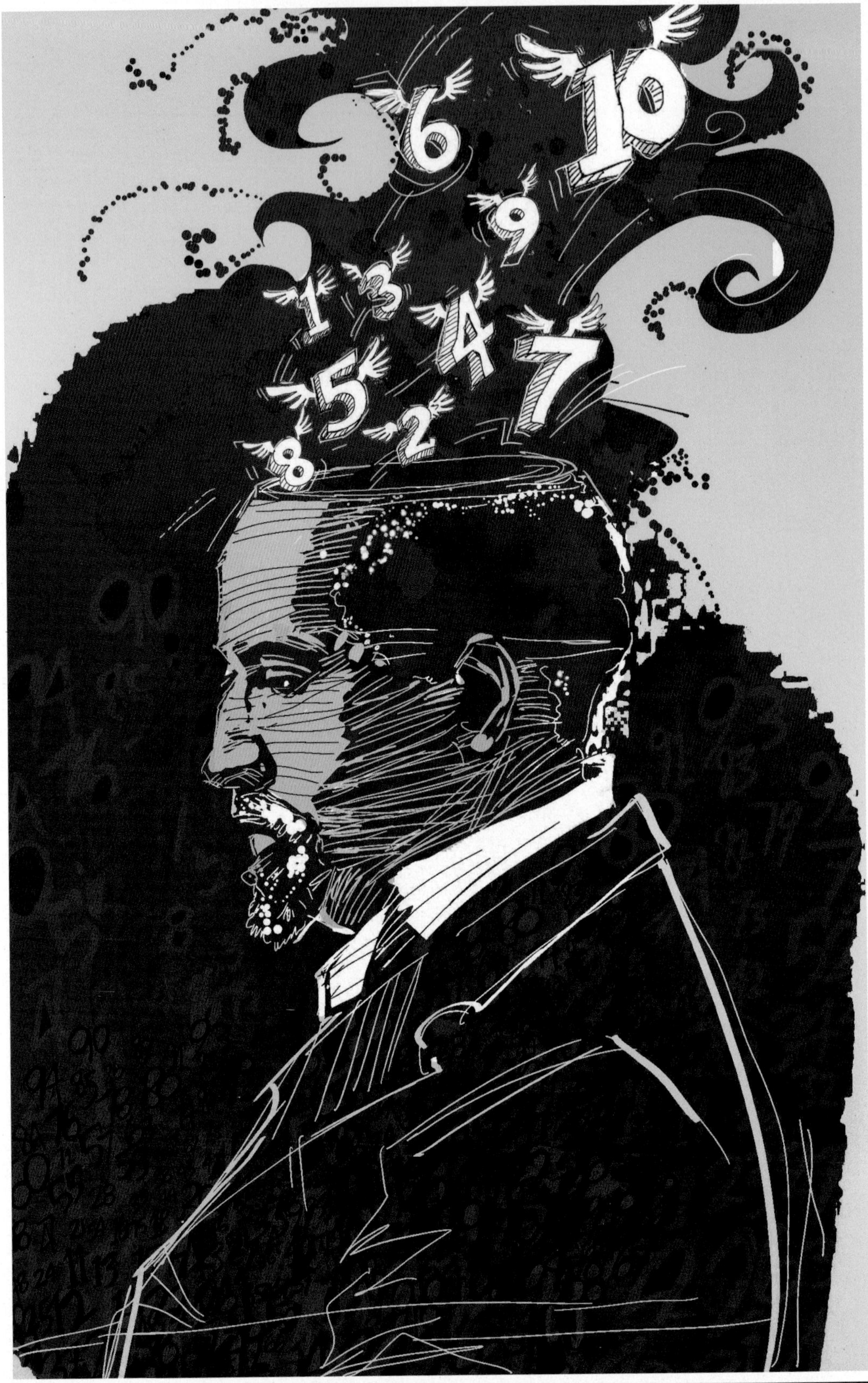

"DREAMING DuBOIS" by JOHN JENNINGS

BITTER TWITTER:

@BITTERROOT18 | @Cbrown803 | @sanfordgreene | @DavidWalker1201

BITTER TRUTHS curated and designed and edited by **John Jennings / tw @JIJennings**
Research Assistant: **Edgardo Delgadillo-Aguilera**

INTO THE AFROWEIRD ABYSS
CONTEMPLATING RACECRAFTIAN HORROR

JOHN JENNINGS is a Professor of Media and Cultural Studies at the University of California at Riverside. Jennings is co-editor of the Eisner Award-winning collection *The Blacker the Ink: Constructions of Black Identity in Comics and Sequential Art.* Jennings is also a 2016 Nasir Jones Hip Hop Studies Fellow with the Hutchins Center at Harvard University. Jennings' current projects include the horror anthology *Box of Bones,* the coffee table book *Black Comix Returns* (with Damian Duffy), and the Eisner-winning, Bram Stoker Award-winning, *New York Times* best-selling graphic novel adaptation of Octavia Butler's classic dark fantasy novel *Kindred.* Along with *Kindred* co-adaptor Damian Duffy, he has also earned a 2021 Hugo Award nomination for their work on the *Parable of the Sower* graphic novel. Jennings is also founder and curator of the ABRAMS Megascope line of graphic novels and recently released the first book in the series entitled *After the Rain.* It is an adaptation of superstar author Nnedi Okorafor's short story *On The Road.*

When we think of symbolism and monsters it's very hard to not be reminded of the work of H.P. Lovecraft. Lovecraft lived from August 20, 1890 to March 15, 1937. In his forty-six years on the planet he managed to create a large body of works for the nascent pulp magazine publications of the time. He was definitely part of why *Weird Tales,* a science fiction and fantasy magazine of the time, was so successful. One could even state that the genre of "weird fiction" was created to describe Lovecraft's oeuvre. This type of horror that focused on the sense of cosmic awe afforded by seeing the unseeable was dubbed "Lovecraftian Horror" and it has influenced so many creators after him like Stephen King, Ramsey Campbell, John Carpenter and Clive Barker. His main contributions were his methods of creating an eerie sense of dread through his antiquated word usage. He also created a deranged pantheon of mad gods who came from outer space and were so ancient and so massive in scope that they were far beyond what mankind could possibly comprehend. He also was very well read and into the latest scientific theories and he integrated these into his stories. Lovecraft was obsessed with the idea that man was basically insignificant in the expanse of the universe and that the cosmos cared not if we lived or died and neither did the Great Old Ones; pitiless gods who barely noticed our existence. His great inventions included the amphibious creatures the Deep Ones, the mystical book of spells called the Necronomicon, and the sleeping god Cthulhu who waited in the ocean to rise and destroy all life on the planet. Lovecraft created an open-source connected universe that he allowed other writers to participate within. They did so and have helped push his ideas into almost every aspect of popular culture. His work gave us a structure on how to utilize the technology of the monster to talk about symbolic representations of our ideas of society. H.P. Lovecraft's other legacy was that for most of his life he was an almost prototypical xenophobe and racist. The horror of the unknown and the lurking monsters in the dark were all allegory for the author's intense fear of people who were not like him.

Because Lovecraft's work was so ubiquitous and influential, it's attracted a great deal of attention by an international collection of fans from various communities and this includes BIPOC creators. Over the last few years there has been an uptick in minority creators making Lovecraftian horror stories but also directly engaging with the inherently problematic racist and anti-immigrant messages in Lovecraft's body of work. For instance, Victor LaValle's brilliant remixing of Lovecraft's story "The Horror at Red Hook" becomes a timely examination of racism and xenophobia in the guise of his novella *The Ballad of Black Tom. Harlem Unbound,* a tabletop role playing game from Chaosium Inc., merges Lovecraft's Cthulhu Mythos with a detective story set in the middle of the Harlem Renaissance. *Bitter Root* also has some Lovecraftian tropes in it as well. From the use of technology to fight monstrously infected humans to unexplainable entities from other dimensons, *Bitter Root* also has some of the Old Ones in its DNA. Of course another prime example of this retooling and critical making oriented literary practice is Matt Ruff's novel *Lovecraft Country.* The book and also the critically acclaimed HBO program do a lot of work related to dissecting H.P. Lovecraft's work while also celebrating his intensely visionary world-building. However, what kind of world was he building with his stories?

I recently came across a book written in 2012 by Barbara J. Fields and Karen E. Fields. The book title of this book is, *Racecraft: The Soul of*

Inequality in American Life. The main argument of the collection of essays is that racism is a belief system and that race is an artifact of that belief system and that over the centuries race has managed to present itself as natural. They get the term "racecraft" from their comparison to how "witchcraft" works. Witchcraft makes these strange leaps in logic around causality that do map very well onto how we have been socialized to think about race. Long ago, when a newborn calf got sick in a village, the townsfolk would automatically think that it had to be witchcraft and not a naturally occurring virus. The witch that cast this spell must then be rooted out and killed. This, of course, led to many women being tortured and killed for no reason. In racecraft, black skin marks a human being as violent, grotesque, evil, hypersexual, lazy and so many other negative traits. This leads to a host of unfair practices projected upon black people. Again, no true causal connection is apparent, as the Fields states but, because of societal beliefs these connections are treated as fact. The very thought of this is horrific because we can see this playing out in the history of our country. We can see it playing out right now in real time with the George Floyd murder case being broadcast every day on CNN.

This existential dread connected to black identity and its dark constrictions is what made me ponder the affordances of what I call "Racecraftian Horror." It borrows from the tenets of Weird Fiction but both subverts and critiques it through changing the viewpoint to a decidely more black cultural lens. The Weird morphs and bends into the AfroWeird.

In Racecraftian Horror, the grotesque monster in the dark is racism and its associated effects. Race itself would function like an ancient technology and its monsters would act as nested destructive systems. Lovecraft wrote about uncaring oblivious gods from other dimensions. I feel that Racecraftian horror would be more focused on the darkness deep within the human psyche. Racecraftian horror would see black protagonists using, as John Akomfrah put it, "black secret technologies" against the ancient evil systems of racial injustice. These technologies would be powerful enough to render victories for black people or at least a draw regarding the resolution of conflicts.

Racecraftian Horror as a genre is still a work in progress, but I think that there are some interesting interventions that can result by looking at the tropes of Weird Fiction and also by interrogating Lovecraft's work and its popularity. In the end, I feel we will parse out which is more fearful a phrase: "the haunter in the dark" or "I can't breathe." That is, if we dare to look into the abyss that is ourselves.

RACECRAFT

*The Soul of Inequality
in American Life*

KAREN E. FIELDS and BARBARA J. FIELDS

"When you believe in things that you don't understand then you suffer."

– Stevie Wonder

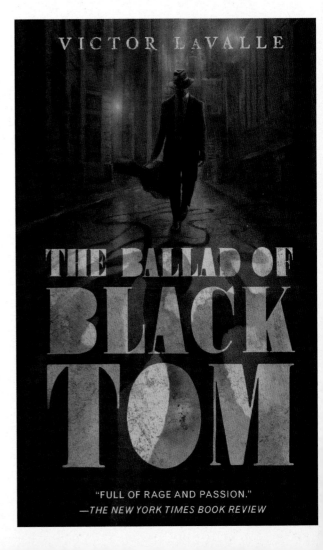

VICTOR LAVALLE

THE BALLAD OF BLACK TOM

"FULL OF RAGE AND PASSION."
—THE NEW YORK TIMES BOOK REVIEW

NEW BLOOD

***an interview with* author**

KENESHA WILLIAMS

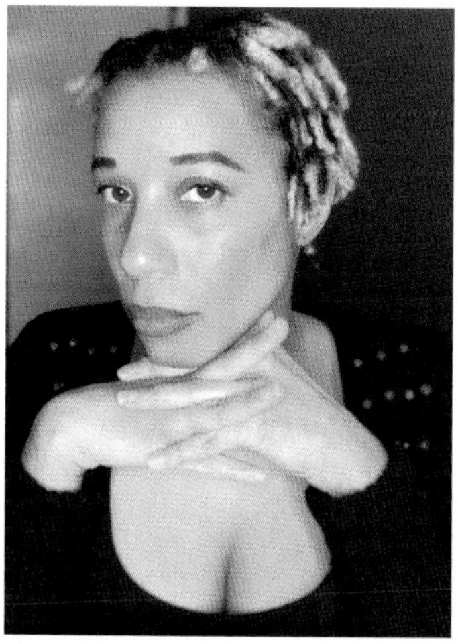

KENESHA WILLIAMS is an author, screenwriter, and essayist. As an essayist she has written for *Time* magazine's millennial imprint, Motto and Fireside Fiction. She lives in the DC Metro area with her husband, three sons, and a feisty cat named Leia. You can catch up with her on her website www.keneshaisdope.com. Kenesha's latest short story, "The Rhythm of War," will be featured in the forthcoming anthology, *Sorghum & Spear: The Way of Silk and Stone.*

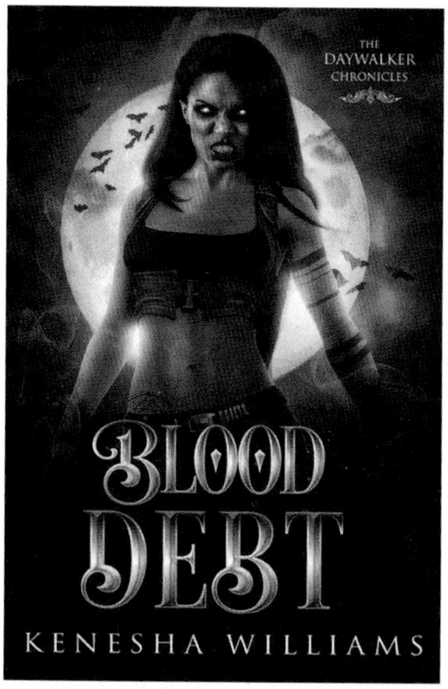
THE DAYWALKER CHRONICLES
BLOOD DEBT
KENESHA WILLIAMS

BT: How long have you been writing professionally and what was the piece that made you realize that this was something that you wanted to do on this level?

KW: In 2012, I was published in a literary magazine, Haunted Waters Press' *From the Depths;* that was the first time I'd submitted prose to a publication that wasn't for school and I thought to myself, hey maybe I can do this. After that publication, I began writing more seriously and started to find my voice as a writer. The second validation was when I started thinking about screenwriting and I entered a contest run by ***The Blacklist's*** blog, Go Into the Story.

I had to send in a logline, a writing sample, and a writer's resume. My resume was pretty thin, my sample was the first three chapters of a novel I was writing, and my logline was for a psychological horror script. I placed, but didn't win. The judge of the contest reached out to me and told me that my writing and concept was really good and took me on as a student. I would say that those two experiences led me to take my writing seriously and consider myself a writer.

BT: Why horror? What is it about the genre that fascinates you?

KW: Horror is universal, but also can be very specific to a culture or a person. I think that's what fascinates me, being able to connect with others over shared fears and exorcise some of our personal traumas through genre because if the main character can make it out alive, so can we.

Horror is cathartic because it gives us a way to face our fears without the actual danger. Although consciously our brains know that we're safe in that theater seat or in our bed with the book light on, subconsciously we still get to experience that instinctual fight-or-flight response we'd have if we were actually in the situation we're reading about or watching. Horror also informs us about what to do in a dangerous situation or what not to do to avoid that situation entirely. It's why we're all screaming at the screen, Don't go in there! I think horror allows us to sharpen our survival instincts without having to actively engage in harm.

BT: Who are your horror heroes and heroines?

KW: My horror heroes and heroines include Tananarive Due, Brandon Massey, Stephen King, Octavia Butler, and L.R. (Lamar) Giles. I was introduced to Due, Massey, and Giles through *Dark Dreams: A Collection of Horror and Suspense by Black Writers*, edited by Brandon Massey. I had gone to a Black bookstore, and I asked the owner if they had any horror books by Black authors. At the time I read mostly literary fiction and contemporary fiction by Black authors, but wondered if there were any "official" Black horror authors. Now I had read horror from Butler and Morrison, but I didn't think of them as horror authors, but rather those who'd incorporated horror into their fiction. Now I don't make that distinction, but at the time I did. The owner pulled out *Dark Dreams,* and I was hooked. I then looked up Due, Massey, and Giles and found everything that they had written. I think that's when I truly felt like there could be a place for me in horror because I saw others like me doing it.

BT: How does your work engage with Black womanhood?

KW: My main characters are almost always Black women and because of that, their race and gender informs the situations that they find themselves in. I think a lot of my stories couldn't exist, as is, if I inserted another character of a different race or gender because the situations I put them in depend on how they navigate womanhood and Blackness and how they're seen by the outside world through the lens of race and gender.

BT: How does being a wife and mother inform your stories?

KW: Motherhood and marriage inform my stories by giving me more things to be afraid of. As a single person, your fears are tied up in your own personal safety and survival. But when you become responsible for others and their well-being, your fears magnify to encompass not only your safety but those who you love as well. I am the mother of three Black sons and although history has never been a safe space for Black bodies, the constant media coverage of police brutality and murder of boys and men who look like the people that I love and care for the most have given rise to new fears which, in turn, leads to more places to mine for horror stories.

BT: In your opinion, how can speculative fiction, especially horror engage with sociopolitical issues? Does your work deal with politics and if so how?

KW: I think horror is one of the best ways to engage with sociopolitical issues without it becoming "preachy." You can show readers the ills of the world and wrap it in entertainment so it's an easier pill to swallow. It lets you challenge a person's worldview without it seeming like an attack, but rather a question and makes the audience come up with the answers themselves.

I do have work that deals with sociopolitical issues, both nonfiction and fiction. I contributed to Journey Planet's, "The Future of Policing" issue, where we took stories in popular culture about policing and what that meant to the present or future of policing. I used Philip K Dick's, *Minority Report* as an example of a writer's work being concerned with the police state and the assumption that someone was a criminal based on factors other than actually committing a crime. That is a present that we currently live in, with arrests and brutality being brought upon Black bodies, because of an assumption of guilt simply because of race.

In my fiction, I often write about sexual or physical violence or the threat of that violence because unfortunately that's a universal experience for women. We're taught how to protect ourselves from becoming victims from a very young age and ironically if we become a victim we're often blamed for the violence inflicted on us. I believe readers are better able to empathize with characters in fiction and by creating narratives where women are victims, but also survivors, it creates empathy for women in those situations in real life. For that reason, I'm ecstatic that The Pixels Project, whose mission is to raise awareness, funds and volunteer power for the cause to end violence against women is including a reprint story of mine, "Sweet Justice" in their forthcoming anthology, *Giving The Devil His Due.*

BT: What are some of your favorite horror comics?

KW: My favorite horror comics are *Bitter Root*, of course, *Killadelphia, Locke & Key, Is'nana the Werespider, Nailbiter, The Chilling Adventures of Sabrina, Abbott, Farmhand*, and *Something is Killing the Children.*

BT: What inspires your stories?

KW: My inspiration comes from a lot of places; history, my own and events or figures in American history, but also from the What If process. Sometimes, just going about my daily life I will observe someone and wonder, what if...conjecturing about their life or who they are and that will inspire a story. Or sometimes taking a familiar trope or monster and saying, what if and turning the trope on its head.

BT: What are you working on now?

KW: I am currently working on the script for a one-shot horror comic with 133 Art. I pitched it with this as the logline: A madam must protect her saloon and a teenage runaway she's harboring from a zombie virus that gold miners unwittingly have unearthed in the canyons of Santa Clarita.

I set the comic during the Gold Rush of 1850 because I wanted to engage with the Old West as it actually was, and that's a hell of a lot more diverse than it's represented in most pop culture. The mythical West isn't an accurate representation of the multi-cultural landscape that was the actual American West. There were immigrants from China to build railroads, the Native Americans that are usually reduced to caricatures and enemies of white cowboys, and of course Black people yearning for freedom and opportunities not afforded to them in the South.

BITTER TWITTER:

@BITTERROOT18 | @Cbrown803 | @sanfordgreene | @DavidWalker1201

BITTER TRUTHS curated and designed and edited by **John Jennings / tw @JIJennings**
Research Assistant: **Edgardo Delgadillo-Aguilera**

WHY THE DARK STILL MATTERS

BY JOHN JENNINGS

SHEREE RENÉE THOMAS is an award-winning fiction writer, poet, and editor. Her work is inspired by myth and folklore, natural science and Mississippi Delta conjure. *Nine Bar Blues: Stories from an Ancient Future* (Third Man Books, May 2020) is her first all prose collection. She is also the author of two multigenre/hybrid collections, *Sleeping Under the Tree of Life* (Aqueduct Press July 2016), longlisted for the 2016 Otherwise Award and honored with a Publishers Weekly Starred Review and *Shotgun Lullabies* (Aqueduct January 2011). She edited the World Fantasy-winning groundbreaking black speculative fiction anthologies, *Dark Matter* (2000 and 2004) and is the first to introduce W.E.B. Du Bois's science fiction short stories. Her work is widely anthologized and appears in *The Big Book of Modern Fantasy* edited by Ann & Jeff VanderMeer (Vintage, 2020). She is the Associate Editor of the historic Black arts literary journal, *Obsidian: Literature & the Arts in the African Diaspora*, founded in 1975 and is the Editor of *The Magazine of Fantasy & Science Fiction*, founded in 1949. She also writes book reviews for *Asimov's*. She was recently honored as a 2020 World Fantasy Award Finalist in the Special Award – Professional category for contributions to the genre and is the Co-Host of the 2021 Hugo Awards Ceremony at Discon III in Washington, DC with Malka Older. Sheree is the Guest of Honor of Wiscon 45 and a Special Guest of Boskone 58. She is a Marvel writer and contributor to the groundbreaking anthology, *Black Panther: Tales of Wakanda* edited by Jesse J. Holland. She lives in her hometown, Memphis, Tennessee near a mighty river and a pyramid.
contact: shereereneethomas.com

When I took on curating and designing *Bitter Truths*, I did so thinking about the good that a space like this could do. I knew that what Chuck, Sanford, and David were planning was going to be special. Once I heard the premise of the story, I was in! For the last thirteen issues of *Bitter Root*, this space has tried to provoke, prod, question, emancipate, and educate. Well, I wanted to take this time to add one more action to that list. I wanted to **celebrate!** Therefore, for this one issue, we're not dealing with the "bitter truth," we are dealing with the **Sweet Truths** of what it means to be Black and alive in this moment. Right now, there has been a huge change across many mediums related to Black speculative cultures. It seems that the so-called "mainstream" has finally seen the power and creative prowess of Black people and the people of the African Diaspora. They've finally caught up to what we've always known and it's about time!

One of the first griots and oracles to see this was the amazing editor, author, and poet **Sheree Renée Thomas**. This prescient Black Southern woman saw the connections. She saw what was coming. Sheree saw the history, the change and the need and she did something about it. A few years after the term "Afrofuturism" was coined, she started re-imagining what Black Literature looked like. While still living in Harlem, she pored over countless tomes at the Schomburg Center for Research in Black Culture; looking for the history of the future. The Schomburg, in some ways, is the repository of the Harlem Renaissance. So, it makes sense that she would look there for the beginnings of Black speculation. What she found was that writers like Zora Neale Hurston, Charles Chestnutt, George Schuyler, and others were really using speculative fiction to write about the tensions of being this thing called "Black" and the problems and joys that came with it. From magical chairs and conjure women to falling comets and ships filled with bones, she sorted out our ancestral imaginings that were right under our noses.

When she came out of her wondrous journey into Black pasts, presents and futures Sheree had put together the groundbreakingly masterful anthology *Dark Matter: A Century of Speculative Fiction from the African Diaspora (2000).* This and the follow-up *Dark Matter: Reading the Bones* (2004) gave us a guidebook to the most beautiful of stars. Here we found our analogs to Wells, Asimov, and Lovecraft. Here we saw the first inklings of W.E.B. DuBois as a writer of science fiction! Sheree tirelessly conceptualized a new way of thinking about the magical aspects of Black speculative work. Fusing the soulful brilliance of Harlem with the sweet red dirt of the American South, she became a pioneering editor, scholar, and author.

These days, you can find Sheree Renée Thomas doing both national and international lectures on her many works, editing multiple journals, and creating brand new collections of her own Black speculative works. Long before this new movement, she was there yelling to the skies that, yes Black lives, Black futures, Black dreams, Black pain, Black love, and Black imagination matters. They always mattered. Sometimes we just need reminding. Sheree, in her wisdom, saw this, and we owe her an eternal debt of gratitude. I know that I would not be doing what I am doing without her insightful and foundational work. We celebrate another Southern-born and bred genius; Sheree Renée Thomas. Thank you for your vision, persistence, courage and talent. We can't wait to see what else you pull from the beautiful darkness that is your glorious imagination!

A CENTURY OF SPECULATIVE FICTION FROM
THE AFRICAN DIASPORA
DARK MATTER
EDITED BY SHEREE R. THOMAS
INCLUDING WORK BY
STEVEN BARNES OCTAVIA E. BUTLER SAMUEL R. DELANY
TANANARIVE DUE JEWELLE GOMEZ WALTER MOSLEY
ISHMAEL REED AND MANY MORE

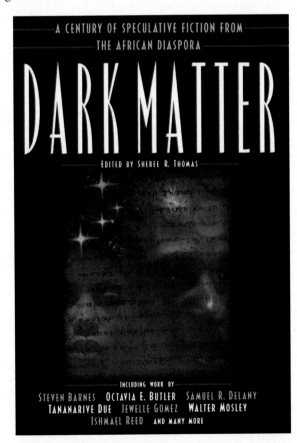

"Love makes your soul crawl out from its hiding place."

– Zora Neale Hurston

THE CONJURE MAN PAINTS

The Magical Canvasses of
PAUL LEWIN

BY JOHN JENNINGS

PAUL LEWIN is a fine artist and illustrator based in Miami, Florida. He was born in Kingston, Jamaica in 1973. His acrylic paintings utilize the folklore of the Caribbean mixed with the speculative storytelling aspects of fantasy, science fiction, and horror. His beautifully detailed work has graced the covers of the re-releases of Octavia E. Butler's *Parable of the Sower* and *Parable of the Talents*. He also illustrated the special edition of best-selling MacArthur Genius grant recipient NK Jemisin's award-winning anthology *How Long 'Til Black Future Month?*.

contact: paullewinart.com

I remember the first time I saw a painting by Paul Lewin. I was in awe of the detail, the care and the love in every canvas. Each piece of art is like a window to an intricate world of magic, mystery and folklore. Paul was born in Kingston, Jamaica and you can see the influences in the subject matter and the style.

His main subject matter tends to be iconic, multi-faceted, Black women who seem to be in tune with some kind of ancient or futuristic technology. Maybe it's both? Working primarily in acrylic paint, Paul pours his significant artistic acumen into something akin to a visual sigil. These ancestral spells weave connections between the disrupted peoples who were scattered by the slave trade via the Middle Passage. However, these images are not images of pain. They are images of wisdom, transcendence, and hope. They heal us when we see them. Paul reaches into his mojo bag and pulls out the right color, the right line, and the right composition to open up the cosmos on every masterpiece he makes. There are souls speaking in the mambos, birds, and shining artifices that decorate his work. There's magic there for sure. I can even see Ma Etta and Blink in these images. Yes, them and so much more.

The Crow and the Carnival Queen

BITTER TWITTER:

@BITTERROOT18 | @Cbrown803 | @sanfordgreene | @DavidWalker1201

BITTER TRUTHS curated and designed and edited by **John Jennings** / tw @JIJennings
Research Assistant: **Edgardo Delgadillo-Aguilera**

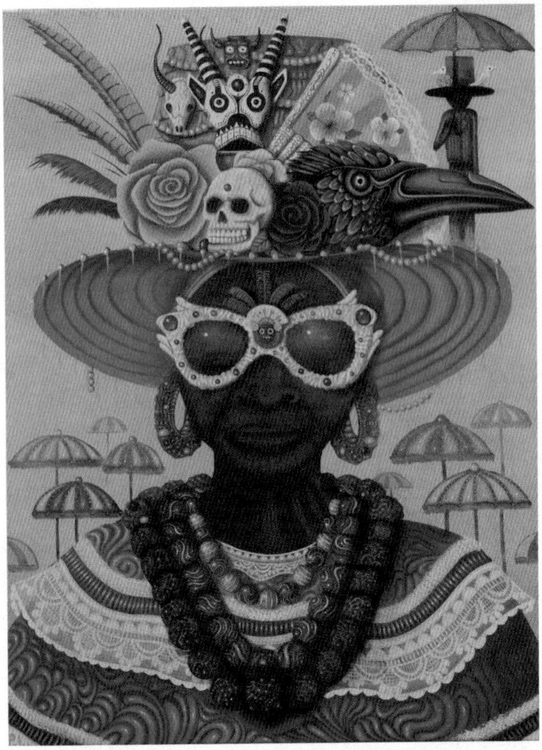

Zyla

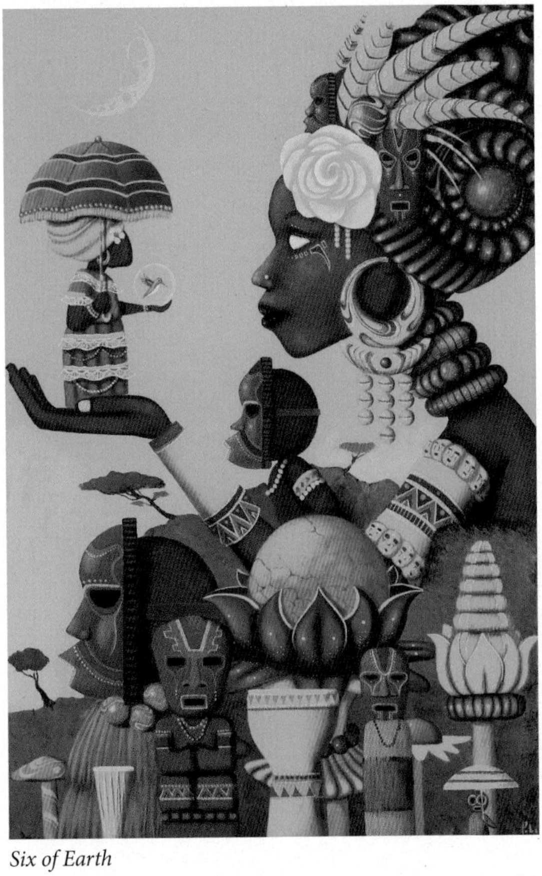

Six of Earth

SHORT INTERVIEW with PAUL LEWIN

What inspired you to become an artist?

I would say sci-fi, fantasy movies, and TV were my first inspirations to create art. I was addicted to getting lost in those worlds. I hated when my favorite movies or TV shows ended and I had to go back to "real life." Once I discovered that I could create my own worlds with pencil and paper, I was gone from there. My motivation to get better was to go deeper and further in my own worlds. Creativity and art were my therapy and my escape growing up. I was also inspired by my father who was a woodworker. He spent his days off from his job working on various woodworking projects. I feel that the same motivation that started me out is what continues to inspire my work today. I ultimately want to go deeper into that place where the visions come from.

Why do you make the conjure-inspired art pieces?

I began working on this series around 2011. I was at a point in my art making where I liked what I was doing visually but I wanted to create content that was more meaningful to me on a cultural level. I was inspired by the history and art of the Bay Area. The seamless fusion of art, politics, and history were very inspiring to me. It made me want to connect my art with my own cultural ancestry of Jamaica and the Caribbean. I began to research it and I came across folktales, rituals, and ways of living that have been passed down from generation to generation through the ancient art of storytelling. Much of it from Ancient Africa. A lot of this storytelling and creativity was a form of resistance. One of the first goals of colonization is to cut off a people from their ancestral roots. Around that time I took a trip back to Jamaica with my mom for the first time since I was a child. It was an incredible feeling to be back in my homeland. That's where the visions for this series began to take shape. Part of my research led me to Jamaican sci-fi authors such as Nalo Hopkinson. Her work was a huge inspiration to me at the time. I was fascinated by the way she infused Caribbean folklore with sci-fi and fantasy. Creating this series of works was my way of honoring the legacy of creative resistance that my ancestors lived.

What's your process like?

My process usually begins with the current piece I'm working on. There is always some part of it that I want to explore more or expand on. It could be a color scheme, a pattern, or a small section in the corner of the piece that I see something more in it. Sometimes that spark will grow into a full vision that becomes my next painting, or it may sit for a while until I'm ready to work on it much later. Some ideas could sit for years before I'm ready to work on them. One of the ways in which I choose my next piece is by whichever one is the loudest in my head. When an image gets to a point where it's all I can think about then I know it's the one I need to make happen. I don't always know the meaning behind the individual pieces. Each image forms after meditating on a few basic concepts: nature, folklore, sci-fi, science, and ancestry. I try to let each painting form on its own by not getting in the way too much.

ON MONSTROSITY

REBECCA WANZO is the author of *The Suffering Will Not Be Televised: African American Women and Sentimental Political Storytelling* (SUNY Press, 2009), which uses African American Women as a case study in exploring the kinds of storytelling conventions people must adhere to for their suffering to be legible to various institutions in the United States. Her most recent book, *The Content of Our Caricature: African American Comic Art and Political Belonging* (NYU Press, 2020), examines how Black cartoonists have used racialized caricatures to criticize constructions of ideal citizenship, as well as the alienation of African Americans from such imaginaries. Her research interests include African American literature and culture, critical race theory, fan studies, feminist theory, the history of popular fiction in the United States, cultural studies, theories of affect, and graphic storytelling. She has published in venues such as *American Literature*, *Camera Obscura*, *differences: A Journal of Feminist Cultural Studies*, *Signs*, *Women and Performance*, and numerous edited collections. She has also written essays for media outlets such as CNN, the *LA Review of Books*, and *Huffington Post*.

On April 9, 2014, white police officer Darren Wilson shot eighteen-year old Michael Brown. In his grand jury testimony, Wilson infamously said Brown's face looked "like a demon." This is just one example of a long history of African Americans being described as monstrous. Emerging from the enlightenment, theories of polygenesis—that there are varied origins for different races—were used to argue that Black people were not fully human. Rapist Gus in Thomas Dixon's *The Clansman* (1905) is a "beast" and sinks his "black claws" into the "soft white throat" of a symbol of pure white southern womanhood. This attack, modified for the sensibilities of delicate audiences, is the most famous scene in D.W. Griffith's *The Birth of a Nation*, the first blockbuster in the United States. Descriptions of "wilding" criminals in the 1980s was justification, to people like the 45th president, for the unethical treatment and wrongful incarceration of the Central Park Five. African Americans have often said, "they don't see us as human," in response to the many, many examples of police brutality. Some who hear the claim treat it as hyperbole, but there is so much evidence that Black people have been seen as something other than human in the long, brutal history of slavery, imperialism, and contemporary discriminatory practices.

Part of the work of *Bitter Root* is flipping the script on the narrative of Black monstrosity, a counter-narrative that Black people have always practiced in both real life and in fictions. James Baldwin argued that white people did not see him as human, and that white people in the United States had become "moral monsters." The refusal to see monstrosity in white supremacist violence is part of how racism does its work. People do not want to acknowledge that their ancestors committed monstrous acts, they do not want to admit that their loved ones are racist, or that structural racism continues. I remember watching the piece on the news about the 1898 Wilmington white supremacist coup d'etat, in which white insurrectionists destroyed the businesses of the Black middle class and drove Black elected officials out of town. A descendant of a white man who participated insisted on the goodness of his ancestor. Many people probably saw goodness in family pictures of family members smiling around lynched Black people. Burnt corpses, castrated men, and faces deformed from asphyxiation are the backdrops of photos and postcards with people celebrating their torturous murders of other human beings. African Americans worked to flip those representations too—as Leigh Raiford documented in *Imprisoned in a Luminous Glare*, white audiences would see the images as "evidence" of Black wrongdoing and construct a discourse of who can belong and be treated as citizens. In contrast, the Ida B. Wells and the NAACP would try to shift the way of looking at audiences, making it a call to arms to protect vulnerable Black people from extra legal violence.

And yet *Bitter Root* is also part of a tradition of Black creators rethinking the idea of Black male monstrosity, and seeing it as something birthed from racism. Richard Wright's *Native Son* (1940), explores what made a young African American man commit monstrous acts. In "How Bigger was Born," Wright writes that he "feels that the environment supplies the instrumentalities through which the organism expresses itself, and if that environment is warped or tranquil, the mode and manner of behavior will be affected toward deadlocking tensions or orderly fulfillment and satisfaction." Jeremy Love's masterpiece *Bayou* depicts spirits of Black people who have died from racist violence and cannot let go of what happened as monstrous Golliwog dolls in the afterlife. Victor

Bayou by Jeremy Love

LaValle takes on H.P. Lovecraft's racist treatment of Black people in his brilliant revision of "The Horror of Red Hook" (1925) with *The Ballad of Black Tom*, as a Black man made into a monster both tragically and triumphantly takes his vengeance. In *Destroyer*, LaValle's revision of *Frankenstein*, a Black boy murdered by the police is reanimated by his grieving mother, and he has the most humanity of all.

Dr. Walter Sylvester is a survivor of the Tulsa massacre in 1921, and was overcome by the loss of his children. He is a "villain" of *Bitter Root*, but his acts of violence are undeniably shaped by his grief. The different types of monsters, as we are repeatedly reminded in *Bitter Root*, are not the same. For the white characters, monstrosity is what happens when they commit acts of racist violence. It transforms their souls. They choose the path. Sylvester had agency, but violence proceeds his shift. To return to Wright—this is how Sylvester "was born," and violence and inequality are the root of intracommunity conflict and violence. To say this is not to say that Black people lack agency or are totally determined by environment. It is simply to say that the effects of anti-blackness are too much for some people to bear.

People often think that the best way to address racist histories and events is with realism—but these excesses cry out for generic recasting into the horror genre. The historical excesses often seem too excessive to be real. We should represent those, even though those representations are sometimes rejected as "trauma porn" and sensationalist depictions of Black pain. But there's something about the speculative imagination that contributes to the project of reframing histories in which Black activists and artists have always participated. Some people do not know these histories, but once they do, there is still something unrepresentable about the excesses of white supremacy, anti-black violence, and grief for what has been lost and what might have been. I think Black folks will always be trying to find new ways to represent events that you wish were fantastic, you hope could not be true. To crib Richard Wright, these monsters have been made up, because America already invented them.

"A monster is a person who has stopped pretending."
–Colson Whitehead

IT'S AFTER THE END OF THE WORLD

MICHAEL GILLESPIE is a film professor at the City College of New York and the Graduate Center, CUNY. His research focuses on film theory, black visual and expressive culture, popular music, and contemporary art. He is author of *Film Blackness: American Cinema and the Idea of Black Film* (Duke University Press, 2016); co-editor of *Black One Shot*, an art criticism on ASAP/J; and editor of Crisis Harmonies, a music criticism series on ASAP/J. His recent work has appeared in *Black Light: A Retrospective of International Black Cinema, Flash Art, Unwatchable, Film Quarterly*, and *Ends of Cinema*. His current book project is entitled *The Case of the 3 Sided Dream*.

Towards the conclusion of James Baldwin's 1976 book-length essay *The Devil Finds Work*, he writes of the "mindless and hysterical banality of the evil presented in *The Exorcist* [William Friedkin, 1973]." Unmoved and unconvinced by the reaction of white moviegoers to the film's seemingly unprecedented display of evil, Baldwin writes, "The Americans should certainly know more about evil than that; if they pretend otherwise, they are lying, and any black man, and not only blacks—many, many others, including white children—can call them on this lie; he who has been treated as the devil recognizes the devil when they meet." Baldwin's brutally sharp comment speaks to the enabling mechanisms of disavowal necessary to be shocked by the Satanic (supernatural) yet unmoved by the antiblack violence of white supremacy (natural). He tacitly suggests an equivalence between white supremacy and the demonic. This correlative gesture is a crucial feature of the *Bitter Root* comic series.

The worldmaking of *Bitter Root* entails a refabulation of the historical record of early 20th century America and African American life. With black visual and expressive culture as its animating force, the series operates as a historiographic operation at once retrofuturist and prescient. The series opens in 1920s Harlem in the midst of the Harlem Renaissance but still very much in the wake of the Red Summer of 1919 and the 1921 Tulsa Massacre. In one sequence from the series, Ford Sangerye discoveries a map that is a cartography of gateways to hell that corresponds to the sites of unrest during the summer of 1919. In this way the map charts a chilling correspondence between white supremacist terror and a trafficking in eternal damnation. *Bitter Root* centers on the Sangerye family's multigenerational hunting of monsters, humans who because of their racism have become demonic. Significantly there are disagreements over the terms and possibility of this saving. It poses an acute understanding of how psychic and spiritual susceptibility to the uncanny horror of America and otherworldly wickedness are dependent on the extent of an individual's wrongdoing or grief-ridden resignation. Attuned to Alain Locke's "New Negro" but with supernatural and arcane accents, the series sets forth the deliberate anachronism of neo-vernacular technology in the service of saving humanity from the underworld and itself. The issue of trauma manifests itself in a deeply affective persistence across the series narrative especially by the ways that it evinces monsters. More than merely a historical fiction or special issue exercise, *Bitter Root* offers a challenging devotion to the vast capacities of blackness as a cultural and aesthetic practice. In particular, its hoodoo alchemy horrorshow envisions history as a resource and not as a finite script.

Within this same vein of a retrofuturist devising, Dawolu Jabari Anderson's "Gullah Sci-Fi Mysteries" series (2007–2009) consists of poster-sized paintings designed as individual comic book covers. Reminiscent of Roy Lichtenstein's Pop Art isolation of a single comic frame with a word balloon, the series engenders a sense of narrativity at the level of the comic cover. With a dog-eared patina conceit, it conveys the worn intimacy of tales regularly revisited. As Anderson has stated, "The function of a comic book cover is to encapsulate the most striking components of a narrative into a one-page composition. Covers are often loaded with ambiguity and will play on what that imagery may possibly suggest. I sample imagery that I find to have a kind of condescending nostalgia transmitted through a one-dimensional narrative. I sample them and then refurbish these images. At the same time, it resuscitates them and gives them a new significance."

Set on and around a southern plantation, Anderson's covers feature figures such as Mammy, Remus, and Rastus. They are antebellum-informed relics that began circulating in the early 20th century in the commercial market transformed into trademarks in the service of Aunt Jemima Pancakes, Joel Chandler Harris's Uncle Remus series, and Cream of Wheat. Other figures include alligator-humanoids, a golem made of grits, John Henry, a Kool-Aid beast, Seminoles, and Madame Ethiopia. Madame Ethiopia, or Emereciana, is an extraterrestrial time traveler from the Bandung Dimension of Saturn. Bandung refers to the Indonesian city that hosted the Afro-Asian Conference (April 18-24, 1955). While the Bandung gathering hinted at the possibility of global and postcolonial solidarity, the series amends this spirit with galactic advocacy. Madame Ethiopia endows Mammy, Remus, and Rastus with cosmic energy that turns these symbols of dutiful domesticity and simple folksiness into super-powered beings. Transmogrified from less-than-human to more-than-human, Mammy becomes "Mam-E" once her cosmic broom is activated by the frequency of her voice. When he wears the Saturn Ring, Remus has the power to use his storytelling to induce mind control and also wields a tar baby, a receptacle for his psychic power that induces the feeling of being fathomlessly stuck in tar. Rastus psionically fashions shapes from the very farina. This symbolic act reclaims and weaponizes the porridge with the remediation of a product historically weaponized and wielded by its trademark. We are witnessing a sort of "Cream of Wheat" war game taking place on the canvas. These figures of Americana/antiblack visual culture demonstrate a kind of revenant materiality; the way that their empowered rendering disputes the deadening circulation and fetishism of their previous incarnation. Mam-E is still apron-clad and wears a gingham shirt with a handkerchief atop her head, but her buxomness is now more muscular than corpulent. Remus appears as raggedy-clad as his Joel Chandler Harris forebear, but in Anderson's work the "old Uncle" storyteller resembles the Hulk. Anderson's science-fictional mutation of the kindly old narrator calls for the destruction of the plantation rather than offering "Zip-a-Dee-Doo-Dah" platitudes. These tales are bannered as "mysteries" authored by the slave descendants of the Sea Islands as an alternate conception and serialization of the plantation tradition. Linking the Motherland and the Mothership, the Afrofuturist charge of the series refashions these figures of dispossession and service as galactic vernacular beings. Be it an epic struggle against demonic hordes on 125th or clashes between cosmically endowed trademarks, *Bitter Root* and the "Gullah Sci-Fi Mysteries" series each demonstrate a staging of the black speculative tradition towards plotting new avenues of pleasure, freedom, and sedition.

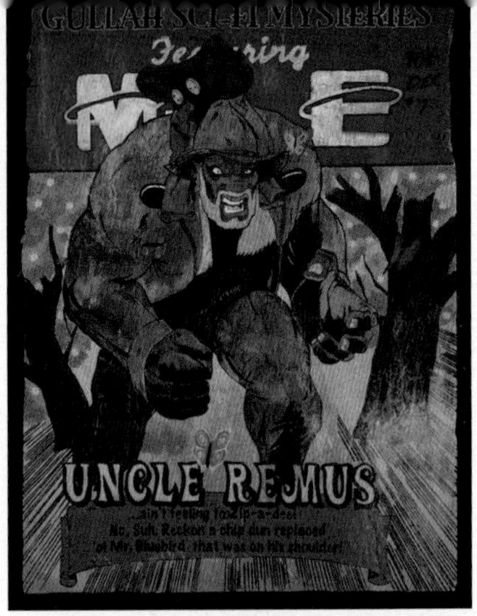
GULLAH SCI-FI MYSTERIES
UNCLE REMUS

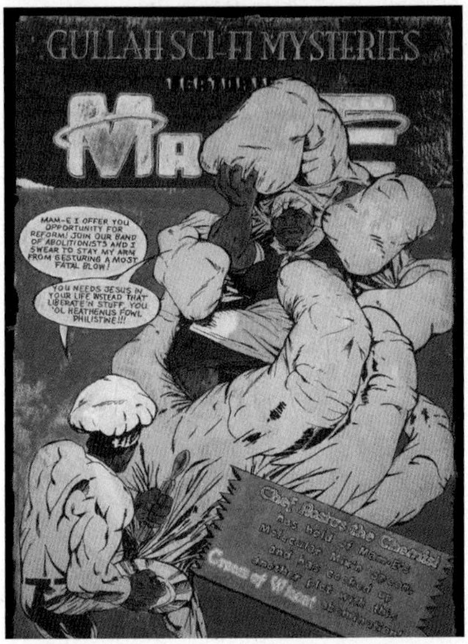
GULLAH SCI-FI MYSTERIES
MAM-E I OFFER YOU OPPORTUNITY FOR REFORM! JOIN OUR BAND OF ABOLITIONISTS AND I SWEAR TO STAY MY ARM FROM GESTURING A MOST FATAL BLOW!
YOU NEEDS JESUS IN YOUR LIFE INSTEAD THAT LIBERATE'N STUFF, YOU 'OL HEATHENUS FOWL PHILISTINE!!!

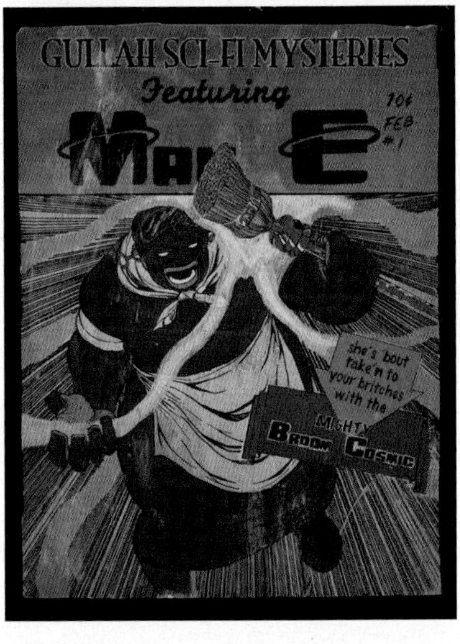
GULLAH SCI-FI MYSTERIES
Featuring
10¢
FEB
#1
she's 'bout take'n to your britches with the
MIGHTY
BROOM COSMIC

BITTER TWITTER:

@BITTERROOT18 | @Cbrown803 | @sanfordgreene | @DavidWalker1201

BITTER TRUTHS curated and designed and edited by **John Jennings / tw @JIJennings**
Research Assistant: **Edgardo Delgadillo-Aguilera**

PROCESS

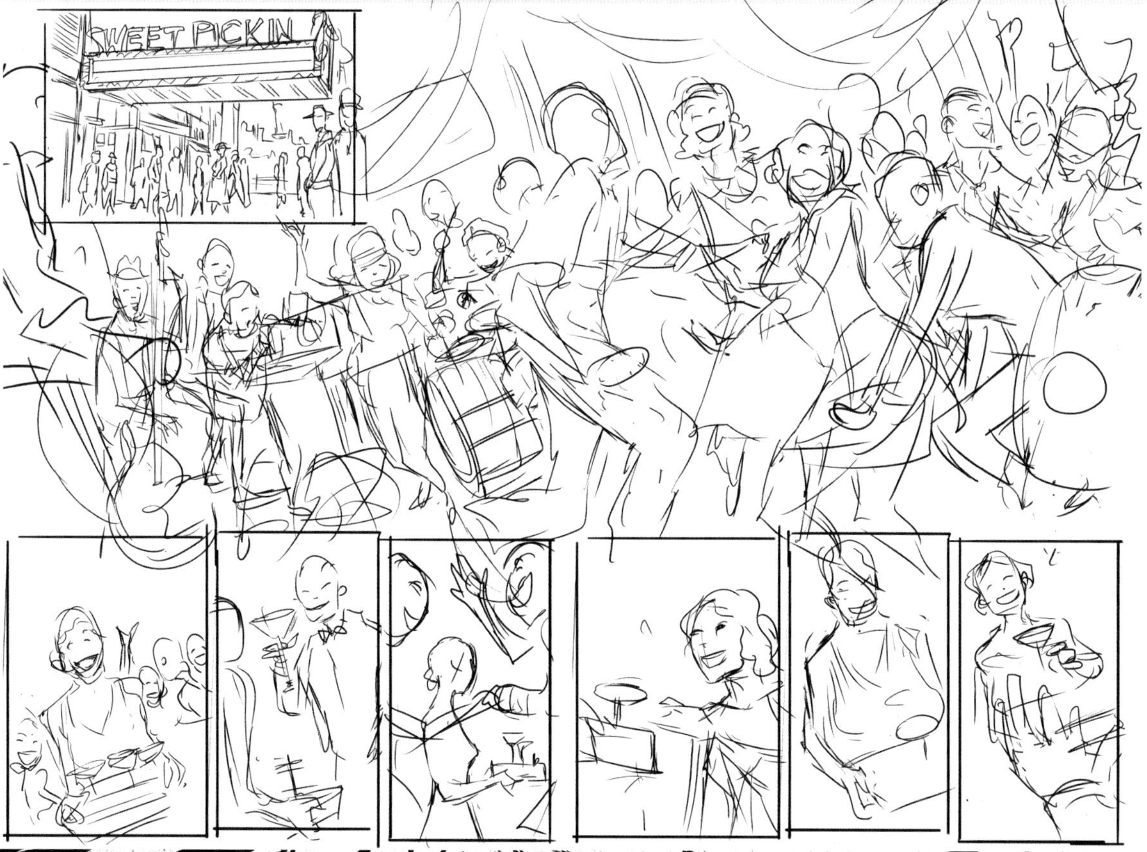
SWEET PICKIN

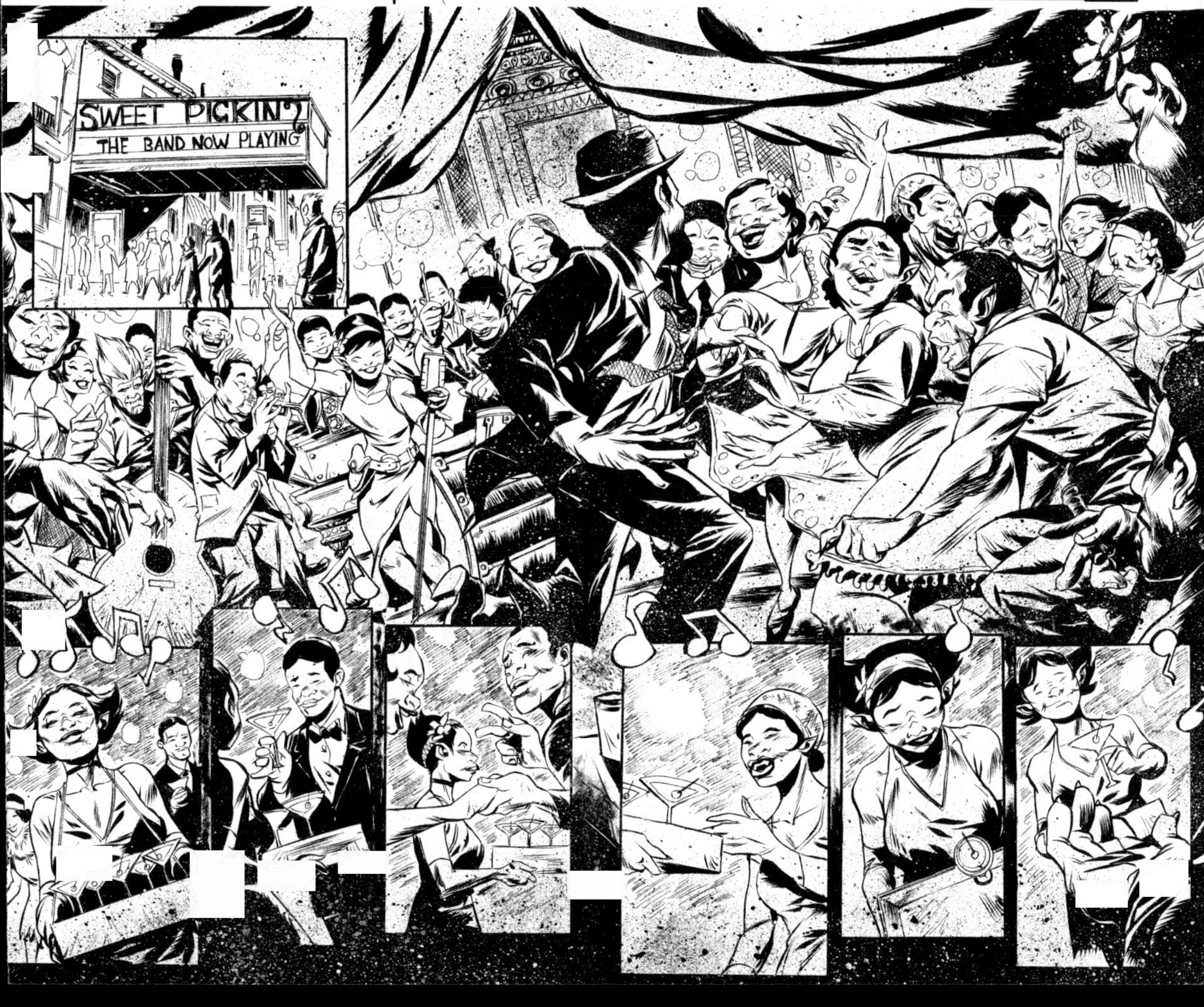
SWEET PICKIN'
THE BAND NOW PLAYING

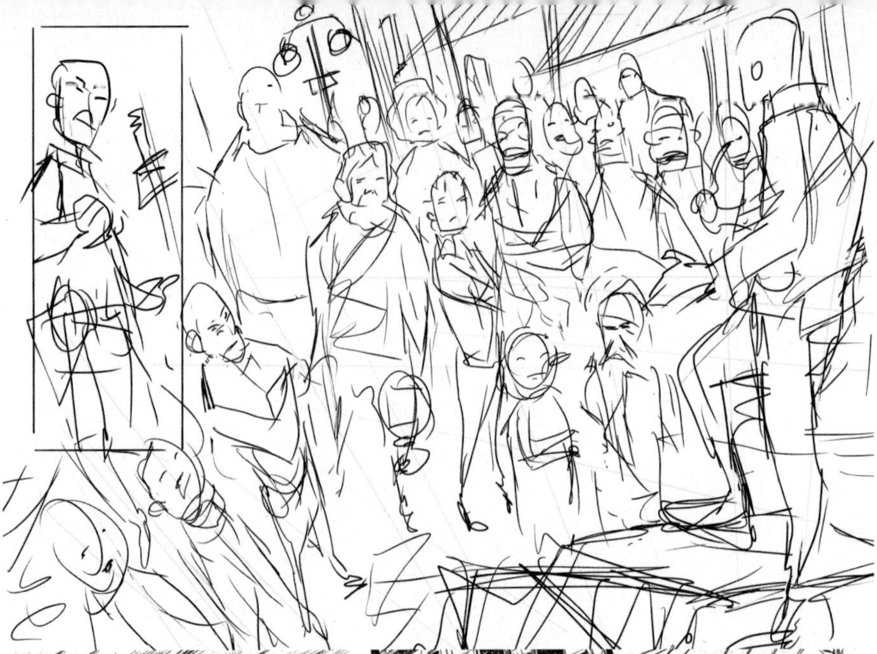
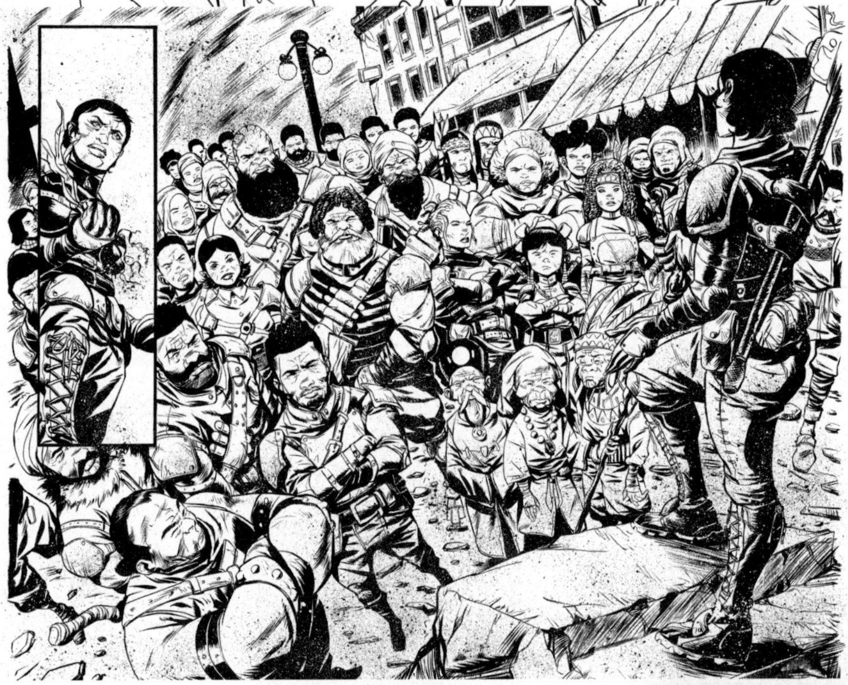
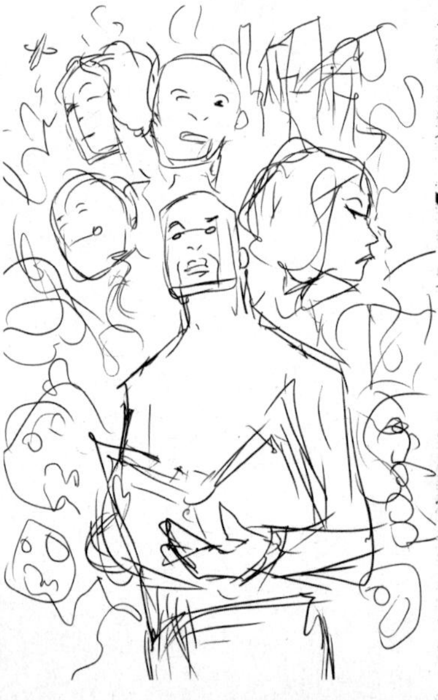
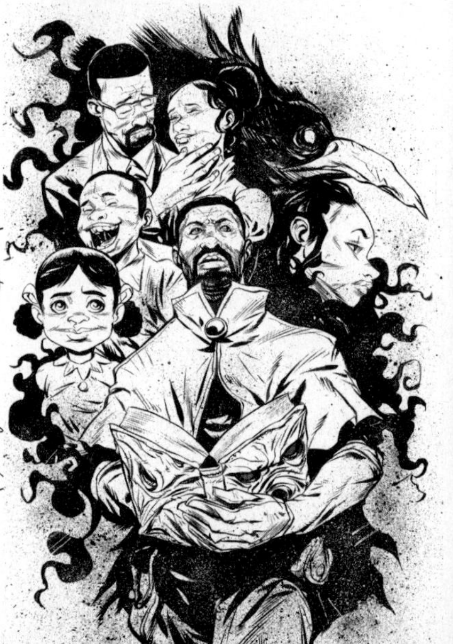
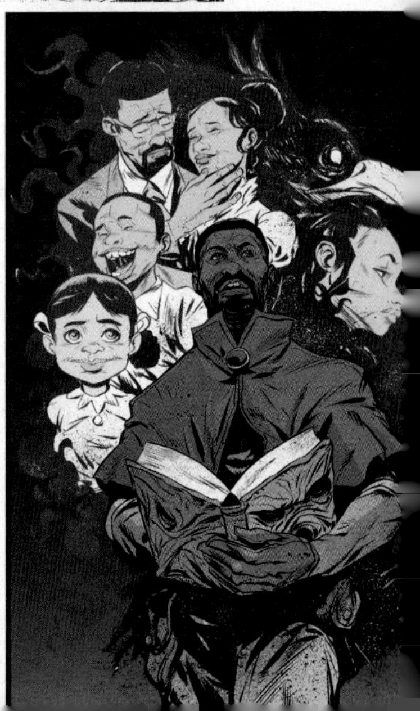

Pencil and inked art by Sanford Greene.

Color by Sofie Dodgson.

Thumbnail roughs on issue #15 pages 8-9, 12-13 by David F. Walker.

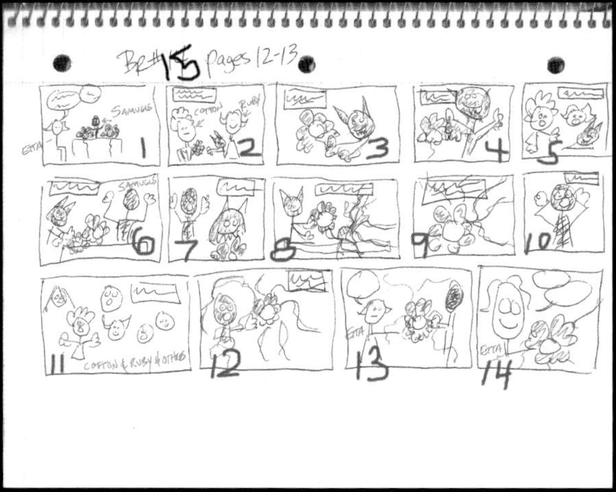
Pages 12-13

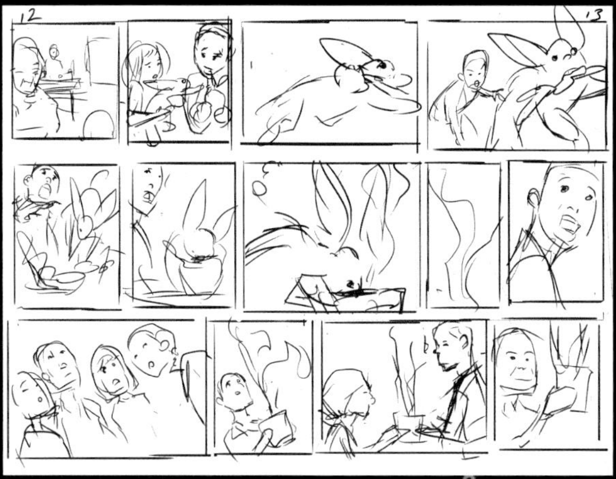

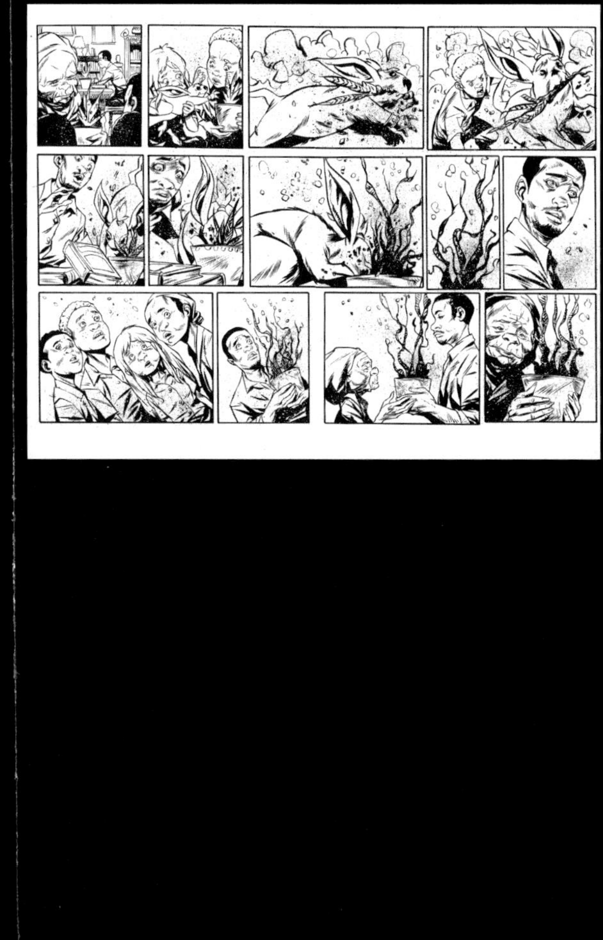

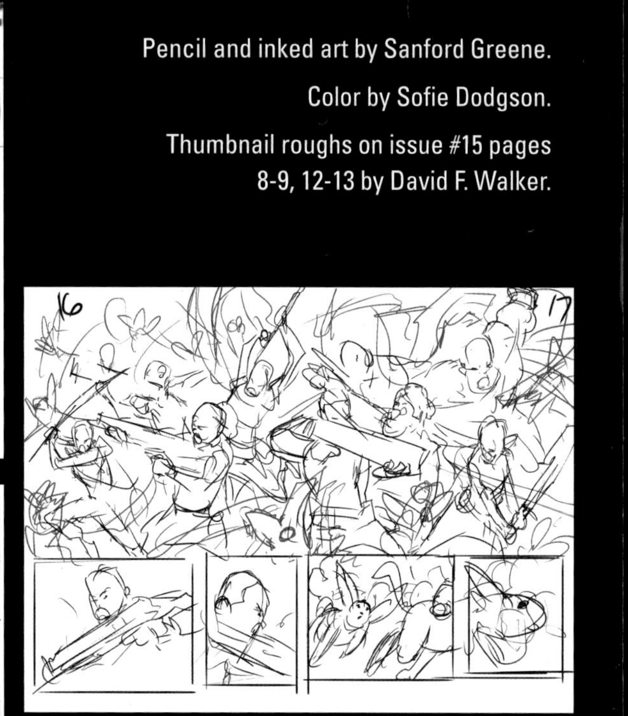

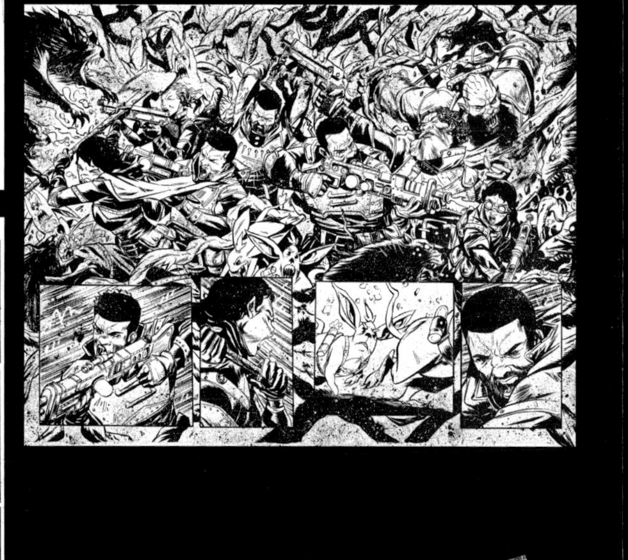

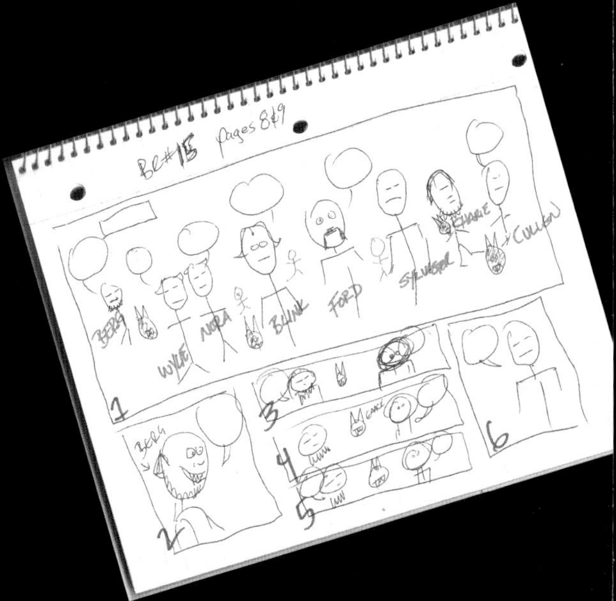
Pages 8&9

DAVID F. WALKER is an award-winning writer, educator, and Sagittarius. He is co-creator of *Naomi* (DC Comics) and the writer of *The Black Panther Party: A Graphic Novel History* (Ten Speed Press). He teaches part-time at Portland State University and prefers Miracle Whip over mayonnaise.

CHUCK BROWN is an Eisner and multiple Ringo Award-winning writer. He has written *The Punisher*, *Wolverine*, and *Black Panther* comics for Marvel. He has written *Superman*, *Black Manta*, and Aquamen for DC Comics. He's also the writer and creator of ON THE STUMP and *Short Complex*.

SANFORD GREENE is an Eisner Award-winning creator as well as a Ringo Award winner for Best Artist. He is currently working on *Justice League* and several soon-to-be-announced DC Comics projects. He is also currently working as a concept designer for the sequel of the Oscar Award-winning animated film *Spiderman: Into The Spiderverse*, coming in 2022.

SOFIE DODGSON is a costume designer who lives by the sea and sometimes colours comic books.

HASSAN OTSMANE-ELHAOU is a British/Algerian letterer, who has worked on comics like *Time Before Time*, *Undone by Blood*, and *Red Sonja*. He's also the editor of the Eisner Award-winning *PanelxPanel* magazine and the voice behind *Strip Panel Naked*.

SHELLY BOND is the writer and art director of *Filth & Grammar: The Comic Book Editor's (Secret) Handbook* featuring artists Imogen Mangle, Laura Hole & Sofie Dodgson. She's been driven to edit comics and aggravate her freelancers since 1988. She lives in Los Angeles with her husband, artist Philip Bond, their son, Spencer, and eight electric guitars.